MODERNISM À LA MODE

MODERNISM À LA MODE

Fashion and the Ends of Literature

ELIZABETH M. SHEEHAN

Cornell University Press *Ithaca and London*

First published 2018 by Cornell University Press

Printed in the United States of America

Library of Congress Cataloging-in-Publication Data

Names: Sheehan, Elizabeth M., author.
Title: Modernism à la mode : fashion and the ends of literature / Elizabeth M. Sheehan.
Description: Ithaca : Cornell University Press, 2018. | Includes bibliographical references
    and index.
Identifiers: LCCN 2018015841 (print) | LCCN 2018021285 (ebook) |
    ISBN 9781501728150 (pdf) | ISBN 9781501728167 (epub/mobi) |
    ISBN 9781501727726 (cloth ; alk. paper)
Subjects: LCSH: English fiction—20th century—History and criticism. |
    American fiction—20th century—History and criticism. | Fashion in literature. |
    Modernism (Literature)—Great Britain. | Modernism (Literature)—United States.
Classification: LCC PR830.F34 (ebook) | LCC PR830.F34 S54 2018 (print) |
    DDC 820.9/112—dc23
LC record available at https://lccn.loc.gov/2018015841

To Mom, Dad, and Chris

Contents

Illustrations

Acknowledgments

One of the guiding assumptions of this book is that we can never fully account for what brings a text into the world. So I am glad to acknowledge many individuals and institutions that made this book possible, but also acutely aware of how partial these acknowledgements are.

Deborah McDowell's work, guidance, and engagement with my writing have shaped this project and my academic career from their earliest stages. Rita Felski's courses and scholarship raise some of the questions with which I continue to grapple, and her support has been crucial. At the University of Virginia, I also benefitted from classes and conversations with Victor Luftig, Michael Levenson, Susan Fraiman, and, especially, Jennifer Wicke, whose encouragement helped to launch this project. My friendships with Gwen Kordonowy, Justin Neuman, Walker Holmes, Melissa Schraeder, Bob Clewell, and Bethany Mabee sustained me during our time together in Charlottesville.

In my years at Ithaca College, Claire Gleitman and Hugh Egan were models of (senior) collegiality, and they helped me to secure time to devote to this project via a Center for Faculty Research and Development grant. Chris Holmes became a dear friend and has given incisive feedback on multiple chapters. Dan Breen, Shauna Morgan, and, later, Jen Spitzer also read and discussed portions of the project with me. Julia Catalano was a fine research assistant. One of the pleasures of being in Ithaca was sharing yet another college town with Liz Anker, who has been generous with her advice and friendship.

At Oregon State, I have found a vibrant and caring intellectual community. I deeply appreciate my colleagues in the School of Writing, Literature, and Film and the Women, Gender, and Sexuality Studies program, particularly for the many ways they make my life and work better. Megan Ward improved every part of this manuscript with her sharp comments and was an ideal companion in book completion. Christina León and Iyun Osagie also generously took the time to read and share their thoughts about chapters of this book. Anita Helle, Peter Betjemann, Susan Shaw, Larry Rodgers, Kristin Griffin, Ehren Pflugfelder, Rebecca Olson, Mila Zuo, Dougal Hencken, Patti Duncan, Ana Ribero, Tekla Bude, Emily Malewitz, Bradley Boovy, Nana Osei-Kofi, Janet Lee, Evan Gottlieb, Tim Jensen, Isabelle Brock, Ben Mutschler, and Hayley Trowbridge provided other key forms of support, as did Deborah Carroll at OSU Library. A fellowship at OSU's Center for the Humanities gave me the space and time to reconceive and expand this project. The work of David Robinson, Joy Jensen, and Ray Malewitz made it possible for me to share portions of this project with colleagues and students at the center. An OSU Internationalization Grant enabled me to conduct needed archival research. Additional support for this project was provided by grants from the Lauretta and Edward Smith Fund for Faculty Professional Development in the School of Writing, Literature, and Film.

I thank librarians, archivists, and curators at the Indiana Historical Society, the British Library, the Courtauld Museum, Charleston House, the Schomburg Center for Research in Black Culture, the New York Public Library, Manuscripts and Special Collections at the University of Nottingham, and the Tate Gallery Archives, where research for this project was conducted. I am particularly indebted to Alexandra Gerstein at the Courtauld for sharing her expertise regarding the Omega Workshops and to Wendy Hitchmough, curator of Charleston, for her advice and generosity. A'Lelia Bundles, Henrietta Garnett, Cressida Bell, and the late Anne Olivier Bell also provided helpful information.

Thanks to audiences at the Block Museum; the University of British Columbia, Okanagan; the Global Modernism Symposium at Ithaca College; and the Ray Warren Symposium on Race and Ethnicity at Lewis and Clark College for engaging with portions of this project and to Christopher Reed and Christine Froula, Chris Holmes and Jen Spitzer, Ilya Parkins, and Rishona Zimring for inviting me to share work in those forums. Ilya has been a brilliant interlocutor, collaborator, and close friend since we first met at a Modernist Studies Association conference over a decade ago. Her work on fashion, femininity, and modernity is a constant source of inspiration. I have also benefitted from the insights of many other fellow modernist scholars who have read or listened to me read portions of this manuscript, including Rishona Zimring, Celia Marshik, Jessica Burstein, and Douglas Mao. Special thanks to Gayle Rogers for his support at a pivotal moment in this book's journey to publication.

It has been a pleasure to work with Mahinder Kingra of Cornell University Press, who has been unfailingly responsive, enthusiastic, and professional. I am grateful to Kristen Bettcher for guiding the manuscript through production and to Anne Davidson for her expert copy-editing. I thank the three readers of this manuscript, one of whom I now know is Barbara Green, whose reports provided the kind of astute, detailed feedback of which every author dreams.

Portions of chapter 3 appeared in "'This Great Work of the Creation of Beauty': Imagining Internationalism in W. E. B. Du Bois's *Dark Princess* and Black Beauty Culture," *Modern Fiction Studies*, 62, no. 3 (Fall 2016): 412–443, published by Johns Hopkins University Press; and in "Fashioning Internationalism in Jessie Redmon Fauset's Writing," *A Companion to the Harlem Renaissance*, edited by Cherene Sherrard-Johnson, 137–153, published by John Wiley and Sons, Inc. I am grateful to Johns Hopkins University Press and to John Wiley and Sons, Inc., for their kind permission to reproduce portions of these essays here. I wish to thank the Crisis Publishing Co., Inc., the publisher of the magazine of the National Association for the Advancement of Colored People, for the use of images first published in the March 1919, July 1923, and March 1927 issues of *Crisis* Magazine.

Finally: my most joyous acknowledgements are to my family. My mother, Beth's, curiosity about the world, commitment to kindness, and love for reading and teaching literature remain guiding principles for me. She and my dad, Bob, have supported me with a deep, unwavering love and generosity that are almost incredible. I want also to thank my wonderful brothers, Rob and Will, for their love, humor, and argumentative skills.

Chris Nichols has been my partner through every step of conceiving, writing, recasting, and revising this book. He read and discussed each page with characteristic care and insight, yet his greatest gift to me and to this project is his breathtaking capacity for love. Thank you, Chris.

MODERNISM À LA MODE

INTRODUCTION
FASHIONING MODERNISM

> Misunderstanding as [*sic*] constitutive element in the development of
> fashion. No sooner is the new fashion at a slight remove from its origin
> and point of departure than it is turned about and misunderstood.
> —WALTER BENJAMIN, *The Arcades Project*

Why and how does modernism matter at this moment? Will the study of
modernist texts become unfashionable, just as modernism itself is no longer the latest thing? Is it inaccurate or unwise for scholars to describe shifts
in how literature is written and studied in terms of fashion? In academic and
literary circles, fashion signifies inconsequence, frivolity, and a capitulation
to market demand. The word *fashionable* describes work that appears
cutting-edge, but is the product of a system that requires constant and periodic change. Modernist writers and humanities scholars are particularly
vulnerable to such charges because they are invested in innovation, and they
emphasize *how* as well as *what* things are expressed. In addition, the uses
and impacts of the knowledge produced in the humanities are not as obvious as in many social sciences and STEM (science, technology, engineering,
and mathematics) fields. Humanities scholars face the suspicion that their
work is driven more by intellectual trends and niche markets than by the
things that matter, especially if they concern themselves with esoteric topics such as fashion or modernism.

   This situation ensures there is a steady stream of books and articles that
explain the importance of the humanities, and literary studies specifically.
These texts frequently point to skills and values such as critical thinking and
close reading, which seem enduring rather than fashionable. Literature and
literary criticism offer those lasting goods. But it is not so easy to distinguish
fashion from enduring principles or substantive transformations. After all,
the phenomenon of constant and periodic change that we call fashion per-
meates modern life and institutions. It touches, moves, and keeps in place
bodies, materials, desires, beliefs, and attachments. In the early twentieth

century, fashion also figured prominently in various political movements; as this book discusses, modes of dress generated alternative black internationalist imaginaries, women's garments were implicated in debates about their right to vote in the United States and Britain, and uniforms exerted the pressure of compulsory nationalism and made palpable the advent of total war and the rise of fascism. Because fashion spurs both frivolous and fundamental transformations, it raises the question of what stylized objects can do—that is, what they can fashion, including perhaps an end to fashion altogether. This book shows that various modernist texts pose and address that question via fashion. I find that fashion functions in texts as a mode of perception, a target of critique, and a means of touching and connecting bodies and objects across time and space. Thus fashion shapes as well as competes with modernism as a practice of sensing out, giving form to, and thereby having an impact on the world. Modernism's modishness is central to how it matters.

Fashion and modernism are entwined conceptually and historically. Modernism and *la mode* spring from the same etymological root: *modo*, Latin for "just now." That connection underscores modernism and fashion's concerns with what distinguishes the present from the past and future, as well as their impulse to "make it new," to invoke Ezra Pound's famous dictum.[1] But as scholars of modernism and fashion will tell you, these phenomena also involve forms of repetition, stasis, and return. Nor is there general agreement about what modernism and fashion are, or when and where they emerge or persist. Yet that is precisely why fashion is vital to addressing what modernism does and what we do with modernism. For fashion is not only a system and a set of objects; it also operates as a contingent, contextual mode of perception that foregrounds how form and meaning shift across space and time. Fashion provides a way of reading that combines an attention to aesthetics with a sense of historicity—that is, with a sense of being situated in history and equipped with particular ways of understanding it. That kind of fashion sense is vital to modernist studies, and literary studies more broadly, at this moment, when scholars are reconsidering prevailing historicist and formalist methods and reassessing the nature and force of material objects. These scholarly trends should be understood in the context of the demands for literary studies to justify itself and its place in the contemporary university. We need to keep in view how present concerns shape our practices of reading cultural objects from the past, even if we situate those objects in relation to their historical moment. Nevertheless, it is not accurate or useful to describe all current critical engagements as symptoms of the prevailing academic-economic order. Instead, we need nuanced ways of thinking about how our critical methods and objects (including modernist texts) inflect, anticipate, resonate, and converge with contemporary concerns. The nexus of modernism and fashion provides tools for that work.

Fashion's historical connection to literary modernism anchors this book's claims about how both phenomena shape current accounts of the uses of literature and literary criticism. During the late nineteenth and the early twentieth centuries, the period most closely associated with modernism, fashion became an increasingly conspicuous cultural force, given the rise of the celebrity fashion designer and the so-called democratization of fashion, whereby stylish dress became more widely available due to changing technologies of mass production combined with cheap labor. Fashion also became a prominent subject of philosophical and sociological inquiry as well as a political tool. Leading social theorists in Europe and the United States, including Herbert Spencer, Georg Simmel, Walter Benjamin, and J. C. Flügel, presented fashion as a clue to the political, psychological, and cultural dynamics of modernity. For example, Spencer, Simmel, and Flügel claimed that fashion epitomized the tension between individuality and collective obedience that defines modern democracies.[2] Benjamin described fashion's capacity to grasp and remake old styles—its "tiger's leap into the past"—as a model for Marxian revolution.[3] Fashion, in short, provided vital philosophical and political material for describing, imagining, and remaking modernity.

Fashion's prominence in early twentieth-century culture, politics, and social theory helps to explain how and why it shapes the form and aims of work by Virginia Woolf, D. H. Lawrence, W. E. B. Du Bois, Nella Larsen, and F. Scott Fitzgerald, among other writers. Each chapter of this book demonstrates that fashion underpins a central way that their texts seek to matter: by offering a distinct way of knowing (Woolf), by stimulating particular bodily desires and inhuman forces (Lawrence), by imagining possibilities for revolutionary self-fashioning (Du Bois and Larsen), and by providing a means to grasp an historical period (Fitzgerald). These ways of mattering are not exclusive to novels, but this study attends to the convergence between fashion and novels' particular capacities to reflect, render, and remake the social fabric, as well as to adjust readers' modes of sensing the world. Those shared characteristics inform how and why the writers whom I discuss frame and advance the aims of their work via fashion. These authors, texts, and issues, then, are not meant to represent literary modernism or even its entanglement with fashion fully. Rather, each chapter demonstrates a way that a modernist engagement with fashion intersects with and might inform current conversations in literary, cultural, and political theory about how such seemingly minor things as ordinary feelings, everyday objects, aesthetic tastes, and anecdotes matter; those topics have resurfaced in a range of fields, along with fresh interest in questions of perception and materiality. The book's necessarily partial vision of modernism also responds to the ways that fashion's ephemerality and contingency confront us with the limits of historicist and formalist approaches that would propose a decisive context for a cultural object or a definitive interpretation of a given style. In Woolf's famous essay "Modern Fiction," she critiques fiction that attempts to describe characters via so much physical detail that, if brought to life, they would "find themselves dressed down to the last button of their coats in the fashion of the hour."[4] Woolf calls for a change in how novels are written, but her formulation also highlights a related problem of interpretation. It reminds us that fashion, like language, is so various and shifting that no amount of archival work will recover its precise meaning—or even perhaps its original appearance.

The inevitable ambiguity of fashion makes it a fitting sibling to modernism, whose formal tendencies—narrative fragmentation, stylistic experimentation, and subjective narrativization—have been described in various and sometimes contradictory ways: as modes of detachment from social and political matters and from mass culture, as expressions of a utopian desire for an alternative to capitalist modernity, as symptoms of imperialism, as marketing strategies, as methods of conceiving difference, and as ways of pursuing various ethical and political commitments.[5] Nevertheless, fashion makes clear that cultural products *do* have material effects at the moment of their emergence and via future audiences, which reencounter and recast them. While connections between literary style and material conditions can seem attenuated, a new or renewed fashion may more obviously fuel and accompany broader cultural and material dynamics, from reinvigorated demands for political representation to shifts in trade patterns and labor practices. At the same time, the power of garments, like the power of texts, is not reducible to their status as commodities, although one cannot simply disentangle modernism or *la mode* from capitalism.[6] It is with those dynamics in mind that this book takes up fashion as an object of analysis and a mode of perception, which operates in modernist texts and shapes how we read modernism. So, as this book engages fashion to understand what modernist texts do, it demonstrates what we can do with modernism to address long-standing and contemporary questions about the material dimensions of collective feeling, the agency of nonhuman objects, and the relationship between present and past. In other words, this book embraces and makes use of the fact that we necessarily read modernism à la mode—that is, contingently, contextually, and in light of contemporary concerns.

Fashion and Politics

This book draws from fashion's flexible, tensile strength as a defining phenomenon of modernity and as a means of describing a given time and place—the *modo* of modernism as well as our contemporary moment. The word *fashion* refers variously to the prevailing or most innovative style, to a set of objects that share that style, to a system of production and consumption that embraces novelty for the sake of novelty (and profit), and to the act of creation. This study explores all of these dimensions of fashion, but remains grounded in Elizabeth Wilson's observation that "fashion, in a sense, *is* change." As Wilson points out, "no clothes are outside fashion; fashion sets the terms of all sartorial behavior."[7] Wilson's formulation helps us to see how fashion functions as a mode of perception that encompasses antifashion and whatever purports to ignore fashion. That includes uniforms and forms of dress deployed by utopian and radical groups to resist and replace capitalism's constant sartorial stylistic change. As a result, one is always dressed in some fashion, and to produce a garment is to fashion it. At the same time, fashion, like modernism, repeatedly breaks free of arguments that try to assign a single, overarching meaning to its prevailing form—that is, "the fashion" in a given time and place and among a group of people. Fashions also usually cannot be traced to a single source. Even during the early twentieth century, when designers had a greater ability to determine the direction of fashion, they could not dictate what would be in style. And fashion theorists long ago relinquished the so-called trickle-down theory, exemplified by the work of Simmel and Thorstein Veblen, which proposes that fashions begin with the economic elite and are imitated by the lower classes. Instead, critics acknowledge that styles flourish in different subcultures and are often inspired by, appropriated, and adopted from economically, culturally, or politically subordinate groups with varying degrees of cultural capital.

Fashion's networked quality moves us away from simplistic accounts of intentionality and agency when discussing modernist cultures. Whether garments are created within the elite, hierarchical realm of haute couture or sewed at home, they are the result of collective labor and a product of creative inspiration, materials, modes of production and consumption, desires, and aesthetic, cultural and political trends, among other forces. It follows that in the texts I examine, the phenomenon of fashion raises questions about what discursive and material resources enable and constrain literature as a seemingly more autonomous mode of cultural production. Since the quality of fashionability is so lambent, clothing also draws attention to the extent to which the dimensions and impact of stylized objects—whether texts or garments—depend on how they are encountered and received. I find, then, that texts draw on discourses and images of dress to address their own capacity to create various effects, including particular ways of knowing and relating. As I show in chapter 2, for example, Lawrence's texts attempt to function like textiles as they touch, orient, and excite the reader's body. Modernist texts imitate as well as represent, and solicit as well as critique fashion as a way of engaging the world.

Not only does fashion have various meanings; ways of understanding fashion also have shifted, particularly since the formation of modern social sciences disciplines over a century ago. These changes, however, are not simply evidence of greater cultural understanding or progress in academic knowledge. Rather, as a contingent, contextual, and fashion-conscious reading of fashion would expect, historical conditions accelerated and brought long-standing dynamics into view. The purported "democratization" of fashion increased over the course of the century with the rise of youth culture and street style. By the interwar period, it became ever more common for middle- and working-class people to purchase ready-made clothing in addition to having garments made by a local seamstress or constructing them at home. Patterns of immigration and migration also shaped the industry in New York, Paris, and London as it employed laborers disproportionately from the recent immigrant population, which also constituted a market for relatively inexpensive fashion. Consuming particular styles of dress could function as a way of claiming citizenship, for clothing was key to the project of assimilation and to the politics of respectability by which subjects' enactments of bourgeois norms signaled their qualifications for political rights.[8] Negotiating the right relationship to fashion was part of the work of cultural and political belonging.

The phrase *democratization of fashion* underscores fashion's relationship to forms of governance and announces that consumption is the foundation and expression of citizenship and democratic freedom. As Minh-Ha T. Pham notes, this discourse reemerged with particular force in the wake of 9/11 with George W. Bush declaring that U.S. citizens could defend American freedom by resuming their shopping habits.[9] The concept of fashion's "democratization" also makes clear that the availability of such commodities promises to mediate tensions between purported equal political rights and obviously unequal economic opportunities and class positions. Giles Lipovetsky's *Empire of Fashion* celebrates the proliferation of fashion on similar grounds. He asserts that the increased availability and diversification of fashion emerges from and facilitates individualism, frivolity, and freedom, all of which, he claims, lead to greater "tolerance" in modern democratic societies.[10]

Lipovetsky's study was published in 1987, but as Pham notes, theories of fashion's democratization are quite old, as "the concept of cheap chic, the idea that fashion should be attainable at lower, mass-market price points and that stylishness is within anyone's reach, has been an unstable but recurring precept of fashion since fashion's inception in 1675."[11] The democratization of fashion is thus not a process within fashion history, but commensurate with fashion itself.

The year 1675 marks the founding of a French trade guild for couturiers— that is, female seamstresses responsible exclusively for the cutting and construction of women's court dress. The creation of this guild coincided with a fashion for looser-cut garments, which could be more easily constructed and altered, and clearly displayed embroidery and decoration. As fashion historian Christopher Breward explains, the guild's restriction on the work of couturiers and the shift in style helped to empower another guild of female garment workers, the *marchandes de modes*, who were responsible for the ornamentation on garments and could respond more swiftly to individual and collective tastes and trends.[12] They set up shops in Paris (in addition to Versailles), and as their businesses flourished, changes in style became increasingly determined by commerce in addition to the dictates of the court. Discussing these shifts, Breward recapitulates the common view that fashion emerges as culture and commerce gain independence from state control. But he also argues that scholars of dress underestimate the role of technology and material in shaping fashion history; Breward thus describes fashion as flourishing at the intersection of aesthetics, commerce, and technology.[13] Breward's more complex account of fashion history is illuminating. Nevertheless, domestic and international regulations regarding materials and designs as well as states' investments in military gear make it clear that fashion often has been shaped by government policy and vice versa. Fashion, then, is more accurately understood as an expression of the complex relationship between commerce, culture, technology, and the state, rather than an expression of the latter's relative weakness. Accordingly, fashion makes up and can make visible the way state, legal, commercial, and technological systems overlap and constitute the material of everyday life.

Because fashion is at the nexus of economics, aesthetics, and forms of governance, it also can help us to avoid reproducing conventional distinctions among those categories. That is needed because, even as those distinctions marginalize particular subjects and groups, they have been leveraged to make implicit and explicit claims for the relevance of modernist studies. In their oft-cited 2008 survey of "the new modernist studies," for example, Douglas Mao and Rebecca Walkowitz assert that scholars were beginning (again) to discuss "Politics as Itself." By that they mean "politics in relatively naked rather than veiled forms," with the latter signifying Foucauldian accounts of political power as ubiquitous, dispersed, and often hidden. According to Mao and Walkowitz, this shift involves "getting out from under the commodity form (at least temporarily) when assaying literature's relation to modern social life."[14] This turn can be understood partly as a reaction against the way that accounts of modernism's complicity with and embeddedness within consumer culture might undermine justifications for studying literary modernism as a distinct and valuable cultural formation. Regardless of such anxieties and their potential effects, the greater challenge for the field is to avoid reinscribing boundaries between economic, cultural, and political practices and phenomena.[15]

Fashion offers an ideal material for addressing that issue, for it functioned as a constitutive limit of political subjectivity and the political sphere, in addition to playing a vital role in political events and phenomena. Thus, for example, in Britain in the mid-1920s, opponents of the "flapper vote"—suffrage for women aged twenty-one to twenty-nine—maintained that young women's purportedly greater interest in clothing indicated their unfitness as political subjects.[16] At the same time, spectacles of suffragettes in prison uniforms and in conventional feminine dress worked to make the "feminine body into a civic body," as the former signaled that protesters should be understood as political prisoners while the latter showed that suffragettes conformed to feminine norms.[17] As fashion marked boundaries between the economic, cultural, and political, it helped to shift the contours of those arenas.

Fashion also delineates what counts as political in the work of early twentieth-century theorists, including the sociology of Simmel and the psychology of Flügel. Simmel and Flügel offer gendered explanations for the incompatibility of fashion and politics, even as they discover underlying structural similarities. Simmel, for example, claims that democratic leaders are like fashion trendsetters in that they do not so much direct the crowd as epitomize its norms; as he puts it, "the leader is the one who is led." Yet he also concludes that women's purportedly greater attachment to fashion stems from their exclusion from the political sphere. Hence, whereas men express themselves through public life, for women, "it seems as though fashion were the valve, as it were, through which women's need for some measure of conspicuousness and individual prominence finds vent, when its satisfaction is more often denied in other spheres."[18] Flügel, for his part, asserts that in the wake of the French Revolution, there was a "great masculine renunciation" whereby men gave up claims to "sartorial decorativeness" and beauty in exchange for being "useful."[19] In *The Psychology of Clothes* (1930), which was published by Virginia and Leonard Woolf's Hogarth Press, Flügel proposes that men's stronger sense of "morality" led to "uniformity" and the "democratisation in clothes," which in turn expresses the "advanced," modern principles of equality and labor. Flügel laments that the world is "aesthetically the poorer for this change," but contrasts women's narcissism with men's sense of equality and commitment to the common good.[20] He thus conceives femininity and fashion as difficult to reconcile with democracy. Flügel's and Simmel's tendency to explain fashion and politics in terms of innate tendencies or progressive historical development naturalizes capitalism and liberal democracy. Yet, as we find in debates about suffrage, such approaches also admit ways that frivolous, feminine modes of cultural production and consumption bear on the composition of the political order and functions of the state. This opens up possibilities for counter-readings that exploit fashion's entwinement with politics.

In the chapters that follow, I show how various modernist texts respond to that possibility and, in doing so, grapple with their own capacity to address and intervene in the formation and practice of politics. This is perhaps most obvious in Woolf's *Three Guineas* (1938), which I discuss in chapter 1. Woolf's feminist antiwar polemic investigates how the masculine public sphere consolidates itself by precluding fashion as a way of perceiving men's garments; Woolf reveals that patriarchal and state power produce the distinction between garments subject to fashion and those (such as uniforms and ceremonial dress) that are supposedly immune to it. *Three Guineas* thus offers the account of a judge decked out in an elaborate wig and robe who holds forth on women's innate and irrational attractions to the pleasures of dress. I argue that much of Woolf's work encourages a fashion-conscious mode of perception, which can sense the uneven texture of the social fabric. Woolf's work does not, however, endorse fashion as a form of production, consumption, or political expression. In *Three Guineas*, a focus on dress helps to unravel distinctions between states that are liberal democratic (British) and those that are fascist (German, Italian, and Spanish) insofar as these categories rest on the assumption that the former are grounded in rational debate between self-transparent subjects, whereas the latter draw force from irrational pleasures such as clothing and performance. Indeed, *Three Guineas* helps us to see how beliefs about how and why states, populations, and individuals invest in vestments underpin distinctions between liberal and fascist modes of collectivity and governance, as well as reasons for war making. Despite Woolf's critique and her prominence in modernist studies, the political dynamics and impact of masculine dress in wartime and interwar culture remain mostly the concern of costume historians and fashion theorists.

Nevertheless, the idea that dressing a certain way might facilitate or result from progressive or utopian individual and collective transformation is a common feature of social theories and movements in the early twentieth century, including feminist, antiracist, eugenicist, and fascist causes. Specific organizations and efforts for "dress reform" were a very visible feature of U.S., British, and Continental culture from the mid-nineteenth century, when Amelia Bloomer promoted bifurcated garments for women. Some of these projects overlapped with modernist and avant-garde ventures, such as the Wiener Werkstätte (which emerged from the Vienna Secession).[21] The logic, aesthetic, and rhetoric of the dress reform movement is also apparent in the dress design work undertaken by, for example, the Italian futurists and even the Bloomsbury group during the existence of the Omega Workshops (1913–1919), a design collective led by Roger Fry that created and sold garments. The dress reform movement also informed social theories of fashion. In Germany, Simmel worked with artist and designer Henry Van de Velde, whose commitment to making dress more rational, beautiful, and healthy resonates with Simmel's worries that modernity meant the dominance of objects over subjects and their needs.[22] Flügel participated in the London-based Men's Dress Reform Party, which counted H. G. Wells among its supporters in the early 1930s.[23] In *The Psychology of Clothes*, Flügel also joins a host of cultural critics who associate the end of fashion with the triumph of democracy; he predicts a future in which people will wear fewer clothes and the exposure of the body will balance the pleasures of narcissism with a commitment to equality. Flügel's theories and the dress reform movement itself can be situated within late nineteenth- and early twentieth-century artistic and scientific investigations into the role of aesthetics and particularly "aesthetic environments" in shaping human behavior.[24] Dress was perceived as a key way to adjust individual and collective modes of feeling, behaving, and perceiving via style.

Even those critics, such as Spencer, who do not express much interest in the aesthetic dimensions of dress saw it as key to the fate of civilization because of its intimate relationship to the body and its impulses. Unlike Flügel, Spencer (writing fifty years earlier) did not predict the end of fashion altogether, but claims that it "has ever tended towards equalization" and describes it as one of the forms of "the regulation of conduct" that "imply the increasing liberty which goes along with the substitution of peaceful activities for war-like activities."[25] Flügel and Spencer link peace and individualism to ideas of fitness, progress, and reproduction in ways that reflect what

Lee Edelman describes as reproductive futurism: that is, a normative politics constituted in the name of future generations.[26] As this book contends, Du Bois, Lawrence, and Fitzgerald also address the connection between clothing and sexual desire in order to offer or replace various visions of reproductive futurism. In the novels *Dark Princess: A Romance* (1928), *Women in Love* (1920), and *Tender Is the Night* (1934), dress emerges as a way to translate erotic force into the capacity to shape the future by generating sexual and material reproduction. Texts and textiles thus reinforce and compete with each other as ways of soliciting and directing erotic and imaginative attachments to objects and between bodies, thereby remaking the social fabric.

No early twentieth-century writer made greater claims for fashion's and writing's transformative political potential than Walter Benjamin, the theorist who figures most prominently in academic discussions of fashion and modernism. Indeed, Benjamin's treatments of modernist culture and the past as potentially revolutionary resources make him a favorite of scholars of modernist studies, as his work authorizes theoretical and archival approaches. This book draws inspiration from Benjamin's claim that fashion illuminates the interdependence of past and present while offering alternatives to positivist and progressive versions of historicism. In his famous late essay "On the Concept of History," Benjamin declares, "Fashion has a nose for the topical, no matter where it stirs in the thickets of long ago; it is the tiger's leap into the past. Such a leap, however, takes place in an arena where the ruling class gives the commands. The same leap in the open air of history is the dialectical leap Marx understood as revolution."[27] Benjamin finds in fashion a nonlinear and nonprogressive vision of history that resides, paradoxically, in the heart of capitalist modernity. He thus returns repeatedly to the topic of fashion in *The Arcades Project*, an uncompleted work that assembles fragments of historical and literary texts along with Benjamin's commentary.

As Ulrich Lehmann points out, Benjamin's writing on fashion builds on Simmel's, Charles Baudelaire's, and Stephen Mallarmé's treatments of fashion as a phenomenon that reveals the nature of modernity.[28] Baudelaire describes both modernity and modern art via fashion; in "The Painter of Modern Life," he says that the modern artist "is looking for that quality which you must allow me to call '*modernité*.' . . . He makes it his business to extract from fashion whatever element it may contain of poetry within history, to distill the eternal from the transitory." Baudelaire goes on to define *modernité* as "the ephemeral, the fugitive, the contingent, the half of art whose other half is the eternal and the immutable"; it means something like a "nowness," which is distinct in every age and which can be best perceived in fashion because of the latter's ephemerality and ubiquity.[29] Drawing on Baudelaire's connection between aesthetics and history via fashion, Benjamin uses fashion to grapple with how modernity might be fundamentally transformed. Benjamin's writing thus also can be located in a tradition of utopian approaches to clothing, although it departs from visions of dress reform that seek to improve individuals and groups through the adaptations of particular styles. Benjamin, after all, does not offer a path into that "open sky" where the revolutionary leap can be made. Instead, his description of the tiger intimates that the means to release it from the "arena" have not yet been found; with its uncanny nose, fashion offers a potentially transformative mode of perception but also may keep one's senses attuned only to that which reproduces bourgeois power. Benjamin's writing, nevertheless, follows the smell; and it, too, resembles fashion insofar as it provides methods and prompts, but not prescriptions or maps.[30]

That approach is typical of modernist texts, which often avoid explicit instruction yet maintain some sort of pedagogical ambition, whether that be to offer a critique of a certain aspect of modernity; to encourage or simply reveal particular ways of knowing, feeling, or being; or even to supply information about a given phenomenon. As my last chapter discusses, for example, Fitzgerald presents modernist literature as a source of data about modern sexual mores. Fashion enables all of these modernist pedagogies, in part because of what Benjamin, following Baudelaire, perceives as fashion's power to express the essence of the contemporary moment, even before it can be felt elsewhere. Thus *la mode* gives form and weight to *modo*, which is at the heart of modernism. In French, *mode* also refers to mood. It follows, then, that fashion provides ways to feel out the construction and contingencies of the "just now," particularly in modernist texts. Dress generates one's sense of the ordinary as well as what Lauren Berlant describes as "feeling historical"—that is, feeling located in a given time and place at a moment when the contours of the present and hence the future seem to be shifting.[31] Fashion, in other words, holds and produces knowledge about the present and future, which may be inexpressible in another mode. One of the aims of this book is to show how and why modernist texts strive to give textual form to sartorial ways of knowing and feeling. It does so both to demonstrate fashion's importance to modernism and to address how fashion as a discourse and a system shapes literary study despite and because of its associations with ephemerality, superficiality, and commodification.

Modes of Reading

I have proposed that we already read modernism à la mode. Accordingly, what constitutes modernism is subject to change. In the last few decades, definitions of modernism as comprised of esoteric texts composed by writers disengaged from politics and popular culture and gathered in metropolitan coteries have given way to temporally, spatially, culturally, and formally capacious visions of plural, even planetary modernisms.[32] More recently, there has been a shift from debates about what modernism *is* to conversations about what various definitions of modernism *do*. This trend can be connected to the move in literary studies toward forms of observation and description rather than diagnosis and taxonomy. Paul Saint-Amour, for example, employs a "weakly theorized" concept of modernism understood as a "nonexclusive shorthand for works that display, even speculatively or intermittently, an anticontemporary or counterconventional temper."[33] Tracing the models of weak theory or weak thought offered by Silvan Tomkins, Eve Kosofsky Sedgwick, Gianni Vattimo, and Wai Chee Dimock, Saint-Amour observes that "weak theory tries to see just a little way ahead, behind, and to the sides, conceiving even of its field in partial and provisional terms that will neither impede, nor yet shatter upon, the arrival of the unforeseen."[34] That is an apt account of weak theory. It also describes fashion as a practice of responding to, anticipating, and attempting to shape the contours of the immediate past, present, and near future without being entirely superseded when new modes arrive. Indeed both Sedgwick and Dimock refer to textiles and thread to explain nontotalizing modes of thinking that allow for surprise and change. Those weak methods, they suggest, are an alternative to strong theory, which maps a much broader temporal and spatial terrain.[35] Sedgwick asserts that texture "comprises an array of perceptual data . . . whose degree of organization hovers just below the level of shape or structure," thereby undercutting attempts to read in terms of overarching systems.[36] This move to the substructural facilitates what Sedgwick (adapting Melanie Klein) refers to as reparative modes of reading, which are "additive and accretive" and attempt to "assemble and confer plenitude" on objects that may thereby offer "resources" for the subject.[37] These formulations help us to see that fashionable fabric invites the kinds of contingent, materially specific, and close readings that weak theory pursues.

I would emphasize, however, that engaging with modernism and/as fashionable fabric helps us to shift between or interweave modes of reading.[38] For fashion and dress also underpin key versions of strong theory—that is, theory that is capable of great "reach and reductiveness" in organizing a vast "domain" of phenomena.[39] The consumption of garments typifies what Marx describes as commodity fetishism. Indeed, as Peter Stallybrass notes, a coat serves as a key example of a commodity in *Capital*, a book made possible by Marx's own coat, which kept him warm on the way to doing research at the British Library, made him a "suitable citizen to be admitted to the Reading Room," and provided financial support since he repeatedly pawned it.[40] Pierre Bourdieu uses fashion to explain how distinction, taste, and cultural capital function, while Roland Barthes's study of the (written) fashion system epitomizes semiotic analysis and treats fashion as an exemplary subject for structuralist analysis. In turn, drag provides key material for Judith Butler's poststructuralist theory of gender performativity. Fashion, then, enables and prompts modes of weak and strong theorizing. After all, when one engages with a garment, one often reads for both texture and structure—that is, for fabric and fashionability.

These ways of perceiving also often are combined and invited by modernist texts as they focus on that which is "irreducibly phenomenological" (as Sedgwick claims texture and affect are) and attend to extant forms and structures.[41] We can thus return to the familiar pairing of text and textile— both deriving from *textere* (to weave)—with a sense of how those related terms suggest types of reading for textures and for the forms and structures that emerge within and encompass texts.[42] Like literature, fashion is a way of reading forms in time, as well as a way of giving form to time. Moreover, fashion facilitates shifts and highlights connections between levels of form and the not-quite-form that is texture.

If fashion and fabric inform how we read, they also stage related questions about why we read. I have emphasized fashion's entanglement with early twentieth-century conceptions and practices of politics. But fashion also can set form and style against politics and history as the grounds for meaning and value. Jessica Burstein, for example, argues that Coco Chanel perfected the aesthetic of timeless chic whereby, paradoxically, that which is absolutely of the moment supposedly transcends time. That aesthetic epitomizes what Burstein dubs "cold modernism," which "engages a world without selves or psychology" and rejects humanity as the source and aim of what matters.[43] According to Burstein, rather than existing in the context of human social change, Chanel's little black dress proposes to simply persist. Judith Brown, in turn, identifies glamour as a characteristic modernist aesthetic that is "cold, indifferent, and deathly," as well as impeccably polished.[44] By these accounts, fashion pits a stringent, apolitical formalism against historicism insofar as the latter takes up social power and change over time as key terms and aims of cultural production and consumption.

While Chanel's glamorous little black dress can be seen as a formalist chal-lenge to history and historicism, other early twentieth-century practices and representations of fashion accept history and politics as measures of meaning while contesting or refusing their forms. Racialized and gendered subjects, for example, deployed dress to insist on their right to redress via political channels. Dress also helped to make other political formations imaginable. As Monica L. Miller shows in her *Slaves to Fashion*, W. E. B. Du Bois imagined the black dandy as a diasporic figure who challenges white supremacy and what he describes as a "color line within the color line," which forestalls political solidarities among people of color across the globe.[45] In his novel *Dark Princess*, Du Bois depicts an African American hero whose love for dress helps to cultivate a love for justice. The third chapter of this book argues that Du Bois's revolutionary vision responds to the way that black women's practices of self-fashioning gave rise to competing, gendered visions of the international order. Putting Du Bois and black beauty culture in conversation illuminates how feminized practices of fashion became a flash point in debates about the role of aesthetic production in political ac-tivism as well as what kinds of communities and connections would define black internationalism. As each chapter of this book shows, fashion posed and addressed the question of how modernist cultural production (includ-ing literature) might reimagine prevailing modes of knowledge, embodi-ment, recognition, and political engagement. In short, fashion dramatizes different ways that form and style matter—to whom, in what way, and at what moment.

Conversations about how and why we read overlap with questions about what we read, which involves addressing what disciplines make up the inter-disciplinary field of "new" modernist studies. New modernist studies emerged in the 1990s as literary scholars challenged prevailing accounts of modernism's apoliticism, conservatism, and aspirations to aesthetic auton-omy to explore its complex entanglement with the culture and politics of its era.[46] Despite an emphasis on interdisciplinarity, modernist studies con-tinues to be populated mostly by experts in literature who draw from other disciplinary approaches and cultural studies methodologies to varying de-grees. We can explain literature's continuing preeminence in modernist studies as a result of existing institutional formations and mechanisms, which may reward interdisciplinary or transdisciplinary work only to the point that it remains legible within existing disciplines. Be that as it may, multiple objects, desires, and attachments make up this academic field. My interest is in grappling with the implications of our continued choice of objects—namely, literary texts and individual writers with varying degrees of name recognition—in order to supply sharper accounts of what texts and our readings of them do, and how. As modernism's seemingly frivolous, ephemeral sibling, *la mode* throws these questions into relief. The writers in this study negotiate the distinctions between literature and other forms of cultural production by aligning themselves with various pedagogical projects that texts offer, but which depend on fashion, whether as an object of critique, a tool, or a model. This strategy is perhaps clearest and most compromised in the case of Fitzgerald. As chapter 4 argues, his celebrity and system of production resemble those of the designer Paul Poiret. Fitzgerald's publication of short stories in popular magazines involves bringing "in house" the work of creating inferior but authorized versions of his greatest creations, a project that Poiret also attempted. In addition, both Fitzgerald and Poiret celebrate their most valued work as unparalleled expressions of their age. Those strategies bolster their reputations as masculine cultural authorities, including their expertise in modern women and their tastes. That dynamic resonates with early twenty-first-century concerns about modernism's value as an object of study. Fitzgerald's work anticipates modernist studies' ambivalent relationship to cultural studies methodologies that might undercut assumptions about the particular importance of literature and of work by individual authors. His efforts to articulate the value of literature as an expression of its historical moment prompts us to reconsider if, why, and how we treat modernist texts as ways to know what cultural forces and structures of feeling characterize a given place and time.

A focus on fashion also helps us to address and negotiate modernism and theory's overlapping temporal logics. Stephen Ross maintains that modernism and theory share a narrative strategy, a "repeated story of critique," which emphasizes a break with what comes before.[47] The same is true of the "new" modernist studies, which announced a rupture between older, purportedly apolitical formalist approaches and newly historicist work.[48] Yet of course not all modernist, scholarly, and theoretical texts endorse or bear out that narrative. As my discussions of Woolf, Lawrence, Du Bois, and Fitzgerald show, fashion's complex temporality—which involves novelty, continuity, and repetition—provides ways to undercut and reconsider the logic of the break. Indeed, skepticism about the logic of the break is a point of continuity between many modernist literary and contemporary theoretical projects. Sara Ahmed is among the recent theorists who question a reliance on claims to novelty. While she does not discuss fashion or modernism, she critiques this rhetoric when discussing recent feminist work in the field of new materialism, which purports to provide fresh accounts of the nature and agency of bodies and objects. Ahmed argues that new materialism's claims to innovation overlook and misread long-standing feminist engagements with matter and biology.[49] That effort to "make it new" erases or misrepresents rather than makes use of what comes before.[50] As she indicates, feminist criticism, like praxis, should orient itself toward change without reinscribing the logic of the break. In modernist studies, that project involves acknowledging that modernism's and critique's narratives of rupture are not equivalent to theoretical or political transformation, while keeping in view how cultural and knowledge production provides resources and opportunities for desired change. It is in that spirit that this book shows how early twentieth-century writers, artists, theorists, and activists draw on fashion and dress to grapple with the pace, possibilities, and implications for modest and radical resistance and transformation.

Modernist and Contemporary Matters

Reading early twentieth-century writers and early twenty-first-century critics together reveals the modernist dimensions of theoretical conversations that are not often connected to early twentieth-century literature—let alone fashion. Links between mood, *la mode*, and *modo*, for instance, suggest how modernism's interest in perception, fleeting moments, material objects, and modes of writing overlap with topics in new materialism and affect studies. These topics are also crucial to renewed debates about methods of literary study, which often hinge on issues of perception. Heather Love's model of reading "close but not deep," for example, provides an alternative to analyses that find in texts the kind of rich, unique, profound interiority that is part and parcel of liberal humanist visions of the individual.[51] Modernism has long been associated with explorations of complex interiority, but precisely for that reason, critics also have shown how various modernist texts and modernist fashions counter, deconstruct, and disperse a liberal humanist version of perception and personhood.[52] Recent scholarship in affect studies and new materialism also attempt to challenge individualist, liberal humanist accounts of feeling, embodiment, and agency. It follows that we can bring modernist texts and fashions together with affect theory and new materialism to address new and renewed questions about how we read and why.

The first two chapters of this book explore convergences between modernist texts and contemporary theories of feeling, embodiment, and materiality by putting texts by Woolf and Lawrence in conversation with work by Ahmed, Berlant, Elizabeth Grosz, and Jane Bennett, among others. These writers share an interest in bodies and objects, although only Woolf,

Lawrence, and Bennett devote much attention to dress. They also share a concern with the possibilities for desired types of transformation in the context of capitalist and imperialist expansion and state-sanctioned violence. And they pursue those possibilities beyond the confines of rationalist visions of political subjectivity or dualistic accounts of a mind-body split. The means and aims of such transformation and the specific historical conditions shaping the work of modernists and contemporary theorists are certainly distinct. Nevertheless, modernist treatments of fashion raise, and provide ways to address, key issues in affect studies and new materialism, including the material dimensions of collective feeling and the extent to which the agency of objects can be separated from their force as commodities.

To that end, chapter 1 argues that Woolf's modernism repeatedly turns to the connection between moods and modes of dressing and writing in order to examine the nature and dimensions of collective feelings in a specific time and place (*modo*). Mood/modes/*modo* thus describes the affective, tactile, formal, material, and temporal aspects of Woolf's modernism. In particular, fashion helps Woolf's texts to locate everyday experiences in the context of broader structures and institutions. As material traces of the "just now," fashionable garments convey the contours of an unfolding present that characters and readers may sense and feel but not be able to articulate. Thus, via mood and mode, novels such as *Mrs. Dalloway* (1925) and *The Years* (1937) refabricate the sensations of a historical present that often takes the character of what Berlant refers to as a "crisis ordinary"—that is, an everyday life that is disordered and ordered by capitalism and geopolitical events (economic collapse, militarization) such that subjects may need to find new ways of feeling their way through the world.[53] Berlant focuses on the turn of the twenty-first century. But, for Woolf almost a century earlier, the crises also are political, structural, material, and psychological (world wars, economic depression); are experienced as shifts in the collective mood and in modes of behavior; and require new ways of sensing out the contours of the present and near future. In this context, fashion provides a way for Woolf's texts to explore how bodies are touched and oriented as well as to touch and orient readers, in part by depicting and conjuring a particular mood.

In making this argument, I deploy a capacious understanding of mood as well as fashion. Following recent cultural theories of "mood work," I do not take mood to refer only or always to a particular, individual feeling; mood also functions like a disposition that makes one more likely to have or encounter certain feelings, as well as thoughts, ideas, sensations, objects, and perceptions.[54] This approach is indebted to Martin Heidegger's description of mood as a form of attunement to the world that shapes what and how things come to one's attention.[55] It is in that sense that I maintain that what Saint-Amour describes as modernism's "counterconventional temper" is a mood and thus a mode of attention. Moreover, via modernism, this mood takes on and is expressed through certain forms or modes. If, as Douglas Mao notes, in the nineteenth century, literature became a principal means of "tuning subjects to their worlds," modernism involves an intensified interest in how describing subjective processes of tuning might produce different forms of attunement.[56] That is, the writers I discuss depict processes of perception in order to alter them. Conceiving modernism in that way helps us to see why it is a rich resource for considering how we are attuned not only to texts, but also to our contemporary moment. We can, in short, learn from how modernist and antimodernist texts attend to and reimagine the world via certain moods and forms, including what they miss or misconstrue.

Modernist engagements with fashion can also draw our attention to the limitations of certain contemporary cultural theories. That is one implication of this book's second chapter, which reads Lawrence's work alongside recent work on corporeality, animality, and agential objects within the sprawling field of new materialism. One of the aims of a certain strand of work within new materialism is to discover an animatedness in matter that exceeds or diverges from Marx's account of how commodities become lively via the reification of alienated human labor.[57] Bennett in particular contends that an enchanted sense of lively matter that exceeds the disenchanted perspective of historical materialism may enable more ethical and sustainable ways of being and acting. Lawrence's work takes up similar questions as it considers dress as a way to counter the deadening and disenchanting effects of modern life. Garments are, after all, particularly affectively saturated and lively materials. They cradle, constrict, and take the shape of human bodies. In that sense, fashion complements and competes with the methods and aims of Lawrence's work, which describes and seeks sensuous contact between living and nonliving objects. Lawrence's primitivist vitalism, however, prompts a fairly suspicious approach to concepts of lively matter, including their ethical and political potentials. His work also suggests why a celebration of the enchantments of objects may merely reinforce the dynamics of consumer capitalism. Lawrence's treatments of dress, then, offer a useful response to certain strands of early twenty-first-century new materialism, which seek to conceive matter's liveliness apart from its commodification in an attempt to promote better ways of existing in the world. At the same time, his depictions of garments as animated matter contribute to new materialist efforts to understand human agency as distributed but also capable of resistance and creativity in the face of catastrophic and imminent destruction. As with Woolf, the modishness of Lawrence's modernism helps it to speak to the contemporary moment. Via fashion, their work responds to unfolding theoretical and political questions.

Fashion, Orientalism, and the Dimensions of Modernism

While engaging with contemporary issues and theories, this book focuses on literature, culture, and politics in Britain and the United States during the 1910s through 1930s, the conventional period of so-called high modernism. Despite these relatively narrow geographical parameters, it shows how the relationship between modernism and the mode helps us to address what is at stake when we delimit or expand our meanings of modernism, including as we move from national to international, global, or transnational aesthetic and political frames. After all, modernism and fashion remain of the moment precisely because of their entwinement with prevailing processes of globalization and their alternatives. In other words, they are embedded in contemporary economic, political, and cultural structures and the ways those structures are understood. The connections between fashion and globality are particularly central to the third chapter, which examines how different approaches to self-fashioning and to modernism fuel competing visions of black internationalism. I note that, as Du Bois's novel *Dark Princess* describes the affair between an African American man and a South Asian princess, it imagines how a love for beauty—in corporeal and artistic terms—might consolidate and reproduce global solidarities among people of color that challenge white supremacy. The novel attempts this, however, by alternating between long-standing literary forms such as realism and romance rather than employing potentially modish modernist techniques. We could apply the label *modernist* to Du Bois's unusual transition between narrative styles if we employ a formally capacious understanding of that term. But to read *Dark Princess* as obviously modernist would be to overlook rather than grapple with the associations between modernist stylistic innovation, consumer culture, femininity, and nonreproductive sexuality as they shape his aesthetic and political vision of black internationalism as the foundation for a new world system. I argue that Du Bois turns to realism and romance as a way to disarticulate the lasting good of beauty from ephemeral fashion, even while drawing on the power of the latter, particularly as he tailors his vision of black masculinity.

The significance of Du Bois's novel, however, does not rest solely on the power of his influential ideas. For *Dark Princess* responds the ways that, thanks to the business of black women's beauty culture, commodified practices of self-fashioning became a platform for black working-class women's political agency as well as a source for alternative visions of black globality. In particular, the prominent black beauty culturalists Madam Walker and her daughter, A'Lelia Walker, drew upon modes of black femininity and the flows of transnational capital to imagine a global (business) empire led by a black woman. Madam Walker also funded and joined black radical efforts to intervene in the formation of the international order in the wake of World War I. I thus read Du Bois's ambivalent treatments of fashion and modernist narrative techniques as an effort to disentangle his aesthetic and political vision from the conceptions of femininity and finance exemplified by the Walkers. Recognizing that Du Bois associates modernist aesthetics with fashion, femininity, and a disruption of heterosexual reproduction enables us to describe modernism's contested role in black internationalist activism and aesthetics, including in the work of Nella Larsen and Jessie Fauset. Fashion's inextricability from aesthetic taste and experience also provides further evidence of how gender and sexuality are woven into visions of globality in this period and should not be secondary concerns for scholars of transnational modernisms.

Reading Du Bois's novel and black beauty culture together demonstrates how fashion requires and enables a textured account of modernism's relationship to imperialist and colonialist practices and imaginaries. In their art and activism, Du Bois and the Walkers (like many other black internationalists) turn to South Asia as well as to Japan and its growing imperial ambitions as the source of aesthetic and political models that might compete with those of the United States and Britain. In this context, imperialist aesthetics of self-fashioning and consumption become interwoven with modernist aesthetics and anti-imperialist activism. Fashion and modernism are implicated in empire and provide strong and weak critical methods and positions from which to grasp and alter its various textures and structures.

Modernism's connections to fashion and empire are part of a long history of fashion's centrality to global trade and global imaginaries. Whether one dates the modern Eurocentric fashion system to the fourteenth, seventeenth, eighteenth, or nineteenth centuries (to list a few popular alternatives), it is inextricable from the exchange of fabrics, styles, and ideas, particularly between Europe and Asia. The links between fashion, capitalism, imperialism, and Orientalism are suggested by the material and etymological origins of the words *cotton*, *muslin*, *silk*, and *taffeta*, not to mention the more obvious *damask* and *cashmere*. Fashion's connection to Orientalism is borne out by what Anne Anlin Cheng notes is the association between the Orient and "excessive" fabric and bodily covering.[58] Affectively, fashion also shares with Orientalism the promise of an elsewhere and an otherwise that involves the possibility of possession, depending on one's position in the global political and economic system. That was certainly the case in Europe and the United States just before the war, when fashion was synonymous with Orientalism thanks to the Ballets Russes and Paul Poiret, the designer known as the King of Fashion, whose promotional activities included hosting elaborate costume parties inspired by fantasies of life in harems and *One Thousand and One Nights*. As Nancy Troy shows, Poiret not only was central to early twentieth-century fashion but also was a pivotal figure in the art world. Arguably the most famous designer of the first two decades of the twentieth century, Poiret's influence on the writers and artists in this study makes clear that Orientalism, like primitivism, is inextricable from modernist forms and thus arguments about the relationship between modernist aesthetics and politics.

More specifically, Poiret's career, including his lecture tours across Europe and in the United States in the 1910s and 1920s, underscores the relations between fashion, modernity, Orientalism, and aesthetic education, to which Fry, Fitzgerald, Du Bois, the Walkers, Lawrence, and Woolf all respond. In Britain and the United States, contact with and consumption of apparently exotic objects and styles was often framed as a form of edification and a sign of sophistication.[59] As I show, these writers and activists pitch their own projects against and through the pedagogical promise of Orientalist fashion, which is represented in part via Poiret. Accordingly, Poiret and his influence thread through the chapters of this book. He first emerges briefly in my discussion of Woolf and the Bloomsbury group due to his impact on the Omega Workshops. Under the leadership of Vanessa Bell and Duncan Grant as well as Roger Fry, the Omega sold textiles, furnishings, and garments, among other products. The letter that Fry circulated to secure support for the Omega cited Poiret's École Martine as a model for his venture. The École was part of Poiret's interior design business; its mission was to teach working-class girls design and then sometimes use their creations for Poiret furnishing and fabrics, which were sold to his elite international clientele. This approach accords with the Omega's primitivist and Orientalist aesthetics and its focus on amateurism, although Poiret represented a far more conventional type of prestige and success than the Omega found (or perhaps pursued). Indeed, Poiret makes a cameo in the second chapter via a diatribe in *Women in Love* in which Rupert Birkin—and, I argue, Lawrence's text—expresses both contempt and envy for Poiret's success as an interior designer. As John Marx contends, Lawrence treats primitivist and Orientalist objects, including garments, as sources of vital knowledge, particularly in the context of declining empire.[60] Lawrence is thus jealous of efforts such as Poiret's to reproduce and thereby mediate people's access to these objects.

Poiret appears again in chapter 4 as a precursor and parallel to what I describe as Fitzgerald's status as a modernist celebrity designer and pedagogue. Like Fitzgerald, Poiret resists Chanel's "cold modernist" mechanized aesthetic, which welcomed (inevitably imperfect) imitations by others. Well into the 1920s, Poiret continued to pursue an opulent, Orientalist style, which appeared more difficult to reproduce than the minimalist designs exemplified by Chanel's little black dress. Peter Wollen understands this split between Orientalist and minimalist aesthetics as a fundamental divergence in modernist form.[61] Yet, as Cheng suggests, the distinctions between Orientalist excess and modernist restraint—as well as primitive nudity—are fundamentally unstable.[62] That slippage implicates both Poiret's and Fitzgerald's aesthetics and careers, for it imperils their attempts not only to distinguish between certain styles but also to differentiate pedagogy from imitation and to celebrate the former as the aim of their modernist projects. Both Poiret and Fitzgerald end up blaming their professional failures on the fact that people learned from them at once too poorly and too well, which results in their having imitators rather than pupils and devotees. This close resemblance between imitation and instruction poses a challenge to twenty-first-century scholars as we consider what and how modernism teaches and how we teach modernism.

The pedagogical ambitions of the Omega Workshops are instructive. The aesthetic education it offered the British public via its primitivist and Orientalist creations overlapped with the pacificist activism undertaken by members of the workshop during World War I. As Woolf's biography of Fry suggests, he understood the workshops as a way to cultivate a shared taste for the very civilization that the fighting threatened.[63] The erotics of Orientalism also facilitated Bloomsbury's exploration of nonnormative forms of intimacy in their art and daily lives. Indeed, fashion's associations with frivolity, sophistication, decadence, and waste bind it to perceptions of nonreproductive and nonnormative sexuality. At the same time, the erotic same-sex interactions and gender ambiguity enabled by fashion can fit fairly comfortably within patriarchal, capitalist structures and norms, thus requiring temporally and cultural specific readings of their forms. Poiret's influence is again relevant, for his "harem pants" epitomize the combination of subjugation and liberation that characterizes modern white bourgeois femininity. The pants simultaneously evoke Orientalist fantasies and recall Bloomer's designs for feminist dress reform, which sought to "rationalize" and improve fashion by offering a purportedly feminine version of a bifurcated garment. This history throws into relief the moment in *Orlando: A Biography* (1928) in which the hero turned heroine dons Turkish trousers after her transition.[64] The pants' appearance in *Orlando* also functions (like much of the novel) as an inside Bloomsbury joke, since Orientalist garments encouraged the circulation of affective, erotic, and economic capital within the group. And in the *Dreadnought* hoax of 1910, Woolf and fellow Bloomsberries used primitivist and Orientalist masquerade to humiliate the British navy. A few years later, in the midst of the war, the production of Omega garments and textiles also helped to support refugees and Bloomsbury's conscientious objectors, including Duncan Grant. In 1916, when Bell was aiding Grant, she exchanged playful letters with Woolf about making her a silk jacket—"a kind of kimono," Woolf proposed. Indeed, Woolf purchased a number of garments from the Omega during the war.[65] In short, the Omega's Orientalist and primitivist designs became both a product of and a bulwark against imperialist violence as they helped to sustain Bloomsbury as a subculture.[66] As is the case with the *Dark Princess* and the Walkers, Orientalist fantasies, fabrics, and fashions function as imperialist anti-imperialist tools. Reading these objects and methods fashionably involves teasing out how they might still be useful and attending to how our own approaches emerge from them.

Bloomsbury's investments in dress suggest the density and reach of modernism's formal and historical entanglement with fashion as well as the impossibility of separating modernism's aspirations for social transformation from its reinforcement of the status quo. This book grapples with modernism's intertwinement with imperialism, capitalism, and heteronormativity. At the same time, it responds to arguments about how suspicious or disenchanting approaches to culture generally and modernism specifically might lead us to reinscribe the terms and systems we critique. Justus Nieland, for example, points out that when we "ironize modernism's historical agon with bourgeois publicity," we may end up reaffirming what constitutes the public sphere and overlook the different forms of publicness that modernism offers.[67] Similarly, if we respond to modernists' denunciations of fashion by reaffirming that the latter denotes apoliticism and a capitulation to the market, we miss ways that modernist texts reconceive and mobilize fashion as a practice, mode of perception, and object of critique. Moreover, suspicious and disenchanting analyses of literature and culture, including fashion, can involve their own disavowals.[68] That is not to say that embracing the enchantments of modernism and fashion is a good alternative to reading suspiciously; as I discuss, Lawrence's fiction in particular both expounds on and demonstrates the trouble with such strategies. Instead, the approach I use to read modernism and fashion involves interweaving enchantment and disenchantment and suspicious and reparative readings to create a textured account of these phenomena. This method responds to the variegated, ambivalent, and inventive ways that writers engage with fashion as a local and global system made up of objects, substances, feelings, practices, beliefs, values, desires, styles, and ideas. What this book undertakes, then, is an *explanation* of fashion and fiction, keeping in view the origin of that word in the term for unfolding or laying flat (*explanere*) what may be and remain dense, thick, crumpled, pleated, and knotted, even when spread across the page.

1 : MOODS, MODES, MODERNISM

Reading Fashionably with Virginia Woolf

> Mood work takes shape as a form that is similarly used or co-recognised between agents in a shared scene, a sense that something is happening and an attachment, however inchoate, to sensing out what that something is. The world composed comes apart all the time and at the same time something is (always) coming, and coming together.
>
> —Jennifer D. Carlson and Kathleen C. Stewart,
> "The Legibilities of Mood Work"

> But my present reflection is that people have any number of states of consciousness: & I should like to investigate the party consciousness, the frock consciousness &c. The fashion world at the Becks— Mrs. Garland was there superintending a display—is certainly one; where people secrete an envelope which connects them & protects them from others, like myself, who am outside the envelope, foreign bodies. These states are very difficult (obviously I grope for words) but I'm always coming back to it. The party consciousness, for example: Sybil's consciousness. You must not break it. It is something real. You must keep it up—conspire together. Still I cannot get at what I mean.
>
> —Virginia Woolf, *Diary*

For anthropologists Jennifer D. Carlson and Kathleen C. Stewart, "mood work" refers to the individual and collective labor of "sens[ing] out what is actual and potential in an historical moment or a situation."[1] This process is both subject and method for Carlson and Stewart. As they seek to make legible "emergent patterns of everyday life and their poetic force," their technique brings together ordinary and scholarly ways of reading, as well as literary, literary critical, and social scientific modes of inquiry.[2] Such an approach draws from a tradition of affectively attuned cultural studies epitomized by Raymond Williams's concept of "structures of feeling," which he defines as the "set" of "characteristic elements of impulse, restraint, and tone" in a given time and place.[3] Williams compares changes in structures of feeling over time to the changes in language captured by "the literary term 'style'" and indicates that "similar kinds of change can be observed in manners, dress, buildings, and other similar forms of social life."[4] Yet, whereas Williams offers an analogy between feelings, literary style, manners, and dress, mood can be conceived more capaciously. In the introduction of the special issue of *New Formations* in which Carlson and Stewart's essay appears, Ben Highmore and Julie Bourne Taylor propose that mood "incorporates the entire situation as well as the 'players' within it" and "is made up of individual and collective feelings, organic and inorganic elements, as well as contingent, historical and slow changing conditions."[5] Like Virginia Woolf's reflections on "frock consciousness," such an understanding of mood foregrounds how seemingly personal feelings are formed with and through objects, bodies, thoughts, experiences, beliefs, and historical conditions.[6]

This approach to mood offers a number of benefits. It shifts us away from an account of feelings as possessions that may pass between individuals toward an understanding of how emotions are produced by contact between objects, bodies, behaviors, and atmospheres.[7] An understanding of mood as made up of multiple "players" also offers a way for theorists of emotion and affect to avoid untenable distinctions between a bodily or "affective-corporeal" realm and one of ideology and history.[8] For example, Carlson and Stewart's mood work, like many of Woolf's texts, attends to how subjects negotiate the political ideas and forces that are woven into the texture and feeling of the everyday, thereby tracing connections between corporeal, affective, aesthetic, and political dimensions of mundane experience. In turn, Stewart suggests that close readings of everyday life may better equip us to grasp possibilities for social and political transformation than do more sweeping accounts of socioeconomic systems.[9] She joins scholars such as Lauren Berlant and Sara Ahmed whose efforts to trace contemporary affective forms and dynamics offer ways of grappling with the possibilities and limitations of the present.[10] Mood provides a particularly powerful tool for doing such work because it enables us to connect and contrast different scales of reading and representation. A mood can characterize a fleeting everyday scene as well as a global affective-material system (as for example in an economic depression). Moods thus offer ways of discussing how and why such temporal, spatial, and conceptual shifts occur. At the same time, mood work involves being attuned to how things might be otherwise or how they may already take unexpected forms. Thus mood work keeps in view questions about what the knowledge it produces does, and how.

The passage from Woolf's diary entry for April 27, 1925 is also concerned with scale and form. Woolf records her thoughts after a morning spent "sitting to *Vogue*"—that is, having her picture taken for a feature that would appear in the magazine a month later. Woolf was photographed by Maurice Beck and Helen McGregor at their studio, where the magazine's assistant editor, Madge Garland, was simultaneously arranging a display. Woolf understands "frock consciousness" as particular to this scene and as a characteristic form or genre of experience. Moreover, her references to the influential British socialite Sybil Colefax and to parties, foreign bodies, and conspiracies invite one to imagine how this "state" might intersect with and translate into other social and political forms and contexts. Woolf's association between fashion and feeling also points to the connection between mood and *la mode*. In French, *mode* means mood and fashion, and it links both to the sense of the "just now" (*modo*) at the heart of modernity and modernism.[11] Accordingly, fashion (understood as a prevailing style of dress) is often said to reflect, express, or capture the characteristic feeling or "spirit" of a given time and place.

In Woolf's work, moods often are generated or expressed through *les modes*—ways of dressing and ways of writing (including writing about dress). For example, Woolf's famous claim that "on or about December 1910, human character changed" describes a change in mood. Woolf illustrates this transformation by asserting that whereas "the Victorian cook lived like a leviathan in the lower depths, formidable, silent, obscure, inscrutable; the Georgian cook is a creature of sunshine and fresh air; in and out of the drawing room, now to borrow the *Daily Herald*, now to ask advice about a hat."[12] This epochal shift in mood is experienced as a change in the fashion system, in weather, and in the texture of everyday life, and it necessitates a change in how literature is written. Of course, Woolf's own modes of representation vary during her career, as she experimented with fictional and nonfictional prose genres and forms. Yet across a range of texts she explores how fabrics and frocks make up the patterns of fiction and everyday life, and how they situate bodies within fashion systems comprising objects, beliefs, desires, corporations, labor, styles, and feelings. If mood helps us to attend to form and to a network of forces, then Woolf's exploration of mood's relationship to fabric and fashion links that project to the dynamics of textuality, style, and representation. Woolf's work shows how mood is inextricable from the terms in which it is expressed, and therefore mood might be imagined and experienced otherwise via writing.

Taking its cue from the idea of "frock consciousness," this chapter shows how Woolf's work draws on the relationship between mood and *la mode* to "sense out," describe, and give form to what is happening in an unfolding, densely textured scene in which local and global forces converge. In such temporally and generically disparate texts as *Mrs. Dalloway* and *Three Guineas*, affectively saturated garments (a green dress, a military uniform) determine "what is actual and potential in a historical moment." As garments locate people within existing networks of objects, beliefs, and emotions, they make those networks and processes more perceptible. Thus representations of feeling and fashion make clearer how accounts of everyday life can provide tools for understanding broader political and historical forces. In addition to making things legible, the connection between mood and *la mode* helps Woolf to grapple with what and how things are sensed and known in the first place. Heidegger's account of *Stimmung*, which is usually translated as "mood" or "attunement," reflects this word's roots as a term for musical tuning. He claims that moods or attunements dictate what "matters to us," what resonates and claims our attention.[13] In the case of Woolf's assertions about 1910, we might note that the cook is not simply different, but nearly indiscernible ("silent, obscure, inscrutable") to the speaker prior to this transformation. As she attends to shifts in class relations, Woolf highlights mood's sociopolitical dimensions. Fashion, too, can draw attention to the situated, contingent nature of perception. Think, for example, of how garments can seem to have changed shape and texture when reencountered after the fashions have changed. (We open a box of our old clothes and wonder: Were those pant legs always so wide?) In that sense, fashion is itself a form of attunement that makes certain forms more or less perceptible in a given time and place. If mood is, as Ahmed says, an "*affective lens*, affecting how we are affected," then fashion is a formal lens, forming our perception of forms.[14]

Woolf's "frock conscious" mode of mood work responds to those dynamics as it offers and endorses what I would describe as fashionable ways of knowing and perceiving. These methods are contextual, contingent, compromised, and materially grounded, as well as textually mediated. In fiction and nonfiction from *Jacob's Room* (1922), *Mrs. Dalloway*, and "Modern Fiction" to *The Years* and *Three Guineas*, Woolf engages fashion and fabric as heuristic devices to develop affectively attuned and materially grounded modes of describing established, emergent, and potential "patterns of everyday life." Fashion, fabric, and feeling thus shape what Woolf's texts attempt to do in the world, and how—that is, what her texts illuminate and how they make an impact. Fashion's influence on Woolf's ideas about the form and purpose of her works is also a matter of context. For example, Woolf supported the experiments in dress design undertaken during World War I by the Omega Workshops, an artists' collective run by members of the Bloomsbury group, including her sister, Vanessa Bell. During the war, the

Omega was a center for both design and pacifist activism. But it provides a counterpoint for Woolf's later thinking about how carefully stylized and intricately textured objects—whether texts or garments—might shift the mood and otherwise make visible and interrupt the functioning of patriarchal imperialist systems. For, as I argue, Woolf comes to distinguish between using dress as a form of political expression and using fashion as a critical mode of perception.

The overlap I perceive between Woolf's modernism and contemporary cultural work on mood includes not only a mutual interest in shared forms of feeling, thinking, and acting but also a vulnerability to charges of modishness. In Woolf's era and our own, fashion provides a vocabulary for dismissing certain forms of knowledge. Certainly we can read Woolf's engagements with the "fashion world" (however ambivalent) as evidence of her complicity with consumer culture. Attending to such connections, many scholars in modernist studies in the last few decades have revitalized the field by demonstrating how various modernist artists and their work at once decry and reinscribe gendered and racialized capitalist and imperialist systems. My emphasis, however, is how modernism and specifically Woolf's works engage with mood, fabric, and fashion to make visible, grapple with, and attempt to work through the resulting entanglements and impasses. The point is to acknowledge and make use of the resonances between the various combinations of critique and complicity that characterize modernist and contemporary academic methods.

Such a Woolfian approach is apparent in much contemporary scholarship on affect and feeling, including Carlson and Stewart's essay, which acknowledges the critic's relation to and implication in the forms they examine, while attempting to offer some critical purchase.[15] Moreover, Woolf's work responds to many of the same issues that emerge with the recent turn to affect and wider debates about methodology in the humanities and social sciences. These include skepticism about totalizing systems of knowledge, attunement to the limitations of institutionalized critique, and doubts about the capacity of art (and writing about art) to effect political change.[16] Discussions of methodology are also matters of feeling. As Rita Felski observes, the interest in new approaches to literary study can be understood as a desire for a change in mood.[17] After all, calls for alternative forms of scholarly inquiry often involve a critique of what Paul Ricoeur describes as the "hermeneutics of suspicion"—a form of interpretation exemplified by Freud, Marx, and Nietzsche that privileges the work of "unmasking, demystification, or reduction of illusions."[18] Contemporary debates about methodology raise questions that Woolf's work addresses via its treatments of mood and mode: Do prevailing affective and material patterns determine what becomes a matter of interest in the first place? How do shared feelings and material practices consolidate or shift in the context of broader networks of power? What groups, individuals, and institutions are positioned to change the mood? This chapter explores how Woolf grapples with these questions across a range of genres and forms. It tracks her fiction's shifting modes of sensing out and giving shape to the world through mood and mode. Through discussions of "Modern Fiction," *Mrs. Dalloway*, "The New Dress," *The Years*, *Three Guineas*, and *Roger Fry: A Biography* (1940), I describe changes and continuities in Woolf's method. Certainly, other works by Woolf address these questions and employ these methods. *Jacob's Room* and *The Waves* (1931), for example, investigate the nature of mood and use garments to interrogate distinctions between interior, individual lives and collective and material forces, while *Orlando* directly addresses the connection between fashion and "the spirit of the age."[19] Indeed, I focus on *Orlando* in chapter 4 because its related treatments of periodicity, exemplarity, Orientalism, and celebrity help us to understand Fitzgerald's and Poiret's efforts to parlay fashionability into lasting influence. My aim in this first chapter, then, is not to provide an exhaustive account of Woolf's methods and their relationship to mood and fashion throughout her career. Rather, I highlight intersections between her writing and certain influential contemporary approaches to affect, mood, and critique in literary and cultural studies. Woolf's engagements with the nexus of mood and *la mode* clarify the stakes and terms of recent debates about the methods and aims of literary study, as well as the forms and strategies of her modernism.

Feeling Modern Fiction

The importance of mood and *la mode* to Woolf's modernism becomes clearer when we read Woolf's reflections on "frock consciousness" in light of the essay "Modern Fiction," in which Woolf lays out her aesthetic principles. In fact, "Modern Fiction" was published in Woolf's volume of essays *The Common Reader* (1925) just days after her visit to "the Becks."[20] In particular, Woolf's image of people secreting an "envelope" invites a more "frock conscious" reading of Woolf's famous essay. As readers of Woolf will recall, "Modern Fiction" describes "life" as a "semi-transparent envelope," which literature must try to "convey."[21] In the diary entry, the envelope is more obviously intersubjective and material as well as defensive and exclusive. Like a stylish garment, it envelops those "in the know" with a material that unites and separates them from interlopers. It operates, in short, like both a mood and *la mode*. A concern with collective forms of feeling and knowing is typical of Woolf's work, which depicts such shared states as having diverse, even contradictory effects, including constraint, oppression, repair, and transformation. In this passage, Woolf's ambivalence about these "states" is suggested by their association with fashion. Although Woolf insists she is "outside the envelope" of this "fashion world," the photography session brought her (temporarily) into its fold; in a diary entry six months earlier, Woolf noted with a mix of pride and sarcasm that *Vogue* was "going to take up Mrs. Woolf, to boom her."[22] Given Woolf's ambivalence, it is fitting that her attempt to describe others' "states of consciousness" becomes an effort to express her own feelings, while the switch to the second person implicates her in these "states." In short, Woolf's shifting relationship to the fashion world epitomizes her position vis-à-vis the patterns of experience that she reads and makes readable through writing.

This process of sensing out and describing the world recalls the modes of reading and writing that Woolf advocates in "Modern Fiction."[23] All involve feeling one's way, and all use fashion and fabric to describe these processes. In this diary entry, writing occurs once Woolf has felt out the situation in this "fashion world" and as she gropes for words to convey it. In "Modern Fiction," Woolf treats feeling as a principle tool of literary criticism and of composition. For instance, Woolf admits that her critique of "the form of fiction most in vogue" (that of Wells, Bennett, and Galsworthy) is based on a feeling of "discontent" that she attempts to "justify" ("MF," 148). And Woolf employs textile metaphors as she concludes that "the proper stuff of fiction" must be able to include "everything . . . every feeling, every thought; every quality of brain and spirit" that the writer can "draw upon" ("MF," 154).[24] Literature is a kind of "stuff" (i.e., fabric) into which feeling and thought can be woven and through which they can be represented. Writers thus need not only a new "design" for fiction but also a more elastic sense of the very "stuff" that makes it up and what that fabric might do. Yet the Woolfian critic must be attuned to and skeptical of fashions in fiction, so as not simply to follow current trends. Fabric provides Woolf with a vocabulary that interweaves form, content, and historicity and establishes the substance of style.

Woolf's references to "stuff" also underscores that, in "Modern Fiction," feeling involves sight and touch. The essay proposes that modern fiction should be attuned to and should explore the places where the emotional, visual, and tactile converge—a realm exemplified by textiles and moods and by the connection between them. Textiles, after all, are often understood to conjure particular moods, while moods shape our experience of objects, including textiles; that relationship reinforces the link between mood and *la mode.*[25] In "Modern Fiction," Woolf interweaves emotion, sight, and touch when she describes fiction's privileged material, "life," both as an "envelope" and in terms of the "myriad impressions" on the mind, which she refers to as "an incessant shower of innumerable atoms"; this "shower" is a process by which the world touches the mind, generating thought and feeling (150). So while Woolf critiques Wells, Bennett, and Galsworthy for being "materialists" who lavish too much attention on "the trivial and transitory" (such as "the fashion of the hour"), her version of modern fiction is realized through material processes and forms ("MF," 148, 149).[26] Woolf's references to "stuff" and "impressions" also suggest that we should not read the envelope simply as evidence of a Woolfian "fixation on surfaces."[27] If "the mind receives myriad impressions," as Woolf says, then its surface has some depth and texture.[28] The task that Woolf proposes for modern writing is not to describe surfaces, but rather to sense out and to convey the particular texture and feeling of "ordinary" life.

This formulation bears on current discussions about literary method—specifically, what has been described as "surface reading." Stephen Best and Sharon Marcus explain that surface reading involves attending to "what is evident, perceptible, apprehensible in texts" rather than what is "hidden, repressed, deep, and in need of detection and disclosure by an interpreter," which they associate with symptomatic reading and the hermeneutics of suspicion.[29] Yet focusing on mood and *la mode* facilitates a move away from a binary between surface and depth and, with it, between scholarship that exerts "minimal critical agency" and scholarship that aspires to political transformation.[30] Mood and fashion also trouble the assumption that one can easily distinguish between "what is evident" and "what is "in need of detection." Although dress might seem to be aligned with surface, Woolf's work often draws on fashion and feeling to examine the process by which, as Ahmed puts it, some issues "surface" or become visible only for some people and at certain times. Ahmed contrasts this attention to the "affective distribution of problems" with "what is described (and perhaps dismissed) as 'ideology critique,' as a critique of what the surface hides."[31] Like mood work, Ahmed's method better equips us to take into account how differences in position and (I would add) transformations over time determine what makes things surface in the first place. In works including the short story "The New Dress," *Mrs. Dalloway*, *The Years*, and *Three Guineas*, Woolf deploys phenomenological approaches that resonate with Ahmed's. Woolf's texts do not so much detect deep, hidden structures as feel out and follow around the traces of complex, shifting systems of power while also imagining how such systems extend beyond the reach of her own and other people's senses. In *Three Guineas*, for example, Woolf develops a method of critique that might be practiced by the "educated man's daughter," who is unschooled in certain forms of institutionalized knowledge but is an expert in sensing out the uneven texture of the social fabric. While Woolf's fiction does not make the same claims to factuality as *Three Guineas*, her experiments with mood and mode describe or comment on how such ephemeral and contingent phenomena as feelings and fashions take hold and travel across space and time. Woolf thus engages in a speculative mode of mood work, which fabricates as well as traverses the threads of connection formed through feeling and fashion. Her mood work involves describing the social as an assemblage of diverse agents, but also takes up the task of imagining and reimagining how the world might be "coming together."[32]

"Modern Fiction" draws on the language and logic of fashion to critique existing narrative forms and conjure alternative possibilities. When Woolf associates the "accepted style" of fiction with detailed depictions of the styling of "Bond Street tailors," she ties it to a fashion system steered by the latest in court dress ("MF," 150).[33] Along with her complaints that a "tyrant" seems to dictate fiction's "design," these references highlight the intertwinement of British fashion and forms of governance—a bond that was, however, weakening in the postwar era ("MF," 149).[34] (*Mrs. Dalloway* registers that relationship when it describes how the car apparently bearing a member of the royal family or the prime minister "left a slight ripple which flowed through glove shops and hat shops and tailors' shops on both sides of Bond Street").[35] We also might read these critiques of "the form of fiction most in vogue" as evidence of Woolf's anxieties about her own work's seeming modishness. Certainly it is ironic that Woolf describes Bennett and others this way when the publication of *The Common Reader* was announced in *Vogue*'s May issue and accompanied by one of the photographs of Woolf taken by Beck and McGregor. As we recognize such anxiety and disavowal, Woolf's associations of tyranny and fashion also attune us to ways that her account of literary history resembles the logic of fashion. Woolf writes, "We do not come to write better; all that we can be said to do is to keep moving, now a little in this direction, now in that, but with a circular tendency should the whole course of the track be viewed from a sufficiently lofty pinnacle" ("MF," 146). Woolf compares authors to warriors who, engaged in the fight, lack perspective on the progress of the war. But this vision of nonprogressive, ultimately circular change also recalls the temporality of fashion, which Walter Benjamin describes as "the eternal recurrence of the new."[36] Even as Woolf critiques forms of literature that are merely fashionable, she offers an account of literary and historical time that resembles a distended version of fashion's cycles.

While Benjamin offers the most famous formulation of this idea, fashion was (and is) popularly associated with repetition, as a cartoon from the *Sketch* illustrates. The image registers the shift in fashion that occurred in 1915 as narrow, high-waisted prewar styles gave way to a so-called war crinoline, which some fashion journalists at the time described as reanimating Victorian styles and epitomizing traditional visions of frivolous, pleasing femininity.[37] The cartoon predicts a quick return to high-waisted modes, but that did not turn out to be the case; like literary historians, fashion historians often cite the war's beginning or end as a moment of epochal change, which the cartoon does not anticipate.[38] By condensing the fashion cycle into three years, the image mocks the women who cannot see beyond the current styles, while the quote from Shakespeare's *Twelfth Night*—"and thus the whirligig of time brings in his revenges"—links the cartoon to an enduring British literary tradition that transcends even as it comments on time's fools. Nevertheless, the cartoon ends up revealing its own inability to master fashion's temporality, which is also a failure to anticipate how the war was impacting everyday life. "Modern Fiction" registers the limitations of occupying both the place of the fashion-conscious women and the creators of the *Sketch* cartoon, who, like Woolf's literary historian, presume to have a better "vantage point" on past and current cultural developments ("MF," 146). Woolf's literary historian is very much like a fashion journalist who, with war raging, presumes to trace the origins and judge the value, endurance, and near future developments of certain forms, yet whose distance from the action makes his or her claims irrelevant.

While the cartoon gets the specifics of fashion history wrong, we also might read this image as signaling that the war was not a complete break in imperialist-capitalist business as usual. In that sense, the seemingly superficial phenomenon of fashion (or, in this case, fashion journalism) displays those underlying continuities and repetitions on its surface. Accordingly, in *Mrs. Dalloway* fashion can make legible the connections between everyday life and the economic, political, and social forces that give rise to repeated yet unanticipated state-sanctioned violence. For example, the green dress that Clarissa repairs and wears to her party displays how certain power dynamics, forms, and structures of feeling survive the war—and thus might bring about another conflagration. As Celia Marshik notes, "British women's evening dress" was understood by twentieth-century commentators, including Woolf, to be a "particularly *conservative* form."[39] This is underscored in *Mrs. Dalloway* by the fact that Clarissa's gown was made before the war by

AS IT WAS. IS. AND EVER WILL BE!

DRAWN BY G. E. PETO.

G. E. Peto, "As It Was. Is. And Ever Will Be!" *The Sketch*, July 14, 1915, 2. © Mary Evans Picture Library.

a now-retired dressmaker named Sally Parker, whose creations Clarissa wore to Buckingham Palace and Hatfield House. The garment enables Clarissa to set the right mood for the party. In a climactic moment, Peter watches as Clarissa "escorted her Prime Minister down the room, prancing, sparkling, with the stateliness of her grey hair. She wore ear-rings, and a silver-green mermaid's dress" (*MD*, 169). The dress's mermaid quality speaks to the way that (as her party demonstrates) elite political and social networks cross into each other and traverse pre- and postwar time. Clad in a glamorous, newly mended gown, with hair tinged by age and illness, Clarissa's stateliness makes her an accessory of the state.

This dress also facilitates the ethically ambiguous moment in which Clarissa imagines that she can feel what Septimus felt at the moment of his death. As Clarissa stands by the window, "her dress flamed, her body burnt," fueling an instant of connection, empathy, projection, and violence via text and textile (*MD*, 178).[40] Yet another green evening dress—this one worn by Miss Isabel Pole, Septimus's beloved lecturer on Shakespeare—is part of the vision of England for which Septimus volunteers to fight. So if "war crino-lines" and uniforms can conjure a patriotic mood, in *Mrs. Dalloway* green evening gowns generate and expose such fantasies of shared feeling between women and soldiers. This dynamic underscores the novel's ambivalence about the power of mood as a form of collective emotion and about its own densely textured narrative form. The novel stitches together characters' con-sciousnesses, but the character that is explicitly described as connected by a "thread" to others is the imperious and imperial Lady Bruton, who is joined to Richard Dalloway and the impeccably dressed Hugh Whitbread (*MD*, 110). Woven out of such strands, social and narrative fabrics smother as well as swaddle and sustain.

Nevertheless, "Modern Fiction" does not advocate for distance or disen-tanglement as alternatives to feeling one's way; Woolf is reluctant to take up the "vantage point" of the literary historian. At the same time, her essay bases its argument on historicist claims about the relationship between literature's form and its cultural context. Woolf echoes the popular association between fashion and the prevailing mood or "spirit of the age" when she asserts that "one of those little deviations which the human spirit seems to make from time to time" has caused realist novels to become "ill-fitting vestments" in which "life . . . refuses to be contained" ("MF," 149). As it connects changes in literature to changes in dress design, however, "Modern Fiction" dodges any straightforward account of what the correspondences between clothing, writing, and history might be; the nature or reason for the "deviations" is unspecified, although references to things such as battles, tyrants, atoms, and

Bond Street fashions hint at a network of forces shifting the mood and the mode. So while the essay gestures toward historicist readings of literary form, it also underscores the inadequacy of such readings. This mode of historicism complements the essay's attempt simultaneously to describe, influence, and stay open to literary-historical developments and, in doing so, to mark the essay itself as both perennial and of the moment.[41] Refusing simple historical accounts of cause and effect helps the essay to escape being pinned to a particular historical moment, even as it comments on contemporary literature. This temporal strategy also is expressed through the mixed form of "Modern Fiction," which offers a partial and slightly belated survey of contemporary fiction as well as a hesitant manifesto.[42] Rather than embracing the avant-gardism of the manifesto, Woolf's modernist vision emphasizes continuity as well as change.

That hybrid genre of the survey-manifesto is perennial and of the moment in twenty-first-century literary criticism, including as the discipline turns to questions of methodology. In Best and Marcus's introduction to the special issue of *Representations* on "The Way We Read Now," for example, they observe and thus consolidate what they see as ongoing methodological shifts toward surface reading. Like "Modern Fiction," their essay begins with a hesitant invocation of a collective subject made up of writers who are also readers and who are formulating their own methods in response to the work of their predecessors. Both essays announce that their description of a particular method emerges from their observations about what techniques are already in use. And they emphasize that they must be somewhat vague in describing their subjects (trends in modern fiction and in contemporary criticism, respectively) and must use terms that may misrepresent or exclude aspects of what they mean to describe.[43] These resonances between Best and Marcus's and Woolf's essays attune us to the ways that current methodological debates echo modernist concerns about method, which are also concerns about what literature can do in the context of capitalism and spectacular yet normalized state-sponsored violence.[44]

This could be understood, in fact, as a matter of attunement. *Modernism* is a notoriously slippery and contested term, designating a range of sometimes contradictory attributes, but it usually refers to work displaying what Paul Saint-Amour describes as an "anticontemporary or counterconventional temper."[45] Such a "temper" does not describe a particular feeling, since it can involve, for instance, euphoria, excitement, anticipation, anxiety, nostalgia, and despair. Like a mood, however, it can make certain feelings more likely; it thus recalls Ahmed's description of mood as an "affective lens," although I would also echo Ahmed's point that distinctions between moods and feelings are situational and performative rather than "intrinsic."[46] Moreover, this modernist "temper" encompasses different perspectives on what constitutes the contemporary and conventional. As "Modern Fiction" demonstrates, it does not necessarily involve a universal hostility to the present or a radical break with the past. It is with that capaciousness in mind that I suggest that modernism's mode of attunement to the world characterizes much literary criticism, including efforts to mark and encourage shifts in critical practices. The next section of this chapter explores how, according to Woolf, moods and modes shape what come to our attention and what that might indicate about what we should attend to when considering literary methodologies.

Fashion and Ways of Knowing

In discussing "Modern Fiction," I have argued that although Woolf critiques the "form of fiction most in vogue," she turns to fashion to describe writing and reading as ways of feeling one's way in a densely textured present that is changing but not radically new. If feeling is inextricable from thought, we might ask: Are there particular kinds of knowledge that fashion involves or encourages? How do mood and *la mode* shape what is known? And how do those ways of knowing and feeling bear on recent discussions of methodology in literary and cultural studies? Answers to these questions are scattered throughout Woolf's oeuvre, but a short story called "The New Dress" offers a case study that was written during the period in which Woolf developed the literary method for which she is most famous. Though published in 1927, the story was composed in 1924 while Woolf was revising *Mrs. Dalloway* and *The Common Reader*, and it focuses on the thoughts and feelings of one Mabel Waring while she attends Mrs. Dalloway's party. Though Mabel is peripheral to Clarissa's event, her methods of feeling her way through the world anticipate the novel's engagements with mood and fashion and, in particular, with frock consciousness as a mode of perception and relation. Before turning to "The New Dress" and then *Mrs. Dalloway*, however, it is worth saying a bit more about how mood has been understood to relate to knowledge in the context of modernity.

"Modern Fiction" implies that the mood of modern life is one of transition and transformation, and it shows some ambivalence and anxiety about the relationship between *la mode* and what we now call modernism. Indeed, if excitement and anticipation are signature moods of modernity and fashion, so is anxiety.[47] Not coincidentally, anxiety also has been theorized as the basis for philosophical thought; Sianne Ngai describes it as "the male knowledge-seeker's distinctive yet basic state of mind."[48] According to Heidegger, all moods entail the "thrownness" of *Dasein* ("Being-in-the-World"), his term for human existence, which signals its situatedness and contingence.[49] In other words, moods underscore that Being is cast into a particular time and place that determine the contours and possibilities of its existence. Yet Heidegger maintains that, unlike most moods that involve "an evasive turning away" from that thrownness, anxiety prompts a confrontation with the meaninglessness of the things that otherwise engage and situate us.[50] As Stephen Mulhall explains, anxiety thus can prompt *Dasein* to "acknowledge [that] its existence . . . is always more or other than its present actualizations" and to take up the possibility that one might be otherwise.[51] In this way, "anxiety individualizes Dasein."[52] Such a response to anxiety amounts to what Justus Nieland refers to as a sort of "existential heroism."[53] This account of anxiety diverges from the form of mood work endorsed by Carlson and Stewart as well as Ben Highmore and Julie Taylor Bourne, for these critics indicate that grappling with mood always turns one toward one's relation to other bodies and objects. But we can see the legacy of Heidegger's concept of anxiety as individualizing in literary critical practices, including those that try to shift away from anxiety and suspicion.

Ngai emphasizes the gendered dynamics of anxiety's "epistemological cachet" by situating Heidegger in relation to "spatialized representations of anxiety in works by Alfred Hitchcock and Herman Melville."[54] Ngai's reading of *Vertigo* compares the Heideggerian subject both to Hitchcock's protagonist, Scottie (James Stewart), a private investigator who ultimately recovers from vertigo after witnessing his lover's fall from a tower, and to an (unseen, briefly mentioned) male engineer-turned-designer who is said to make a fortune off of a design for a strapless bra that uses the principles of bridge construction to cause a woman's body to "throw" the chest out by using its own weight. For Hitchcock's designer and investigator, catapulting femininity is a way for the masculine intellectual to "regain his equilibrium."[55] In Scottie's case, moreover, he lost that equilibrium after a policeman plunges to his death while attempting to rescue Scottie from the edge of a rooftop; hence, Scottie must recover from causing the fall of a man in uniform, which in turn has cast him out of the public realm and into the private sphere.

Ngai does not discuss representations of anxious women, but her cinematic example points us toward a feminized counterpart to the figure of the anxious modern male knowledge seeker: that of the fashion victim, who anxiously yet seemingly mindlessly turns to dress to regain a foothold within modernity's disorienting flux. But of course, dressing and knowledge seeking are not mutually exclusive. "The New Dress" contrasts these two anxious activities and traces gendered hierarchies between ways of knowing, including dress, literature, religion, politics, and science. These hierarchies are amplified by the story's minor status in Woolf's oeuvre and the apparent triviality of the story's subject matter. "The New Dress" employs free indirect discourse to convey the anxious thoughts of an unremarkable if oddly dressed middle-aged woman (Mabel Waring) as she arrives at, moves through, and quickly leaves Mrs. Dalloway's party. Mabel feels deeply ashamed of what she decides is her "idiotically old-fashioned" new dress, and it becomes clear that she has invested in clothing as well as literature as objects that might stave off the mood of anxiety and disappointment that often envelops her.[56] This dynamic returns us to current discussions about possible alternatives to the hermeneutics of suspicion—an anxious form of critical inquiry that might seem increasingly outmoded. For Mabel's patterns of thought and feeling overlap with those of Heidegger's anxious individual and of his intellectual cousin, the paranoid reader, whom Eve Sedgwick presents as the exemplary practitioner of the hermeneutics of suspicion.[57] Like Sedgwick's discussions of paranoid reading, "The New Dress" explores the limitations of anxiety and suspicion as signature moods of inquiry. But the story also dramatizes the impediments to and consequences of shifting to a different mood and mode of thinking. In Woolf's story, unlike in Heidegger's account, such transformative projects falter as they rest on a (somewhat) socially marginal individual. Woolf's story thus attunes us to the ways that our debates about methodology invest us in forms of progressive, individual transformation, even as we describe broader changes in "how we read." By linking the intransigence of mood to *la mode*, "The New Dress" keeps in view the material dimensions of methodological questions that often are described in psychic, affective, or epistemological terms and in ways that privilege the individual's relation to a cultural object.

The opening sentences of the story could be read as a parody of Heideggerian anxiety and the hermeneutics of suspicion. They describe Mabel's arrival at Mrs. Dalloway's party:

> Mabel had her first serious suspicion that something was wrong as she took her cloak off and Mrs. Barnet, while handing her the mirror and touching the brushes and thus drawing her attention, perhaps rather markedly, to all the appliances for tidying and improving hair, complexion, clothes, which existed on the dressing table, confirmed the suspicion—that it was not right, not quite right, which growing stronger as she went upstairs and springing at her, with conviction as she greeted Clarissa Dalloway, she went straight to the far end of the room, to a shaded corner where a looking-glass hung and looked. No!

It was not right. And at once the misery which she always tried to hide, the
profound dissatisfaction—the sense she had had, ever since she was a child,
of being inferior to other people—set upon her, relentlessly, remorselessly.
("ND," 61–62)

As Jessica Burstein observes, the "it" that is "not right" seems to refer both
to Mabel's dress and to Mabel herself.[58] Mabel's anxiety and suspicion appear to encompass rather than stem from her concerns about the garment.
Anxiety also undercuts Mabel's senses of cause and effect and of interior and
exterior; Mabel's "first serious suspicion" is provoked by the same gestures
that "confirmed the suspicion," and that suspicion comes "springing at her,"
yet also originates from a "conviction" that seems to be her own ("ND," 61).
As in Heidegger's account of mood, Mabel's anxiety "comes neither from
'outside' nor from 'inside,' but arises out of Being-in-the-world."[59] Mabel
also is "thrown back" on herself after discovering that "it" fails to provide the
sense of meaning and plenitude that she already lacks. Yet Mabel's flight to
the "looking-glass" implies that this anxious return to the self is a cul de sac.
Throughout the story, Mabel's anxiety makes it extremely difficult for the
reader to distinguish her assumptions and misperceptions from observations
of other guests' behavior, to the extent that it is sometimes unclear whether
Mabel hears or imagines the statements attributed to other guests. The result
is an exaggerated version of the subjective, interiorizing technique of high
modernism. As Woolf says of Joyce's work in "Modern Fiction," we have "a
sense of being confined and shut in" and "feel neither jovial nor magnani-
mous, but rather centred in a self which, in spite of its tremor of susceptibility, never embraces or creates what is outside itself and beyond" ("MF," 151).
Mabel's anxious ruminations—and hence Woolf's method of narration—are
often frustratingly recursive and self-referential.

Mabel's anxiety sets in motion a way of thinking that more closely resembles Sedgwick's account of paranoid reading than Heidegger's description of anxious philosophizing.[60] Drawing on Silvan Tomkins's theories of
affect, Sedgwick asserts that paranoia is anticipatory, mimetic and reflective, a strong theory, and a theory of negative affects, and that it places its
faith in exposure. Throughout her time at the party, Mabel anticipates other
guests' criticism and rejection and, as in the opening paragraph, her unreli-
able perspective generates yet more suspicion in the reader. Like the "strong
theory" of paranoia, Mabel's suspicion is capable of "accounting for a wide
spectrum of phenomena," since everything she feels and observes is explained in relation to her own inferiority and weakness.[61] Mabel even diag-
noses her own pervasive mood of dissatisfaction as a symptom of her place

within British society—specifically, as one of ten children in a family of fading country gentility who ends up marrying a man with a "safe, permanent underlings job in the Law Courts" ("ND," 70). Mabel also places great faith in the bracing effects of confronting such facts about herself. She lashes out against what she decides are the false courtesies of her fellow guests and castigates herself for indulging in the fantasy that the new dress reveals her hidden, beautiful self: "She saw the truth. *This* was true, this drawing-room, this self, the other false" ("ND," 64; emphasis in original). Even as she exposes and feels exposed, however, Mabel reinvests in rather than de-mystifies the romance of empire and gender norms. She laments, for example, her lost "dreams of living in India, married to some hero like Sir Henry Lawrence, some empire builder (still the sight of a native in a turban filled her with romance)" ("ND," 70). Mabel's tendency to see her own attachments as symptoms of broader sociopolitical forces resembles methods of suspicious reading. Her self-diagnoses also seem to accomplish the Woolfian project of showing how historical and political systems are experienced and become legible in the realm of the everyday. The reader who is attuned to the dynamics of Orientalism and imperialism, however, will perceive the ways Mabel and perhaps the story nevertheless reaffirm such systems. Mabel's mode of attunement, we might say, is such that these things do not surface or come to her attention.

Mabel fails to perceive what is on the surface. But if we read her story as a symptom of imperialism, capitalism, and heteronormativity, we do not so much reveal what is hidden as take into account what Mabel Waring is wearing and how it was made. Mabel believes she cannot afford a fashionable dress because "fashion meant cut, meant style, meant thirty guineas at least." Instead, she has had an outfit made by a modest, unfashionable dressmaker after an illustration in an "old fashion book of her mother's, a Paris fashion book of the time of the Empire." Mabel imagines, paradoxically, that wearing such a style will make her "original," and indeed this imperial era represents for Mabel a kind of maternal origin point, when femininity and beauty were not yet eroded by fashion ("ND," 62). Mabel thus wears her attachments on her sleeve, although only some viewers might see what stylistic and financial investments her yellow dress displays.

A reader of British *Vogue* in 1924 might also perceive that Woolf is implicated in Mabel's tale of sartorial disaster. That May, the magazine's monthly spread on men and women of achievement called "We Nominate for the Hall of Fame" included a photograph of Woolf clad in a late-Victorian dress that belonged to her mother, Julia Stephen.[62] A descendent of aristocratic French and Anglo-Indian families, Stephen served as an icon of British beauty in the work of her aunt, Victorian photographer Julia Margaret Cameron. It is not clear what Woolf intended in posing in this garment, nor is the impact of this gesture obvious. Like much of Woolf's work, it can be understood variously as protesting, reflecting, or reinscribing capitalist, imperialist, racist, classist, and gendered systems of power. Yet to diagnose Mabel and Woolf's work in these cases puts us in a position oddly akin to that of Mrs. Dalloway's more discerning guests or *Vogue*'s readers who grasp the aesthetic, social, and economic meanings of these garments perhaps better than the wearers themselves. Understood in these terms, such critique is, like the account of writing and reading in "Modern Fiction," a form of entanglement and implication rather than the achievement of distance or critical mastery.[63] Of course, it does not follow that politically interested critique should be abandoned. Ellen Rooney, for example, advocates for symptomatic reading by reminding us that Louis Althusser calls for a process of "guilty reading" that must declare what it is guilty of—in other words, what it is reading for—but does not thereby absolve itself of its interests or the unanticipated effects of such readings.[64] Rooney points out that Althusserian symptomatic readings do not assume a surface-depth model by which hidden truths are brought to light but rather draw on the metaphor of terrain to describe how readings occur within yet also might shift the existing landscape of thought and experience. To reformulate this point in terms of mood and mode, we would say that all readings are carried out in a certain affective atmosphere and with the material and forms that are within view and reach. The question then becomes, how might a change in mood and mode be brought about?

Mabel's story tracks impediments and dead ends in the pursuit of such transformation. She is eager to change her mood and her dress (or her dress and thus her mood) so that she might recapture the sense of transcendence and fulfillment she has felt only fleetingly in the past. We learn that Mabel, while reading in bed and being fitted for her "new dress," has experienced "divine moments," which resemble what Woolf later describes, in "A Sketch of the Past," as "moments of being."[65] Mabel also has a habit of calming herself by reciting "tags of Shakespeare," a phrase that intertwines fashion and fiction because *tag* referred originally to "one of narrow, often pointed, laciniae or pendent pieces made by slashing the skirt of a garment."[66] Like an old-fashioned cut of dress, decontextualized fragments of text are imbued with personal and cultural meaning. The *Sketch* cartoon's deployment of a line from *Twelfth Night* represents a version of this practice, as Shakespeare's words become a commentary on women's petty competitions over dress. Mabel, for her part, conceives "classic" literature and clothing

Virginia Woolf photographed for *Vogue*, 1924. Maurice Beck & Helen MacGregor / Vogue © The Condé Nast Publications Ltd.

as ways to escape fashion, which for her epitomizes anxious, everyday time; she envies and scorns those who are "dressed in the height of fashion, precisely like everybody else, always" ("ND," 63). In this story, however, reciting lines and reanimating styles are empty because isolated gestures; we never hear any of Shakespeare's phrases, only the fact of their repetition. The dress and the quotations fail Mabel when she attempts to shore them against the ruins of her self-image. So while "The New Dress" links moods to modes of

dressing and writing, it does not imply that choosing the latter can transform the former. A shift in mode and mood must be legible in relation to
broader trends and cannot be an individual project, even if it rests on the
recognition and effects of achievements such as those of Joyce, Eliot, or
Woolf—or Heidegger and Sedgwick.

More specifically, "The New Dress" helps us to see what is at stake in Sedgwick's focus (via Klein's account of infant and mother) on the relationship
between a cultural object and its reader as a way to facilitate broader shifts
across a critical field. Fashion's expense and normative force make clothing
an object of suspicion and source of anxiety. But Mabel—like the Kleinian
subject for whom the "depressive position is an anxiety mitigating achievement" that is possible "only sometimes, and only briefly"—is able "to use
[her] own resources to assemble or 'repair' the murderous part-objects into
something like a whole," which then provide one with "nourishment and
comfort in turn."[67] Importantly, Mabel's resources in creating this reassembled maternal object (the new dress) are not only psychic and volitional but
also materially determined; while she is too poor to afford cutting-edge fashion, she can employ a modest dressmaker, Miss Milan, to realize the design
according to her "specifications." It is in fact when she looks in the mirror
while the dressmaker adjusts the hem that Mabel has her moment of being;
she sees "the core of herself, the soul of herself" and feels "pity" and "love" for
Miss Milan, who "is crawling on the floor with her mouth full of pins," although, tellingly, she does not encourage her to stand ("ND," 65). Mabel's
story, then, reminds us what might be missed if we rely predominantly on
an individual psychic model to describe the work of criticism, which involves
not only a relation between subject and cultural object but also a broader affective atmosphere and a material context.[68] Furthermore, Mabel's story underscores the question of what material, cultural, and political positions the
reader occupies in the first place. Who can or should occupy the position of
Sedgwick's reparative reader? Will shifting between paranoid and reparative
positions be enough if the kind of self-reflexive suspicion that Mabel demonstrates may not illuminate our most pernicious attachments? As Mabel's
fantasies of political and religious conversation suggest, such problems are
compounded if we misread Sedgwick's critique as a call to leave behind
suspicion and anxiety altogether.[69]

In a rather Eliotic turn, Mabel's disappointment drives her toward modes
of impersonality as well as textual, epistemological, sartorial, and political
orthodoxies. Leaving the party, she determines to be transformed by the discovery of "some wonderful, helpful, astonishing book . . . a book by a clergyman, by an American no one had heard of" or by listening to a speech by

a miner about "the life of the pit." These experiences, she imagines, will lead her to join a religious order: "She would wear a uniform; she would be called Sister Somebody; she would never give a thought to clothes again" ("ND," 72). In short, they will lift her into a permanent state of rapture that at once evacuates her subject position and crystallizes it by detaching it from the vicissitudes of mood and mode. Mabel Waring will never again have to worry about what she is wearing. In her distress, Mabel also imagines that academic subjects might offer a way of knowing that will be unclouded by mood. Earlier in the evening, she castigates herself for not "being seriously interested in conchology, etymology, botany, archaeology, cutting up potatoes and watching them fructify, like Mary Dennis, like Violet Searle" (two women who do not appear elsewhere in the story) (67). Such disciplines seem to Mabel to be alternatives to the work of feeling one's way. Heidegger critiques the conception of scientific inquiry as unaffected by mood and contends that "by looking at the world theoretically, we have already dimmed it down to the uniformity of what is purely present-at-hand, though admittedly this uniformity comprises a new abundance of things which can be discovered by simply characterizing them."[70] As we have seen, uniformity is precisely what Mabel seeks. She perceives ecstatic religious conversion as well as systematic, empirical, positivist academic disciplines as alternatives to the anxiety, failure, and passionate attachment more commonly associated with such moody objects as dress and literature. While my reading of "The New Dress" risks repeating Mabel's gesture of seeking reflections of herself in the Dalloways' mirrors, Woolf's story illuminates anxieties about fashion and literature that fuel contemporary efforts to establish literary criticism's connections to more "serious" forms of academic inquiry. What, then, are the forms of critique that fashion facilitates for Woolf? How might literature and dress orient us toward productive, sustaining ways of knowing and acting?

"Frock Consciousness," Intersubjective Feeling, and Repair in Mrs. Dalloway

Like "The New Dress," *Mrs. Dalloway* investigates the intertwinements of mood and *la mode*. This includes examining how particular investments in literature, dress, and academic knowledge arise from and fuel desires for uniform modes of being and believing. For instance, in addition to Septimus's devotion to Shakespeare and "Miss Isabel Poole in a green dress," the novel describes Doris Kilman's craving for absolute faith and superior academic knowledge. These desires as well as Kilman's self-consciousness about not being able to afford fashionable clothes recall Mabel. Kilman, however, has undergone the kind of religious conversion that Mabel only imagines, and she even dons a sort of uniform; as Marshik notes, by the 1920s, Kilman's "older style of mackintosh" specifically recalls the versions worn by soldiers on the front.[71] Moreover, while Kilman's critiques of British nationalism and the class system are more robust, extensive, and historically informed than Mabel's, her mackintosh—and especially her fraught attachment to it—points to the difficulties of paranoid and reparative modes of being, thinking, and feeling. In particular, the association of Kilman with uniformity anticipates *Three Guineas* and *The Years*'s skepticism about forms of feminist critique and resistance that reinscribe militarist epistemologies and tactics (which I discuss below). At the same time, Woolf's depiction of Kilman does not indicate that suspicion, anxiety, and critique should or can be abandoned, for Kilman's attempts to *escape* anxiety and suspicion lead her to what Woolf treats as insipid orthodoxies and compensations, including attempts to soothe herself through prayer and the thought that "her knowledge of modern history was thorough in the extreme" (*MD*, 122). The implications and effects of Mabel's and Kilman's reparative methods are as circumscribed as their anxieties and suspicions.

If "The New Dress" offers a claustrophobic, myopic version of high modernist style via Mabel, however, *Mrs. Dalloway*'s form is characterized by its exploration of multiple affective and epistemological positions and orientations. The novel multiplies and extends the short story's investigation of fashion and feeling as linked phenomena through which the world is sensed, touched, and known. As I have suggested, *Mrs. Dalloway* treats garments (such as the green dresses) as material expressions and aids to its own textual method of weaving together disparate perceptions and times into a whole through which readers feel their way. Clothing is key to *Mrs. Dalloway*'s depictions of feelings as intersubjective and circulating with and through objects. It enables Woolf's speculative accounts of how moods shape perception and generate affective and material worlds. Woolf's approach anticipates Carlson and Stewart's "mood work" in that the composition of the world through fashion and feeling is both Woolf's subject and method. Such methodological correspondence emerges in the novel's opening pages, when Clarissa imagines how the postwar June day will unfold. Engaging in a kind of textual world making, Clarissa senses that "everywhere, though it was still early, there was a beating, a stirring of galloping ponies; Lords, Ascot, Ranelagh and all the rest of it; wrapped in the soft mesh of the grey-blue morning air, which, as the day wore on, would unwind them, and set down on their lawns and pitches the bouncing ponies whose forefeet just struck the ground and up they sprung, the whirling young men, and laughing girls in their transparent muslin who, even now, after dancing all night, were taking their absurd woolly dogs for a run" (*MD*, 5). This vocabulary of dress and fabric is apt for a society woman. The language of textiles conveys Clarissa's social milieu and her confidence in the inevitability and repetition of these scenes of aristocratic leisure, which would have been interrupted by the war: "soft mesh" naturally gives way to "girls in their transparent muslin" as the day wears on, while the image of sounds, places, and figures being unwrapped and placed grants them a solidity and endurance in the midst of transformation and movement. While such images are particular to Clarissa, however, the passage's links between mood and weather recall Woolf's famous description of the change in "human character" in 1910; in both cases, weather seems to affect mood and mood operates like an affective atmosphere.[72] And in *Mrs. Dalloway*, many of the characters experience their intimacy with and disaffection from other characters and social worlds via frock consciousness—that is, a mutual focus on clothing that generates and delimits collective thoughts and feelings, which often are experienced as atmospheres.[73]

Frock consciousness even offers a respite from the despair and damage produced by war when Septimus and Rezia are once again "alone together" as they collaborate on a woman's hat (*MD*, 141). As they "conspire together" (to use the language in Woolf's diary entry), the "envelope that connects and protects them" in this moment is described in terms of atmosphere.[74] Moments before his death, Septimus finds he can "wait in this warm place, this pocket of still air" generated by Rezia sewing beside him (*MD*, 141, 140). Septimus, moreover, recalls that he proposed to Rezia in part because he was insensible to yet protected by the scene of "scissors rapping, girls laughing, hats being made" that she and her sisters inhabit in Italy (*MD*, 85). Unable to share the mood in Italy, Septimus attempts to stay in proximity to it. He relies, that is, on the sisters' mood work—their creation of a shared affective form through their aesthetic and material labor—to avoid sensing his misattunement to the world around him. In turn, as Septimus works with Rezia to create the hat, the couple engages in frock consciousness as a mutual and mutually reparative process.

This intimate, immediate experience of shared peace and happiness stands out in the novel, since other pleasurable moments of intersubjective connection are more ambivalent or are recalled by a single character, as is the case with Sally and Clarissa's kiss.[75] At the same time, fashion's centrality to this moment underscores the material conditions that enable and limit it. The hat for Mrs. Peters, "Mrs. Filmer's married daughter," facilitates and represents heteronormative domesticity and attendant boundaries between domestic and public spaces (*MD*, 138). While Septimus jokes that it is "an organ grinder's monkey's hat" (unfit for a lady in public), Rezia is thrilled that they are once again "poking fun privately like married people"; this instance of frock consciousness confirms, for Rezia, her belonging to a state-sanctioned couple that, thanks to its resemblance to a normative heterosexual unit, enjoys the privileges of privacy and satire and the intimacy they yield (*MD*, 139). Rezia and Septimus repair marriage (and, with it, domesticity, gender, and feminized labor) "into something like a whole," which is *"not necessarily like any preexisting whole"* and which provides them, briefly, with "nourishment and comfort in turn."[76] Of course, their privacy is soon violated by Dr. Holmes, who is particularly irritated by Septimus's failure to fulfill his duties as a husband. Yet this instance of frock consciousness provides a glimpse of collective repair that, unlike Clarissa's and Mabel's textual imaginations, does not aim to reconstitute an imperial prewar social world. This moment allows more space for critique, however partial and oblique.

This scene also indicates how Shakespeare's words can facilitate reparative modes of mood work while also making clear that such work might involve misperception, misreading, and even delusion. Moments before Septimus begins to design Mrs. Peters's hat, he hears waves, watches a shifting yellow light, and recalls part of the lines from *A Winter's Tale* that have reverberated in Clarissa's mind ("fear no more the heat o' the sun / Nor the furious winter's rages"). Septimus's reveries culminate with a vision of Nature as a woman using her "plumes" and "mantle" as well as "Shakespeare's words" to "show . . . her meaning" (*MD*, 136). The image of Nature as a well-dressed woman is particularly fitting given that Clarissa—and perhaps Septimus—picks up Shakespeare's lines from a book in a shop window on her way to Bond Street and later recalls them as she mends her green dress.[77] It remains unclear, however, whether Septimus's belief that "Shakespeare's words" contain Nature's "meaning" is an insight or a sign of insanity. His sensations and revelations at this moment anticipate aspects of Woolf's much later account of "the most important of her memories"—that of hearing the waves, watching the light made by "a yellow blind," and "feeling the purest ecstasy I can conceive," while lying in bed at St. Ives.[78] Yet Septimus only imagines the sound of the waves, and, as Rezia observes him, she finds his smile "strange" and links it to his increasingly frequent outbursts and claims to know "the truth" (136). Moreover, we could also understand Septimus's reparative misreading of Shakespeare as a means to reconstruct if not simply renew his attachment to Britishness. The linked forms of reparative work undertaken by Septimus, Clarissa, and Rezia, however, do point to collective yet intimate and private means to reconstruct sustaining worlds of thought and feeling by working and reworking texts and textiles.

"The Connection between Dress and War Is Not Far to Seek"

In "The New Dress" and *Mrs. Dalloway*, fashion makes up the material and affective texture of modern life, but these works are skeptical about attempts to change the mood by changing one's dress or turning to a beloved text.[79] Yet at other points, Woolf was involved in projects that connected dress making and dress buying to social change; during World War I, the Bloomsbury group's efforts to challenge the nation's militaristic mood involved designing, producing, and consuming garments. These included items created for Woolf by artists at the Omega Workshops, among them Vanessa Bell, who launched a "dressmaking department" in 1915.[80] Throughout the war, clothing design helped Bloomsbury to sustain itself as a subculture.[81] It was a group that—like the "fashion world" that Woolf observed at the Becks in 1924—"connects and protects" its members, particularly those engaging in nonnormative forms of intimacy and, from 1914 to 1918, pacifist resistance. As many critics have noted, this period is a touchstone for Woolf's writing, but little has been said about how the Omega and its political and aesthetic projects might have influenced how her work conceives, depicts, and responds to war.[82] I propose that this moment in the history of Bloomsbury offers a counterpoint to Woolf's thinking about the political dynamics of dress and mood and about the varying visibility of systems of power and violence in the late 1930s. In particular, the history of Omega dress design sheds light on the ways that mood and *la mode* shape Woolf's forms of critique and representation in *Three Guineas* and *The Years*, both of which were written when the rise of fascism and the threat of war made shared feeling and clothing matters of public concern. In *Three Guineas*, dress helps Woolf to develop a method of critique that anticipates aspects of Ahmed's approach to queer phenomenology as "a phenomenology of 'being stopped,' a description of the world from the point of view of those who do not flow into it."[83] Woolf's phenomenologist—the educated man's daughter—is first brought to a halt when she encounters men in their elaborate "public" dress. The Omega also exploited the capacity for garments to stop a person short. And Omega clothing supported Bloomsbury's efforts to create a space apart from (but at times flowing into) the masculine public sphere. At the same time, the Omega's primitivist and Orientalist designs bring to the surface the ways that Bloomsbury constituted itself through its access to non-Western "worlds."[84] For Woolf, Omega garments represent the promise and limitations of Bloomsbury's efforts to promote "civilization" and conjure countermoods in the face of war and compulsory nationalism.[85]

Bloomsbury has often been described in terms of particular moods and modes of expression and behavior. Christopher Reed, for example, dubs Bloomsbury's visual aesthetic "the Amusing Style," a term that alerts us to the ways the group was constituted through aesthetic and social forms and shared feelings in addition to philosophical, ethical, and political commitments.[86] Together these made up the distinctive texture of everyday life in Bloomsbury—right down to the furnishings; many group members, including the Woolfs, decorated their personal spaces with objects and textiles designed by fellow Bloomsberries.[87] Aesthetic theories and unusual domestic arrangements (encompassing interior designs and forms of intimacy) brought together and flourished within this group of friends and collaborators.[88] But though scholars have discovered a distinctive look and feel to Bloomsbury's visual art and design, the group's sartorial style seems less coherent and distinctive. This has not stopped late twentieth- and early twenty-first-century fashion designers from referencing Bloomsbury. Christopher Bailey, designer for the British firm Burberry, for example, listed Bell and Woolf as inspirations for his sober, recession-conscious women's ready-to-wear fall/winter 2009 show, and he titled his far more relaxed and whimsical fall/winter 2014 collection "Bloomsbury Girls." In 2009 Bailey presented garments in earthy colors with military-inspired tailoring, whereas in 2014 he showed bright, hand-painted scarves, bags, shoes, and loose-fitting coats that paid homage to the interior design at Charleston House and showed the influence of Bloomsbury's Omega Workshops.[89] Then in fall 2016, Bailey offered a collection that was inspired, in part, by *Orlando* and that leaned heavily on military references (especially in vintage-inspired jackets) to signal its innovations with respect to gender and time; the show was unusual (if not groundbreaking) in that a major house sent similarly fashioned men's and women's garments down the runway together and made the garments immediately available for sale rather than producing them for the next season. Bailey's different collections indicate that Bloomsbury can signify whatever moods and modes of Britishness might seem to sell at a given moment. But his references to militarism, Charleston, and the Omega also remind us that it was during World War I that members of Bloomsbury extended the group's signature postimpressionist style into the realm of clothing.

When Vanessa Bell began supervising dressmaking at the Omega, the workshops were becoming a center for experimental design and pacifist activism. Projects included creating textiles, furnishings, and garments, as well as employing conscientious objectors, publishing antiwar books, and supporting Quaker relief work in France.[90] As designers and patrons, members of the Bloomsbury group—including Bell, Roger Fry, and Woolf—invested in Omega garments as a means to sustain and express aesthetic, affective, and political commitments. In a letter to Bell praising a dress made for her by the Omega, Woolf jokes, "I think even as an advertisement I should pay the Omega, as I'm always being asked who made my things."[91] At least a decade before Woolf's image began circulating as a symbol of British and specifically Bloomsbury's intellectualism, she imagined herself as a representative of the Omega.[92] Fashion offered a way for Bloomsbury to express and underwrite itself as a subculture that sheltered political as well as sexual nonconformity, both of which could result in imprisonment and public humiliation. In this sense, the clothing gave weight and heft to the tentative connections between sartorial, social, and state formations and foreign bodies that one finds in Woolf's reflections on "frock consciousness" and her visit to the Becks. But it also raised the question of whether the public circulation of Bloomsbury aesthetics (in this case via dress) would have meaningful effects.

Though Bell did not describe her designs as a response to war, her creations presented a marked alternative to the sober colors and ladylike silhouettes that filled fashion magazines in 1915. Surviving photographs, descriptions, and examples of Omega garments show they were influenced by prewar fashions associated with the designer Paul Poiret, the "King of Fashion," and by the Ballets Russes; as in Poiret's designs from that period, one can see the influence of the early nineteenth-century directoire silhouette, modernist primitivism and Orientalism (especially via references to Turkish, Russian, Chinese, and Japanese styles), and dress reform movements associated with British aestheticism and Viennese Secession.[93] The Omega's simpler silhouettes and hand-painted silks, however, generally demonstrate a less polished, more bohemian look than Poiret's couture creations. And it would be a mistake to conclude that Bell simply was a few years behind the times, given that what was cutting-edge in mainstream fashion was framed as a return to Victorian styles, values, and commitments. Bell's designs demonstrate an unwillingness to relinquish a prewar mood of iconoclasm despite the backlash against what came to seem like comparatively foreign styles.

As Bloomsbury invested in vestments, so did the British government—and not only by funding the mass production of uniforms. During the war, sartorial style was linked to patriotic moods and to national economic and military survival. Posters sponsored by the National Savings Committee admonished women, "Dressing extravagantly in wartime is worse than bad form. It is unpatriotic." A number of recruiting posters focused on men's dress, including one that demanded "Why Aren't *You* in Khaki?" and another that asked "Which Ought You to Wear?" as it displayed various men's hats, including one military cap.[94] On the "home front," men were publicly shamed for not bearing the marks of war or wearing uniforms, and the refusal to wear khaki was a point of resistance for conscientious objectors. In turn, the process of getting such men into uniform became the subject of illustrated newspaper articles that associated adopting military garments with accepting the mantle of British masculinity.[95] As *Mrs. Dalloway* and *Three Guineas* suggest, dress registered and reinforced war's enmeshment in the texture of everyday life even at a spatial, temporal, and even ideological distance from the fighting itself.[96]

Militarization, imperialism, and violence provided the backdrop and a vocabulary for the Omega's forays into fashion. These included garments for men and women, although Bell focused on women's dress. In a letter to Fry in April 1915, Bell proposed to launch the project with "a sort of dress parade, perhaps in Ottoline's drawing-room," thus using a term that fashion borrowed from the military to describe an event in the home of two prominent pacifists, Ottoline and Philip Morrell.[97] Ottoline Morrell became one of the dressmaking department's most important patrons, and Omega garments seem to have circulated as a sign of being "in the swim" of the elite pacifist subculture that gathered at her estate, Garsington Manor.[98] The actress and socialite Iris Tree apparently purchased bathing suits—one black and one with a hand-stitched avant-garde appliqué effect—to wear in Garsington's pond, which makes a thinly disguised appearance in D. H. Lawrence's *Women in Love*.[99] Tree's handmade suit is in keeping with what Fry, in the preface to the first Omega catalog, asserts is the workshop's intention to replace "shop finish" with the rougher textures and stronger feelings of a "savage's handiwork," whether in "a pot or a woven cloth."[100] According to Fry's modernist-primitivist theory of affects and aesthetics, such textures can reflect and inspire "disinterested delight" in ways that factory-made products cannot.[101] This formulation exposes some of the ironies of Fry's theories and Bell's related concept of "significant form" (which describes aesthetic experience as a realm apart from other cultural and social phenomena, including politics), as well as Fry's insistence elsewhere that his aim with the Omega was to "develop a definitely English tradition."[102] It makes clear that the circulation and success of Bloomsbury's aesthetics, including the Omega,

depend on their engagement with primitivism, which of course was interwoven with racism and colonialism and was popular thanks to existing
European and American modernist and avant-garde movements.[103]

Indeed, in a letter to Bell, Woolf describes Bell's designs not as creating
"disinterested delight" but as producing the kind of shock associated with
the avant-garde:

> My god! What colours you are responsible for! Karin's [Stephen's] clothes
> almost wrenched my eyes from the sockets—a skirt barred with reds and
> yellows of the vilest kind, and a pea green blouse on top, with a gaudy hand-
> kerchief on her head, supposed to be the very boldest taste. I shall retire into
> dove colour and old lavender, with a lace collar, and lawn wristlets.[104]

Though playful, Woolf's comments register in the realm of sartorial taste
the paradoxes of a pacifist, primitivist avant-garde that would "fight for
peace" by shocking the bourgeois with styles that draw inspiration from imperialist fantasy.[105] However unwittingly, Woolf's joke also echoes the shift to
more Victorian styles then occurring in British fashion, and in doing so indicates how fashionable performances of feminine passivity or resistance intersect with issues of peace and war. After all, divergent views of femininity underpin different visions of pacifism. A rejection of Victorian ideas of femininity
as passive and retiring might challenge patriarchal systems that (as *Three
Guineas* argues) fuel war. Yet, an embrace of the "very boldest" forms of
modern femininity might reinforce the mechanisms, mood, and logic of
violence, not least because it encourages women to invest in consumer culture
as a means of self-expression.

These contradictions emerge in *Three Guineas* as Woolf attempts to articulate a feminist pacifism in the context of gendered capitalism. But Woolf's
ambivalence about the Omega's project can also be discerned in her biography of Roger Fry, which she wrote in the shadow of war. *Roger Fry* is haunted
by questions about whether her fellow Bloomsberry had made an impact,
and how "civilization, art, personal relationships"—core Bloomsbury
values—might survive and even assist in preventing war.[106] Although Woolf
does not ignore the Omega's wartime activities, she presents the workshops
as part of the lost promise of the prewar era's "new ferment" (*RF*, 195). Woolf
uses Fry's attempts at "tackling the subject of women's dress" *before* the war
to illustrate the aesthetic and pedagogical ambitions and failures of the
Omega, which Fry hoped might spread "civilisation, a desire for things of
the spirit" (*RF*, 201, 199). Woolf cites an exchange between Fry and a newspaper reporter who visits the Omega and reports seeing, among other daz-
zling items, "a radiantly coloured dress in gossamery silk" decorated with

the image of "a mass of large foliage and a pastoral scene, and maidens dancing under the moon, while a philosopher and a peasant stood by" (*RF*, 195).
As Randi Koppen observes, this dress exemplifies the "spirit of fun" and the
"modernist project of playful allegorical defamiliarisation" that characterized Bloomsbury's visual aesthetic.[107] Yet, while the interviewer admits the
dress is "beautiful," he asks, "Would English women ever have the courage
to wear it? 'Oh,' said Mr Fry, 'people have to be educated . . .'" (*RF*, 195). In
Roger Fry, Woolf celebrates her friend's capacity to generate in others an
excitement about and attunement to the world around them, and especially
to art. Yet Woolf's rendering of this exchange undercuts Fry's apparent confidence in his capacity to create such an atmosphere for the Omega's products. The ellipsis gestures toward a future that the war would forestall, and
thus admits some skepticism about Fry's pedagogical project. When considered from Woolf's perspective in the late 1930s, Fry's attempt to remake
British sensibilities through dress seems at once belated and premature.

It is in this period, however, that *Three Guineas* takes up the project of
cultivating the modes of perception and forms of behavior that might help
to end such violence.[108] The text is made up of multiple letters to various
interlocutors, but Woolf returns repeatedly to address the "educated man"
who has written to ask her, an "educated man's daughter," how they might
"prevent war." Dress plays a key role in this effort, but not as a vessel or symbol of aesthetic theories and orientations, as in *Roger Fry*. Rather, clothing
and fabric offer heuristic devices to develop Woolf's mode of "sens[ing] out
what is actual and potential" in a given scene into more explicit forms of social critique. That shift both within *Three Guineas* and within Woolf's oeuvre
involves altering the mode, scale, and mood of her writing; *Three Guineas* is
distinguished by its strategic, variable deployment of anger and the imperative mood.[109] In this context, clothing connects what the "educated man's
daughter" feels and senses about the world to an understanding of and a desire
to affect global systems whose intricacies and force necessarily remain out of
view and reach. The first letter begins by explaining to the "educated man"
why "though we look at the same things, we see them differently" (*TG*, 7).
Woolf's initial example of seeing differently refers to dress: "The noble
courts and quadrangles of Oxford and Cambridge often appear to educated
men's daughters like petticoats with holes in them, cold legs of mutton, and
the boat train starting for abroad while the guard slams the door in their
faces" (*TG*, 8). This equivalence between Oxbridge and well-worn garments (as well as certain tastes and experiences of exclusion) may seem to
denigrate the latter. Yet it also lays the groundwork for Woolf's claim that
dress is part of the education that men apparently lack. She refers to this as

women's "'unpaid-for education'—that understanding of human beings and their motives which, if the word is rid of its scientific associations, might be called psychology" (*TG*, 9). Accordingly, when Woolf describes her vision of what a college for women (or indeed, men) should teach in order to prevent war, she mentions, "It should teach the arts of human intercourse; the art of understanding other people's lives and minds, and the little arts of talk, of dress, of cookery that are allied with them. . . . It should explore the ways in which mind and body can be made to co-operate" (*TG*, 43). Woolf relinquishes these demands as she imagines the weary face of the headmistress and, with it, the paltry financial support the college already receives. As in *Roger Fry*, the "little ar[t] . . . of dress" is a form of education that must be described subjunctively and conditionally, for it can be taught only if other lessons of peace have been learned and put into practice—including the funding of education for women. But rather than turn away from the pedagogical promise of clothing, the first section of *Three Guineas* advocates and offers that sort of education by other means, for it undertakes a sartorially attuned phenomenology of patriarchy.

"Sensing out" the nature and meaning of garments is a central concern of the first section of *Three Guineas*. While Woolf declares, "the connection between dress and war is not far to seek; your finest clothes are those you wear as soldiers," the text pursues a number of strategies to draw out the nature and implications of that connection. Though Woolf discusses at length how she and her imagined interlocutor would react to a photograph of civilians killed in the Spanish Civil War, the only images reproduced in *Three Guineas* are those of British men in different ceremonial outfits; the illustrations are of "A General," "Heralds," "A University Procession," "A Judge," and "An Archbishop" (*TG*, 3). This selection of images underscores that these supposed opponents of fascism are part of the same violent patriarchal order. Indeed, in the final pages of *Three Guineas* Woolf insists that a picture of a uniformed "Man himself"—the image of a "Tyrant or Dictator"—has come to demand as much attention as that of the ruined houses (*TG*, 168). But long before this assertion, the text has taught the reader to see this way. Although many of the individuals in the photographs would have been recognizable to British readers of the time (and the images appeared originally in newspapers that identified the principal figures), Woolf treats these men like anonymous subjects of social scientific interest. They are presented as if in an academic study like psychoanalyst J. C. Flügel's *The Psychology of Clothes*—an influential work published by the Woolfs' Hogarth Press in 1930—which offers illustrations of various forms of "historical dress" or "primitive costume" for its readers' edification.[110] In

Three Guineas, however, this social scientific method of using unnamed, representative subjects to display sartorial trends is complemented and undercut by detailed narratives conveying the particular feelings and sensations of the educated man's daughter when she encounters such elaborately dressed men in their natural habitat, "the world of public life": "Your clothes in the first place make us gape with astonishment. How many, how splendid, how extremely ornate they are—the clothes worn by the educated man in his public capacity!" The woman's combination of heightened feeling and naïve empiricism ("Now you dress in violet; a jeweled crucifix swings on your breast; now your shoulders are covered with lace") defamiliarizes men's clothing, allowing what is in plain sight to expose the ideology of the masculine public sphere (*TG*, 23).

This approach seems to invert the paradigmatic structure of viewing that characterizes consumer culture and modern epistemological regimes in which an invisible male subject sees and thereby comprehends hypervisible feminized and racialized subjects.[111] In addition, it highlights how this epistemological structure is linked to forms of ideology critique that deploy the language of illumination and exposure to present their insights. Yet *Three Guineas* also experiments with an alternative form of perceiving and knowing that might emerge when the feminized subject feels her way into this masculine scene. Hence Woolf's descriptions and photographs of clothing do more than trace what is on the surface or make visible what was hidden; they recover and develop ways of perceiving that are discredited or ignored. Woolf's use of the language of fabric establishes this point. Woolf refers to her descriptions of "public life" as "a crudely colored photograph" of the world as seen by those who view it "through the shadow of the veil that St. Paul still lays upon our eyes"—that is, in keeping with St. Paul's injunction that women be veiled in public (*TG*, 22–23). Tellingly, this passage precedes the critique of elaborate masculine dress, thus implying that women's association with fabric—though a result of patriarchal prohibition and an apparent sign of occluded vision—may enable her to perceive and weave together associations and connections not grasped by men. And rather than simply afford women the kind of invisibility presumed by the male spectator, it initiates a process by which the woman with the veil exercises her talent for bringing together and following the threads where they lead.

This contrast between assuming the position of the distant, invisible spectator and feeling one's way overlaps with film theorist Laura U. Marks's distinction between optical and haptic visuality. According to Marks, optical visuality follows from "European post-Enlightenment" concepts of vision in which a "disembodied" subject gains knowledge about an object through sight and at a distance.[112] Haptic visuality, by contrast, destabilizes boundaries between viewer and object and prompts a more textured, less determinative, and decentered way of looking. The "crudely colored" and shadowed nature of the photograph that the educated man's daughter offers to her reader is in keeping with Marks's claim that haptic visuality involves attending to the textures and surfaces of images rather than their symbolic dimensions.[113] Moreover, Marks claims, haptic visuality's intimate process of touching changes both the viewer and that which is viewed.[114] *Three Guineas* describes and offers textured pictures of public life in order to emphasize how they affect the educated man's daughter, to transform the way that men in public are viewed, and to alter her readers in the process. In that sense, Woolf claims for her text the capacity for transformation that Marks attributes to haptic visuality in film.

The nature and impact of the educated man's daughter's method of perception is also described in terms of orientation and perspective: "Your world, then, the world of professional, of public life, seen from this angle undoubtedly looks queer" (*TG*, 23). Woolf's use of *queer* recalls its etymological roots in words for "twist" and "oblique" and as well as Ahmed's proposal that "queer phenomenology would function as a disorientation device . . . allowing the oblique to open up another angle on the world."[115] While Ahmed insists that the term *queer* should not be disarticulated from non-normative sexuality, she also draws on this method when examining diversity work as "a phenomenological practice" that "generates knowledge of institutions in the process of attempting to transform them" (rather than knowledge necessarily preceding or dictating practice).[116] In this scene, Woolf imagines a phenomenologist—the white, middle-class educated man's daughter—whose diversion from normative lines and angles may involve only momentarily wandering from the private home into the masculine public sphere. *Three Guineas* takes up the insights generated from such collisions to formulate a critique of patriarchy. But in doing so, it reifies the phenomenologist's unfamiliarity with class, sexuality, and race as "veils" and as disorientation devices—and thus as potential epistemological tools. Yet it is this particular *method*—rather than the specific knowledge it offers—in which *Three Guineas* ultimately places its faith.[117]

Alternative Modes and Moods through The Years

I have argued that *Three Guineas* takes up aspects of Woolf's earlier mode of describing and giving form to what is happening in an unfolding, densely textured scene to offer a sartorially attuned phenomenology of patriarchy. We can see Woolf working out a related fictional approach to "sensing out" via mood and *la mode* in *The Years*, which was first conceived with *Three Guineas* as part of a single work that would alternate between novelistic scenes and essayistic social critique. *The Years*, like *Three Guineas*, is particularly interested in developing ways to "sense out what is actual and potential" in the present and for the future. As Thomas S. Davis notes, "The novel seems to want to train its contemporary readers to look, observe, and read everything with the same intensity before the catastrophe of an historical event."[118] In contrast to this implicitly (though not cheerfully) optimistic aim, Davis argues that the novel "can only demonstrate the possibility of [the] desire" for historical progress and that it offers a "recursive historicism," in which violence repeats and is amplified. This recursive temporality, however, also recalls the rhythm of fashion that characterizes the account of the ongoing "battle" that is literary history in "Modern Fiction." And while the novel does track patterns of violence as they shape the texture of everyday life, it also opens itself to future readings that might find contrasting recursive patterns of resistance and creativity in its pages. Such patterns are suggested through mood, fabric, fashion, and texture.

It is in keeping with the history of the realist historical novel that Woolf draws on fashion and garments to reimagine the genre. As *The Years* follows the lives of various members of the British Pargiter family between 1880 and the "Present Day," it more closely resembles what Henry James described as the "loose baggy monster" of the nineteenth-century novel than any of Woolf's other texts, even *Night and Day*.[119] Fashion's relationship to the novel extends well beyond James's quip, however. Timothy Cambell argues that the early historical novel, epitomized by Sir Walter Scott's work, took from fashion—and in particular, representations of fashion in print culture—a sense of the past as made up of distinct historical moments that are irretrievable yet imaginable via cultural objects, including clothing and texts.[120] Fittingly, the chapters of *The Years*, which are titled for different years (save for the last "Present Day"), often begin with brief references to current sartorial fashions and consist of snapshots of various relatives and friends during particular moments. Thus *The Years's* treatment of periodicity reflects the ways that, as Campbell argues, print cultural fashion fuels modern, periodized understandings of history, including the idea of annualization, which remains fundamental to literary history.

The Years both composes and undoes the historical novel and its temporality via fashion. While it organizes its chapters by year, it offers scraps of time, fragments of thought, and no clear resolution. Its use of free indirect discourse also undercuts the presumption of an overarching and coherent narrative design or a single prevailing consciousness. As it shifts in and out of the minds of a number of daughters of educated men, *The Years*, like *Three Guineas*, often describes the world from the perspective of those who see it through a veil of fabric. Dress, for example, is a material through which Kitty Lasswade feels her way through Oxford's gendered and classed social terrain. It also fuels and gives her terms for expressing her attraction to a visiting scholar's American wife who, unlike the women in Oxford, is "in the fashion."[121] In addition, the scene set in 1907 in which Sara Pargiter lies in her attic bedroom reading her uncle Edward's translation of *Antigone* draws attention to the way the blinds shape the view of the party next door as well as how the bedsheet influences her perception of the relationship between mind and body. "Where did thought begin? In the feet? she asked. There they were, jutting out under the single sheet. They seemed separated, very far away" (*TY*, 124–25). This sheet, which modestly covers her crotch, seems to facilitate this misperception and epitomize her mood of boredom and frustration. But it also brings to the surface how this scene recalls and revises the forms of patriarchal prohibition and resistance that *Antigone* dramatizes. Sara's gestures, mood, and covering offer a faint echo of Antigone's experience of emotional, physical, and political suffocation, as well as the "white sand" with which she coats her brother's naked corpse (*TY*, 128). In this way, the scene shows the connections between, on the one hand, Sara's mood and mode of attunement and, on the other, her bodily orientation, physical and historical location, vesture, and the objects within her reach, including the translation of *Antigone*. In effect, it brings together an attention to orientation and objects with an understanding of the power of mood and mode.

The scene also returns us to questions about how mood and orientation shape modes of reading and writing. Sara's experience repeats with a difference—one might say, translates—a scene in which Edward reads *Antigone* in Greek in his room at Oxford in 1891. Edward pictures Antigone as Kitty Lasswade in a "white and blue dress," and looks out his window at the Master's Lodge where he imagines that, behind the blind, she is entertaining visitors (*TY*, 49). In conflating Antigone and Kitty, however, Edward remakes them in the traditional mode of heterosexual romance and commits an error in literary interpretation that *Three Guineas* cautions against. *Three Guineas* cites *Antigone* as evidence that "things repeat themselves"; this phrase refers most obviously to patriarchal patterns of violence, but also anticipates how the patterns of resistance in *Antigone* might be taken up by subsequent readers—as have late twentieth- and twenty-first-century feminist, queer, anticolonial, and antiracist theorists, artists, and activists. Nevertheless, in an endnote, Woolf advises readers against trying "to squeeze these characters into up-to-date dress," as "it is impossible to keep them there" (*TG*, 201). If in "Modern Fiction," "the form of fiction most in vogue" can provide only "ill-fitting vestments" for life, in *Three Guineas*, propaganda provides badly cut garments for literature. Throughout the novel, clothing helps to make things surface and offers glimpses of what Woolf in "A Sketch of the Past" refers to as "the pattern hid behind the cotton wool."[122] What the novel undertakes, however, is not so much a tearing away of the "cotton wool" to reveal a hidden design, as an attempt to put pressure on the fabric so as to feel out the pattern beneath. This approach resembles *Three Guineas*'s mode of haptic visuality, which combines a close, intimate attention to texture with a method of feeling one's way through and around existing arrangements of thought, feeling, space, and time. Accordingly, the scene in which Sara reads about Antigone drapes this figure only loosely over the girl's form, allowing the momentary overlay of these two literary characters to make perceptible patterns of experience and resistance that have not yet surfaced.

The Years features a series of scenes in which characters' attunement to and perception of texture and fabric gives way to a sense of a pattern that is felt but not fully exposed. For example, during Eleanor's visit to the Chinnerys' country estate in 1911, she looks up at a star through the elm trees whose "leaves hung in a fretted pattern like black lace," hears "country people going home" and has the feeling that "This is England"; that revelation, in turn, is experienced as a slow "sinking into some fine mesh made of branches shaking, hills growing dark, and leaves hanging like black lace with stars among them" (*TY*, 197). As is the case with Sara, thought occurs with and through the perception of texture and fabric. Earlier in the novel, at the close of the 1910 chapter, Maggie stitches the last bit of "stuff" into her party dress as she and Sara realize that the contempt they feel for the poor, drunken people on their street is like the feeling that people in the future will have for Sara and Maggie and "this room—this cave, this little antre" in which they live (*TY*, 179). One of the aims of *The Years* is to make perceptible such overlapping patterns over time and (social) space—in this case, the way the affective structure of class relations resembles and anticipates that of historical distance. In this scene, the tactile, sensational quality of class and temporal distinctions is emphasized by Maggie's construction of a silk party dress, since clothing materializes social and historical distance in particularly obvious ways. At that moment, Maggie and Sara get a grip on these related historical logics, although they cannot undo or reconfigure them.

In the chapter "Present Day," however, dress prompts Eleanor to attempt some alternative historical thinking. The appearance of a "well-dressed woman" makes Eleanor feel she has seen this scene before and to wonder, "If so, is there a pattern; a theme, recurring, like music; half remembered, half foreseen? . . . a gigantic pattern, momentarily perceptible?" (*TY*, 350–51). As the chapter's title indicates, this section as a whole invites readers to consider what aspects of the Pargiters' "Present Day" might characterize their own moment. In keeping with the novel's interest in multiple forms of difference, including the temporal, however, this necessarily draws attention to what does not fit a given reader's "Present Day," as well as what (even in the 1930s) could never have been "present" for that reader given their geographic and social position. That dynamic responds to the mode of critique undertaken in *Three Guineas*, in which the educated man's daughter feels out certain qualities of the social fabric but misses others. *The Years* does not presume to transcend such limitations by providing a vision of the whole, but rather prompts readers to sense those limits and attempt some comparative thinking about how various modes of difference overlap and work together. The novel, then, uses fabric and dress to teach one to feel and read against the grain of historical distance and to experience the proximities and repetitions, as well as the foreclosures of the past, present, and future.

These textured engagements with dress contrast with the trivialization of fashion and the embrace of military "decoration," which Woolf associates with militant suffragism via Rose Pargiter (*TY*, 341, 399). When the novel turns to Rose in 1910, it finds her, a middle-aged suffragette, in the midst of the city, catching a glimpse of herself in a shop window and reflecting "it is a pity . . . not to dress better, not to look nicer" (*TY*, 153). A moment later, however, she associates her dress with her tendency to speak out loud in public, which she considers "one of the consolations, like her coat and skirt, and the hat she stuck on without giving a look in the glass" (*TY*, 154). This idea of "consolations" recalls *Three Guineas*'s commentary (in an endnote) on the judge who, swathed in "a scarlet robe, an ermine cape, and a vast wig of artificial curls," holds forth on women's purported attachment to fashion, which he describes as one of "nature's solaces for a constant and insuperable physical handicap" (*TG*, 177). Woolf asks, sarcastically, whether the judge also might be seeking such "solace," given "the singularity of his own appearance together with that of Admirals, Generals, Heralds, Life Guards, Peers, Beefeaters, etc." (*TG*, 177). *The Years* associates Rose's brand of suffragism with masculine war making; Rose is repeatedly described as a would-be soldier, and the novel draws attention to the fact that militant suffragettes joined the war effort. While Rose does not share the judge's "blindness to the remarkable nature of one's own clothes," her particular consolation for femininity seems to be her feeling that, unlike most women, she can ignore fashion and embrace a kind of uniformity (*TG*, 177). Rose then represents yet another Woolfian figure whose attempts to repair fashion into something less anxiogenic and costly ultimately upholds existing systems of power.

The role of textiles in *The Years*'s textual method is also apparent in the novel's tendency to offer what John Whittier-Ferguson describes as "tag-lines associated with every character" and fragments of narrative that the reader can assemble into different patterns.[123] Whereas in "The New Dress" the "tags of Shakespeare" are empty signifiers, in *The Years* it is possible for various repeated scraps of language to be reanimated and reassembled in different ways. Accordingly, while the chapters proceed in a clear temporal order, this densely textured novel is made up of narrative threads that often fray or seem to be part of a fabric that extends beyond our spatial and temporal view. There is no clear narrative arc, the narrative focus seems to move between the characters almost at random, and the final scene brings them together but offers no obvious conclusions. Like *Three Guineas* and *Roger Fry*, *The Years* is concerned with not only tracing the past but also what might be possible in the future. Ahmed proposes that rather than invest in utopian visions that involve a radical break with the present, the queer phenomenologist might notice "the lines that accumulate through the repetition of gestures, the lines that gather on skin already take surprising forms."[124] Ahmed uses *lines* to refer to lines of sight as well as lines of direction, of movement, and within patterns that are created by and that steer bodies. We might also understand it to refer to lines of writing and the lines of garments, which may suggest new forms that are perceptible only when encountered from a different angle. Ahmed's formulation also resonates with Eve Sedgwick's account of texture. As Sedgwick observes, drawing on the work of Renu Bora, when perceiving texture, one wonders, "How did it get that way? and What could I do with it?"[125] In *The Years*, this engagement with the historicity and potential of texture describes how we might understand the aesthetic of the novel and the various scraps of daily life it offers the reader.

This sense of the manipulability and mutability of the social fabric and the texture of daily life, however, operates in tension with the ambient power of a prevailing mood, which in *The Years* is again expressed via *la mode* and the weather. The opening sections of each chapter feature a seemingly omniscient narrator whose descriptions of the weather at a particular moment in England (and once in France) recall the sweeping vision of the realist novel. Strikingly, all of these episodes draw on the language of garments, textiles, or fashion. Yet in the first four chapters (titled "1880," "1891," "1907," and "1910") these opening pieces refer to specific items of clothing, while in the remaining six chapters ("1911," "1913," "1914," "1917," "1918," and "Present Day") the narrator refers to fabric or dress metaphorically. Thus that pivotal year 1910 marks a subtle shift in modes of representation, and specifically a new way of wielding the language of clothing to conjure the physical and affective atmosphere of a given moment in time. This shift is, to be sure, not a break. As Elizabeth Evans points out, all of these opening set pieces describe the world metaphorically and betray some uncertainty about what they observe; in that way, "Woolf exposes the subjective and fallible underpinnings of that [narrator's] vision."[126] The fallibility of the seemingly omniscient narrator underscores that perceiving and describing mood is also a process of shaping it, which does not, however, mean that moods are subject to individual will. Nevertheless, the countrapuntal movement between these sections (which provide sweeping accounts of contemporary life) and the rest of the narrative (which is focalized through particular characters) prompts readers to shift in and out of a supposedly collective mood while observing how unevenly the weight and force of mood is distributed between bodies and objects.

The atmospheric quality of mood and the moody effects of atmosphere are signaled in the novel's first sentence: "It was an uncertain spring." The opening paragraph then traces the meteorological and affective contours of the season, first observing that "the country farmers, looking the fields, were apprehensive" and then moving into London's West End shopping district, where "umbrellas were open and shut by people looking up at the sky." In London, objects and apparel circulate feeling, and the connections between mood and *la mode* underscore the affective dimensions of economic life; the narrator observes that "shop assistants" pass on soothing banalities about the weather along with "neat parcels" to "ladies in flounced dresses" (*TY*, 3). That sense of repetition and reassurance, however, also draws attention to the variable and exclusive nature of mood. The passage focuses on middle-class activities and perspectives, only glancing into the basement where "servant girls in cap and apron prepared tea," or toward "broad stretches of darkness" on unilluminated streets. Rather than exposing all of London to the reader's gaze, the passage observes and undertakes the labor of perceiving, constructing, and maintaining a given atmosphere.

The movement in and out of a shared mood is in fact the subject of the novel's first scene involving the Pargiters. After the opening prelude describing life in London in 1880, we find Colonel Pargiter at his men's club first enjoying and then breaking off from a group of "men of his own type," as he feels suddenly that their discussion of a recent political appointment "was disagreeable to him." The result of this disaffection, however, is not any lasting estrangement. Rather, this moment of feeling "out of it" at the men's club puts the Colonel in the mood to see his mistress, Mira (*TY*, 5). For her part, Mira recognizes that she always must be in the mood—meaning both sexually available and able to bolster his mood. Via this episode, we see that the possession of economic and sexual power makes being out of the mood an inconvenience rather than a potential disaster and places the responsibility for one's mood on others—in other words, it requires other people to do a certain kind of mood work. For those people, in turn, sensing out the texture of a given scene is a means of survival.

Like *Three Guineas*, however, *The Years* invites us to imagine what might occur if mood work were redirected for different ends. The novel's final moment offers a last description of the weather via a sartorial metaphor that connects mood work to the project of reading the text and the world. The characters turn toward the door to leave a family party, but the narrator swivels back toward the window to direct the reader's gaze outward. The final sentence reads, "The sun had risen, and the sky above the houses wore an air of extraordinary beauty, simplicity and peace" (*TY*, 412). It recalls the lines "This City now doth, like a garment, wear / The Beauty of the morning" from William Wordsworth's "Composed upon Westminster Bridge, September 3, 1802," which also registers the glories of London in a time of peace.[127] In the case of Wordsworth's poem, the speaker experiences an unprecedented mood—"Ne'er saw I, never felt, a calm so deep!"—moments before the city resumes its daily activities, and during a temporary pause in the Napoleonic wars thanks to the Treaty of Amiens. Addressing the performative nature of Woolf's words (if not specifically its reference to dressing or Wordsworth), Sarah Cole finds in them "a certain strained willfulness, a consciousness of their fictionality." She emphasizes that the open sky registers the city's vulnerability to air raid.[128] Accordingly, we could say that Woolf and Wordsworth's metaphors of dress invite us to conclude that this mood and these forms are temporary and deceptive—like a cloak or veil. I would not discount such readings, but simply suggest that it coexists with other possibilities, some of which may not yet be perceptible. We might read this reminder of these texts' fictionality as pointing to the artificiality of stopping time at any given point, which is underscored by the eternal recurrence of the "Present Day" enacted by the title of the last chapter of *The Years*. Such cessation and retrospection are essential to narrative and to Wordsworth's poetry, but also lead us to perceive and prioritize certain patterns and forms; in the case of *The Years*, that form is war. Yet if encountered from another point in space or time, this line of text might also fit into a pattern that leads toward peace. Moreover, if we consider the way that certain moods and forms of attunement shape what comes to the surface, then orienting ourselves toward what is peaceful might highlight how such things come together and how they unravel. In that sense, the language of adornment points us to how "sensing out what is coming together" helps things to cohere. In addition, Woolf's final gesture to a romantic poem in a text more often described as a revision of the realist novel recalls the cyclic vision of literary history presented in "Modern Fiction." It marks Woolf's late modernism as a renewed romanticism, turning back to the early nineteenth century for alternative ways of experiencing the "Present Day." At the same time, the allusion to Wordsworth underscores what has and may again be created in and about similar moments of peace.

This approach involves a mode of reading in the subjunctive mood. It is a way of experimenting with what might happen if we read while imagining that something else has come to pass.[129] *The Years*, like many of Woolf's texts, uses garments to conjure that mode of engagement: fashion and fabric provide vocabularies for describing the feeling but also the contingencies of a given historical moment. Fashion enables fiction to offer speculative and subjunctive modes of thought while making clear that such imaginative and intellectual work is entwined with and dependent on material and historical conditions, locations, objects, and bodies. If, as Campbell argues, fashion provides the historical novel with a model for conjuring the past, *The Years* employs fashion to imagine how we might read past and present differently via a future that is hoped for *and* one that is feared. In that sense, *The Years*'s engagement with fashion complements *Three Guineas*'s treatment of the "ar[t] . . . of dress" as a subjunctive mode of education—that is, a subject that cannot yet be taught, but which shows what needs to be learned. Both texts, then, exemplify a Woolfian commitment to the possibility that how one reads texts, garments, and the world might make a difference—without knowing precisely what that difference is. Reading fashionably helps us to see what Woolf's modes of modernism might do if and as we try to do certain things with Woolf's modernisms.

Fashion's frivolity as well as its historical and economic force provide a vocabulary through which to conceive literature's agency (and lack thereof) in the context of imperialism, war, and consumer capitalism. The next chapter argues for the centrality of fashion to the work of a very different early twentieth-century British writer, D. H. Lawrence, who at times positioned himself in contrast to Bloomsbury's fashionable milieu. Like Woolf, Lawrence draws on the relationship between mood and *la mode* to offer alternatives to individualist and rationalist accounts of agency and subjectivity. He is also suspicious of fashion's status as a theoretical and material phenomenon. But while Woolf's texts use fashion as a tool for thinking and feeling one's way, Lawrence's describe and aspire to garments' capacity to excite, exalt, and prioritize the body. His oeuvre represents a distinct way of understanding how modernist fiction uses, imitates, and competes with clothing, and his approach bears on contemporary questions in literary and cultural theory. In particular, Lawrence's use of dress to explore distributed, nonintentional forms of human and nonhuman agency as well as the vitality of living and nonliving bodies anticipates a range of early twenty-first-century new materialist projects. The next chapter thus shows how Lawrence's engagements with fashion reveal the possibilities and limitations of new materialist attempts to imagine more ethical and sustainable forms of interpersonal and interspecies relations.

2 : MATERIAL CONCERNS
D. H. LAWRENCE, GARMENTS, AND THE MATTER OF FICTION

Now that is the line to take. Start with externals, and proceed to internals, and treat life as a good joke. If a dozen men would stroll down the Strand and Piccadilly tomorrow, wearing tight scarlet trousers fitting the leg, gay little orange-brown jackets and bright green hats, then the revolution against dulness [*sic*] which we need so much would have begun.

—D. H. LAWRENCE, "Red Trousers"

In the beginning, I would like to entrust myself to words that, were it possible, would be naked.

—JACQUES DERRIDA, "The Animal that Therefore I Am"

D. H. Lawrence is not known for having a good sense of humor or for prioritizing "externals."[1] Many of his texts explore a version of what he describes (in a famous letter to Bertrand Russell) as "blood-consciousness," a bodily, instinctual way of knowing that he contrasts with "mental-consciousness," which he associates with visuality and the intellect.[2] According to Lawrence, the subordination of such corporeal knowledge is a cause and product of modernity's ills, including rampant industrialization, mechanization, rationalization, and commodification, as well as technological warfare and social conformity. Given Lawrence's antipathy to consumer culture and its spectacularization of bodies, it is striking to find him claiming in this essay, which was published in the September 27, 1928 issue of London's *Evening News*, that matching outfits are the way to incite a men's "revolution."[3] Lawrence's aim is to make the present more like the "really great periods like the Renaissance," when "we treated life as a joke" and "young men" wore outrageously bright, mismatched clothing: "One leg bright red, one leg bright yellow, doublet of puce velvet, and a yellow feather in a silk cap."[4] He claims that reviving such styles will spark a revolution that will outlast the women's "emancipation crusade" and will offer men an alternative to the pursuit of money and to "Politics Socialism preaching of any kind."[5] The facetiousness of this proposal helps to establish its import, since the essay announces the transformative power of humor. Lawrence's article aspires to function like these colorful outfits on a London street, bringing some unexpected color and levity to the pages of London's popular evening paper and thus to the hands and bodies of its readers.[6]

As this chapter shows, garments appear in a number of Lawrence's texts—including *Women in Love,* "Education of the People," and *Lady Chatterley's Lover* (1928)—when they imagine how society might be reoriented and renewed on a collective and individual basis.[7] As in Lawrence's article, clothing suggests how his work might precipitate or participate in that transformation. In such instances, Lawrence grapples with the nature of political and social change. He seeks to identify and generate the kinds of feelings and attachments that enable individuals and groups to pursue desired transformations. In particular, Lawrence's work repeatedly returns to the problem of how disenchantment—rendered here as "dulness"—unfits people for the right kinds of social and political action. Such dullness also is the product of misguided activism; Lawrence claims that "our modern crusades, like Votes [for women] or Socialism or politics, freedom of little nations, and the rest" simply produce more dullness because their outcomes, even when successful, are profoundly disappointing.[8] Like Woolf, Lawrence links moods to modes of dress in a certain time and place; his red trousers gain their affective force via their difference from and hence relation to current fashions. Yet Lawrence is more sanguine than Woolf about the possibilities for deploying clothing's capacity to shape individual and collective feeling. He even asserts that the red trousers are a more reliable way to dispel dullness than love is. Although love banishes dullness, it "is a thing you can do nothing about. It's like the weather."[9] Thus we find this "priest of love" offering red trousers as a way for men to exert some control over the conditions in which they live.[10]

"Red Trousers" concedes that phenomena such as the women's "emancipation crusade" may be *temporarily* enlivening. This raises the question of how one can know for sure what kinds of animation or enchantment are desirable and how to generate them. And, once one has created the right kind of engagement, how can and should one proceed? In Lawrence's work, that problem is particularly complicated because his texts seek out continuities between human, animal, and nonliving bodies and forces. On the one hand, ideas that involve corporeal forms of knowledge and power, such as blood-consciousness, suggest that the human body has agential capacities well beyond those associated with the rational, intentional actions of a sovereign individual. But on the other hand, Lawrence's vocabulary of flows and energies ushers in accounts of agency as dispersed and of bodies entangled with a range of forces. Such visions of distributed agency undercut simplistic causal visions of how transformation might be brought about, whether through texts, textiles, or the bodies that encounter them.

Lawrence's thinking about connections between human and nonhuman bodies and matter have prompted fresh interest in his work among scholars in the overlapping fields of critical animal studies, posthumanism, and science and literature.[11] Dress, clothing, and fashion have not figured significantly in such conversations or in those fields more generally.[12] It is not coincidental, however, that questions about human agency, objects, and collective transformation emerge repeatedly in Lawrence's work through the language of dress and textiles. On the one hand, fabric demonstrates the agential force of nonliving matter, and on the other, it poses questions about how humans can best draw energy from and direct those forces.[13] Fabric, after all, is the most obvious point of contact between the human body and nonliving matter. Clothing also demonstrates the human practice of fitting, twisting, and remaking animals, plants, and minerals into things that shelter, extend, enhance, and excite the body. Garments seduce and enchant, making the blood flow more quickly, but they also constrict its circulation, making the impress of social convention a matter of touch and feeling. All of these phenomena inform Lawrence's treatments of fabric and dress, through which he takes up a set of related questions: How might we conceive the relationship between the human body and the material world so as to spur productive attachments and entanglements? That is, how can thinking about the connections between living and nonliving matter bring about desired forms of change? In turn, must that change be revolutionary, absolute, and perhaps violent, or can it be gradualist and reformist? Should old forms be unraveled or readjusted and refitted?

Lawrence's efforts to formulate and address these questions resonate with the twenty-first-century interdisciplinary field of new materialism, which urges us to consider and reconsider how matter matters. As Diane Coole and Samantha Frost explain in the introduction to their influential collection *New Materialisms*, such scholarship is characterized by a resurgent interest in "matter; about how to approach it, and about its significance for and within the political."[14] This project overlaps with and sometimes draws from a wealth of feminist work that examines the dynamics and legacy of femininity's association with matter and corporeality in contrast to masculine form, intellect, and rationality. Much of this feminist criticism and theory intersects with Lawrence's work insofar as it is skeptical of and seeks alternatives to Cartesian dualism—the purported split between mind and body, and hence between thinking and embodied matter.[15]

New materialism also has a complex and varied relationship to historical materialism. Coole and Frost emphasize that the new materialisms they describe respond to the perceived failures of "structural Marxism" to attend sufficiently to the agency and particularity of matter. But Coole and Frost also maintain that important strands of new materialist scholarship take up the Marxist "opposition to dominant neoliberal trends" in various ways.[16] Revealingly, one of the most direct attempts to articulate a divergence between historical materialism and a form of new materialism hinges on a reaction to garments—trousers, in fact. In *The Enchantment of Modern Life*, Jane Bennett—a leading theorist in new materialisms—draws out the implications of her reaction to a GAP advertisement in which "young people" clad in khakis dance to Louis Prima's "Jump, Jive and Wail" and the camera occasionally "freezes the image of the foregrounded dancer in midflight."[17] Bennett says she is enchanted by this ad, having defined enchantment as "a state of wonder" that involves a "temporary suspension of chronological time and bodily movement," which gives way to "an energizing feeling of fullness or plenitude" as well as a sense of the world's unrealized possibilities. Enchantment involves "a mobilizing rush as if an electric charge had coursed through space to you. In enchantment, a new circuit of intensities forms between material bodies."[18] Bennett acknowledges that one could describe her enchantment as commodity fetishism, in which commodities become animated and attractive as they reify and obscure the labor of human bodies. Bennett's claim, however, is that the feeling of enchantment and vitality sometimes generated by consumer culture—in her case, by the representation of these khakis—exceeds the kind of vampiric animation described by Marx. Bennett places this ad in the "tradition of works of art that explore the phenomenon of animation—of dead things coming alive, of objects revealing a secret capacity for self-propulsion," including stories by Franz Kafka and E. T. A. Hoffman.[19] "The swinging khakis," she writes, "emerge from an underground cultural sense of nature as alive, as never having been disenchanted."[20] In acknowledging and enhancing this sense, Bennett's enchanted materialism recognizes agential capacities in matter that historical materialism does not. Bennett also describes this enchantment with lively matter as a political and ethical resource, arguing that it inspires a more generous orientation toward the world, whereby "humans must reckon with a much larger population of entities worthy of ethical concern" and the possibilities for changing the world seem closer at hand.[21] Such change, however, is not revolutionary or radical. Bennett's "enchanted" or "vital materialism" assumes the persistence of capitalism and consumer culture but leads people to "participate" more ethically within that world.[22]

This frankly reformist vision is by no means characteristic of new materialism. But it puts pressure on questions about how new materialist theories relate to political programs and praxis. It also helps us to draw out the ways that Bennett's and Lawrence's ideas converge and diverge as they explore the causes of and limits to social and political transformation through their engagements with garments and fiction. Like Bennett, Lawrence treats garments and texts as compromised, commodified means to enchant people. And, like Bennett, he aims to revitalize and shift how people conceive and engage with each other and the material world. Indeed, one reason Bennett's *The Enchantment of Modern Life* pairs well with Lawrence's work is that, although it challenges the concept and privilege of the human, it—like Lawrence's oeuvre—does not ultimately decenter people altogether (as do some posthumanist approaches such as object-oriented ontology). Lawrence, however, is less sanguine than Bennett about the dynamics of enchantment and its relationship to transformation, whether reformist or revolutionary. He also is attracted and committed to gendered and racialized social and political ideas and formations that are not in keeping with Bennett's implicit and explicit ethical commitments. At various points in his life, Lawrence flirted with authoritarianism, insisted on women's subordination to men, and endorsed primitivist and racist ideas and orders. The extent and nature of Lawrence's fascism, misogyny, and racism are a matter of debate, as are his precise attitudes toward democracy, socialism, and communism at different points in his life.[23] But we can safely say that he and Bennett—or likely any other theorist of new materialism—would not quickly agree on a vision of what it might mean to live ethically with others. Tracing the connections between his work and contemporary theories can thus both show how old "new" materialism is and prompt us to reconsider the political and ethical implications and effects of certain ideas about lively matter.

As in the first chapter, my analysis bears on debates about the possibilities and limitations of critique. Citing Max Weber's claim that modernity is characterized by disenchantment, Bennett aligns disenchantment with rationalist modes of critique, including historical materialism. She works, in part, to point out the affective, political, and ethical limitations of this approach. "In the cultural narrative of disenchantment," she claims, "the prospects for loving life—or saying 'yes' to the world—are not good. What's to love about an alienated existence on a dead planet?"[24] As an alternative to disenchantment, Bennett turns to work, such as Giles Deleuze and Felix Guattari's, that challenges the rationalist foundations of psychoanalysis and much philosophical thought. As Anneleen Masschelein points out, Deleuze and Guattari identify Lawrence as a model for the ways he critiques

psychoanalysis, undertakes "criticism of literature," and conceives the relationship between philosophy and art.[25] In her subsequent book *Vibrant
Matter* (which develops many of the ideas in *The Enchantment of Modern
Life*), Bennett again engages vitalist thought—including that of Henri Bergson, who influenced Lawrence—as she undertakes to "theorize a vitality intrinsic to materiality as such."[26] This network of influences helps to explain
why Bennett's enchanted and vitalist materialisms, particularly her vocabulary of energies and flows, may seem familiar to those acquainted with
what Bruce Clarke describes as Lawrence's "electrovitalist schemes" in
which living and nonliving bodies, from cats to stars, contain irreducible
energetic forces.[27]

Lawrence, however, offers a more complicated and troubling story than
Bennett does about enchantment and disenchantment and their relationship
to practices of demystification, commodification, and social transformation, whether revolutionary or reformist. In Lawrence's work, enchantment with the right kinds of things is harder to distinguish from enchantment
with the wrong kinds of things, including disenchantment itself. The stakes
of such difficulty become clearer when we also take into account Sarah Cole's
discussion of enchantment and disenchantment as opposing and related
ways of understanding and depicting political violence, particularly in
modernist texts.[28] Indeed, aesthetic objects have a pressing role to play in
thinking about enchanted and disenchanted engagements with the world,
since—as Cole and Rita Felski point out in different ways—art and literature have long been seen as sources of "(re)enchantment" in the context of
modernity.[29] The relationships between enchantment, disenchantment,
and critique become particularly tangled with respect to modernism since
it is often defined as having a critical stance toward modernity. Yet even
when modernist texts do use disenchantment as a form of critique—when,
for example, *Mrs. Dalloway* offers a disenchanting portrait of a great doctor
as a way to critique the treatment of shell-shocked soldiers—it may be that
readers are enchanted by precisely that approach. In other words, modernist texts show us that the association of critique with disenchantment is too
simple.[30] At the same time, as Cole's discussion of the modernist enchantment with violence suggests, it behooves us to be somewhat suspicious of
the enchanting power of aesthetic forms. Moreover, when we consider the
power of aesthetic experience in terms of the enchanting effects of stylish
dress, the implication of aesthetic experience with consumer culture and *its*
violence comes to the fore.

Lawrence makes precisely this move in *Women in Love*. In doing so, he
prompts us to reconsider what it might mean to try to find transformative

possibilities in commodified aesthetic objects, including clothing and texts. Focusing on Lawrence's treatments of fashion and fabrics also contributes to our understanding of his theory of agency. In *Women in Love* in particular, Lawrence critiques both the subordination of the individual to the machine of industry, and liberal individualism with its focus on self-expression, self-development, and personality. These phenomena correspond with contrasting theories of fashion and fiction: one in which fashion and fiction demonstrate how external forces make the self, and one in which fashion and fiction are a means of expressing the self. Lawrence's alternative to this binary schema is to understand human desire and embodiment as manifestations of universal forces, which nevertheless take unique form through each individual. Fashion and fiction are evidence of the content and direction of these fancies and desires. At the same time, they can catch the fancy, encouraging people's desire to take certain directions and forms.

This dynamic at once opens up possibilities for agency and dramatizes the difficulty of controlling or determining in advance what form agency might take or what impact it might have. These are political issues because they involve how matter works to assemble, arrange, shift, and hold in place bodies, institutions, and systems. Indeed, Lawrence places greater emphasis than Bennett on the ways that matter works to constrain and oppress human bodies. This difference notwithstanding, one benefit of putting Lawrence's work in conversation with new materialist work—particularly by political theorists such as Bennett or Coole and Frost—is that it helps us to see that Lawrence's depictions of what and how things have agency amount to an expanded vision of what it might mean to be a political subject or object. This in turn shifts the terms of the debate about Lawrence's politics. Existing arguments usually hinge on an understanding of politics as concerned with systems of collective governance or as defined in terms of legible political philosophies (such as liberal democratic, communist, fascist).[31] Thus Lawrence's work is often described as apolitical—and, more specifically, as rejecting politics in favor of sex or myth—or as ascribing to or critiquing certain established political positions.[32] Understanding Lawrence's relationship to various political movements is of course important, and I touch on such issues in this chapter. But if we employ the expanded sense of political agency offered by new materialists such as Bennett, Coole, and Frost, the extent and nature of Lawrence's political engagement becomes clearer.[33] Again, pursuing this argument through dress and garments is not a trivial choice. Doing so adds a further dimension to our investigation of what matters, including with regard to how we discuss how matter matters. Rather than being epiphenomenal and superficial, fashion and dress emerge for

Lawrence as an important route into politics and toward theories of agency and materiality, especially in the context of state-sanctioned violence. In that respect Lawrence's work overlaps with feminist projects that seek to show how various things often coded as feminine and hence marginal—such as fashion and matter—are actually vital to understanding and addressing various issues from the constitution of modernity and modernism to the nature of political subjectivity and the causes and prevention of war.

While much of my argument in this chapter rests on *Women in Love*, I turn first to the beginning of Lawrence's career as a writer and his first published novel, *The White Peacock* (1911), to understand how he treats dress as a way of linking erotic desire to aesthetic creativity, and both to modern politics. *The White Peacock* also makes clear that, in discussing clothing in Lawrence's work, one also has to confront nudity, so to speak. After all, while I have been focusing on clothing, Lawrence is more famous for his depictions of bare flesh in his writing and his painting. Yet, in Lawrence's texts, the distinction between adornment and nakedness often does not hold, particularly as it operates to differentiate between human and nonhuman animal life. As I discuss below, the collapse of distinctions between adornment and nakedness and human and animal in Lawrence's work overlaps with aspects of Jacques Derrida's late writing on animality; in turn, this resonance between Derrida's and Lawrence's texts clarifies how the seemingly human, intellectual acts of writing and reading texts might discover and generate connections between human and nonhuman animal life as well as corporeal modes of agency and knowledge.

In *The White Peacock*, slippages between nakedness and dress demand more nuanced and generative ways of conceiving the relationship between flesh and fabric, which *Women in Love* pursues. As I discuss, *Women in Love* offers a vision of agency that is "intent" yet not consciously intentional—a process by which a focus on the task at hand opens up future possibilities for individual and collective transformation. Lawrence also explores related forms of agency in his treatise on education, "Education of the People," and in *Lady Chatterley's Lover*, the last novel published during Lawrence's lifetime. In their treatments of garments and fabric, these texts respond to various late nineteenth- and early twentieth-century beliefs about the connections between dress, sexual difference, and political formations, which are exemplified by Italian futurism and by the theories of Herbert Spencer, J. C. Flügel, and Georg Simmel. Drawing out these connections in Lawrence's work helps us to see how fashion and dress inspired and underpinned competing theories of "human nature" and political life in the early twentieth century.

No "Decent Suit": Art, Eroticism, and Clothing in The White Peacock

Fashion was not only a theoretical problem for Lawrence; it mediated his access to publishers and writers and thus to a career as an author. His letters and diaries from 1909 to 1911 attest to his experience of fashion as a constraint on his professional and artistic aspirations.[34] In that period he gained the attention of Ford Madox Hueffer (later Ford Madox Ford), then editor of the *English Review*, and began to be invited to events hosted by members of Ford's literary and artistic circle, including the writer Violet Hunt's celebrated "at homes" at the Reform Club. While Lawrence was characteristically skeptical of this coterie, he knew his connection to the group was a brilliant professional opportunity, as well as a potential relief from the oppressive solitude he was experiencing as a teacher in Croydon. Yet his lack of a "decent suit"—and his consequent need to decline invitations to various events—is a common refrain in his letters to his fiancée, Louie Burrows.[35] When Lawrence did attend social events, his clothing and his boots became a focus for his anxieties and resentments about his class position vis-à-vis Hueffer and his milieu.[36] Lawrence, for example, reports to Burrows in late November 1909 that he is going to tea with his new acquaintance Ezra Pound, "as we are going out after to some friends who will not demand evening dress of us. He knows W B Yeats and all the Swells. Aren't the folks kind to me: it is really wonderful."[37]

As Lawrence quickly realized, it was not just a matter of having the wrong clothes, but also of having clothes that were wrong in the wrong way. In contrast to Lawrence's drably inappropriate suits, which signaled his poverty and class origins, Pound's outlandish dress, recorded in great detail in Lawrence's letters, represented a bold rejection of middle-class values and a deliberate attempt to startle—if not quite shock. Lawrence reports (to Grace Crawford, a friend of Pound and member of Ford's circle) that Pound's "David Copperfield curls . . . were cut" and "his great grandfather's black satin stock . . . had given place to a tie of peach-bloom tint and texture. He wore a dark blue cotton shirt, no vest, and a Panama hat. What is the guise?—sort of latest edition of a jongleur?"[38] In Lawrence's account, this new style offers a sartorial parallel to—and parody of—Pound's poetic investment in the tradition of Renaissance troubadours. Pound's 1909 collection *Personae* included poems in which he took up the "guise" of a troubadour. Lawrence's letter, however, mocks Pound for imitating a mere troubadour's assistant. Lawrence's reference to Pound's Dickensian haircut also indicates that this look may not so much make the old new as take up a mid-Victorian trend; rather than an innovator drawing inspiration from Robert Browning and his collection *Dramatis Personae*, Pound is a Dickensian hangover. Lawrence thus witnesses and undercuts Pound's self-conscious attempt to "modernize" via a haircut and outlandish cravat. Given Lawrence's particular anxiety about his own boots, it is telling that he concludes the letter by joking that, "having had all the experiences possible for a poor man, [Pound] will now proceed to conquer riches" in America, where "he will sell boots—there is nothing in that blown egg, literature."[39] This joke skewers Pound for his interest in marketing and advertising and for collapsing the distinction between selling apparel and selling literature.[40] Yet it also suggests some envious fascination with Pound's performance of the role of the modern poet. As Lawrence complains to Louie Burrows, "This black suit of convention is most gênant. I feel like a very wicked and riotous person got up to look and behave like a curate."[41] By contrast, Pound's dress demonstrates a seemingly easy mobility between acceptable and outré, and rich and poor. In a 1913 letter to editor Harriet Monroe, Pound asserted that Lawrence's poems in the *English Review* showed that he had "learned the treatment of modern subjects before I did."[42] While Pound may not have tutored Lawrence in the ways of modern poetry, he certainly presented an obvious model for the modern poet, one that Lawrence both suspected and envied.

Pound's earlier "look" and flair for marketing impressed Lawrence enough that they appear in *The White Peacock*. The novel, which is set mostly in the countryside near Nottingham, focuses on a love triangle between the middle-class Lettie; George, the handsome son of a neighboring farmer; and Leslie, the heir of the local mine owner. Lettie marries Leslie, whose career as a businessman and conservative politician flourishes, but whose attitude toward Lettie becomes at once indulgent and disengaged. After her marriage, Lettie remains emotionally entangled with George, who achieves financial success and marries his cousin, but then declines into alcoholism. Near the end of the novel, after George finally breaks off contact with Lettie, she begins patronizing "a young literary fellow who affected the 'Doady' style—Dora Copperfield's 'Doady.' He had bunches of half-curly hair, and a romantic black cravat; he played the impulsive part, but was really as calculating as any man on the stock-exchange. It delighted Lettie to 'mother' him. He was so shrewd as to be less than harmless."[43] This character is never again mentioned, but the passage establishes Poundian fashion as the symbol of literary culture's emasculating dependence on bourgeois society. Early Anglo-American modernism is reducible to the latest fashion—and not a particularly fresh one at that.

The references to Lettie's mothering and Dora Copperfield's nickname for her husband also offer a parallel between contemporary literature's relationship to the feminine bourgeois sphere and what *The White Peacock* suggests is modern men's enthrallment to women via love and marriage. This early novel has received relatively little critical attention, perhaps in part because it does not break from naturalism, Victorian realism, and romance to the extent that Lawrence's later works do. But *The White Peacock* addresses concerns and paradoxes that occupy Lawrence for the rest of his life. These include a critique of conventional heterosexual romance and matrimony as well as an examination of the relationship between human and nonhuman life; the tale unfolds in a fertile but rapidly developing landscape and includes lavish descriptions of its flora and fauna. The novel also explores the contrasts and convergences between heterosexual and homosexual desires, as do many later works, including *Women in Love*. *The White Peacock* is narrated by Lettie's brother, Cyril, whose love for George represents an early version of Lawrence's exploration of the possibilities for male-male companionship as a substitute or supplement to heterosexual romance. Whether classifiable as heterosexual, homosexual, or autoerotic, characters' desires are directed, blocked, and spurred by artworks and garments. Through the sexual dynamics of dresses and shirts as well as songs, poems, and paintings, the novel engages Lawrence's lifelong concern with the intimate relationship between aesthetic and erotic experience. It is because of this relationship that art and fashion can determine political, social, and cultural life. So, for example, Leslie and George's original sexual contest over Lettie, which is spurred and directed by garments and artworks, gives rise to their later political battles, which pit Leslie's conservatism against George's socialism and then liberalism. This early novel thus draws attention to the political implications of Lawrence's investigations of sexuality, embodiment, and interpersonal relations, which unfold in subsequent works.

The novel's nod to formal politics also dramatizes the social consequences of women's ascendency in the spheres of modern art and fashion. Perhaps most obviously and predictably, depictions of dress in the novel expose the economic logic of matrimony and the corrupting effects of feminine consumer culture on heterosexual desire. In one of the book's first scenes, Lettie dismisses any possibility of marrying George by focusing on the more pressing question of what frock she can wear to an outing with Leslie. This contest between her interest in George and her interest in the clothing of Leslie's "set" is replayed in a climactic scene soon after her engagement to Leslie. When Cyril shows George some of Aubrey Beardsley's erotic prints, George is inspired to try to convince Lettie to run away with him. But George's erotic appeal cannot overcome the attractions of the clothing that Lettie has acquired on a prematrimonial shopping spree. Lettie refuses George's plea to run away with him, chiding him for thinking she could live as a simple "farmer's wife" (*WP*, 167). This scene registers what many critics note are pervasive modern anxieties about how the seductions of fashion and consumer culture might turn women away from their proper roles. Allison Pease describes a version of this dynamic in Beardsley's illustrations for Oscar Wilde's *Salomé*, which evoke the dangerous autoeroticism of the New Woman.[44] Beardsley emphasizes the link between contemporary fashion and autoeroticism by depicting Salomé in the pleasurable process of dressing herself. Beardsley's revision of the scene of the toilette, which was common in fashion illustrations, thus plays on and recirculates the alternate sexual economy of feminine self-fashioning.

While reflecting such anxieties, *The White Peacock* also undercuts distinctions between naked masculine desire and women's sartorial delights and blurs the line between art and fashion. George, for example, prepares for his meeting with Lettie by fantasizing about what frock she will wear, imagining that it will resemble the "naked lines" of the Beardsley print (*WP*, 166). Only when he sees the "soft stuff" she actually is wearing does he sense that she will not play out the scene as he had hoped (*WP*, 166). As Lawrence underscores, form and style as expressed through dress and art are central to how George— and Beardsley—imagine and reproduce erotic desire.[45] Thus George adorns himself carefully for this meeting with Lettie, asking the narrator, Cyril, what he should wear. George's growing awareness of his own physical desirability is treated as a sort of fall from innocence, an example of the corrupting modern self-consciousness that Cyril and Lettie help him to develop. But there is no clear alternative; George's eroticism in the novel is always conveyed via his relationship to clothing. For instance, Cyril registers George's powerful appeal when he sees—or imagines how Lettie sees—George's strong white throat emerging from his opened collar. The meeting of tan and untanned flesh—the trace of clothing on the white body, which is also a mark of class, race, and occupation—is George's most erotic feature. In short, George's pastoral masculinity is desirable because of its particular relationship to clothing, just as Lettie's appeal as a "modern woman" is constructed through dress. In this early novel, then, Lawrence emphasizes the difficulty, even impossibility, of recovering a corporeal or sensual register that is not marked by clothes. Even as the novel emphasizes the force of bodily desire reaching across boundaries of class and education, it suggests that this desire is fueled precisely by the play between body and clothing, "natural" desires, and the social values woven into clothing and marked on the flesh.

The mark of clothing is also the mark of language, and Lawrence's own art is caught in this knot of corporeality, adornment, and desire. Linda Williams explores this contradiction through Lawrence's treatment of visuality. As she notes, Lawrence negatively associates visuality with modern femininity, intellectualism, and mere "sex in the head," yet he also enjoys it and does so, moreover, via the visual process of reading.[46] In *The White Peacock*, Lawrence's project is further complicated by the censorship laws of the day, which require him to omit or to cloak references to the body and its desires in metaphor and symbol; the result is that Lawrence's novel performs a kind of striptease.[47] Yet even frank and extensive descriptions of nudity—such as Beardsley's erotic prints—are, at best, fabrications of real bodies. Nor can they be disentangled from the titillation of breaking social mores.[48] Given these dynamics, the problem that *The White Peacock* poses is how the relationship between aesthetic and erotic experience might be used to discover, recover, or sustain less destructive forms of desire. It is a question that Lawrence returns to repeatedly in later work, including *Women in Love* and *Lady Chatterley's Lover*.

One possible response, which Lawrence begins to explore in *The White Peacock*, is to conceive of language and adornment as continuous with rather than opposed to forms of animal embodiment and behavior. That is, language and adornment not only can describe or represent connections between human and nonhuman animals, they also can partly constitute that connection. In exploring that possibility, the novel, like many of Lawrence's works, grapples with Darwinian arguments about man's animality. In addition, the paradox of nudity suggested by tan lines and "naked lines" dovetails with Derrida's discussion of nakedness as a founding distinction between human and animal. Derrida begins "The Animal that Therefore I Am" by considering a moment in which he stands naked in his bathroom in front of his female cat and feels ashamed. As Derrida points out, animals are always and never naked, for they are "naked without knowing it," which also means "without consciousness of good and evil."[49] In Lawrence's novel, this paradox is captured in the symbol of the "white peacock," which concatenates distinctions between human and nonhuman animals, nakedness and adornment, nature and culture, morality and amorality, and art and fashion, as well as female and male. In one of the novel's most discussed scenes, a burly gamekeeper named Annable recounts to Cyril his disastrous marriage to an aristocratic lady, who (he claims) was attracted to and then tired of his physical charms. As many critics note, Annable appears to be a precursor for Mellors in *Lady Chatterley's Lover*, although (as we will see) the later novel addresses and redresses some of the failures—both philosophical and sexual—that Annable represents. As Annable and Cyril talk in an abandoned churchyard, a peacock appears and defecates on the head of a stone angel, prompting Annable bitterly to declare that the bird epitomizes "the soul of a woman," "all vanity and screech and defilement" (*WP*, 148, 149). The gamekeeper admits, however, that his former wife may not have been entirely at fault; she is thus "a white peacock," Cyril proposes. The "white peacock" is at once guilty and blameless, unadorned and extravagantly ornamented, as well as male and female, since of course peacocks are distinguished from peahens by their elaborate tails. Annable's anthropomorphism and zoomorphism are thus fundamentally unsound ways to describe the supposed essence of womanhood or the nature of human or animal existence. Instead, his misguided attempt to translate prevailing ideas about intention, guilt, and gender across the human/animal divide exposes the inadequacy of all of those concepts to describe the world, including himself and his experiences.

Annable's condemnation of the white peacock reveals the trouble with connecting—but also the need to connect—human and nonhuman animal behaviors. The white peacock represents not only Annable's lady, but also Lettie, whose vanity and fickleness help to destroy George. In a scene in which she preens before him and Leslie, Lettie is described as letting her "white shoulder" slip out of a cloak that is "a peacock's gorgeous blue" (*WP*, 254). This image recalls Beardsley's depiction of Salomé adorned in peacock feathers, which in turn suggests the defiance and usurpation of male authority.[50] Yet, as with George's encounter with Beardsley's "naked lines," this moment of exposure (in which Lettie's body and the meaning of the book's title seem to be revealed) gives way to further layers of meaning. As Cyril notes, Annable's motto is "Be a good animal, true to your animal instinct" (*WP*, 147). For Annable, this means fathering nine children, whom he neglects along with his long-suffering second wife. While he flouts certain conventions, however, Annable's condemnation of the peacock suggests his understanding of animality remains entangled with an androcentric moral schema and concepts of vanity and adornment. This leads him to overlook his own resemblance to the bird, even as he admits to Cyril that he was too proud of his own (white) body and its capacity to captivate the lady.[51] Nor does he seem cured of this vanity, for he invites Cyril to admire the look and feel of his bare forearm. As Kathryn Sproles points out, Annable and his failed marriage suggest what might have transpired if Lettie had chosen George.[52] We can thus read Annable as one of the many instances in which Lawrence has a character express a simplistic or misguided version of a Lawrentian idea—in this case, the need to reconstruct and reconceive the relationship between human and nonhuman animal life, especially through men's recovery of their bodily instinct. The paradoxes and contradictions in Lawrence's text keep us shuttling between different approaches to these ideas as well as various interpretations of the white peacock.

This ongoing work of interpretation might seem to invest Lawrence's reader in forms of "mental-consciousness," which he would decry in his 1915 letter to Bertrand Russell. Leonard Lawlor's reading of Derrida's confrontation with his cat, however, suggests another possibility. Taking up Derrida's association between dressing and writing and their links to techne and technology, Lawlor argues:

> When Derrida is most human, most technological, most concealed, he is most indeterminate, and when he is most indeterminate, when he is only appresented, when he is imperceptible and clandestine, he most resembles a cat. In still other words, Derrida is most catlike when he is most human: when he is writing aporias, he most resembles a cat pacing back and forth before a door, waiting to be let out or to be let in.[53]

This formulation provides a way of understanding why the texts that Lawrence kept producing so furiously throughout his relatively short life are often characterized by contradiction and inconsistency. Lawlor conceives paradoxes and aporias as a way to move humans closer to the conditions of unknowability and vitality that, for Derrida (and Lawrence), characterize an encounter with a naked/adorned nonhuman animal and the uncategorizable nature of an individual animal's existence. Lawlor's account also acknowledges that it is the particularly human work of writing that brings the cat and the man together, thus also attending to the difference between these creatures. This version of unknowability and being human, then, is not equivalent to a purportedly "natural" or brute ignorance possessed by people who have been less exposed to modern forms of knowledge—as George is at the beginning of *The White Peacock* and as Annable's children are. That is not to say that Lawrence does not develop and endorse racist, primitivist ideas about the vitality of "less civilized" peoples, especially in works such as *The Plumed Serpent* (1926), which belongs to his "leadership period." On the contrary, I want to point out that such views coexist and intertwine with ways of bringing together human and nonhuman animal life that inform twenty-first-century critical animal studies.[54]

Derrida's attention to the proliferation of difference within and beyond the category of the animal also sheds light on *The White Peacock*'s treatment of adornment as a spur and muffler for sexual desire and thus for forms of difference. For Derrida, the category "animal" fails, in part because it cannot accommodate the many forms of difference that flourish and exceed its boundaries. Lawrence's production of contradictions is also a way of maintaining and promoting varieties of difference, which disrupt and exceed attempts at categorization. Moreover, in *The White Peacock* the production of difference via textual contradiction develops through and alongside the proliferation of difference in natural life, which Darwin's work had made part of popular consciousness. As Elizabeth Grosz emphasizes in her feminist, Deleuzian reading of Darwin's *The Descent of Man* (1871), however, it is *sexual* selection rather than natural selection that generates myriad degrees of intra- and interspecies difference. Whereas natural selection works via the logic of survival, Grosz writes, "Sexual selection is above all creative. . . . [It] provides the artistic raw materials for song, dance, painting, sculpture, and architecture, or at least for the animal preconditions of these human arts."[55] Grosz explains that "the laws of sexual selection are the principles of aesthetics" and make unpredictability, taste, and individuality part of animal life.[56] One of the things that Darwinian sexual selection creates is sexual difference, which is not fully explainable in relation to reproduction or judgments of biological "fitness." Grosz echoes Darwin's use of the peacock to describe the gendered dynamics of taste and adornment: "Generally, the more adorned one sex is, the more discerning the other seems to be, otherwise there hardly seems to be any reason for the continuity in and intensification of male ornamentation over time."[57] *The White Peacock*'s descriptions of birds, insects, and plants attest to this flourishing of aesthetic forms in the natural world, while the scenes in which Lettie, George, and Cyril encounter or reflect on works of art in this pastoral setting mark continuities between human and nonhuman animal aesthetic-erotic experience. At the same time, the gendered confusion produced by comparing a woman to a peacock announces an impending crisis in aesthetic production. Together, the stories of Lettie and of Annable's lady suggest that modern women are both the "more adorned sex" *and* "the more discerning," since both women choose their lower-class would-be lovers because of their shapely bodies. Meanwhile, men's aesthetic expression—exemplified by Cyril's narration, the poetry of the Poundian dandy, and George's and Annable's bodily displays—fails to transcend the logic of feminine consumer culture and the restrictions of bourgeois norms as they attempt to appeal to or at least accommodate women's tastes. In short, the result of women's becoming both those who display and those who choose is aesthetic impoverishment. According to Lawrence, such impoverishment also entails a loss of masculine vitality and bodily decay; hence the final chapters of the novel track George's physical decline as he drinks himself to death.

The loss of richness and vitality is also experienced through the novel's own citational style, for *The White Peacock* takes up classical pastoral, aestheticist, impressionist, realist, and romantic modes (among others). And the appearance of the Poundian poet near the end of the novel suggests that his literary modernism is merely a recycling of the old. In the novel, aesthetic and corporeal exhaustion are exacerbated by what Lawrence observes is the culture's alignment of sexual selection with reproduction through the enshrinement of motherhood and child-rearing as the purpose of marriage and the goal of a woman's life. Grosz emphasizes that the decoupling of sexual selection and reproduction is key to Darwin's vision of life as "the infinite elaboration of excess, the conversion of the excesses of bodies, of natural objects and forms, into both new forms of body and also new forms of culture, new modes of social organization, new arts, new species."[58] It follows that Lawrence's characteristic antipathy to modern motherhood, which surfaces in *The White Peacock* and extends through much of his work, stems partly from how this means of producing bodies (through the strict logic of reproduction) conscribes ways of producing new *forms* of bodies (through the wild workings of sexual selection). In short, nonreproductive sexuality prompts and is prompted by innovative aesthetic forms, including forms of adornment.

Grosz emphasizes that aesthetic production and individuation follow from and amplify types of difference, since sexual selection follows the vicissitudes of taste rather than the logic of survival. For Grosz, this proliferation of difference offers an alternative to "egalitarian feminism," whose goal is the achievement of equality between the sexes and which assumes their fundamental sameness.[59] Grosz's and Lawrence's political commitments and their aims in reconsidering the relationship between desire and difference are certainly quite distinct, but this objection echoes Lawrence's attacks on modern democracy as enforcing homogeneity and mediocrity.[60] So too does Lawrence share Grosz's investment in nonmechanistic and nonteleological ideas of life as a way to promote new ways of living. Thus Grosz emphasizes that Darwin's vision of change over time is not dominated by a grim, deterministic logic of natural selection. Instead, she finds in Darwin new energies and new possibilities for political transformation. According to Grosz, selection and difference do not function only along binary gender lines, and Darwin invites us to conclude that "homosexuality, like racial diversity or difference . . . is one of the many excesses that sexual selection introduces to life, like music, art, and language."[61] This particular formulation risks flattening the very different differences that race, sexuality, and art make, as well as naturalizing the category of race as a way to describe phenotypical differences. Such a move is in line with Lawrence's treatment of the generative, vitalizing effects of difference, which includes the circulation of desire between disparate men—most famously, Birkin and Gerald in *Women in Love*. Nevertheless, for Lawrence, human gender binarism remains the fundamental motor of creativity and hence of personal, social, and political transformation—even while, as feminist and poststructuralist critics including Williams have noted, such binaries always threaten to collapse in Lawrence's work. As we will see in *Women in Love*, Lawrence continues to engage adornment as a vital material that, crucially, can sustain or interrupt gender binarism's functioning as a generator of individual differentiation. Attending to such dynamics helps us to see how Lawrence's vision of the autonomous individual involves and depends on particular intersubjective and material connections.

Dress and Redress in Women in Love

I have argued that Lawrence's interest in dress responds to nineteenth-century Darwinian theories and resonates with twenty-first-century work that considers adornment as it recovers continuities between human and nonhuman animals in order to imagine routes for ethical and political transformation. Such connections extend through Lawrence's oeuvre. In later texts, particularly *Women in Love*, Lawrence attends more closely to the nature of the relationship between living and nonliving matter, at times offering vitalist visions of the world as animated by irreducible forces, flows, and energies. Dress remains a crucial, though critically overlooked, aspect of Lawrence's writing; it is a material through which ideas about the relationship between living and nonliving matter interweave with theories about how desired transformations might be brought about, and about what that transformation might entail. Using the language of design, we might say that, especially in *Women in Love*, dress shows what affordances there are for individual and collective change, given the erotic, bodily, political, aesthetic, and imaginative material at hand.

In *Women in Love*, Lawrence's engagements with dress also overlap with those of early twentieth-century artists and cultural theorists, including Woolf, who turn to dress to understand and spur individual and collective formations and transformations, often in the context of catastrophic violence. For members of the Bloomsbury group, Italian futurists, and (more obliquely) social scientists such as Flügel and Simmel, fashion was an important medium for describing the nature of sexual difference and its relationship to political and social structures. Lawrence's work and futurist manifestos on dress, for example, engage garments to present visions of historical causality that hinge on the relationship between what Lawrence's "Red Trousers" refers to as "internals" and "externals." But while the futurists draw on dress to encourage war making, Lawrence, like Woolf and the Omega artists, investigates if and how garments might serve to prevent it. Such differences notwithstanding, Lawrence and the futurists invoke dress to express concerns with how conventional, disenchanting forms of knowledge stifle or at least fail to revive desired modes of engaging the world. In turn, *Women in Love* draws on the language of fabric and textiles to describe forms of embodiment that draw energy from the human body's entanglement with non-human objects and forces. The novel also skirts the possibility that such energy might be derived from the act of producing garments. That possibility is addressed more directly in "Education of the People," a collection of twelve essays begun in 1918 and finished in 1920.[62] While shifting away from issues of production, *Lady Chatterley's Lover* also considers how the right kind of garments might inspire social and political change, in part by reconnecting bodies to the vital forces and flows that Lawrence associates with "blood-consciousness." Yet all of these works falter on questions of causality and individual agency.

Written largely during World War I but not published until 1920, *Women in Love* is both Lawrence's most sartorially attuned novel and the most explicitly engaged with contemporary British and European artistic movements, particularly Italian futurism and Bloomsbury's visual art. While in the foreword to the American edition of the novel Lawrence declares, "I should prefer the time remain unfixed, so that the bitterness of the war may be taken for granted in the characters," the novel registers the cultural and historical trends shaping Britain and Europe, especially the flourishing of artistic subcultures in London just before and during World War I.[63] Bohemian fashions such as those sported by Pound in 1909 and ridiculed by Lawrence were a widely recognized feature of these groups. Of course, artistic movements before the 1910s had experimented with clothing design, most notably William Morris's arts and crafts movement, which influenced many of the artists and designers of the early twentieth century, including the Wiener Werkstätte and Omega Workshops. But the period just before and even during World War I saw an unprecedented flourishing of artists designing clothing across Europe. Of the Italian futurists, Giacomo Balla issued the first of the group's many manifestos on dress in 1914 and designed futurist outfits worn by Filippo Marinetti. In Germany, Gustav Klimt and Emilie Flöge designed dresses for the Wiener Werkstätte. Lawrence seems to have been one of the artists in the 1910s who did some dressmaking—at least for private use. In a letter to the *Nottingham Journal* soon after D. H. Lawrence's death, local luminary William Hopkin claimed that Lawrence "seemed to do anything he desired. He was a fine cook, could design and, if necessary, make a women's dress. In fact, he was a genius of a peculiarly all-around kind."[64] Lawrence trimmed hats and made garments for his wife, Frieda, and he was intimately familiar with the craft of haute couture, for he would refit Frieda in the designer frocks that her sister occasionally sent.[65] He also obliquely connected that labor to the war. A former acquaintance of Lawrence claimed that in 1919 he equated "[u]npicking a Poiret gown" with "taking the Rheims Cathedral to pieces," both disenchanting tasks he may very well have simultaneously regretted and relished.[66] Though playful, the comparison of a couture gown to the Rheims Cathedral establishes clothing as a medium through which one might consider if and how human life continues in the midst and wake of war; images of the badly damaged cathedral were widely circulated as evidence of the barbarity of the German forces that bombed it, and in 1919 reconstruction was begun. It is fitting then that in Lawrence's wartime novel, *Women in Love,* aesthetic theories and modes of living are fabricated and dismantled through dress. Characters use dress to make social, artistic, and political statements, and the novel examines competing ideas and practices of aesthetics and politics through the image and metaphor of fashion. Dress also foregrounds the material dimensions of these discursive negotiations. Accordingly, in *Women in Love,* dress's aesthetic, affective, and material affordances suggest what resources and possibilities there are for remaking everyday life and collective systems. As Lawrence seeks to move and persuade his own readers, fashion operates within—and alongside—the novel as a material and discursive means of shaping and reshaping human desires. Like Woolf and the artists of the Omega Workshops, Lawrence treats dress as central to efforts to reconfigure affective and social life in the context of modern violence.

The associations between fashion, art, and desire that Lawrence establishes in *The White Peacock* emerge in the first scene of *Women in Love.* As Ursula and Gudrun sit "working and talking" by the window, they tentatively discuss whether they *"really want* to get married" (*WL,* 3, emphasis in original). Ursula's embroidering and Gudrun's drawing echo their process of spinning out their ideas about themselves and their lives in this scene. Both efforts, however, are partial, imperfect, and limited by the material at hand. As Gudrun complains, *"Nothing materializes"* (*WL,* 5, emphasis in original). The novel, however, traces the process by which the women's desires do gain material shape and force. In doing so, the text puts aside conventional ideas of how women's desires are fulfilled: namely, through marriage. As Maria DiBattista notes, "no actual desire motivates this decision to marry or not" for the sisters.[67] Instead of following the usual marriage plot, then, the novel recognizes the heft and force of these women's as yet unarticulated desires as they lead not to marriage necessarily, but to the dynamic state of being "in love." It is the furious but unspoken thrust of these women's desires—rather than novelistic or social conventions—that steers the novel into uncharted waters.

While the sisters' words fail to represent what they "*really want,*" the narrative offers up the sisters' appearance (and particularly Gudrun's dress) as a clue to what these women desire but cannot articulate. There is an intimate and immediate connection, the narrative suggests, between one's fantasies and one's fashion. Gudrun has costumed herself for a dramatic and defiant part; she displays "emerald-green stockings" and a "perfect sang-froid" that makes her an outsider among the "provincial people" (*WL*, 4). This emphasis on dress, however, establishes that neither Ursula nor Gudrun are shaping their dreams out of thin air; rather, they are adopting and adapting marriage as the material they are given, which itself combines older traditions with modern modes of living. As in *The White Peacock*, Lawrence uses the metaphor of cloth to convey how tradition and modernity shape and inform his character's desires. Gudrun's dress, after all, features "ruches of blue and green linen lace," a material that was fashionable in the early to mid-1910s, thanks especially to the British designer Lucile, Lady Duff Gordon, whose dresses often were made of materials, including linen lace, which were associated with lingerie (*WL*, 4). Lace is also interwoven with more conventional modes of feminine dress—hence its use in wedding gowns in Lawrence's day and our own—as well as traditional women's work, such as Ursula's embroidering. So too are Gudrun's hopes and beliefs tied to older values and contemporary trends. Though her deep-green stockings retain the ability to startle, this technique of adapting existing material, like the women's conversation about marriage, is essentially cold-blooded and disenchanted.

Different characters' engagements with dress play out the tensions between enchantment and disenchantment and between revolutionary and reformist visions of change. Accordingly, in the novel, fashion often operates as an imperfect and compromised form of self-expression and conscious defiance. By manifesting her iconoclastic ideas through dress, Gudrun invites opposition, critique, and discipline. In the opening chapter, she even encounters a sort of Midlands fashion police after walking through the collier town, which she experiences as hellish. When Gudrun and Ursula arrive at the Crich wedding, they step onto the red carpet laid out in front of the church, where a policeman stops them and a group of colliers' wives jeer at Gudrun's outfit. "What price the stockings!" someone shouts (*WL*, 9). For Gudrun, this mockery prompts a fantasy of complete destruction: "She would have liked them all annihilated, cleared away, so that the world was left clear for her" (*WL*, 9). As Michael Levenson notes, this dream of anni-hilation, which Birkin and Ursula also have, is the basis from which *Women in Love* builds new visions for heterosexual relationships and then commu-nity, all the while circling back to this original fantasy of near extinction at various points in the novel.[68] Birkin, for instance, fantasizes about the oblit-eration of all nonhuman and human animal life or simply the destruction of humanity, but his enchantment with Ursula helps to draw him away from this fantasy. Throughout the novel, a vision of eradication contrasts with the process of fabricating new modes of living from the material at hand. A ten-sion develops between these two means of remaking the world: one that demands a complete destruction and rebuilding and the other that imag-ines how to harness and adapt the conditions of modernity to allow new ways of living.

The distinction between these visions depends in part on particular modes of enchantment and disenchantment with violence. When he indulges in fantasies of the earth cleared of humanity, Birkin exemplifies what Cole describes as the tendency to be enchanted with violence by seeing "in [it] some kind of transformative power."[69] What I want to draw attention to is that such a vision first emerges in the novel at a moment of fashionable display—and specifically one that recalls a mannequin parade (that is, a fash-ion show) and anticipates a Hollywood red carpet. As Caroline Evans notes, fashion and mannequins have often been associated with deathliness; she cites Susan Buck-Morss's gloss of Walter Benjamin: "The modern woman who allies herself with fashion's newness in a struggle against natural decay represses her own reproductive powers, mimics the mannequin, and enters history as a dead object."[70] Gudrun's fantasy is the apotheosis of this vision of the self as perpetually new and dead to history, for she reimagines her ob-jectification as a form of cold-blooded persistence (if not exactly liveliness) in the midst of apocalyptic destruction. The scene also highlights the historical materialist dimensions of Benjamin's link between fashion and death. Esther Leslie observes that Benjamin's assertion registers "the reifying operation of commodity fetishism" by which "capital's organisation murderously consumes life."[71] While Gudrun moves among colliers' wives rather than textile workers, the deathly conditions in which they live are "the price" of the stockings, since Gudrun's livelihood comes from teaching the colliers' children and from the bourgeois patrons who purchase her art. In that sense, the emerald-green stockings absorb and artificially reproduce the vibrancy of the human and natural world.

As it converges with Marxist critiques of commodification, this scene un-derscores what is at stake in Bennett's claim that animated, commodified garments like the swinging khakis might inspire an enchanted engagement with the world that, in turn, directs us toward desired forms of transformation. In offering her account of the enchanting effects of lively garments, Bennett seeks an alternative to the disenchanting narratives offered by Marx's account of commodity fetishism and by Theodor Adorno and Max Horkheimer's critique of the culture industry. Lawrence seems to stick with disenchantment as he emphasizes the deathly quality of Gudrun's striking outfit. Yet in focusing on Gudrun's clothing in the opening of the novel and in this early scene, Lawrence also exploits their enchanting effects to engage his readers—to guarantee, in effect, that they are enchanted enough to keep reading. This implicates the reader in the dynamics of attraction and attachment that will play out between Gudrun and Gerald as well as Ursula and Birkin (despite Birkin's claim that he wants "a woman I don't see") (*WL*, 151). Following Cole, then, we might acknowledge how enchantment with violence (and, I would add, with fashion) coexists with disenchantment. Lawrence's work puts pressure even on that formulation, however, since it shows how difficult it may be to differentiate disenchantment from an enchantment with disenchantment. This suggests that one must be alert to both the enchanting power of aesthetics and the allure of critique as well as the ways that the two become intertwined. Birkin, for example, seems to suffer from an enchantment with disenchantment, since he gets caught up in his own denunciations of modern life. So even as Birkin expounds on the need for people to reject "intellectualism" and to find "the great dark knowledge" of the blood, he remains uninspired (*WL*, 39, 40). Throughout the novel, the appeal of dress dramatizes the difficulty of ensuring that one will be enchanted by and hence attached to the right kinds of things or people, and in the right way.

Fashion, Futurism, and Political Formations

The allure of Gudrun's sartorial performance demonstrates this problem. It also plays out in *The White Peacock*'s concern with the role of sartorial display in fueling erotic attraction. If, according to Lawrence's first published novel, women's ascendancy in the realms of dress and taste threatens erotic and aesthetic production, in *Women in Love*, Gudrun's fashionability fuels a modern, mechanistic, and violent version of heterosexual desire. Stylish clothing catalyzes Gudrun and Gerald's affair, for Gerald's furious attraction to Gudrun is spurred by her efforts to wear her ideas on her sleeve—or rather, on her stockings. In the scene at the Criches' estate in which Gerald

and Gudrun experience a "mutual hellish recognition" of their sadomasoch-
istic desires as they handle a terrified rabbit, textiles fuel and express the
nonhuman forms of attraction and repulsion that characterize their explo-
sive relationship (*WL*, 250). After one of Gerald's sisters is drowned, Gudrun agrees to be an art tutor for the youngest child, and she arrives at the
estate while the family is in mourning. Gerald, who is always correct and
conservative in his dress, is clad in a black suit that—like Lawrence's in
1909—barely conceals the "wicked and riotous" nature of his desire. Gerald is struck by Gudrun's bold appearance: "She was dressed in blue, with
woolen yellow stockings, like the Bluecoat boys. . . . Her stockings always dis-
concerted him" (*WL*, 245). He is annoyed that she comes "dressed in startling colours, like a macaw, when the family was in mourning." Yet he is
roused by her call to battle: "It pleased him very much. He felt the challenge in her very attire—she challenged the whole world. And he smiled
as to the note of a trumpet" (*WL*, 246). This simile echoes the reference to
the "trumpets" of the flowers that Gerald watches Gudrun caress and admire just a moment before (*WL*, 246). Hence Gudrun's garments are associated with sight, sound, and touch as they play out through militant
display, music, and floral sexual reproduction, which often involves interspecies contact, since many flowers must attract the touch of insects.[72]
Indeed, *Women in Love* repeatedly associates dress with flowers. Such associations extend *The White Peacock*'s examination of the relationship
between varieties of human and nonhuman forms of aesthetic and erotic
experience, and, via Gerald and Gudrun, dramatize the violent, destructive dimensions of these forms of enchantment.

Gudrun's dress and her relationship with Gerald also expose the limitations of avant-garde strategies for transforming everyday life and social and
political structures in the 1910s, particularly as they emerge via experiments
in dress design. Discussions of futurism in *Women in Love* usually focus on
how Birkin, Gerald, or Loerke represent the movement's mechanism, mas-
culinism, individualism, and antihumanism, although a few critics do associate Gudrun with futurism.[73] In these scenes, Gudrun's dress exemplifies
the antitraditional, chromatic, and militant ideals of the futurists in the face
of Gerald's conventionality and the Criches' mourning. In fact, the futurists
embraced dress as a medium for their aesthetic and political program and
issued multiple manifestos about clothing, usually accompanied by designs.
The first, titled "Le Vêtement masculine futuriste: Manifeste" ("Futurist
Manifesto of Men's Clothing"), was written by the painter Giacomo Balla
and appeared in May 1914. In September, Marinetti published an expanded
and revised version in Italian titled "Il vestito antineutrale" ("The Anti-Neutral

Suit"). That "interventionist tract" (to borrow Jeffrey T. Schnapp's words) appeared as Italy was hesitating to join the war.[74] "The Anti-Neutral Suit" begins: "Humanity always dressed itself with modesty, fear, caution, and indecision, forever wearing the mourning suit, the cape, or the cloak. The male body was habitually diminished by neutral shades and colors, degraded by black, and imprisoned by folds of fabric."[75] The manifesto imagines dress as a means of transforming bodily comportment and individual and collective feeling and behavior. It proposes that remaking clothing will remake the character of the Italian people: "One thinks and acts as one dresses. Since neutrality is the synthesis of all tradition, today we Futurists display these antineutral, that is, cheerfully bellicose, clothes." The aim is "to color Italy with Futurist audacity and risk, and finally give Italians joyful and bellicose clothing," so that they will embrace nationalist politics and leap into the fray of World War I. The suit that will accomplish these changes will have "the most violent violet, the reddest red, the deepest of deep blues." It will encourage free movement and be "dynamic, with textiles of dynamic patterns and colors (triangles, cones, spirals, ellipses, circles) that inspire the love of danger, speed, and assault and loathing of peace and immobility." Yet, in keeping with the futurists' individualist bent, the "anti-neutral suit" is not a uniform. Rather, it includes detachable and changeable items that are "warlike" and will be complemented by an "asymmetrical" and "exuberant" hat and mismatched shoes. The futurists thus embrace change as a sartorial principle, while emphasizing the power of the individual rather than the fashion cycle to dictate such shifts.

Lawrence may not have read any of the futurist manifestos on dress while composing *Women in Love*, but Balla's "The Anti-Neutral Suit" resonates with Lawrence's earlier complaints about the "black suit of convention," as well as his search for patterns and forms that spur and make perceptible the violent energies flowing through bodies. As Lawrence explains in an oft-cited letter to Edward Garnett in 1914, he is sympathetic to what he perceives as the futurists' rejection of conventional ideas of human personality and morality. Lawrence admires their pursuit of "the non-human, in humanity," and compares that project to his own in *The Wedding Ring* (then the title of *The Rainbow*). According to Lawrence, that novel departs from previous literature by having "a different attitude to my characters," which requires, he tells Garnett, "a different attitude in you."[76] The word *attitude* suggests how Lawrence's aesthetic might involve and require reciprocal shifts in modes of feeling, thinking, and bodily comportment. Lawrence, however, does not claim an automatic or mechanical correspondence between form and behavior, as Balla's manifesto does. In a letter to another friend a few days

IL VESTITO ANTINEUTRALE

Manifesto futurista

Glorifichiamo la guerra,
sola igiene del mondo.
MARINETTI.
(1° Manifesto del Futurismo - 20 Febbraio 1909)

Viva Asinari di Bernezzo!
MARINETTI.
(1° Serata futurista - Teatro Lirico, Milano, Febbraio 1910)

L'umanità si vestì sempre di **quiete,** di **paura,** di **cautela** o d'**indecisione,** portò sempre il lutto, o il piviale, o il mantello. Il corpo dell'uomo fu sempre diminuito da sfumature e da tinte **neutre,** avvilito dal nero, soffocato da cinture, imprigionato da panneggiamenti.

Fino ad oggi gli uomini usarono abiti di colori e forme statiche, cioè drappeggiati, solenni, gravi, incomodi e sacerdotali. Erano espressioni di timidezza, di malinconia e di **schiavitù,** negazione della vita muscolare, che soffocava in un passatismo anti-igienico di stoffe troppo pesanti e di mezze tinte tediose, effeminate o decadenti. Tonalità e ritmi di **pace desolante,** funeraria e deprimente.

OGGI vogliamo abolire:

1. — Tutte le tinte **neutre,** « carine », sbiadite, *fantasia,* semioscure e umilianti.

2. — Tutte le tinte e le foggie pedanti, professorali e teutoniche. I disegni a righe, a quadretti, a **puntini diplomatici.**

3. — I vestiti da lutto, nemmeno adatti per i becchini. Le morti eroiche non devono essere compiante, ma ricordate con vestiti rossi.

4. — L'equilibrio **mediocrista,** il cosidetto buon gusto e la cosidetta armonia di tinte e di forme, che frenano gli entusiasmi e rallentano il passo.

5. — La simmetria nel taglio, le linee **statiche,** che stancano, deprimono, contristano, legano i muscoli; l'uniformità di goffi risvolti e tutte le cincischiature. I bottoni inutili. I colletti e i polsini inamidati.

Noi futuristi vogliamo liberare la nostra razza da ogni **neutralità,** dall'indecisione paurosa e quietista, dal pessimismo negatore e dall'inerzia

Vestito bianco - rosso - verde
portato dal parolibero futurista Cangiullo, nelle dimostrazioni dei Futuristi contro i professori tedescofili e neutralisti dell'Università di Roma (11-12 Dicembre 1914).

Il Vestito Antineutrale: Manifesto futurista (1914). Courtesy of the Istituzione Biblioteca Classense, Ravenna.

earlier, Lawrence distinguishes his vision from the futurists', in part by emphasizing how art might involve exchange and interaction, albeit in a heterosexual frame. Whereas the futurists "will progress down the purely male or intellectual or scientific line" and offer a mechanistic vision of the world, Lawrence claims that "re-vivifying art" requires men to "expose themselves" to women and for women to "accept" men.[77] This idea of self-exposure and acceptance in the process of sexual selection contrasts with the violence of Gerald and Gudrun's interaction, in which the charge created by their contrasting garments gives way to a moment in which the "veil of [Gudrun's] consciousness" is "torn" and they are unwillingly revealed to each other (*WL*, 249).

Of course, Gudrun's sartorial militancy also undercuts the futurists' masculinist vision of the machinic, individualized body by suggesting how women might grasp the mantle of antitraditionalism, bellicosity, "audacity and risk." This issue emerges in "Education of the People" when Lawrence attacks the "modern woman" for wanting to become a mere product of the clothing she wears:

> She wants to derive her own nature from her accoutrements. Put her in a khaki uniform and she's a man shrilly whistling *K-K-K-Katie*. Let her wear no bodice at all, but just a row of emeralds and an aigrette and she's a cocette before she's eaten her hors d'oeuvres, even though she was a Bible Worker all her life. She lays it all on from the outside, powders her very soul.[78]

This furious passage spells out the potential implications of Balla's theory that "one acts as one dresses," since that would suggest that clothing can inspire "danger, speed, and assault" in a woman as well as a man. Anyone can put on or discard masculinity and militarism like a frock. Lawrence thus traces an easy trajectory from masculine, nationalist futurism to feminine self-indulgence via fashion. Lawrence's comment also registers the ways that discourses of dress were entangled with suffrage debates and responses to women's donning uniforms and taking up traditionally masculine jobs during the war. Suffragettes in Britain, for example, advanced their campaign for equal voting rights by deploying dress in various and sometimes contradictory ways, such as insisting on their femininity, increasing their visibility, announcing their solidarity, and demonstrating their seemingly unwomanly militancy.[79] Yet, as in "Education of the People," this link between bodily display and political subjectivity intersects and at times collides with the familiar binary between women's purported materiality and corporeality and men's rationality. An article published in the *Times* in April 1914 titled "Fashions and the Vote: Women's Dress as Hindrance to her Cause" provides an example of such discourses. It insists that "[man] cannot believe in a woman being capable of efficient, vigorous, or independent action when hampered by the skirt of the period. It is equally hard for him to suppose that a woman can get a clear view of public affairs or vote intelligently when wearing her hat over one eye."[80] A distinction between material and epistemic concerns undergirds this explanation of women's exclusion from the public sphere, for women's focus on material objects—especially those related to the body—proves their unfitness as rational political subjects. Yet while women's interest in fashion implies a narrow focus on the self and on the material, the author assumes, paradoxically, that men can create theories about women's nature by contemplating those very same fashions. In short, the topic of fashion knits together gendered concerns about the nature of modern liberal political subjectivity, its dependence on forms of Cartesian dualism, and related fears about the corrupting influence of irrational, sensual consumer culture.

The "Manifesto della moda femminile futurista" ("Futurist Manifesto of Women's Fashion"), published in 1920, represents one attempt to address fashion's association with femininity and the possibility that it might challenge masculine authority. Composed by "Volt," it declares, "Women's fashion has always been more or less Futurist. Fashion: the female equivalent of Futurism." It even claims, "We don't need to start a revolution. It's enough to multiply a hundredfold the dynamic virtues of fashion." Yet the manifesto balances these assertions of fashion's revolutionary power with an emphasis on masculine authority, asserting, "a great poet or painter must take over the directorship of all the great women's fashion houses."[81] Like a number of other futurist manifestos on dress, it also links changes in dress to the stimulation of the Italian economy, thus imagining consumer capitalism as masculinized and rationalized as well as nationalized. According to Lawrence, the modern woman desires to surrender control of her desires by making herself and her sexuality a mere reflection of fashionable, sometimes foreign tropes. The futurist manifesto nevertheless attempts to assert masculine and national control over popular culture as a way to assure political ascendancy.

The mobility of styles and garments across borders bolsters *Women in Love*'s disenchanting critique of nationalism. The novel repeatedly refers to nationalism as "old hat," and early in the novel, Gerald, Birkin, and Hermione use the metaphor of haberdashery to debate whether international conflict is essentially a justified defense of a nation's possessions (its hats writ large). Birkin announces that the "hat" is simply not worth defending, and that a man is more profoundly free without such belongings and beliefs. Much later, Gudrun dismisses British nationalism as an "old bowler hat," aligning conformist styles, materialism, and outmoded beliefs (*WL*, 435). These references recall the military recruitment posters that I discuss in the first chapter, since they sought to secure a sense of national belonging and duty by associating British masculinity with a series of hats. Lawrence's metaphor of the hat also undercuts the futurists' attempt to replace one hat with another. However colorful or asymmetrical, the hat seems like a dull attempt to refashion traditional nationalism and commercialism for Italy, which will fail to revivify the Italian body politic. The novel's commentary is perspicacious; in 1933 Marinetti published "Il manifesto futurista del cappello italiano" ("The Futurist Manifesto of the Italian Hat"), which announces a continuation of the "clothing revolution" begun by Balla's "celebrated manifesto *The Antineutral Suit.*"[82] The manifesto complains of Italian men's adaptation of "the American and German way of the bare head." Instead, it asserts that there will be a variety of colorful hats created for different times of day and different purposes, including "an intelligence imparting hat for the idiots who criticize this manifesto."[83] Rather than laying out a viable program for dress or politics, the manifesto relies on the enchanting nature of the descriptions of these hats to shift the orientations and attachments of its audience, such that they even forestall critique. *Women in Love* deflates such rhetoric as it suggests that one nation's commercial-nationalist rhetoric could easily be swapped for another's.

In keeping with that point, there was in fact a slippage between Italian futurism and British fashion in the popular British press in the early 1910s. The term *futurist* came to stand for artistic and design efforts that seemed boldly modern, from postimpressionist paintings to brightly colored frocks.[84] In particular, futurism had become popularly aligned with bohemian fashion in Chelsea and Bloomsbury. Newspaper coverage of the design and clothing produced by the Omega Workshops often labeled it "futurist." When the war broke out, however, the status of "futurist fashion" became more contested. The nationalism that swept the country deeply marked the British fashion press, and to many newspapers and fashion magazines, futurist styles were associated with the iconoclasm and "foreign influences" of the bohemian avant-garde. In November 1915, one fashion periodical declared,

> Futurism as a force sickened when the war broke out, and has steadily grown more anaemic. A couple of years ago London Society took up Futurism as if its life depended on it. . . . The cult grew and grew. It even gave its name to a certain style of dress—the negation of every accepted canon of sartorial good taste. Then came the war, and Futurism fled. . . . Instead of Futurist frocks, we have the nurse's uniform and the war worker's eminently practical "get-up."[85]

Yet coverage of fashion and art during the war also sometimes reconciled the prewar language of daring, futurist fashion with patriotic efforts. One fascinating spread on the Omega Workshops in the popular *Illustrated Sunday Herald* on October 24, 1915, for example, featured a photograph of one of the Omega artists, Winifred Gill, decked out in an Omega dress and stand-ing in the Omega display room, with the caption "A West End Futurist smiles on you." The image was part of a set of pictures of the workshops ti-tled "Women Who Do the Most Original War Work of All." As the caption suggests, the newspaper conflates the Bloomsbury avant-garde and futur-ism and construes them as a feminine enterprise supporting the British war effort. It even relocates the Omega from bohemian Bloomsbury to the fash-ionable "West End." A few months earlier, an editorial in the *Sketch* focused on the trend of the "shocking stocking"—a fashion that the women in *Women in Love*, especially Gudrun, prominently display; according to the fashion magazine, "The point of the stocking is that it should be shocking—pleasantly so, of course. That is, it should give a positive impression. . . . Our insteps even respond to the patriotic impulses of the moment, for a common de-vice is to show the Allied flags in emphatic embroidery."[86] Gudrun's daring stockings, it seems, are just a few embroidery stitches away from being per-fectly patriotic.

In *Women in Love*, such stylistic slippage highlights the difficulty in se-curing distinctions between militant nationalist and cosmopolitan pacifist aesthetics. In addition to exploring links between beauty, violence, and death, Lawrence's novel is skeptical about the possibility that a given fashion bears a particular political message. Instead, like Woolf's *Roger Fry*, it admits the difficulty of transmitting a specific lesson via sartorial form itself. So in *Women in Love*, futurist art and fashion easily translate from Italy onto Gu-drun's body and the walls of the Soho flat owned by the frivolous artist Ju-lius Halliday, which features rather forgettable "pictures . . . in the Futurist manner" (*WL*, 72). Gudrun's style in particular seems to declare an opposi-tion to British nationalism and conventional mores, but that apparent defi-ance helps to make her a social success in various aristocratic and bohemian circles in Britain and across Europe; she has "touched the whole pulse of so-cial England" (*WL*, 352). As with the Pound-like figure that appears in *The White Peacock*, Lawrence's portrait of Gudrun highlights the modish mo-bility of bohemian and avant-garde modernism and its compatibility with Englishness. The novel in that sense represents Gudrun in ways that recall the representation of the Omega in the *Illustrated Sunday Herald*. Law-rence insists that the avant-garde's interest in dress provides evidence of the superficiality of its attempt to transform everyday life, and what is at stake is the political efficacy of literature. Given their entanglement with changing fashions, neither beauty, nor avant-garde experimentation, nor existing literary forms seem adequate to address the violence and failures of modernity.

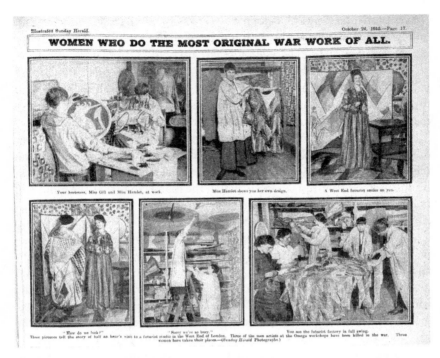

"Women Who Do the Most Original War Work of All," *Illustrated Sunday Herald*, October 24, 1915, 17. © The British Library Board (Illustrated Sunday Herald).

The absence of the war as a clear referent in the novel heightens avant-garde and bohemian modernism's appearance of apolitical modishness. This is exemplified by Lawrence's reimagining of Ottoline Morrell as Hermione Roddice and Garsington as Breadalby. Lawrence aligns Hermione's extravagant, unusual clothing with the accoutrements of culture and the various reform movements in which she dabbles. We learn that she strives to keep herself "well dressed" in clothing, and ideas, and through her commitment to "public action" (*WL*, 12). Yet while Lawrence describes Hermione's clothing and her enthusiasm for dress in great detail, the narrative is relatively vague about the content or purposes of her political and social causes. This attenuates connections between clothing and political opposition but not between fashion and politics. As in *The White Peacock*, Lawrence minimizes fashion as a form of political expression, yet suggests that fashion manifests the impulses that dictate public life. This amounts to a vitalist theory of the relationship between aesthetics and politics, which involves the flow of forces through living and nonliving things; while aesthetic form fails to contain and convey particular political ideas, it can stir and direct the erotic energies that fuel individual and collective action. Dress and literature are ways of shaping the raw material or energy that makes up politics. In that respect, Lawrence's work recalls early twentieth-century theories of fashion, such as those of Simmel, Spencer, and Flügel, who understand fashion as a medium through which contrasting political impulses between autonomy and obedience are expressed and, at times, worked out.

As with the futurist manifestos, those theories raise the question of whether dress might be not only a symptom but also a tool of social and political reform. As I have been suggesting, *Women in Love* seems to reject such a possibility. But it also invests in the idea that the man who breaks the mold will manifest his difference visibly and even sartorially—though not intentionally. Hence, Birkin's first appearance in the novel focuses on his relationship to conventional styles of dress and thought: "Although he was dressed correctly for his part, yet there was an innate incongruity which caused a slight ridiculousness in his appearance. His nature was clever and separate, he did not fit at all in the conventional occasion. Yet he subordinated himself to the common idea, travestied himself" (*WL*, 16). Even though Birkin puts no effort into dressing differently, the relationship between his body and the garments conveys a sense of his individuality. Birkin's "innate incongruity," moreover, fuels the energetic attractions between him and Gerald, whose conventional clothing always fits him faultlessly.[87] Such homosocial connections through difference suggest incipient forms of affiliation that defy modern European democracy's emphasis on immersion and similarity.

Naked Force

It is through nudity that fabric's potential to render alternative forms of embodiment and agency emerges in *Women in Love,* specifically in the famous scene in which Birkin and Gerald wrestle. Tellingly, this episode takes place after the novel critiques those who would shed their clothes as a way of adapting a subcultural style. In the earlier scene in Halliday's London flat in the chapter titled "Totem," the bohemians from the Pompadour Café wander naked before the futurist paintings as a sign of their fashionable liberation. In this episode, flaunting nudity is akin to flaunting outrageous clothing; Halliday and his coterie try it out, as they do other bohemian fashions. The presence of the "wood-carvings from West Africa" reminds us that primitivism also facilitated the traffic in cosmopolitan styles such as the Omega's, which, according to the novel, are nevertheless compatible with militant nationalism (*WL*, 72). Birkin is profoundly uncomfortable with the display, while Gerald is discomfited when he mistakes the "Hindu" servant for a "gentleman" because of his secondhand clothing. To Birkin, moreover, the servant's body, "tinged slightly with grey under the skin," is evidence of "corruption" and encapsulates his feelings about this milieu (*WL*, 71, 80). This account of the servant provides further evidence for Anne Cheng's claim that modernist treatments of racialized skin often bear anxious witness to the instability of visual and ontological distinctions between (natural, immutable) skin and (artificial, alterable) garments. As Cheng shows, this is also a crisis in visual perception more broadly, since racial difference is not simply something we see; rather, it "teaches us *to see*"—specifically, to extrapolate purportedly fundamental characteristics from certain exterior signs.[88] Equipped with Cheng's analysis, we can see that Birkin's perception of the skin of the "Hindu" as an inadequate covering for a fundamental corruption amounts to a reassertion of the legibility of race and being, which contrasts with Gerald's sartorial confusion. Yet Lawrence's use of the language of skin and fabric to describe Birkin's and Gerald's naked bodies also suggests he is grappling with the potential failure of such visual signs, including distinctions between skin and dress. In that later scene, Lawrence works toward other modes of sensation while confronting fashion's paradoxical status as frivolous and transformative.

The wrestling scene in "Gladitorial" draws on the language of fabric to reimagine nudity as a means of a physical and spiritual connection. That connection is sightless and mindless, yet involves touch and sound, and it leverages and draws energy from racial difference. Lawrence uses the language of textiles to describe the men's physical contact. This contact, in turn, is a form of enchantment; Birkin's body weighs on Gerald's "like a spell," which also is cast on the reader via Lawrence's mesmerizing description (*WL*, 279). If Lawrence's antipathy to fashion stems, in part, from his desire to feel rather than see the body and its relation to other bodies, then that feeling and that mode of attachment nevertheless are expressed through the touch and composition of fabric, for it helps him to describe the kind of intimate, knotted, yet impermanent modes of interrelation that support his desired version of subjectivity.

In the passage describing the climax of Gerald and Birkin's match, the sensuous qualities of fabric and thread enable and express new embodied relations and ways of knowing. At first, "Birkin impinged invisibly upon the other man, scarcely seeming to touch him, like a garment" (*WL*, 279). Such contact gives way to a more intimate entanglement:

> So they wrestled swiftly, rapturously, intent and mindless at last, two essential white figures working into a tighter closer oneness of struggle, with a

strange, octopus-like knotting and flashing of limbs in the subdued light of the room; a tense white knot of flesh gripped in silence between the walls of old brown books. Now and again came a sharp gasp of breath, or a sound like a sigh, then the rapid thudding of movement on the thickly-carpeted floor, then the strange sound of flesh escaping under flesh. Often in the white interlaced knot of violent living being that swayed silently, there was no head to be seen, only the swift, tight limbs, the solid white backs, the physical junction of two bodies clinched into oneness. (*WL*, 280)

The phrase "knot of flesh" confuses distinctions between the interior and exterior of the men's bodies as well as the boundaries between them.[89] This reference to knots also marks continuities between the substance of the men's bodies and the material against which they push and thereby gain force, for the "knot of flesh" forms on a "thickly-carpeted floor," which is itself composed of knots made up of animal or plant matter. An earlier chapter, "Carpeting," draws our attention to such matters via a discussion of the "silky" Persian carpet with a "pile" that Hermione gives Birkin (*WL*, 140). This substance, then, is a nonliving and nonwhite product of imperial contact and expansion. In the wrestling scene, the connection between these knotted substances is underscored by the list of human and nonhuman sounds they produce; as the two men become one, the sounds created by flesh on flesh and by flesh on carpet alternate with sounds produced within bodies ("breath") and those ("like a sigh") whose source cannot be determined. It is also unclear whether the men grip each other and themselves or whether they are gripped by an external force; the "tense white knot of flesh" is "gripped in silence between the walls of old brown books." Once again, force emerges from the contact between living and once-living matter, since the "old brown books" are presumably leather. These dynamics draw out the particular nature of the men's agency; they are "intent" yet mindless, forceful yet entangled in external forces, and they are intimately revealed yet subject to a depersonalizing, abstracted narrative gaze. Indeed, the reference to books as well as the dramatic shift to a more abstracted, painterly narrative style draws attention to the reader's role in animating this scene—that is, making it exist through reading—which involves the contact of a living body with the once-living matter of a printed page. Simultaneously human, animal, and nonliving, as well as white and of color, this "knot of flesh" offers a vital, intersubjective alternative to the machinelike, brightly clad yet fully transparent futurist body.

When we put this scene in conversation with Bennett's account of enchanted materialism, we get a deeper sense of how the language of textiles facilitates Lawrence's gendered and racialized vision of what resources might exist for individual and collective transformation. For Bennett, the spectacle of garments animated by forces other than human bodies makes clear "the ever-present possibility of bursts of vitality that violate an order ranking humans incomparably higher than animals, vegetables, and minerals." [90] That spectacle and that possibility generate for Bennett a sense of enchantment that, in turn, prompts a more capacious and generous sense of what bodies and objects deserve ethical consideration. *Women in Love* also explores how a sense of the world's liveliness might produce forms of enchantment that enhance one's attachment to what might otherwise seem a disenchanted world. But as Birkin's fantasies of a world of flora and fauna wiped clean of humanity suggest, the task is not (or not only) to challenge humans' superiority, but to justify humanity's existence, invest in it, and determine what form it will take. In this scene, then, we see the vitality of animals, vegetables, and racialized objects helping to establish a sense of (white) humanity's vitality that at once depends on and tries to disrupt a sense of (white) humanity's radical difference from or superiority to those things. In this context, textiles highlight a continuity between human and nonhuman substances, which suggests that the human body, if "intent" in the right ways, may access—if not self-consciously steer—agential forces well beyond its apparent capacities without succumbing to mechanism or relying on machines.

As the "knot of flesh" moves on the thick carpet, the men become entangled and enchanted with each other and thereby revive their attachment to the world. Having wrestled, Birkin recovers from his anger at Ursula for refusing his proposal and admits to Gerald that he loves and wants to marry her. Indeed, these scenes could be said to prepare Birkin for his union with Ursula, for the descriptions of her "unrevealed nudity" and "forever invisible flesh" as they make love in "Excurse" recall his contact with Gerald. For his part, after wrestling, Gerald ceases to feel "an agony of inertia, like a machine that is without power," as he regains feelings of warmth and "wonder" (*WL*, 275). This is not a permanent transformation, of course. At the end of the novel, Gerald is an inert, frigid mass. Yet as Birkin contemplates the "last terrible look of cold, mute Matter" on Gerald's dead face, he contrasts this lifelessness with the "clasp," the "warm, momentaneous grip of final love" Gerald gives him after they wrestle (*WL*, 498). At once momentary and momentous, dissolvable and secure, the related images of the clasp, grip, and knot underscore what it might mean to undertake what Michael Lackey describes as "the endless re-creation of everyday life and the human psyche" that Lawrence's work pursues.[91] They are the clue to Lawrence's project of reviving bodies and thus the world.

The fragility of this project is also dramatized when, in the wake of the wrestling match, the narrative shifts from descriptions of tactile contact and the "knot of flesh" to accounts of fashionable dress and class difference. As Gerald gets back in his evening clothes, Birkin notices Gerald's "silk socks, and studs of fine workmanship, and silk underclothing, and silk braces," and muses on "how scrupulous Gerald was in his attire, how expensive too. . . . Curious! This was another of the differences between them. Birkin was careless and unimaginative about his own appearance" (*WL*, 283). This move from an intimate, sensual, and defamiliarizing description of "a tense white knot of flesh" to a detached catalog of Gerald's clothing and its cultural and economic value operates similarly to a camera's switch from a fuzzy close-up to clear wide-angle shot. In the previous chapter, I used Laura U. Marks's account of the distinction between haptic and optical visuality to describe the different ways of touching and viewing clothing, and thereby understanding and representing the world, which operate in *Three Guineas*. Woolf's "daughter of an educated man" employs a haptic mode of perception when she zooms in on specific points of strain in the social fabric and feels her way along its uneven texture, in part via dress. But *Three Guineas* also presents wide-angle views of the world that put things, including men's garments, in perspective and at a critical distance. In this scene in *Women in Love*, haptic perception occurs between Gerald and Birkin and between their bodies and the reader. Marks asserts that in a "haptic relationship . . . we become amoebalike, lacking a center, changing as the surface to which we cling changes."[92] But, she notes, this change does not preclude one from reestablishing an optical mode of viewing, by which one reasserts one's "mastery" and distance from that which one perceives.[93] Marks describes that oscillation between haptic and optical and "between near and far" as "erotic." She equates it with "the ability to have your sense of self, your self-control, taken away and restored."[94] That erotic experience occurs for Birkin and potentially the reader, as the intimacy and abstraction of the description of the men's bodies can disorient and bring the reader (and reading) close. Yet Birkin's and the text's reestablishment of optical visuality also makes clear that it is both a mode of dominance and the dominant mode of perception. Moments of haptic contact and thus erotic experience can only be intermittent.

Birkin describes a neat contrast between Gerald's excessive attachment to conventional dress and his own more virtuous disregard for such superficialities. Yet Birkin's relationship to dress and appearance is quite complex; as with Birkin's preaching about "the great dark knowledge" of the blood, the narrative suggests that Birkin's attachments and beliefs are more ambivalent than he might admit. Birkin is not entirely careless about his appearance. Earlier in the novel, as he wanders naked in the fields, stunned by Hermione's attempt to crush his head with a paperweight, he acknowledges his "horror of being observed by some other people. If he were on an island, like Alexander Selkirk, with only the creatures and the trees, he would be free and glad" (*WL*, 109). But Birkin is not Selkirk, nor is *Women in Love* like *Robinson Crusoe* (which was inspired by Selkirk's experiences as a castaway). If *Women in Love* is to find a way out of Birkin's misanthropic fantasy, it must grapple with such mundane questions as how to dress and live among others.

In "Chair," Birkin and Ursula struggle to translate ideals into the material realities of everyday life. During a shopping trip to the "jumble market" to furnish their marital abode, Birkin and Ursula argue about the value and meaning of possessions. Ursula, who shares her sister's affection for clothes, agrees with Birkin that they should give up their plans to settle in England and should travel instead, but she desires a "definite place" and "some beauty in my surroundings." Birkin retorts,

> You'll never get it in houses and furniture—or even clothes. Houses and furniture and clothes, they are all terms of an old base world, a detestable society of man. And if you have a Tudor house and old, beautiful furniture, it is only the past perpetuated on top of you, horrible. And if you have a perfect modern house done for you by Poiret, it is something else perpetuated on top of you. It is all horrible. It is possessions, possessions, bullying you and turning you into a generalisation. You have to be like Rodin, Michael Angelo, and leave a piece of raw rock unfinished to your figure. You must leave your surroundings sketchy, unfinished, so that you are never contained, never confined, never dominated from the outside. (*WL*, 371)

The passage begins with a rather predictable diatribe about the corruptions of fashion and consumer culture. Yet in typical Lawrentian style, Birkin's argument hits a snag. Even as he describes a route to independence, his own argument ties him in knots and entangles him with other objects. Birkin begins by disavowing an interest in houses, furniture, and clothes and then seems to insist that one must take the utmost care in practicing precisely the right form of deliberate, artistic neglect. By declaring that he and Ursula must understand their lives as an act of artistic creation or fantasy, like a sculpture or a sketch, Birkin paradoxically grants houses, furniture, and clothes enormous power. Moreover, Birkin's comparison of crafting one's life to crafting one's "figure" invites a confusion between one's body and the material world. While he insists that neglecting objects will allow one to avoid being "dominated from the outside," his comparison between the self and a statue troubles the distinction between self and object, inside and outside. Reading Birkin against himself, then, we see that the problem with Poiret is not his interest in houses, furniture, and clothing per se, but that he will finish "your figure" for you, doing the work of self-fashioning that the individual must undertake. Here we might recall that earlier in the novel, Hermione insists on decorating Birkin's rooms for him. Clearly Birkin objects to her controlling his surroundings, yet he finds it even more uncomfortable to state his desire to decorate his own rooms. His unsatisfactory solution is to feign carelessness, as he does with his clothing. The problem resurfaces in this argument with Ursula, as Birkin seems to insist on separating the self from the material while describing their interdependence. His initial attack on materialism and consumption as a whole slides into an attack on the wrong kinds of materialism and consumption, where the distinction between good and bad uses of houses, furniture, and clothes remains sketchy at best.

Having read "Gladiatorial," we might conclude that Birkin's tirade unwittingly touches on the vitalizing effect of an "intent" (rather than intentional) struggle with the raw material that is human flesh. In that sense, we might see this as drawing a distinction between fashion and fashioning, where the former refers to the acquisition or achievement of a settled form and the latter denotes an ongoing process of creation. At the same time, the contradictions in his thought—as well as their emergence via a dialogue with Ursula—register the limitations of conscious individual agency as the locus for transformation. That is, the passage keeps in view the intersubjective dimensions of this knot of flesh, as well as its dependence on its material surroundings. Lawrence states in "Education of the People," "The system, after all, is only the outcome of the human psyche, the human desires. . . . The machine is in us, or it would never come out of us. Well then, there's nothing to blame but ourselves, and there's nothing to change except inside ourselves" ("EP," 90). Accordingly, *Women in Love* emphasizes that the individual and his desires are the origin and root of broader social structures, so that the war becomes a less important focus than his characters' personal and interpersonal struggles. Yet Birkin acknowledges that clothing maintains the power to turn the wearer "into a generalisation"—to direct and reshape the desires that Lawrence also insists are anterior to them. The battle to alter the "system" seems to require certain external conditions. This situation turns us to the question of whether it might be possible to help to create such conditions for others yet avoid imposing one's vision on them. It is precisely that paradox that Lawrence confronts in "Education of People" via the question of boots.

Causality and Relation in "Education of the People" *and* Lady Chatterley's Lover

"Education of the People" insists that the sociopolitical system is a reflection of human desires, but sets out to describe how to change the system in order to cultivate certain desires. Lawrence describes how children ought to be educated in order to realize a society based on the "ideal" of a "living, spontaneous individuality in every man and woman" ("EP," 107). The educational system, led by the "school inspectors," must recognize and develop "the true nature in every child," whether it be for manual or intellectual labor, though all children should be taught to be self-sufficient, down to the darning of their own socks. As a result, each individual will take a job and a position in society that is suited to his or her inclinations and abilities, and the society will dispense with the myth of democratic equality in all things.

Throughout the essays Lawrence avoids the use of the first person, taking on a didactic, impersonal tone and even omitting any reference to his own very pertinent experience as a schoolteacher. Yet, when Lawrence gets to the matter of teaching boys to sew their own clothes and make their own boots— the foundation, we might say, of Lawrence's corporeal materialist philosophy of everyday life—his own body and experience become visible for the only time in this extended treatise. He complains, "I object to the abstract Mr Everyman being clapped over me like an extinguisher. I object to wearing his coat and his boots and his hat." He admits, "If I could, I would make my own boots and my own trousers and coats. I suppose even now I could if I would. But in Rome one must do as Rome does: the bourgeois is not worth my while, I can't demean myself to *epater* him, and I am much too sensitive to my own isolation to want to draw his attention" ("EP," 151). This is a startling moment in the text, not least because in writing and attempting to publish these essays, Lawrence has gone very far out of his way to *épater le bourgeois* and draw his attention. It is worth considering why the question of dress precipitates Lawrence's appearance in the text in this way.

In the passage that follows, Lawrence defers the question of his own sartorial behavior by imagining a moment when "Rome will fall again" and the Lawrentian pupils will be able to enjoy their new skills:

> It is to prepare for this fall of Rome that we conjure up a new system of education. When I say that every boy shall be taught cobbling and boot-making, it is in the hopes that before long man will make his own boots to his own fancy. . . . He'll sit happily devising his own covering for his own feet, and machine-made boots be hanged. . . . He'll be gay-shod to the happiness and vanity of his own toes and to the satisfaction of his own desire. And the same with his trousers. If he fancies his legs, and likes to flutter on his own elegant

stem, like an Elizabethan, here's to him. And if he has a hankering after scarlet trunk hose, I say hurray. *Chacun à son goût*: or ought to have. Unfortunately nowadays nobody has his own taste, everybody is trying to turn himself into a eunuch Mr Everyman, standardized to his collar-stud. ("EP," 152)

As with Birkin's speech in "Chair," this passage doubles back on itself. At first it seems that the new sartorial exuberance will be a product of the new order in which each man's "own fancy" will be manifest and his "desire" satisfied through clothing. In this reading, Lawrence's own refusal to break the sartorial mold signals his recognition that dress will be a mere offshoot of deeper social changes. But then Lawrence decries the fact that "nowadays" "everybody" is actively shaping himself into "a eunuch Mr Everyman" via his dress, thereby depicting fashion as an emasculating and destructive force maintaining the status quo. Wearing "machine-made boots" becomes a form of subjecting oneself to the standardizing "machine" of modern society. This vacillation brings to light a similar uncertainty in Lawrence's prescription for education; it appears that this system of education, like the change in dress, will not be the cause of the "fall of Rome," but rather will accompany it. As the reference to Rome underscores, the text's uncertainty about the causal relationship between the political system and the means of production are particularly topical given that the decline of the British Empire would help to expose the interdependence of supply chains and systems of governance. Lawrence's vision of individuals making their own boots thus anticipates the sense of Britain as a "shrinking island," as Lawrence at once admits that such change will occur regardless of British men's footwear, but also imagines that their bodies might be the locus of such transformation; that formulation accords with what Jed Esty notes is the modernist turn to "revivalist" visions of "little England" in the 1930s.[95] Having set out his vision, however, Lawrence retreats from asserting that it—even if enacted—can bring about desired change.

All of this brings to the fore Lawrence's ambivalent treatment of the issues of agency and causality. In refusing the supremacy of the self-transparent, individual human will, Lawrence struggles to discover a way to incite change in a system via the shifting aims and forms of individual and collective desire. As we see in the wrestling scene and in "Red Trousers," Lawrence partially addresses this by thinking about such transformation as a collective material and affective endeavor. If Gerald and Birkin become a tight but dissolvable knot of flesh, then the men in red trousers are bound temporarily by their shared dress and feeling. This vision flirts with the appeal of fascist marches and futurist sartorial defiance, including Gudrun's "trumpet" of an outfit. But Lawrence imagines this particular jaunt as a more open-ended, even nonviolent gesture. "It is not particularly brave to do something the public wants you to do," "Red Trousers" concludes. "But it takes a lot of courage to sail gaily, in brave feathers, right in the teeth of a dreary convention" ("RT," 138). The repetition of "brave," particularly given its older meaning of "finely-dressed," suggests that this quality does not so much come from the men's bodies as inhere in their garments and their acts.[96] Whereas the futurists argued that "one acts as one dresses," here, Lawrence describes the circulation of feeling whose origin cannot be so easily pinned down, despite his claim that one should "start with externals." As in a knot, the external quickly becomes the internal, and vice versa, and the boundary between the two is more difficult to discern. That dynamic recalls Elizabeth Grosz's account of the body as a Möbius strip.[97] Yet it also takes Grosz's theory a step further by taking into account how bodily matter can become entangled with and enhanced by the fabric in which one is swathed.

Lawrence's writing of course shows the courage and bravery that "Red Trousers" celebrates; the essay appeared in the midst of efforts to censor *Lady Chatterley's Lover*. But the previous year, Lawrence also flirted with the idea of a bold sartorial display. In August 1927, after leaving Florence and convalescing in Villach, a town in the Alps of southern Austria, Lawrence wrote eagerly of the local costume to his friend Arthur Wilkinson, a socialist and pacifist activist, painter, and puppeteer who had been a generous neighbor to the Lawrences in Italy. Lawrence notes, "There are such amusing men's jackets, that the people wear—all colours, in checks—am so tempted to buy you one—& myself—we'd look such shoots—I'd buy you a green and purple check—myself, I think, yellow & pea-green—shall I?"[98] With its reference to new plant life, the word *shoots* suggests the reenergizing corporeal and affective force the men's unusual appearance might have. Lawrence himself was regaining strength and life after his tuberculosis caused a frightening series of bronchial hemorrhages, during which time the Wilkinsons helped care for him in Florence. But Lawrence also describes this energy as particular to Villach's cultural and political milieu. In his letter, Lawrence praises people's tendency to go nude or nearly so when bathing, and he finds the atmosphere pleasantly "queer": "It's queer to be in a country with practically no government—a queer shabby kind of populace—quite nice—and no bosses or bossing at all—a queer empty sort of feeling, all the *forza* of Italy suddenly removed, and the *sforza* too."[99] Here Lawrence puns on the fascist and futurist rhetoric of *forza* (strength) as well as the conflict between the ruling fascists and their opponents, since Count Carlo Sforza was a recently exiled antifascist leader and a member of a powerful aristocratic family.

This "backwater" in the Alps, surviving in the wake of economic and political destruction, and in a liminal space between Italy and a newly reorganized Austria, emerges as an alternative to the push and pull of existing political conflict.[100] The traditional Tyrolean jackets seem to catch some of this "queer" atmosphere; in a letter dated three days later, Lawrence reports that he bought himself a purple and green jacket but may still send one to Wilkinson, though he warns "they'll look mighty queer in Italy & England."[101] Lawrence's fantasy of (mis)matching outfits suggests how the corporeal, political, sexual, and affective spirit of the milieu might be carried into the heart of Italy and England—or perhaps grafted onto their roots. It implies that at least some of the queerness of this place—where force, activity, gendered forms of comportment, and even time are suspended—might be experienced in Italy and England via an encounter with these garments. In this instance, stylish clothing's paradoxical status as a frivolous phenomenon and overdetermined cultural and political signifier enable it to translate the kinds of "queer"— strange, off-kilter, nonnormative—modes of feeling and living that Lawrence values.[102] As in *Three Guineas*, the sense of bodies being out of place makes visible the oddity and potentially queer effects of certain masculine garments.

Lawrence's interest in the feeling of political and cultural suspension also reveals a further dimension to the dynamics of enchantment. Writing to artist and art patron Mabel Dodge Luhan later that August, Lawrence again repeatedly uses the word *queer* to describe Villach, announcing, "This queer vacuum is the centre of Europe." He muses, "A German wrote a book called *Schöpferische Pause*—Creative Pause. I don't know whether this is one. It seems more than pause, even more than a blank full stop. Yet such healthy bodies bathing and lying by the lake, you never saw."[103] *Die schöpferische Pause*, published in 1922, was a book of educational theory by Fritz Klatt that advocated a kind of individual development, just as Lawrence had in "Education of the People." Recall that Bennett describes this rhythm—a stop following by a surge of energy—as that of enchantment; she refers to a "temporary suspension of chronological time and bodily movement" followed by "an energizing feeling of fullness or plenitude." But if Lawrence devoted more attention to how one might be enchanted with the wrong things, he also has a more ambivalent view of what might fill the gap and follow the pause that enchantment creates and intensifies. When Lawrence wonders "what will fill this void," the possibility of yet more catastrophic violence, such as that which followed the crisis of power in August 1914, looms. Lawrence's references to a vacuum and a void also recall the attack on the staid prewar cultural scene by vorticists such as Ezra Pound and Wyndham Lewis who took a page from the futurists but chose the vortex—a swirl of energy around a vacuum—as their symbol. In short, Lawrence may be enchanted by Villach, but he also recognizes that this stop, however profound, is not an end point and may be an opening for further violence, as indeed was the case. Lawrence thus returns to the questions that he grappled with in *Women in Love*—namely, how to not only dismantle existing systems and challenge particular hierarchies (as do the futurists and vorticists) but also direct latent energies and forces so as to realize better forms of feeling, thought, and relation.

Lawrence did not relinquish the possibility that dress may help to reorient and renew society along desired lines. In *Lady Chatterley's Lover*, he assembles an enchanting outfit of red trousers and jacket in a passage in which Mellors describes how he would regenerate bodies and communities. As he and Connie plan their own future, he explains what he would say to the colliers in order to save them from the debilitating effects of the pursuit of money and hence overwork. He imagines he'd tell them to "take yer clothes off an' look at yourselves," and he would persuade them to wear new outfits. "Why, if men had red, fine legs, that alone would change them in a month. They'd begin to be men again, to be men! An' the women could dress as they liked. Because if once the men walked with legs close bright scarlet, and the buttocks nice and showing under a little white jacket: then the women 'ud begin to be women. It's because th' men *aren't* men, that th' women have to be."[104] The transformation brought about by these "red, fine legs" is relational and intersubjective, and it recalls the dynamics of sexual selection organized via a gender binary; the men's beauty turns the women's interest away from their own adornment and toward the men's bodies, which in turn enforces the men's distinction. By covering the men's bodies, the garments make up the texture of the relation between men and women as well as between men. In doing so, they revive the flesh and renew the social fabric. They also offer a potential solution to the problem of sexual and aesthetic production, which Lawrence raised in *The White Peacock*.

The conclusion of *Lady Chatterley's Lover* invites a comparison between the novel as a whole and these splendid, speculative skin-tight garments. Mellors returns to his vision of "scarlet trousers" in the letter to Connie that concludes the book, and adds the suggestion that the men "ought to learn to be naked and handsome, and to sing in a mass and dance the old group dances, and carve the stools they sit on, and embroider their own emblems."[105] Mellors insists, however, that this transformation is impossible, because "it needs money"; "There's a bad time coming," he predicts.[106] This formulation announces the urgency but also the impossibility of disentangling materiality from (economic) materialism. No matter how enchanting it may be to think it can be done, believing they can be disentangled means ignoring the signs and the extent of the impending disaster. Nevertheless, in the letter, Mellor pledges his faith in touch and describes the text as a poor substitute for bodily contact: "Well, so many words because I can't touch you. If I could sleep with my arms round you, the ink could stay in the bottle."[107] This line has been read in many ways, including as a reminder that the body is always constituted in and through historical circumstance as well as a commentary on writing as erotic sublimation or expression.[108] Accordingly, we can read Lawrence's writing the novel as a way to touch the reader, although he must make contact with the page instead of our bodies. In that sense that the text operates like a textile, which separates and brings bodies together and, in doing so, constitutes the relation between them. If Birkin and Gerald come together to form a knot of flesh, then *Lady Chatterley's Lover* is a fabric in which Lawrence and his reader become at least partially entangled. It follows, then, that the essay "Red Trousers" is a scrap of *Lady Chatterley's Lover*'s "scarlet" material, which Lawrence attempts to circulate more widely via its publication in a daily rag.

This chapter has explored the antagonistic and symbiotic relationship between fashion and fiction that emerges via Lawrence's work and that responds to the ways that various early twentieth-century artists, intellectuals, and activists in Britain and Europe used texts and textiles to describe and reimagine modes of comportment, connection, and community. Although Lawrence celebrates the naked body and critiques fashion, his work relies on the language of textiles to describe human flesh and to capture the agency of living and nonliving matter. As Lawrence attends to such forms of agency, his work converges with contemporary theories of animality, corporeality, aesthetics, and materiality offered by Derrida, Grosz, and Bennett. Lawrence's work thus contributes to the ongoing projects of reconceptualizing the relationship between human and nonhuman bodies, including animals and objects, and of reconceiving what constitutes political agency and collectivity. Yet Lawrence's pessimistic, primitivist, and vitalist visions help us to see how approaches to new materialism that set disenchanting critique aside to celebrate the liveliness of matter greatly underdescribe what it might take for such animating visions to produce ethical as well animating modes of engaging with other beings in the world.

The next chapter continues to investigate how the phenomenon of fashion figured the potential and limits of aesthetic production as a means to generate and reconfigure modes of knowing, feeling, and relating in the early twentieth century. It finds, for example, that W. E. B. Du Bois's novel *Dark*

Princess, like Lawrence's works, simultaneously critiques and invests in fashion as a means to spur and sustain heterosexual desire and, with it, desired forms of community. Yet by turning to a radically different context—that of black internationalist activism and cultural production based in the United States and extending to the Caribbean and South and East Asia—the next chapter also indicates the scope and variety of fashion's role in shaping aesthetic and political thought and activity. In addition to W. E. B. Du Bois, I touch on texts by Nella Larsen and Jessie Fauset as well as the work of black beauty culturalists Madam C. J. and A'Lelia Walker. My discussion of the Walkers also expands this study's exploration of fashion beyond clothing to practices of self-fashioning such as hair care. If Lawrence's work at times treats skin and fabric as related substances, *Dark Princess*, the Walkers' beauty work, and Larsen's and Fauset's texts link sartorial fashions to commodified, racialized practices of skin and hair care as well as the fashionability of black art and black bodies in the 1920s. And while Bloomsbury's primitivism and Orientalism helped to put its aesthetic ideas and practices into circulation (as legible and fashionable), the next chapter explores Du Bois's and the Walkers' strategies for mobilizing black internationalism with and against reductive visions of Pan-African and Pan-Asian aesthetics and politics. The flourishing of black beauty culture in the early twentieth century posed new questions about how the phenomenon of commodified, shifting styles might enable aesthetic practices to fuel political transformation.

3 : "THIS GREAT WORK OF THE CREATION OF BEAUTY"

W. E. B. Du Bois, Black Internationalism, and Beauty Culture

Today both children came home from school
talking about spring and peace
and I wonder if they will ever know it.
I want to tell them we have no right to spring
because our sisters and brothers are burning
because every year the oil grows thicker
and even the earth is crying
because black is beautiful
but currently going out of style
that we must be very strong
and love each other
in order to go on living.
—AUDRE LORDE, "Equinox"

The problem of raiment. The astonishing transformation of the
hoyden and hiker and basketball expert into an amazing butterfly.
We parents had expressed loftily disdain for the new colored beauty
parlors—straightening and bleaching, the very idea! But they didn't
straighten, they cleaned and curled; they didn't whiten, they delicately
darkened.
—W. E. B. Du Bois, "So the Girl Marries"

In "Equinox" (1973), Audre Lorde interweaves her personal history with
African American, African, and Southeast Asian experiences of racial and
colonial violence in the 1960s. Observing that "the year my daughter was
born / Du Bois died in Accra," she describes how she came to see that events
in "Hanoi Angola Guinea-Bissau Mozambique Pham-Phen / merged into

Bedford-Stuyvesant and Hazelhurst Mississippi."[1] The final stanza with its nod to the slogan "black is beautiful" hints at the capacity and failure of black aesthetics to provide a foundation for struggles by people of color to survive and flourish. In particular, the phrase "going out of style" registers that, in the context of global capitalism, blackness can become a passing trend rather than the grounds for sustained collective action.[2] The poem thus makes clear that the phenomenon of fashion is inextricable from claims to beauty, even or especially when it is mobilized for political ends.

Lorde's reference to W. E. B. Du Bois is particularly fitting given his efforts to forge cultural and political connections among people of color across the globe via aesthetics, especially discourses and representations of beauty. This project is epitomized by his 1928 novel *Dark Princess: A Romance*, which he later claimed was his "favorite book."[3] At the heart of the novel is a love affair between an African American former medical student and a South Asian princess, which gives rise to revolutionary anti-imperial racial solidarities that are cemented and symbolized by the birth of their son. Du Bois's novel links the pursuit of beauty to that of justice, as the hero's love for the beautiful princess fuels the development of his aesthetic, ethical, and political sensibilities. In *Dark Princess*, as in "Equinox," the discourse of fashion draws attention to how aesthetic objects and values circulate with and despite the routes of global capital. In short, *Dark Princess* takes up the questions that Lorde's poem also raises almost fifty years later: What role might beauty—and aesthetic experience more generally—have in the formation of anti-imperialist global collectivities for people of color? How might the production and appreciation of beauty enable the reproduction and survival of nonwhite bodies? How does the phenomenon of changing styles, which goes by the name of fashion, fuel and undercut beauty's force? These questions also concern contemporary scholars of black and modernist studies, particularly given the continued emphasis on the diasporic, transnational, and international dimensions of these subjects and fields. Indeed, though *Dark Princess* was relatively neglected in the twentieth century, it has drawn quite a bit of scholarly interest in the twenty-first, as critics increasingly recognize the era of the Harlem Renaissance as one of black internationalism, featuring the rise and decline of the Pan-African and Garvey movements and the flourishing of black radicalism.

The recent interest in Du Bois's novel also makes clear that a shift from national to transnational and international frames returns us to questions about how gender shapes the relationship between aesthetics and politics. Early twentieth-century black internationalism is usually invoked (implicitly and explicitly) as a masculine project. This reflects the predominance of male leadership, including Du Bois's, across various instantiations of liberal and radical black internationalism that challenged and adapted discourses of nationalism and internationalism exemplified by the League of Nations, the Comintern, and European imperialism. A growing body of scholarship, however, addresses women's involvement in black internationalist movements while shifting our understanding of what constitutes black internationalist aesthetic and political work and thought in the first place.[4] This chapter joins those efforts by putting *Dark Princess* in conversation with a relatively neglected realm of early twentieth-century black internationalist cultural and political activity: that of black beauty culture and in particular, the advertisements, activism, and internationalist imaginaries associated with the businesswomen, celebrities, and beauty culturalists Madam C. J. Walker and her daughter, A'Lelia. The Walkers offer modes of theorizing and enacting beauty, fashion, and internationalism that proliferated in beauty salons and on the pages of black-authored periodicals in the late 1910s and 1920s. As with *Dark Princess* and Marcus Garvey's United Negro Improvement Association (UNIA), the Walkers drew on images of racialized beauty and empire to consolidate racial belonging and transcend national boundaries and geopolitical asymmetries.[5] In Madam Walker's case, her beauty work also briefly supported an organization called the International League of Darker Peoples (ILDP). Though short-lived, the ILDP offered a radical challenge to Du Bois's leadership at the end of World War I and sought ties between Pan-Africa and Pan-Asia. My aim, however, is not to demonstrate that the Walkers shaped world-historical events. Rather, by treating black women's beauty culture as a source of black internationalist aesthetic and political imaginaries, this first half of this chapter explores how the Walkers' black business empire converges and competes with Du Bois's imperial and anti-imperial visions. In the second half of the chapter, I turn to work by Jessie Fauset and Nella Larsen to show how their treatments of fashion, beauty, and Afro-Orientalism offer alternative accounts of the relationship between aesthetic practices and international politics. In my discussions of Du Bois, the Walkers, Fauset, and Larsen, I trace the international dimensions of feminized discourses, practices, images, and spaces that usually are treated as unrelated to geopolitics.[6] Particularly in my discussion of A'Lelia Walker and Larsen, I also tease out how their versions of fashionable modern black femininity challenge Du Bois's and Madam Walker's romantic visions of how beauty fuels black international politics.

This chapter begins with an analysis of how *Dark Princess* attempts to link the pursuit of beauty to internationalism and to disinvest from capitalism and imperialism by undoing the links between beauty, fashion, and feminine self-fashioning that the Walkers epitomized and mobilized. Du Bois's novel undertakes this by describing how the natural, unselfconscious beauty of the woman of color transcends fashion as it stimulates and reproduces masculine radicalism. The Walkers, however, use the serial reproduction of black women's beauty by other black women in quasi-domestic spaces to generate an imagined international community. At stake in Du Bois's and the Walkers' contrasting accounts of the nature of beauty is which subjects, modes of agency and intimacy, and aesthetic, economic, and political formations might realize and sustain a black internationalist vision.

For Du Bois and the Walkers, these visions involve connections with Pan-Asia forged via India and Japan. Those connections are conceived through discourses and practices of fashion, self-fashioning, and beauty, all of which operate as lubricants and glue between black and Asian bodies and cultures. These dynamics converge with what Bill V. Mullen describes as Afro-Orientalism, a "counterdiscourse" that is often grounded in "Marxian analytical contributions on colonialism and imperialism" and draws on Orientalist tropes while seeking forms of black-Asian solidarity and resources for opposing white supremacy.[7] I follow Mullen in examining *Dark Princess* as a key instantiation of this heterogeneous discourse. However, by reading the novel and texts by Fauset and Larsen in relation to the Orientalist dimensions of modernism and 1920s African American beauty culture, including A'Lelia Walker's celebrity persona, I emphasize the tensions and slippages between Afro-Orientalist and Orientalist, Marxist and capitalist, imperialist and anti-imperialist, and queer and heteronormative dimensions of black internationalism.[8] Such tensions emerge from associations between the Orient and nonnormative sexuality, as well as what Thomas W. Kim observes are constructions of "the Orient as the a priori signifier of beauty and grace, but also of goods and merchandise" in the late nineteenth- and early twentieth-century United States.[9] Kim refers specifically to fashionable perceptions of East Asia, but Du Bois, Fauset, Larsen, and the Walkers' engagements with South Asia as well as Japan embrace and confront ideas that such spaces are available via aesthetic perception and the routes of global capital; in particular, Orientalism's fetishization and flattening of cultural difference and geopolitical asymmetries facilitate Du Bois's and Madam Walker's imagined anti-imperialist empires. As a nexus of concepts and practices of beauty, fashion, gender, sexuality, commerce, and radical politics, Afro-Orientalism emerges as a key site for theorizing the production of black internationalist aesthetic and political formations.

Afro-Orientalism and the "Unstable Good" of Beauty

Both early twentieth-century black beauty culture and *Dark Princess* put beauty to work. The novel follows the development of its hero, Matthew

Towns, as he transforms from a medical school dropout into a spy, then Pull-
man porter, prisoner, Chicago politician, and finally, revolutionary leader
and husband to his beloved Kautilya, princess of an East Indian kingdom
called Bwodpur. *Dark Princess* emphasizes that Matthew's attraction to
beauty in the forms of art, ethical perfection, and the "colored" female body
helps him to become an activist.[10] In turn, Matthew's ascension challenges
both white supremacy and the "color line within a color line," which forestalls anti-imperialist interracial solidarity (*DP*, 22). Kautilya is part of the
Great Council of the Darker Peoples, an elite cadre of representatives from
North Africa, the Middle East, and South and East Asia, including Japan,
whose victory in the Russo-Japanese war in 1905 Du Bois celebrated as her-
alding the "awakening" of the "darker races" and whose imperial ambitions
he countenanced well into the 1930s.[11] The council, which is led (we later
learn) by a Japanese member, is reluctant to admit the "world of Black Folk"
into their ranks because of a supposed lack of cultural heritage and collective spirit (*DP*, 19). Matthew attempts to change their minds by launching
into a spiritual during an elegant dinner party hosted by Kautilya at which
the group plots the overthrow of "white hegemony" while discussing Picasso
and Schönberg (*DP*, 24). This scene hints at Matthew's capacity to represent "an allegedly authentic black folk voice" and signals the novel's efforts
to explore the ethical and political value of art and beauty while expanding
these categories to include cultures and bodies of the black diaspora.[12]

The novel undertakes these projects by exploring beauty's relationship to
justice. In his famous 1926 speech-turned-essay "Criteria of Negro Art," Du
Bois declares, "It is the bounden duty of black America to begin this great
work of the creation of Beauty, of the preservation of Beauty, of the realization of Beauty." Beauty's work is twofold: beautiful depictions of African
Americans challenge prevailing racist stereotypes and policies, thereby increasing black people's "right . . . to love and enjoy," and at the same time,
this beauty itself is a source of pleasure.[13] Similarly, in *Dark Princess* beauty
is enjoyed, created, and realized through Matthew and Kautilya's sexual relationship and through Matthew's growing attraction to great art. His taste
flourishes alongside his love for the beautiful princess and his disgust with
the ugliness of his life as part of the Chicago political machine and as the
husband of a cynical, ambitious woman named Sara. Kautilya returns to rescue Matthew from this sordid life and barren marriage, but they part again to
develop further as revolutionaries by working among the masses. Shifting
between the realism of U.S. politics and the romance of global solidarity, the
novel ends with a fantastic scene in which Matthew is swept away to his
mother's home in rural Virginia, where he is reunited with Kautilya, who

reveals she has given birth to a son.[14] Kautilya and Matthew are married, at which point members of the princess's entourage emerge from the forest and perform a pageant before the baby, Madhu, who is declared the "Messenger and Messiah to all the Darker Worlds" (*DP*, 311). Interlacing the aesthetic, biological, and political, this conclusion exemplifies what Alys Eve Weinbaum describes as Du Bois's tendency to use interracial romance to create "racially essentialist representations of reproductive heterosexuality as the motor of black belonging in both the nation and the world."[15] It also demonstrates what Michelle Ann Stephens shows is a paradoxical use of imperialist discourses by black internationalists to challenge imperialism and to imagine a diasporic, transnational community led by a black male head of state and sustained through the body of the woman of color. Such imperial aesthetics bolster what many critics note is the novel's messianism.

This messianism depends on the novel's disavowal of the ephemeral and feminine phenomenon of fashion, even as *Dark Princess* traces Matthew's refashioning and self-fashioning into a revolutionary subject. As Monica L. Miller argues, the novel investigates "the relationship between character and clothing, activism and *accoutrement*" through the depiction of Matthew as a black "cosmopolitan activist-dandy."[16] Beauty and the formation of the revolutionary black masculine subject, however, are carefully distinguished from feminine self-fashioning, which, nevertheless, haunts attempts to demonstrate beauty's political uses. Matthew's good taste in dress—signaled from the beginning of the novel—foreshadows his growing appreciation for art and his ethical and political development, but for the female characters a marked interest in their appearance carries the usual associations with narcissism, materialism, and imitation.

In an article on race and beauty, Maxine Leeds Craig writes,

> Beauty is a resource used by collectivities and individuals to claim worth, yet it is an unstable good, whose association with women and with sex, and its dependence upon ever-changing systems of representation, put its bearer at constant risk of seeing the value of her inherent beauty or beauty work evaporate. If beauty is ever capital, it is a somewhat stigmatized capital. It must appear unearned if it is to be authentic, as opposed to purchased, beauty. Nonetheless it is a suspect form of capital if it is unearned.[17]

Craig's observations about shifting standards and the feminization of beauty help us to understand why Du Bois distances his visions of beauty and revolutionary black subjectivity from self-fashioning and fashion—the engine of those "ever-changing systems of representation." The novel is, in effect, seeking to fix the terms, time, and value of the "unstable good" of beauty.

Thus it celebrates Kautilya's beauty as natural and unselfconscious and establishes her body as a stable sign under which international activism, radical black masculine selfhood, and racial community can be formed and perpetuated. This dynamic also converts Kautilya's "suspect form of capital" into radical goods, thereby leveraging while critiquing the dynamics of capitalism and commodified beauty. In *Dark Princess*, the possession and use of women's beauty is a pivot on which distinctions between liberal versus radical political visions turn.

The novel's Orientalism situates Kautilya's beauty outside of modernity and fashion and away from women's control, while paradoxically underscoring the inextricability of beauty and fashion. When Matthew first meets Kautilya, he notices her vibrant color, her beauty, and the "hint of something foreign and exotic in her simply draped gown." The novel repeatedly associates her "golden brown skin" with textiles—silk, a veil, and even a carpet (*DP*, 8). Kautilya wears her body, like her garments, unselfconsciously: "She arranged nothing, glanced at no detail of her dress, smoothed no wisp of hair. She seemed at once unconscious of her beauty and charm, and at the same time assuming it as a fact, but of no especial importance" (*DP*, 15). Yet even as it establishes the timelessness and exoticism of Kautilya's beauty, *Dark Princess* relies on the circulation of images of supposedly Indian beauty to establish her appeal. The vague descriptions of her appearance—her "purple" hair, gloriously "colored" skin, and "royal" bearing—prompt the reader to generate their own exotic fantasy of her beauty.

In the late 1910s and 1920s many African American–led periodicals—including the *Crisis*, which Du Bois edited—published ads for the East India Toilet Goods and Manufacturing Company and the Kashmir Chemical Company (both led by African American men) that featured images of a representative "East India Girl" and "Kashmir Girl," which play on and collapse distinctions between what it means to appear black or "Indian." Given the emphasis on long, straight hair and pale skin, we can see the East India Company ad (Figure 3.1) as evidence of the impact of white supremacist aesthetics.[18] But I think we can read it simultaneously as an arena, however compromised and fantastic, that brings Pan-Africa and Pan-Asia into contact.[19] Indeed, the ad intersects with *Dark Princess*'s attempts to unite Pan-Asia and Pan-Africa via the body of a beautiful "colored" woman. The ad also provides an alternative to the novel's critique of women who try to manipulate or make use of their appearance. It mediates between discourses of natural and artificial beauty by promising that the "East India Hair Grower" will "stimulate the skin, helping nature do its work" and that it "restores Gray Hair to its Natural Color." In the ad, beauty is not (or not only) something

East India Company advertisement, *Crisis*, July 1923, 142. Reprinted with kind permission from Crisis Publishing, Co.

one might naturally possess for others' benefit, but also a commodity, method, and tool.

While the ad and the novel discover the beautiful female body as the imagined site for Pan-Asian and Pan-African contact, they disengage Indian beauty from contemporary Indian culture and politics. Despite the extensive coverage of the noncooperation movement in the *Crisis* during Du Bois's editorship and his relationships with Indian activists, Gandhi does not figure in *Dark Princess*'s geopolitical vision; one of the few references to

Gandhi's movement occurs when Kautilya laments that she could not persuade Bwodpur's people to join his boycott against foreign goods.[20] In a
revealing moment, the princess asserts that this failure persuaded her to try
to establish her own kingdom as "a new *Empire* of India, a new vast union
of the darker peoples of the world" (*DP*, 246; emphasis added). And an
empire, the princess acknowledges, requires a male leader and heir. In the
novel, the aesthetic, corporeal, geopolitical, and ethical resources of Pan-Asia
become available through the romance of empire and require the intervention of black—and specifically African American—masculinity.

This logic culminates with the consummation of Kautilya and Matthew's
relationship, the conception of their child, and the commencement of
Matthew's career as a revolutionary. All of those events occur in a secret
apartment Matthew maintains during his marriage to Sara. That coinci-
dence introduces another strand of my argument: that for Du Bois and
for the Walker Company, black-authored spaces become ways to sustain
alternative social and political formations and to convert the suspect capital
of feminine beautification into the goods of aesthetic or political expression. While ascending Chicago's political ladder, Matthew buys and stores
furnishings and art (including a Picasso and a Matisse nude) in an apartment
in a poor, predominantly black neighborhood, where he flees with Kautilya
after leaving Sara. This apartment, where the lovers luxuriate while listening
to Dvořák, replaces the dining room in which Matthew meets the council as
the incubator for a more radical vision of the union of the "darker races." In
Matthew's apartment, the modernist visual art admired by the elitist,
antidemocratic council is recontextualized to serve radical, romantic purposes. When, however, Kautilya and Matthew recognize that they must part
yet again to pursue their revolutionary callings, Matthew realizes that the
objects he collected represent parts of Kautilya. He resolves to live without
such physical reminders:

> The Chinese rug was the splendid coloring of your skin; the Matisse was the
> flame of your high spirit; the music was your voice. I am going to move to
> one simple, bare room where again and unhindered by things, I can see this
> little place of beauty with you set high in its midst. And I shall picture you still in
> its midst. I could not bear to see any one of these things without you. (*DP*, 263)

This passage suggests that Matthew has been living beside and within Kautilya, a dynamic that establishes her as lover and mother, although Matthew
accomplishes his own parturition. As he rejects "things" yet still preserves
the image of Kautilya among them, Matthew ascends from the arena of capitalist accumulation, Oriental furnishings, and modernist primitivism to a

decorporialized realm of ideals. In doing so, he displaces Matisse as the author of Kautilya's nonwhite beauty. Matthew, then, is learning to do beauty—to reproduce beauty as a resource for world making through romance. His internalization of Kautilya marks his radical internationalization, preparing him to rule Kautilya's kingdom, which, like Kautilya herself, serves as a boundary and meeting point between cultural, economic, and political traditions. "Breasted against Russia and China and in the path of the projected new English empire in Thibet [*sic*]," Kautilya's kingdom promises to be simultaneously imperial, democratic, and anticapitalist (*DP*, 242).

Sara Ahmed writes that the desire of "the Occident" for "the Orient" is "a wish that points to the future or even *to a future occupation*. The directness toward this other reminds us that desire involves a political economy in the sense that it is distributed: the desire to possess, and to occupy, constitutes others not only as objects of desire, but also as resources for world making."[21] Matthew's desire for Kautilya leads him to a new place to occupy and an occupation, for his son's birth enables Matthew to rule Bwodpur with Kautilya. Moreover, Du Bois offers up the dark princess (simultaneously a character and a novel) as an object that will direct his audience's desires beyond the United States and even Africa to East India as the material for world making. The novel, that is, invests in Orientalism as a bodily orientation as well as an aesthetic and political formation. Drawing on Michael Warner's work, Ahmed observes, "Directing one's attention to a shared object is enough to create the public, which then exists by virtue of being addressed."[22] As Du Bois's Orientalism establishes the appeal and power of the dark princess and *Dark Princess* as "shared object[s]," it is inextricable from his more frequently noted use of romance to invite readers to imagine and create an oppositional transnational community.

This unrealized global community of readers, however, emerges in competition with a feminized domestic racial community that is also brought into being through a shared orientation toward beauty—or rather, toward dress and self-fashioning as ways of doing beauty. Matthew's first wife, Sara, consolidates her power within the Chicago political machine and manipulates groups of African American women through fashion—via both her impeccable outfits and their desire to dress differently. The novel describes her pale skin and ensembles in great detail, down to a string of beads or pearls, but deliberately states that she is "not beautiful" (*DP*, 109). These modest, polished outfits recall the rhetoric of uplift and respectability that saturated black women's political and beauty culture.[23] They also underscore the novel's prescient political commentary. Sara creates and controls women's groups—including a "Marching Club" and "Flying Squadron"—to help

"The Chicago Flying Squadron," *Crisis*, 1927, 86. Reprinted with kind permission from Crisis Publishing, Co.

elect Matthew as the first black U.S. senator, a position that Oscar de Priest of Chicago achieved in 1928 thanks in part to the support of his wife, Jessie, and black women's clubs (*DP*, 178). The May 1927 edition of the *Crisis* shows the members of the Chicago Flying Squadron, the first permanent women's division of the National Association for the Advancement of Colored People (NAACP), founded in 1926 by the de Priests. The women are dressed strikingly similarly to Sara.

In *Dark Princess*, this sartorial aesthetic is associated with an imitation of whiteness as well as a lack of racial loyalty, ethical principles, and (appropriate) sexual and maternal desire. Moreover, garments emerge as objects that generate feminized, failed counterpublics, for Sara mobilizes and controls these groups of working-class black women by promising them "uniforms and rituals." This seduction implicates not only middle- and working-class women's groups but also the Garvey movement, which was famous for its pageants and costumes. While such trappings were part of the UNIA's masculinist internationalist vision and rhetoric of black beauty, *Dark Princess* reinforces associations between femininity, frivolity, provinciality, and costume. The narrator sniffs that trifles like outfits and rituals merely tempt Sara's followers with access to "woman's 'new sphere,' of which they had read something in the papers" (*DP*, 178). (One wonders whether those papers might include the *Crisis*.)[24]

Of course, as it critiques the power and pleasure of dress and performance, *Dark Princess*—like a number of Du Bois's other works—leverages them to support his particular vision of black internationalism.[25] In Matthew's case, these pleasures are sanctioned through their reinscription in a heterosexual (if adulterous) mode of reproduction and their eventual subordination to the more substantial delights of art and justice. Nevertheless, the pleasures of the dark princess and *Dark Princess* exceed their political intention or effects. Du Bois's text registers the difficulty of harnessing and directing the force of feminine beauty. Shane Vogel's reexamination of Du Bois's infamous review of McKay's *Home to Harlem* (1928) clarifies the stakes of Du Bois's attempt simultaneously to unleash and direct the forms of pleasure and desire derived from beauty. Noting that Du Bois praises McKay's emphasis on "the beauty of colored skins" and the characters' awareness of their "new yearnings for each other," Vogel argues that Du Bois recognizes "the intimacy and relationships in McKay's novels" as "enactments of emergent alternative sociality."[26] Yet Vogel also observes that Du Bois's much earlier essay "The Problem of Amusement" offers a contrast to what Du Bois described as McKay's vision of the "lascivious sexual promiscuity" of Harlem's lower classes because the essay seeks to situate those yearnings within a bourgeois heterosexual matrix (specifically, by celebrating structured, chaperoned social dance as an ideal form of entertainment).[27] We might then see *Dark Princess* as a continuation of what Vogel shows is Du Bois's earlier project. At the same time, while *Home to Harlem* does not condemn women's sexuality in the moralizing terms of racial uplift, it does privilege male homosocial intimacy as the space for what Gary Holcomb describes as McKay's "queer black proletarianism."[28] Thus both Du Bois's and McKay's visions hinge on the circumscription of women's political agency.[29] This dynamic turns us to women's beauty culture, for it represented an arena of feminine intimacy, aesthetic self-fashioning, new yearnings, and global fantasies that challenged Du Bois's vision both through its capacities and refusals to direct these forces toward international political activism and solidarity.

Madam C. J. Walker's Black (Business) Empire

Beauty culture was a unique site of political organizing and activism for working-class African American women in the 1910s and 1920s, and learning the "art" of beautification enabled many women to leave domestic service.[30] In the case of the Walker Company, agents who sold its products and performed the Walker method of pressing hair were invited to enter a "new sphere" by becoming part of a national organization, complete with a convention. During the first gathering in 1917, delegates petitioned President Wilson to protect African Americans in the wake of the East St. Louis race riots, announcing themselves to be not only Walker "representatives" but also "in a larger sense representing twelve million Negroes."[31] Another statement decries the hypocrisy of Americans fighting abroad for freedoms not provided at home and calls on "the women of the country to uphold the equality of rights guaranteed by our laws and constitution."[32] Like Sara's women's groups, Walker agents organized themselves around practices of fashioning the body, which facilitated their self-fashioning as national and international political subjects. Walker's organization also offered its own brand of romance, as accounts of her remarkable rise from an impoverished laundress to a wealthy businesswoman through the creation and sale of her Wonderful Hair Grower were central to the company's marketing, especially before the mid-1920s. Walker agents were not uncritical consumers of this narrative, however; dissatisfaction with the company's profit-sharing and product-distribution arrangements led to at least one boycott among her agents.[33]

The potentially international political power of black beauty culture became clear in the wake of World War I, as Walker's efforts to intervene in global affairs overlapped with and at times challenged Du Bois's. At the National Race Congress for World Democracy, Walker was selected to attend the Paris Peace Conference as an "auxiliary" delegate of the National Equal Rights League, whose leader William Monroe Trotter had criticized Du Bois's call for African Americans to join the war effort.[34] The U.S. government, however, denied Walker's visa and placed her on a list of "Negro Subversives."[35] From December 1918 through February 1919, Walker also funded and served as treasurer for the ambitious if short-lived ILDP, which brought together an unlikely set of activists including Reverend Adam Clayton Powell as well as Garvey (briefly) and A. Philip Randolph; Garvey and Randolph both publicly critiqued Du Bois's views and leadership in that period.[36] The ILDP's goals were announced in the single issue of the *World Forum*, which was conceived as "the Organ of the International League of Darker Peoples" along the lines of the UNIA's *Negro World* and featured Walker prominently in its pages. As the *World Forum* declares, one of the ILDP's long-term aims was "to maintain a permanent council of dark peoples."[37] Its "immediate program" was to influence the outcome of the Paris Peace Conference by meeting with the Japanese delegation on their way to that gathering and by holding "an international conference of the darker peoples in Paris," which would have offered an alternative to Du Bois's First Pan-African Congress of 1919.[38]

The *World Forum* does not mention the source of Walker's fortune, but it refers to feminine grace, taste, and beauty to describe the founding of the ILDP. An article about the launch of the organization at Walker's "palatial home," Villa Lewaro, even anticipates *Dark Princess*'s depiction of exquisite rooms as wombs and stages for international political subjectivity and the spectacular performance of reproductive futurism. Walker's influence on the ILDP is at once acknowledged and partially mediated through her gorgeous home. Titled "Villa Lewaro-on-the-Hudson, Birthplace of the International League of Darker Peoples," the article praises the villa as "a model of architectural beauty and design, displaying the rarest, most exquisite taste, refinement and culture. Here and there, the International League of Darker Peoples made its debut to the world."[39] Walker figures as hostess and mother or midwife as her feminine aesthetic expertise creates spaces that shelter and produce radical subjects and collectivities. Strikingly, however, the ILDP appears not only as an infant but also as a (presumably well-coiffed) debutante or performer, thus suggesting an ambiguously gendered compound subject.

This celebration of Villa Lewaro resonates with aspects of *Dark Princess* and with the Walker Company's advertising strategies. Images and descriptions of Villa Lewaro and the Walker building in Harlem—especially the beauty salon (or "Parlor"), including a "Tea Room" with Japenese styling—often featured in advertisements and articles on the company in the 1910s and 1920s.[40] These buildings and their interiors were described as benefitting and bringing together both Walker agents and "the race" as a whole.[41] As for Du Bois and Garvey, objects, spaces, and forms of sociality associated with imperialist fantasies constitute key objects around which Walker's imagined community is oriented.[42] The ads, however, stress Walker's role as a property owner and hostess rather than a mother or midwife, while the salon and the Villa Lewaro blur boundaries between commercial, artistic, and political as well as public and private realms—distinctions that often did not hold in African American women's lives. This rhetoric is particularly fitting given that these advertisements were themselves a way that Walker supported the commercial, intellectual, and political forum provided by black periodicals in this period; such diverse publications as the NAACP's *Crisis*, the UNIA's *Negro World*, the *Chicago Defender*, and Randolph's *Messenger* published myriad ads for various black beauty products and relied on Walker's financial backing, even as they published critiques of black beauty culture.[43] In that sense, black women's self-fashioning and beauty expertise fueled the serial reproduction and transnational circulation of black art and politics via these predominantly black-authored forums.

In the case of the ILDP, beauty culture provided the means to seek solidarity with other people of color. As in *Dark Princess*, the article in the *World Forum* celebrates exquisite taste and the ability to throw a dinner party as among its heroine's contributions to global racial alliances. Describing the ILDP's inaugural meeting, the article notes that after the "the guests sumptuously feasted . . . the spirit of race internationalism was manifest by the welcomed suggestion to present the Japanese Peace Delegates with a bouquet of flowers, as a token of friendship and brotherhood."[44] (In December 1918 the Japanese government had announced its intention to raise the issue of racial discrimination in international affairs at the Paris Peace Conference. In February 1919 the Japanese delegation petitioned unsuccessfully to include a clause prohibiting such discrimination in the League of Nations's covenant.) To the apparent discomfort of military intelligence, Walker did not stop at sending flowers and a note. As the *World Forum* reports, Walker was part of a gathering at the Waldorf Astoria between members of the ILDP and Kuroiwa Shūroko, a prominent Japanese publisher and member of the delegation. A military intelligence report at that time specifically credits Walker with seeking connections with the delegation in order to influence the Peace Conference.[45] At the Waldorf, Randolph presented Kuroiwa with an ambitious "Memorandum of Peace Proposals," which the *World Forum* appears to have reproduced in its pages.[46] Kuroiwa seems to have been reticent about the memorandum and his delegation's plans, but the *Forum* recasts his reaction as racialized affect, noting that the group was received "with the characteristic calmness and stolidity of the Japanese."[47] This turn to Orientalist stereotype downplays the possibility that the ILDP's actions were ineffectual. It also underscores Kuroiwa's role as "representative" of Japan and hence helps the ILDP to present the gathering as a meeting between peoples. A photograph of the event shows Madam Walker seated next to Kuroiwa at the center of the group, and a report on the meeting published in the *Philadelphia Tribune* lists Walker first among the ILDP committee.[48] Thus at a decisive period in the history of internationalism, an icon of black beauty culture figures as a potential link between Pan-Africa and Pan-Asia on the pages of periodicals whose reproduction depended on the business of producing beautified black female bodies. While overlapping with matriarchal and patriarchal logics, this proliferation of images, ideas, and activism points toward alternative modes of reproduction facilitated by the "stigmatized capital" of black beauty.

Walker's involvement with the ILDP is not the only link between black internationalism and beauty culture. A global imaginary became a business model and what the Walker Company was selling as it reimagined the routes of global capital as paths to racial solidarity and profit.[49] In the year or two before the United States invaded and occupied Haiti in 1914 and 1915, Madam and A'Lelia Walker worked to expand their access to markets in Central America, Cuba, and Jamaica, as well as Haiti, which held a crucial place in the black internationalist imagination as the first black-ruled nation in the Western Hemisphere. Walker's well-publicized trip to the Caribbean in 1914 deployed the Du Boisian idea that art could cross national borders and build transnational racial networks, as she arranged her tour to correspond with that of African American soprano Anita Patti Brown. Coverage of the trip in the African American press emphasized the hospitality Walker received, thus establishing continuities between the forms of polite sociability promoted in Walker's elegant homes and salons and those in Afro-Caribbean communities.[50] Walker's account of her visit to Haiti, published in the Indianapolis *Freeman*, exemplifies her trip's conflation of beauty work and political work. She finds the land and the women "beautiful" but emphasizes the split between rich and poor and the need for economic and political development.[51] Walker decries the treatment of political prisoners, which she attempts briefly to mitigate by ordering them "a regular Christmas dinner," although she acknowledges that the meal probably never reached the victims. She nevertheless praises the Haitians she met "away from the theater of political activities," particularly the men who make her think of "bygone days when knighthood was in flower." Yet she criticizes the men's "self-centered indifference," which she attributes to their lack of exposure to "the wide awake hustling and progressive American customs and habits." Such attitudes, she suggests, make the island a fertile ground for the more ambitious "American Negro." The account thus implies that such "bygone" days perhaps are well past and offers a democratic, liberal feminist, and capitalist vision of how Walker's company might enable Haiti to fulfill its revolutionary potential through beauty work.

With its references to Christmas dinners and polite hospitality, Walker's report invites a contrast between, on the one hand, the uncivil, masculine space of the jail and, on the other, the widely circulated images of the Walker beauty parlor as a realm of polite intercourse. This contrast in some respects anticipates the dynamic that Mimi Thi Nguyen identifies when discussing early twenty-first-century U.S.-sponsored "beauty schools" established in Afghanistan: in such spaces, it is imagined that "beauty might nurture a horizontal relationship among women brought together as a community of care" as "the beauty salon operates as an oasis amid the ugliness of war."[52] As Nguyen notes, this rhetoric reflects ideas about beauty's civilizing power imbued in Kantian aesthetics.[53] Indeed, Walker's emphasis on development recalls the claim of U.S. politicians and intellectuals who favored commercial and cultural imperialism over overt political intervention in Haiti. Yet Walker's suggestion that Haiti has beauty emphasizes that the nation is already highly civilized, even if in need of cultivation. This approach echoes editorials in the *Crisis* that call for "help" for Haiti without violating its sovereignty, and her company would have been one of the only African American–led organizations with the capital and stature to pursue such a policy.[54] Walker's embrace of capitalism to drive progress also intersects with Garvey's vision of a black-controlled global economy, although Walker replaces Garvey's masculinist rhetoric with her image of an economic network constructed by mobile, cosmopolitan, entrepreneurial black women and held together by a series of beauty salons stretching from Harlem to Buenos Aires that would help to grow democratic and capitalist principles along with women's hair.

Walker's account of the opportunities for Haiti's development also resonates with *Dark Princess*'s vision for the mobilization of the black diaspora. In particular, Walker's belief that the contemporary, ambitious "American Negro" might mitigate Haiti's inequality by modernizing a static elite and uplifting the poor resembles *Dark Princess*'s celebration of Matthew as the figure who brings together the princess and her council with the black masses. Walker's descriptions of Haiti also anticipate the vision of the black diaspora that Kautilya shares with Matthew during her retreat in rural Virginia: "From Hampton Roads to Guiana is a world of colored folk, and a world, men tell me, physically beautiful beyond conception; socially enslaved, industrially ruined, spiritually dead; but ready for the breath of Life and Resurrection" (*DP*, 278). Weinbaum notes the similarity between aspects of Kautilya's rhetoric and Comintern policy in the 1920s, which emphasizes the potential for global black resistance beginning in the United States, although Weinbaum further observes that Kautilya conceives the Black Belt not only as a "nation within a nation" as the Comintern did in 1928, but also as a global phenomenon.[55] The connections between Kautilya and the Comintern are clear, but the echoes between Kautilya's and Walker's claims remind us that this rhetoric of development characterizes communist and capitalist as well as imperialist visions. While aspects of *Dark Princess*'s vision intersect with a Marxian analysis of imperialism, its engagement with beauty does more to open up rather than answer questions about the relationships between various strands of black internationalism.[56]

The connections I have traced between imperialist aesthetics and politics in Du Bois's and Walker's international visions dovetail with a debate that continues to structure accounts of Walker's aesthetic and business practices: namely, whether her hair care was a system of hair straightening and to what degree it recapitulated white supremacist beauty standards.[57] Faced with criticism to that effect, Walker denied that her products or techniques straightened hair, let alone that she had encouraged clients to model themselves after white women. In his tribute to Walker after her death, Du Bois weighed in on this debate in the pages of the *Crisis*; he dismisses claims that "Negroes" using the Walker technique were "'straightening' their hair in order to imitate white folk," although he admits such charges "led to some modifications of the methods used."[58] He praises Walker as one of those rare individuals who "transform a people in a generation" because, he claimed, she improved African Americans' hygiene practices. Du Bois, however, omits any mention of Walker's political activities and international travel, or the thousands of black women she trained and employed, thus anticipating *Dark Princess*'s division between feminine self-fashioning and progressive politics. Nevertheless, reading Du Bois and Walker together prompts us to see discussion of the racial politics of hair as part of early twentieth-century debates over what aesthetic and political formations would counter global white supremacy and, in particular, to what extent such oppositional methods drew from the forms and forces they sought to overcome.

Du Bois's obituary of Walker overlooks the political dimensions of her life and work. But Walker Company advertisements in this period used Du Bois's words—specifically, his redeployment of the metaphor of the Black Belt—to trace a feminized network of relations in the black diaspora generated by Walker agents and beauty practices. An ad published in the *Crisis*'s "Overseas Number" of March 1919 (and republished in almost every subsequent issue of the magazine that year) adapts the title of Du Bois's 1906 essay "The Color Line Belts the World" to announce the Walker Company's global reach. Du Bois's title draws out the international implications of his more famous claim that "the problem of the Twentieth Century is the problem of the color-line."[59] The 1906 essay reimagines the color line as a means of revolutionary solidarity while anticipating aspects of the 1920s Comintern policy by associating that vision with the familiar metaphor of the U.S. South as a black belt. In the essay, Du Bois declares that Japan's victory over Russia "marked an epoch" that promised the end of white supremacy and the "awakening" of first the "yellow races" and then "the brown and black races."[60] As the ad's appearance suggests, 1919 revived such dreams via liberal and communist internationalisms. Activists including Walker and Du Bois hoped the Paris

Walker Company advertisement, *Crisis*, March 1919, 256. Reprinted with kind permission from Crisis Publishing, Co.

Peace Conference might begin to dismantle a racist, imperialist world order, particularly through the intervention of the Japanese delegation.

The phrase "We belt the globe" is not the only allusion, however oblique, to the importance of Japan to Walker's vision of a black global network. The advertisement places the name of Walker's most popular product, Wonderful Hair Grower, within a sun that invokes Japanese imperial iconography; the war flag of the imperial Japanese army, or Rising Sun flag, features a disc and rays that closely resemble those in the Walker ad. Thus it appears that within a few weeks of the ILDP meeting with Kuroiwa, Walker approved the design of an ad that invoked Japanese imperial power to celebrate the transnational reach of her own product. In fact, this sun offers a potential symbol of Pan-African and Pan-Asian solidarity, as references to black people as "children of the sun" proliferated in the early twentieth century, including in the pages of the *Crisis*.[61]

This allusion to Japan coexists with the ad's invocation of three overlapping imagined communities, each held together by Walker products and Walker herself: a global community suggested by the phrase above Walker's stately half-profile, which announces her power even after her death; a hemispheric community, implied by the distribution of tins bearing Walker's image; and finally, a domestic one, indicated by the striking declaration "Sold Everywhere in U.S.A." This last phrase is at the center of the ad, near the latitude dividing Central and South America and just above the global belt of the equator. The ad thus suggests a relay of locations and identifications from the United States at the heart of the ad, to the Americas, and finally to the globe. This dynamic also characterizes the play of gazes in the ad. Most of the people at the bottom of the page turn away from the reader, whose gaze is directed along with theirs toward the sun and the tins of Walker products. This orientation recalls the way that Orientalism functions as a way to turn bodies in the same direction. In turn, the Walker products face outward, radiating the power of the Walker Company and welcoming more agents and prospective clients into its simultaneously national, hemispheric, and global communities. Thus the ad addresses the potential conflicts between national, transnational, diasporic, and international modes of belonging, which the Comintern and Du Bois grapple with in their own treatments of the Black Belt. The ad offers a turn to Walker products as a way to ameliorate if not resolve such tensions. The tins conjure communities of users that exist within but are not identical with the nation, hemisphere, and globe, such that an allegiance to one community belts one to the others. Instead of a global racial community united under a patriarch such as Garvey, or even through the bodies of the effortlessly beautiful woman and the ancient black mother as in *Dark Princess*, we find a network led by a mobile, cosmopolitan matriarch and sustained through the tools of beauty culture taken up by women who create, enhance, and profit from their own and other women's beauty. This is an internationalism in which black women become the agents of a black (business) empire.

Discussing black beauty culture as a source of representing, theorizing, and enacting national and global forms of belonging helps to expand our accounts of black internationalism beyond organizations and movements led by men and conventional realms of aesthetic and political expression. That said, Walker's vision of black women becoming agents by laboring for her corporation reinforces familiar notions of uplift and self-help and accords with liberal, capitalist conceptions of subjectivity and collectivity. Walker's vision of women's agency also dovetails with particular theories of beauty, as both Walker and Du Bois deploy what Vanita Reddy notes is "a dominant post-Enlightenment view of beauty" as a "redemptive force which, for those deemed lucky enough to possess it, facilitates social advancement through its alignment with liberal democratic ideals such as empowerment and freedom."[62] Moreover, "the conferral of beauty has depended upon the erasure and denial of the realities of race and nationality, among other axes of social difference." Walker and Du Bois do grapple with some "realities of race," but they rely on beauty's purported ability to transcend national differences as a way to imagine transnational communities. And, crucially, Walker and Du Bois challenge the exclusion of only certain racialized bodies from the category of the beautiful and hence from political subjectivity. Nevertheless, they differ from one another with regard to which bodies might be deemed beautiful. The Walker Company represented beauty as a practice as well as a way of appearing and implied that any agent or client who used its products might challenge their exclusion. *Dark Princess*, on the other hand, further delimits the category of the beautiful in order to protect it as an ethical and political resource to be directed toward the development of revolutionary black (male) subjects.

Unproductive Beauty, Nonnormative Sociality, and the Dark Tower

Du Bois's efforts to disarticulate fashion from beauty in *Dark Princess* suggest that his objections to some of the more daring literature of the Harlem Renaissance, such as *Home to Harlem* and *Fire!!*, involve matters of form as well as content.[63] Just as *Dark Princess* takes up ideas of empire to suggest the staying power of the novel's vision, it also chooses realism and romance over fashionable modernist aesthetics. After all, such potentially transient literary forms might reinforce the perception that the efflorescence of black arts was merely a moment "when the Negro was in Vogue," as Langston Hughes would later assert.[64] In fact, Hughes's famous chapter on the Harlem Renaissance in *The Big Sea* (1940) offers A'Lelia Walker as a symbol of the era.[65] Hughes turns Du Bois's fantasy of a revolutionary Afro-Oriental empire on its head by mocking any equivalence between art and protest and by associating the Harlem Renaissance and A'Lelia with pseudoaristocratic, cosmopolitan decadence. Hughes describes her as "a gorgeous dark Amazon, in a silver turban" and declares that the "vogue" was a moment "when the parties of A'Lelia Walker, the Negro heiress, were filled with guests whose names would turn any Nordic social climber green with envy," including royalty.[66] Indeed, A'Lelia was known for her lavish lifestyle, dramatic turbans, and multiple marriages, and (in certain circles) her alleged affairs with women. Her personal style suggests what Fiona I. B. Ngô has described as the "particularly queer" qualities of Jazz Age Harlem's Orientalism, in which boundaries between black and Asian bodies and styles were disrupted, often through imperialist fantasies that facilitated expressions of nonnormative desires.[67] While A'Lelia's turbans have been read in relation to African and African American modes of head wrapping, they also draw on Orientalist styles.[68] A'Lelia appears to have reveled in the way that such exotic fashions might defy sartorial gender norms; she seems, for example, to have circulated a photograph of herself in what appears to be a luxurious silken imitation of an antique Cossacks uniform, a choice that recalls constructions of Russia as Asiatic.[69] The handwritten note underscores the photograph's combination of intimacy and performance, exclusivity and publicity. Smiling at the camera and sitting on a table with one leg bent, as if in the midst of a gathering, A'Lelia seems to display her enjoyment of the jaunty, masculine posture the trousers afford her.

Photograph of A'Lelia Walker, signed and dated April 1926. Photographs of Prominent African Americans. James Weldon Johnson Collection in the Yale Collection of American Literature, Beinecke Rare Book and Manuscript Library.

A'Lelia's celebrity persona reinforces what Kate Dossett observes is a contemporary shift in the Walker Company's branding away from uplift to pleasure, as well as a change in milieu: "Whereas in the second decade of the twentieth century Madam Walker invested in race work in order to enter black political circles, A'Lelia created and used her celebrity status to gain access to the New Negroes, the black cultural leaders of 1920s Harlem."[70] The Walker Company's global vision also transitioned from political internationalism toward Orientalist and imperialist fantasy. In the early 1920s, A'Lelia traveled around the world in high style, visiting, for example, Ethiopian empress Waizeru Zauditu, and the company began "Trip around the World" contests in which customers voted for the candidate of their choice (often a preacher) to be taken on a global tour.[71] Access to international spaces was framed through discourses of cosmopolitan privilege, personal development, Oriental pleasures, and consumer citizenship rather than diplomacy or political activism. A'Lelia Walker and her mother's divergent pursuits could be perceived as demonstrating a dichotomy between art and politics and the incompatibility of beauty culture and political justice.

Du Bois certainly seems to have had that impression. His article on A'Lelia published in the *Crisis* after her death intertwines discourses of beauty, reproduction, and descent and anticipates the narrative of generational decline often applied to the Walker Company. He describes this "only child of Madam C. J. Walker" as "without beauty but of fine physique" and asserts, "She loved beauty—beauty of women, beauty of home, sea and sky and strength of young men."[72] Regardless of what Du Bois believed about A'Lelia's sexual object choice, this reference to her love for "beauty of women" provides a link between A'Lelia's profession and her intimate relationships with women, although that is tempered by the mention of masculine strength. In turn, Du Bois describes her life and relationships in terms of spectacular but unproductive sociality; many "lived upon her bounty" and she "died because she was tired of living." "Without beauty" and fascinated by beautiful women and glittering, fashionable parties—the things Matthew recognizes are stepping-stones and impediments to the pursuit of ethical and political beauty—A'Lelia did not realize the reproductive logic that *Dark Princess* endorsed. A'Lelia may have donned her imperial style to insist on her right to be (arguably) the nation's first black heiress, but Du Bois uses gestational language to imagine another fate: "With different training and contacts, she would now have been at the *fullness* of her power and ability *to carry into realization* her mother's great dreams" (emphasis added). While A'Lelia's parasitic friends and spectacular parties might seem far from Sara and her women's groups in *Dark Princess*, in both cases Du Bois grapples with the implications of self-fashioning as a realm of aesthetic engagement as well as feminine intimacy and sociality. For Du Bois, these women's interests in themselves and each other's bodies direct them away from (re)productive political or social activity and cause them to expend their energy in the wrong place.

A'Lelia was well known for providing places in which people could engage in nonnormative intimacy and seemingly waste their time. In 1927, she drew on her reputation as a hostess when she established the Dark Tower, a fashionably and elegantly decorated space at the top of the Walker building that functioned as a salon and private club, although by 1929 it was open to the public.[73] The Dark Tower took its name from a Countee Cullen poem, "From the Dark Tower," which also became the title of Cullen's column on black art in *Opportunity*, published by the liberal National Urban League and edited by sociologist Charles S. Johnson. Cullen's sonnet was painted on one wall, while another bore Hughes's "The Weary Blues." This was a suggestive pairing. On the one hand, it stages an apparent division within the Harlem Renaissance between Cullen, Harlem's unofficial poet laureate who situated himself in an established European poetic tradition, and Hughes, its "poet low-rate," whose more experimental works engage with modernist primitivism. On the other hand, it draws attention to the ways that these works defy such simplistic distinctions. After all, while Du Bois and Alain Locke embraced Cullen as representative of the movement, the poem "From the Dark Tower" was published in the single issue of *Fire!!*, which broke with Du Bois's and Locke's aesthetic and political strategies. The sonnet itself exemplifies what Jeremy Braddock describes as Cullen's "poetics of conjecture," which invites overlapping and at times conflicting queer, heteronormative, and racialized readings via seemingly traditional textual forms.[74] When encountered in the context of the Dark Tower, the poem's opening lines "We shall not always plant while others reap / The golden increment of bursting fruit" could be read as a justification for a black-owned space in which commerce, art, and pleasure overlapped. Insofar as the poem is a space in which multiple cultural registers and readings jostle against each other and recombine, it provides a fitting complement to A'Lelia Walker's luxurious and multipurpose Dark Tower.

"The Weary Blues" also was a canny selection given that the Dark Tower offered opportunities for those who, like the speaker in Hughes's poem, might want to observe and identify with black artists. The invitation to the opening invoked the tradition of the artistic salon: "We dedicate this tower to the aesthetes, that cultural group of young negro writers, sculptors, painters, music artists, composers, and their friends."[75] The reference to "aesthetes" suggests a place for those with a disinterested if decadent love of beauty, but A'Lelia capitalized on the fascination with "young negro writers" by charging guests. Thus the Dark Tower—like the Walker beauty parlor and Lelia College (for aspiring agents), which were on the ground floor of the Walker building—offered a mélange of private intercourse and public display, sold access to those who specialized in the creation of black beauty, and promised patrons that they would be more fashionable on the way out than on the way in. Still, beauty parlors supported modes of respectability and community that might develop into more conventional, legible forms of political organizing and activism, even if, according to *Dark Princess*, they were shortsighted. The Dark Tower, however, was better known for harboring forms of decadent interracial sociality and commerce that fit less easily with Du Boisian ideas about how aesthetics might give rise to political community and commitment.[76] Indeed, we can contrast the Dark Tower—with poems by Cullen and Hughes on the walls, crowds of fashionable white and black customers, and a flamboyant hostess—with Matthew's secret apartment in which he consummates his relationship with Kautilya, comes to possess her natural beauty, and secures the collective future of the "darker races." Both A'Lelia's venue and Du Bois's book organize and direct fantasies of black empire as they function as objects in and around which Harlem Renaissance-era counterpublics form.

Cullen's lingering presence in the Dark Tower provides a further twist to this comparison. In April 1928, the same month *Dark Princess* was published, Cullen married Du Bois's daughter, Yolande. Their wedding was the "Harlem social event of the decade" and was celebrated with much fanfare in the pages of the *Crisis*.[77] The union appeared to situate Du Bois and the Harlem Renaissance within the heteropatriarchal logic celebrated in *Dark Princess*, anointing Cullen and his more formally conservative works as the heirs to a select African American artistic tradition.[78] Du Bois even put down a deposit to hold the wedding reception at the Walker Studio, which included the Dark Tower, but he cancelled when the guest list became too large.[79] Yolande and Cullen's marriage, however, quickly failed after he left for Paris with his best man, Harold Jackman. The Dark Tower, then, stands witness to the failure of one of Du Bois's most personal efforts to ensure that an attraction to beauty might produce and reproduce ethical, corporeal, and political goods. Yet the Tower also suggests the role that the Walkers' work played in Du Bois's visions of reproductive futurism. This extends to the project of feminine beautification, for Du Bois's essay in the October 1928 *Crisis* about Yolande's marriage notes how "the new colored beauty parlors" transformed her from a tomboy into a nubile woman.[80] In this piece, titled "So the Girl

Marries," Du Bois even repeats a version of the defense of Walker's methods that he had offered in her obituary. In the essay about his daughter's marriage, he claims the "[parlors] didn't straighten, they cleaned and curled; they didn't whiten, they delicately darkened." Du Bois also connects "the problem of raiment"—what to wear and how to afford it—with the "problem of marriage," which in turn is vital to solving the problem of the color line. In this essay, black beauty culture and dress help to secure the collective future represented in the "great pageant" that is the Du Bois–Cullen wedding. According to Du Bois, the wedding procession "was not simply conventional America—it had a dark and shimmering beauty all its own; a calm and high restraint and sense of new power; it was a new race."[81] If *Dark Princess* uses fashion, beauty, and Afro-Orientalist fantasy to distinguish between cosmopolitan internationalism and cynical domestic politics as a means of pursuing racial advancement, in "So the Girl Marries" Du Bois's romantic vision of individual and racial progress depends on fashion and beauty culture. The essay acknowledges, in effect, that dress and cosmetics function along with Du Bois's own texts as indispensible if imperfect and sometimes ineffective tools to secure a utopian future.

Jessie Fauset's Black Internationalist Beauty Work

This chapter has shown how fashion underpins Du Bois's and Madam Walker's visions of how aesthetic production and perception fuel political struggle and solidarities across multiple forms of difference. In both cases, fashion highlights Du Bois's and both Walkers' simultaneous deployments of and oppositions to capitalist and imperialist modes of individual and collective movement and development. Given its association with femininity, fashion reveals the hydraulics of gender and sex within Du Bois's and the Walkers' versions of black internationalism and Afro-Orientalism. Du Bois and the Walkers, however, were not the only producers of black beauty to address the relationship between aesthetics and international politics via fashion, beauty culture, and Afro-Orientalism. The rest of this chapter shows how Jessie Fauset's and Nella Larsen's work turns to black beauty culture as a site of Afro-Orientalist imaginaries to describe how particular aesthetic practices and certain public and domestic spaces might cultivate modes of internationalist subjectivity and belonging. My analysis, then, contributes to efforts to trace the global dimensions of Fauset's and Larsen's work, and especially their engagements with the aesthetics and politics of internationalism in the 1910s and 1920s.[82] More specifically, I show that these writers' depictions of beauty culture provide ways to imagine and describe how black internationalist and Afro-Orientalist discourses and practices operate when access to international travel or conventionally political arenas become impossible or undesirable.

Larsen's and Fauset's works feature black women who move great distances, but their texts return to beauty and its cultivation to examine and sometimes expand the limits of political agency and belonging. Fauset's first published novel, *There Is Confusion* (1924), for example, links beauty work to an emerging black internationalist consciousness via a character who serves as a nurse for African American soldiers in France but returns to the United States determined to open a domestic chain of beauty salons. In Larsen's *Quicksand* (1928), the protagonist, Helga Crane, resembles the Afro-Orientalist figures of 1920s black beauty culture, but the entanglement of beauty and fashion in this text highlights the incommensurability of aesthetic experience and political belonging as they are configured in the southern United States, Chicago, Harlem, and Denmark. Larsen draws specifically on modernist visual aesthetics to highlight the difficulty of translating an attraction to beauty into political activism. Fauset and Larsen thus present contrasting accounts of the possibilities for linking aesthetic experience to political belonging via beauty culture. But both writers use black beauty culture's Afro-Orientalist dimensions to interrogate Du Boisian distinctions between seemingly decadent versus properly political forms and spaces of beauty and black internationalism.

The issue of what spaces might harbor desired forms of belonging also shaped Larsen's and Fauset's social lives in the 1920s, as they hosted and attended the gatherings of writers, painters, performers, intellectuals, friends, and spectators that were central to the Harlem Renaissance. Fauset hosted a particularly well-known salon in her Harlem home, which brought together young and established black artists and intellectuals and occasionally, foreign dignitaries. According to Hughes's account in *The Big Sea*, only the most "distinguished" white people were invited since Fauset did not want to host "mere faddists" who were simply attracted by the "vogue."[83] Hughes contrasts the dignity and occasional stuffiness of Fauset's "literary soirées" with A'Lelia Walker's gatherings, though both women with their different modes of cosmopolitanism sought to attract "that cultural group of young Negro writers."[84] Fauset, then, sponsored her own vision of a Harlem Renaissance counterpublic, which overlapped and competed with Du Bois's and the Walkers' configurations of space, race, gender, and fashion.

In her work, Fauset, like Larsen, depicts black women whose aesthetic expertise situates them within global economic, cultural, and political matrixes, while dramatizing the difficulties and losses involved in translating aesthetic experience into political praxis. Fauset's fiction—including "The Sleeper Wakes" (1920), *There Is Confusion, Plum Bun* (1928), *The Chinaberry Tree* (1931), and *Comedy: American Style* (1933)—features dressmakers, artists, and beauty culturalists for whom fashion is a means to navigate the racialized structures of capitalist modernity, including the distinctions between domestic and public spaces and between unremunerated and paid labor, which at once structure and fail to describe black women's experiences. Fauset's engagements with fashion and beauty culture prompt us to reconsider Russ Castronovo's claim that her fiction, specifically the story "The Sleeper Wakes," suggests that "beauty has no social value" and thus upholds the "deprecatory gendering of aesthetics."[85] Instead of dismissing beauty as ineffectual, Fauset differentiates between different ways of conceiving beauty and putting it to work, including via fashion and beauty culture.

There Is Confusion refers indirectly to Walker's business. One of the novel's two heroines, a working-class woman named Maggie Ellersley who longs for middle-class respectability, trains as a hair culturalist and, after a divorce from her first husband, supports herself by supervising beauty salons owned by one Madam Harkness.[86] The novel also comments on Du Bois and the NAACP: Maggie's childhood sweetheart and second husband, Philip Marshall, is a noble, idealistic, and well-educated man who, like Du Bois, conceives "an organization . . . among the colored people which should reach all over the country," in part via a magazine, which he edits.[87] As Nina Miller points out, the novel invites a comparison between Madam Harkness's business—with "Branch offices" in New York, Washington, D.C., Baltimore, and Philadelphia—and Philip's fledgling institution with its antilynching, civil rights platform, and thus between Walker's empire and the NAACP.[88] The novel does so, moreover, within the setting of World War I and with an eye to how the experience of being abroad and the white American backlash against black soldiers and communities reconfigure African Americans' artistic, cultural, economic, and political strategies and aspirations. The war's effects are played out through Philip's and Maggie's narratives and in relation to their disparate political and economic projects. The couple is reunited in wartime France, where Maggie works as a nurse for black soldiers and Philip receives what soon proves to be a fatal wound while fighting on the front. Although the war ends up killing Philip and (it seems) his vision of a national antiracist organization that would benefit "the interests of the country," it provides a backdrop for Maggie's dream of self-reliance and community via beauty work (*TIC*, 129). It is while working in France that Maggie first imagines establishing a set of beauty parlors in America, and she returns to that project after Philip's death. The novel leaves her contemplating her new venture, "bulwarked by the Marshall respectability," her own business acumen, and a new sense of generosity (*TIC*, 289). Thus, as the war highlights the limitations of U.S. nationalism as a framework for black activism and aspiration, it also marks a shift from Philip's vision of masculine, American political leadership to feminized, commodified aesthetic practices that seem poised to flourish in the postwar milieu. That transition registers the apparent failures of black claims for national inclusion, which rely on service to the nation or conventional routes of political protest and expression. But the novel does not embrace high art or the strategy of "civil rights by copyright," as David Levering-Lewis describes the Harlem Renaissance's aspirations.[89] *There Is Confusion* responds to a relative absence of black patronage for black art and the limitations of the nation as a site of attachment and hope by turning to beauty culture as a sustainable site for enabling black survival and solidarity.

It is worth lingering over the details of Maggie's aspirations, as they suggest the novel's treatment of beauty culture as a means of black women's empowerment and belonging in the context of imperial violence and geopolitical upheaval. Through Maggie, the novel addresses the collapse of Philip's national project by providing a blueprint for black beauty work in which black women's philanthropic, antiracist, and capitalist cosmopolitanism flourishes within the semipublic space of the beauty parlor. The specific terms by which Maggie first imagines her business are revealing; she decides "when she returned to America she would start her hair work again, she would inaugurate a chain of Beauty Shops. First-class ones" (*TIC*, 261). This phrasing combines the class-bound project of uplift with the suggestion that Maggie's venture might spark a new "chain" of spaces stretching beyond her initial vision or even control. This rhetoric is bolstered by her belief that her shops might reconcile individualism and ownership with collective belonging and egalitarianism; she imagines the business will allow her to be "serene, independent, self-reliant" and surrounded by "friends, simple kindly people whom she liked for themselves: who would seek her company with no thought of patronage" (*TIC*, 261). The novel also invites us to see her scheme as a way of bridging gendered generational divides and marking progress, as it closes Maggie's narrative by reporting that she and Philip's father—Joel Marshall, a successful caterer—spend "many pleasant hours in consultation" over her plans (*TIC*, 289). The transition from Joel to Maggie is a move from a black business catering to a predominantly white clientele to one appealing to black patrons. In short, key aspects of Maggie's vision echo the rhetoric that the Walker Company used to promote its salons particularly during Madam Walker's lifetime, establishing them as sites of racial solidarity and women's economic empowerment that fit within a generational logic of racial progress. In Maggie, it also depicts the kind of woman who, unlike A'Lelia, might "carry into realization" the "great dreams" of Madam Walker as Du Bois seems to have imagined them.

As with much of Fauset's work, however, the novel's happy ending only partially resolves the "confusion" that the narrative introduces. For example, the novel establishes associations between hair work and an intraracial "color line within the color line." During their courtship, Maggie explains to her first husband, Henderson Neal, that Madam Harkness has "invented a method of taking the harshness out of your folks' locks" and suggests "there's a big future in it. It ought to mean a lot to us. Everybody likes to be beautiful, and every woman looks better if her hair is soft and manageable" (*TIC*, 83). Maggie, who has "a mass of fine, wiry hair, that hung like a cloud" and is repeatedly described as having "yellow" or "golden" skin, admits that she "fortunately" does not need the treatment, but that she is "glad to help those that do" (*TIC*, 57, 83). Echoing the rhetoric of uplift, she presents herself as aiding a community to which she belongs and from which she claims some distance; note, for example, the shift from "your folks" to "us," and then "everybody." The term *manageable* also ties the feminine work of corporeal and domestic management and the image of a docile black body to Maggie's understanding of marriage as the manipulation of black masculinity. She mistakenly, indeed almost fatally, trusts in her ability to "manage" her first husband, misperceiving the management of the body as a way to secure safety and autonomy via men (84).

Maggie's shifting sense of racial belonging alerts us to the ways that her tale of vulnerable beauty facilitates comparative readings of narratives of racialized women's suffering and agency in the context of imperial violence. In a pivotal scene, Fauset describes Maggie via Orientalist tropes, including a gesture to Madame Butterfly; the novel thereby points to what Daniel Y. Kim describes as the "catachrestic set of meanings that congregate around the term" *yellow*, including as a description of Asian and biracial people.[90] Maggie has divorced Neal after she discovers that he is a gambler rather than a respectable businessman, and she believes that the only way to escape from the narrow confines of her life is through a second marriage—this time to Peter Bye (the once and future fiancé of Philip's sister, Joanna). Maggie's feeling of entrapment is exacerbated by her physical confinement; she spends her days going between Madam Harkness's salon and her room in her mother's boardinghouse, where the narrator finds her. Maggie is dressed in a "black silk kimono" embroidered with "silver butterflies" with her hair braided and "brushed to a smooth luster," while she stares "unseeingly" in the mirror at the "golden oval of her face" (*TIC*, 205). Maggie's braid and her gaze recall the figure in the advertisement for East India Hair Grower, while the oblique allusion to Madame Butterfly foreshadows the violence that soon erupts in this domestic space. In the next scene (set in the same room a week later), Peter visits her to break off their engagement before his departure for the French front, but accidentally leaves behind the new British-made surgical instruments that are his military equipment. After Peter departs, a jealous Neal, who has been stalking the house, breaks in and attempts to use one of Peter's knives to kill Maggie, who nevertheless remains calmly defiant. What I see as Fauset's gesture to Madame Butterfly, and to the figure of the geisha more generally, reinscribes Orientalist tropes and erases social difference while pointing to potential proximities and connections between the positions of black and Japanese women in the context of U.S. militarism and imperialism. The geopolitical dimensions of this episode are suggested by the fact that Peter's military tools (and thus Neal's weapon) are made of "British steel"; this reference neatly encapsulates critiques of U.S. involvement in the war, which emphasized that it would mean increased participation in the European imperialist systems and methods that the United States already engaged in through, for example, its occupation of Haiti and, in 1898, the annexation of the Philippines, Puerto Rico, and Guam. The United States's "opening" to Japan in 1853, which serves as the backdrop for "Madame Butterfly," already had signaled that the Pacific would be a site for the United States's global ambitions. It is thus particularly fitting that, in *There Is Confusion*, the reanimation of the nostalgic and retrospective tale of Madame Butterfly via Maggie treats gendered imperial violence as iterative and overlapping.[91]

As this episode stages gendered domestic violence as gendered imperial violence, it also depicts beauty as failing to manage or forestall that violence. Yet, as we have seen, this brush with death does not cause Maggie (or, I would argue, the novel) to reject feminine beauty and beautification as altogether ineffectual or superficial. Rather, the novel marks a shift from understanding beauty as a possession and means of manipulation to pursuing beautification as a practice and tool that facilitates black women's economic independence and racial belonging, as well as the establishment of semipublic spaces controlled by black women. This is a transition that many of Fauset's stories narrate.[92] Like Madam Walker, Fauset invests in commodified aesthetic methods as modes of women's economic empowerment within the framework of global capitalism and geopolitical conflict. Walker and Fauset treat the capitalization of beauty as an opportunity for black women to create semi-public spaces that provide some protection amidst geopolitical violence and that might incubate responses to that violence.

The question of beauty's role in antiracist and anti-imperialist political struggle shaped Fauset's career—specifically, her relationship to Du Bois and the NAACP in the late 1910s to mid-1920s. It determined her position as literary editor at the *Crisis*, which she made a key forum for black fiction and poetry, thus developing the connection between art and politics that Du Bois would theorize in the journal's pages in "Criteria of Negro Art." Fauset's cultivation of artistic beauty also helped her to access black internationalist communities, since her work with Du Bois led to her organizing and attending the Second Pan-African Congress, which took place in 1921 in London, Brussels, and Paris; at the Brussels session, she gave a speech about African American women's lives and accomplishments. We can understand Fauset's depiction of Maggie Ellersley as an effort to imagine further possibilities for aesthetic and political engagement beyond Fauset's own exceptional experiences and milieu. But *There Is Confusion* also includes a more explicit consideration of the relationship between black art and politics via the relationship between Philip Marshall and his talented and ambitious sister, Joanna. Joanna is a singer and dancer with "a beautiful full voice," and "beautiful dreams" of success, as well as a deep appreciation for and desire to create beauty (*TIC*, 229, 162). Yet she becomes famous because of her ability to perform ethnic, racial, and national types; her big break is getting to play "America" in three parts ("black," "white," and "red") in a production called *The Dance of the Nations* (*TIC*, 229, 226). The show is put on by self-consciously progressive white people in Greenwich Village, and it recapitulates the racist structures that shape both Joanna's artistic career and wartime international politics. Like Philip's hopes for a national organization, Joanna's project falters in the face of American racism as it appears on and shapes the international stage. Joanna chooses to abandon her career and her pursuit of artistic beauty in order to be a good wife to Peter (who did not marry Maggie) and mother to their son. But while Joanna's career is a disappointment, the narrative does not depict art or beauty as necessarily ineffectual. Rather, the novel investigates how the conditions for the production and reception of black art shape its potential effects. And although it apparently fails, Joanna's career points to art's capacity to facilitate or set the stage for political critique.

The Dance of the Nations reflects the limitations of prevailing forms of liberal internationalism and cultural pluralism.[93] Though the production's title suggests that the nations might join together through artistic performance, the *Dance* naturalizes the United States's military alliances with other nations against Austria-Hungary and Germany, as it does not include representatives of Germany and her allies (*TIC*, 226). In the *Dance*, the United States is the only nation represented by multiple "roles," which bolsters pluralist narratives of American exceptionalism and assumes the whiteness of the colonial powers England and France (which are, tellingly, the only other nations that are mentioned as part of the performance). The links between nationhood, war making, and artistic and political representation also surface when Joanna defends her ability to play "white" America by citing her male relatives' generations of military service to the nation (*TIC*, 232). This rhetoric is particularly ironic in a novel that emphasizes the virulent racism and "ingratitude" faced by African American soldiers, including Joanna's brother (*TIC*, 269). *The Dance of Nations* also brings to mind the performance of collaboration by representatives of different nations on the world stage at the Paris Peace Conference. As Fauset well knew, the conference, like the *Dance*, used the rhetoric of inclusivity while shutting out Germany and her allies in addition to representatives of colonized and oppressed peoples. Thus the *Dance* dramatizes how the conference elaborately staged but did not realize the promises of liberal internationalism. The pageantlike quality of *The Dance of the Nations* also brings to mind the final scenes of *Dark Princess*, which offers its own romantic, spiritual, and heteronormative performances of solidarity among people of color. *Dark Princess*'s pageant of marriage and baptism admits modes of belonging that multiply and divide the national forms that are reproduced in the *Dance* and underpin liberal internationalism, for it includes Christian, Muslim, Hindu, and Buddhist representatives from the United States and India. Du Bois's final scene, then, offers a vision of what *other* kinds of performances might take the stage when the dance of liberal internationalism, with its white supremacist modes of cultural pluralism, is ushered off.

The connection that *There Is Confusion* makes between domestic cultural pluralism and liberal internationalism via the *Dance* also reframes the well-known narrative of the novel's reception, for the publication of Fauset's first book famously provided the impetus for what David Levering-Lewis describes as the "dress rehearsal of what was soon to be known as the 'Harlem Renaissance'": the dinner hosted by Charles S. Johnson at the New York Civic Club in March 1924.[94] Though Fauset was the guest of honor, Alain Locke, as master of ceremonies, focused on introducing the "next generation" of young black writers to the assembled crowd, which included many white editors and philanthropists who subscribed to pluralist concepts of citizenship and inclusion. Recent international and transnational work on the

Harlem Renaissance challenges Levering-Lewis's account in which the New York Civic Club dinner helps to represent the movement's supposedly national cultural and political horizon and aims. For example, in the introduction to his coedited collection *Escape from New York: The New Negro Renaissance beyond Harlem,* Davarian L. Baldwin emphasizes that the Harlem Renaissance is only part of a broader New Negro movement that unfolds on a "world stage," and he contrasts Locke and the Civic Club dinner with the more insistently global dimensions and ambitions of the Garvey movement.[95] Yet, given that *There Is Confusion* dramatizes the entwinement of cultural pluralism and liberal internationalism, the novel's shadowy presence at the Civic Club dinner offers another way to describe how the event's seemingly national or even local stage was already international, though of course not in Garvey's terms.

As students of the Harlem Renaissance know, the Civic Club dinner led to Locke's editing of the issue of the *Survey Graphic* that became the collection *The New Negro.* Locke nearly did not include work by Fauset in *The New Negro,* though he ultimately accepted an essay titled "The Gift of Laughter," in which Fauset meditates on the legacy and future of black performance. The essay strikes an optimistic note, but also points back to *There Is Confusion*'s less sanguine vision of the possibilities for black women's art in the context of 1920s liberal internationalism and pluralism. In "The Gift of Laughter," Fauset insists, "The question of color raises no insuperable barrier, seeing that with chameleon adaptability we are able to offer white colored men and women for *Hamlet, The Doll's House* and the *Second Mrs. Tanqueray*; brown men for *Othello*; yellow girls for *Madam Butterfly*; black men for *The Emperor Jones.*"[96] As a number of critics have noted, in *There Is Confusion,* Joanna's talents seem to bear out the essay's assertion that African Americans have a particular "dramatic genius," which has been demonstrated through comic, minstrel roles but which now deserves expression in more substantive drama, particularly tragedy.[97] The essay's celebration of physical "adaptability" and tragic performance also provides a framework for seeing Maggie's enactments and practices of femininity as continuous with Joanna's career as a performer.[98] Yet the essay also clarifies why Joanna—and the novel—become disillusioned with her success on the stage. In *The Dance of the Nations,* this "question of color" is addressed by having Joanna wear a mask to perform "white" America and use the familiar tools of minstrelsy—"a wig and greasepaint"—to represent "red" (*TIC*, 231). Moreover, Joanna comes to regret her fame when she realizes that people on the street react to her as they do when laughing at a "dark colored girl wearing Russian boots and a hat with three feathers sticking up straight, Indian fashion" (274). Together these examples suggest that the legacy of comic racial performance as well as the vicissitudes of cosmopolitan fashion overdetermine the terms and reception of Joanna's art by white and black audiences. While Maggie may be able to perceive and pursue a "big future" in black women's beauty practices and parlors, the future of black women's performance is still too distant for Joanna to attempt to stage it, no matter how great her love of and capacity for beauty.

Joanna's narrative concludes in the terms and realms of domesticity and reproductive futurism.[99] So while the novel does not question the hierarchy that ranks artistic beauty above beauty practices, it suggests that the latter may generate and sustain semipublic spaces for working- and middle-class black women that do not yet exist for the former.[100] Indeed, given Fauset's use of her own salon as a "mode of rehearsal" for young black artists (in andré m. carrington's words) and the importance of the parlor as a semiprivate stage for the Harlem Renaissance, we can understand Maggie's beauty shops as sites for black women's performance in which the audience participates in the action.[101] The relationship between the parlor and a more public stage also dramatizes the move that young black artists might make from Fauset's living room to the pages of the *Crisis*. Nevertheless, the novel never actually enters the space of the beauty parlor, positioning it both off the main stage and in the near future or next act of the drama. This absence makes it difficult to grasp beauty parlors as a solution to the problems with public-private space and thus with the conditions for black cultural production and political belonging. But it preserves a sense of privacy and possibility associated with the parlors. It also helps to distance the vision of the beauty parlor from the more mundane mechanisms of commerce, which underwrite such privacy. Like Walker's company, the novel romanticizes black women's entrepreneurship, as Maggie's story ends with a business venture rather than a marriage. In effect, *There Is Confusion* positions the beauty parlor alongside the cabaret, the salon, the street, the stage, the novel, and the periodical as a key space for the formation of Harlem Renaissance–era counterpublics.

Nella Larsen and the Quicksand of Afro-Orientalist Aesthetics

Nella Larsen's *Quicksand* is also intimately concerned with the relationships between beauty, fashion, wealth, space, international mobility, and (Afro-)Orientalism as they enable and threaten black women's survival.

Helga Crane even combines key features of Maggie's and Joanna's characters and narratives. Like Maggie, Helga clings precariously to middle-class status, aided and endangered by her appearance (light-skinned, "attractive," associated with East Asia) and hindered by family background.[102] Helga also, like Maggie, travels from Harlem to Europe and back, albeit under quite different circumstances. Like Joanna, she strains against the limitations of black women's aspirations but ends up a housewife, and critics have described Helga as a "failed artist."[103] She also shares with Joanna a love for beauty as well as a taste for brightly colored clothing, which defies the black middle-class insistence on wearing dull shades of brown and black. Helga's "aesthetic sense" and her geographical and personal trajectory also recall Matthew and his journey, but while Helga's wanderings from a southern school to Chicago to Harlem to Europe and back to the South parallel and intersect with Matthew's movements, her narrative of decline contrasts with his path of discovery (*Q*, 76). Moreover, both novels conclude in the rural South with the births of infants who mark Matthew's and Helga's very different fates: whereas Matthew and Kautilya's child can be understood as emerging from their secret, Oriental womb/room and as symbolizing their revolutionary future, Helga's children trap her in exhausting, deadly domesticity and mark her distance from the beautiful, semiprivate space decorated in chinoiserie where the novel first finds her (and even that space represents a form of entrapment, given that it is located within Naxos, the stifling institution where Helga teaches). Whereas Du Bois celebrates cosmopolitan, male-authored domesticity as a site for the production of Afro-Asian internationalist aesthetics, subjectivity, and futurity, and while Fauset gestures to the beauty parlor as a public-private arena that might help to incubate politically attuned black feminist cosmopolitanism, Larsen underscores the precariousness of both public and domestic spaces, even and especially when they enable the expression of her protagonist's "aesthetic sense." Thus we could describe Helga as a failed or impossible diasporic dandy whose fate underscores how that figure depends on forms of masculinity even as it contests them. While the dandy might revise the terms of black masculinity, Helga's tale dramatizes the dangers of this pose for a black woman with no family support and no independent means.

The parallels and discrepancies between Matthew's and Helga's stories also emerge via narrative form; *Dark Princess* concludes with the triumph of romance over realism, albeit with some loose ends and lumpy seams, but *Quicksand*'s "hybrid form" does not resolve the sense of disjunction created by the movement between scenes that resemble tableaux.[104] These "painterly" episodes (to borrow Cherene Sherrard-Johnson's label) present modernism, fashion, and Orientalism as entangled in ways that challenge Du Bois's attempts to disarticulate beauty from fashion.[105] And they call into question the visions of international and cosmopolitan belonging offered by the Walker Company. Consider, for example, the novel's oft-discussed first passage, which finds Helga in her private room within the Naxos "machine":

> Helga Crane sat alone in her room, which at that hour, eight in the evening, was in soft gloom. Only a single reading lamp, dimmed by a great black and red shade, made a pool of light on the blue Chinese carpet, on the bright covers of the books which she had taken down from their long shelves, on the white pages of the opened one selected, on the shining brass bowl crowded with many-colored nasturtiums beside her on the low table, and on the oriental silk which covered the stool at her slim feet. It was a comfortable room, furnished with rare and intensely personal taste. (*Q*, 35)

The shade's combination of black and red reads as Chinese, and Sherrard-Johnson shows that the decor and the subsequent description of Helga as having "skin like yellow satin" recall Eugène Delacroix's Orientalist paintings of the "mulatta."[106] It is particularly striking that this shade filters the light from the "single reading lamp," which determines what is visible to Helga and the reader. The shade thus draws attention to the way that Helga and the text filter things (at least momentarily) through a dehistoricized, Orientalist lens, which might offer an alternative to Naxos's black and white optical and racial regime. It follows, then, that the book to which Helga turns for "forgetfulness" is Marmaduke Pickthall's *Said the Fisherman*, an Orientalist tale by a white British writer (36). Nevertheless, the scene recapitulates the contrast between black and white via the shade and the "white pages of the opened book." We might then say that the scene's color scheme dramatizes the entanglement and interdependence of different racialized forms of viewing. At the same time, however, the bold, contrasting colors recall the abstract and defamiliarizing techniques of modernism. This convergence between racialized (black, Orientalist) and modernist aesthetics establishes their mutuality and inextricability. So while, as Sherrard-Johnson argues, Larsen draws on Orientalist imagery to depict a "mulatta" figure that is "more modernist and less New Negro," *Quicksand* also interrogates the distinctions between those categories.[107]

The scene's use of modernist technique also interrupts a reading of these colors only in terms of racial or ethnic signification. That is, it prompts us to consider precisely how and why we might perceive certain things as (mis) representative (e.g., Orientalist, New Negro, realist) but others as more abstract (e.g., modernist). The narrator's assertion that the room is "furnished with rare and intensely personal taste" compounds this issue, since this claim is not borne out by the description of the room's fashionable decor. Once Helga gets to Harlem, she finds that her taste in interior design matches that of Anne Grey, the wealthy and stylish socialite who rails against white supremacy but disdains African American culture. The room's decor, then, is "intensely personal" only in the context of Naxos's conservative, uplift-oriented aesthetic—that is, when it is perceived in the school's "soft gloom" rather than in light of bourgeois Harlem fashion.[108] Similarly, the aesthetic and political impact of Helga's clothing, which also expresses her "aesthetic sense," shifts dramatically when moved across the ocean from Harlem to Denmark, where clothing that seemed daring is suddenly too conservative to fulfil the Danes' taste for exoticized nonwhite bodies. Through these shifts, the novel traces the terrain of fashion, which is the terrain of aesthetics inevitably shaped by geopolitics and racial capital. In doing so, the novel points to the contingent distinctions between Orientalism, modernism, and New Negro art and politics, as well between the personal and the collective. In *Quicksand*, beauty, including Afro-Orientalist beauty, does not generate possibilities and desires for immediate or legible political action, but rather highlights the incommensurability of aesthetic practices and political forms of belonging and expression, at least as they are currently configured.

The narrative, however, does not dismiss the particularity and force of Helga's "aesthetic sense" when it is associated with fashion. Her interest in dress and beautiful objects is not held up to ridicule, even if it does prove to be misguided and shaped by (and against) various investments, attachments, desires, and beliefs, including ideologies of uplift, primitivism, and Orientalism. After all, the opening passage of the novel draws the reader into the text through its stylish descriptions of the objects that Helga chooses. Thus Orientalism/modernism/fashion ushers readers into the space of the text where they will linger with Helga. Moreover, *Quicksand* pursues the possibilities that black beauty culture's Afro-Orientalist aesthetics make more proximate, if not practical. As Chandan Reddy and Julia H. Lee argue, *Quicksand*'s engagements with Orientalism gesture to possibilities for black and Asian (particularly Chinese) affiliation, while contesting the available terms for nation-based subjectivity and belonging. Reddy reads Helga's association with Oriental objects and hence silence as connecting her to the silencing and exclusion of Chinese people in the United States, since the nation at once relied on Chinese labor and effectively refused Chinese claims to citizenship and further immigration. Still, as Reddy observes, "in the aesthetic another structure of feeling emerges" and points to modes of belonging that are not otherwise palpable.[109] Certainly Helga's "aesthetic sense" does not translate into a secure form of belonging, and indeed, it proves fatal, as it leads her to an ill-advised marriage to a southern preacher and thence to pregnancy and illness. Yet it offers Helga and the reader access to sensations, attachments, and configurations that are at once close at hand and barely perceived. This function of the aesthetic is continuous with and enabled by the various, sometimes conflicting images and practices of Afro-Orientalism that circulated via black beauty culture. In particular, the history of the Walker Company shows how an Afro-Orientalist aesthetic already existed in relation to (if not necessarily in support of) black internationalist politics and what Reddy describes more broadly as the emergence of black counterpublics in the interwar period.

Weinbaum also reads *Quicksand* in relation to beauty culture, though her emphasis is on how the novel responds to the tropes of racial masquerade in white U.S. beauty culture and in sociological theories of race and assimilation in the 1920s.[110] Weinbaum argues that the novel exposes the ways that participation in such masquerade and thus belonging in U.S. (consumer) culture is premised on whiteness; Helga, in short, discovers that such tactics and subject positions exclude her. Equipped with Weinbaum's reading, we might say that *Quicksand* exposes not only the limitations of white American beauty culture's promises of belonging and of the Du Boisian vision of the diasporic black dandy, but also the failures and pitfalls of black beauty culture's Afro-Orientalist imaginaries. More specifically, *Quicksand* suggests the contingent, contextual, and potentially destructive effects of Afro-Orientalist visions of feminine beauty. For example, when deployed in white liberal cosmopolitan spaces such as those of Copenhagen's bourgeois and artistic elite, such images become indistinguishable from the dominant terms and effects of white European primitivism and Orientalism. However, I would emphasize that *Quicksand* and black beauty culture's Afro-Orientalist imaginaries do not simply imitate the dynamics of racial masquerade in white beauty culture (even if they cannot be disarticulated from them). Rather, as I have sought to show, they are part of an unfolding tradition of reimagining how "black" and "Asian" forms, bodies, and political interests converge and overlap, particularly via concepts and practices of beauty.

A pivotal scene in *Quicksand* set in a Harlem cabaret draws on Afro-Orientalist beauty and its association with fashion and, in doing so, enables a more detailed exploration of what structures of feeling and ways of relating and belonging this aesthetic might make available. In particular, the episode, which occurs just before Helga departs for Copenhagen, stages the challenge of translating aesthetic sensation into potentially politically legible modes of attachment and relation. Across the crowded cabaret, Helga catches sight of Audrey Denney, a girl in a "shivering apricot frock" with "pitchblack eyes, a little aslant . . . veiled with long, drooping lashes" and skin that Helga thinks is "almost like an alabaster" (Q, 90). As described from Helga's perspective, Audrey is an assemblage of Orientalist aesthetic details associated with the Middle East and East Asia, which appeared in 1920s European and American fashion. Yet, as in the novel's opening description of Helga (which this passage recalls), such details point to multiple, overlapping representional schemas. Accordingly, critics have discussed Audrey as Helga's object of desire and identification; as the embodiment of a "complex, messy, and socially unsanctioned racial and sexual subjectivity" that defies both the ideology of uplift and the terms of the Negro "vogue"; and as the model for a world yet to come in which race is transcended.[111] As Anne angrily informs Helga, Audrey hosts scandalous interracial gatherings at her apartment on West 22nd Street (that is, far from Harlem and just outside Greenwich Village); although "colored," Audrey "gives parties for white and colored people together" (Q, 91). Helga, for her part, feels "envious admiration" for "the beautiful, cool, calm girl who had the assurance, the courage, so placidly to ignore racial barriers and give her attention to people" (Q, 92). This is an ambivalent and unsettling moment in the text. The movement of Helga's gaze from the crowd in the cabaret to Audrey invites us to read the woman as a metonym for the bodies gathered there, which display the many "gradations within this oppressed race of [Helga's]." In the crowd, Helga sees "Africa, Europe, perhaps with a pinch of Asia, in a fantastic motley of ugliness and beauty, semibarbaric, sophisticated, exotic" (Q, 90). The extended description of the crowd tests the limits of a singular idea of race or location, and reminds us that Helga herself might "belong" to two races but for the fact that one of them is "oppressed" by the other. The passage thus participates in the aestheticization of Audrey's racialized body and at the same time enables an understanding of the term *colored* that resembles something closer to a concept of people of color, which, however, is not experienced in opposition to a stable or singular whiteness.

Despite this connection between Audrey and this diverse collectivity, Helga's interest in the woman is contrasted with her insensibility to the attractions of the crowd; she is "blind to its charm, purposely aloof and a little contemptuous" (Q, 90). Sianne Ngai points out that Harlem Renaissance novels by black and white writers often feature "paeans to skin color," and she argues that Helga's ambivalence toward the crowd and attraction to Audrey help us to see that the novel refuses "*either* clear identification *or* disidentification with existing constructions of black identity."[112] According to Ngai, the novel thereby resists the "closely related demand that artforms by racialized subjects be expressive at any cost."[113] The aestheticization of "gradations" of racial difference also is in keeping with internationalist visions of harmonious diversity, including Fauset's *Dance of the Nations* and Du Bois's pageant. Certainly, Du Bois's descriptions of Matthew and Kautilya's child, which appears "like a palpitating bubble of gold," participates in the aestheticization of mixed-race bodies as expressions of such desired harmony (*DP*, 307). Understood in this framework of aestheticized internationalisms, Helga's different reactions to the crowd and to Audrey raise questions about what particular forms of attachment and structures of feeling become available via her "aesthetic sense." Helga's wavering attention suggests that her "taste" may be "intensely personal" not only in that it may be unique and can set her apart, but also in that it seems to attach her mostly to individual subjects and objects rather than to collectives.

This attachment, moreover, never becomes a sustained relation. As Laura Doyle points out, a meeting between Helga and Audrey is repeatedly blocked by heterosexual couplings; when Audrey beings dancing with Robert Anderson (Helga's former boss at Naxos, for whom she later discovers a passion), Helga follows an impulse to flee, and at a later party that Helga attends after her return from Denmark, Helga is diverted from meeting Audrey by encounters with her ex-fiancé from Naxos and with Anderson himself.[114] Accordingly, critics have read Audrey as a figure of inadmissible queer desire, which Larsen explores more fully in *Passing* (1929) via the protagonist Irene Redfield's attraction to Clare Kendry.[115] Without dismissing such readings, I want also to suggest that the correspondence between singularity and "aesthetic sense" dramatizes the difficulty of translating aesthetic and erotic attraction into stable forms of relation.[116] Whereas *Dark Princess* imagines that a particular sensitivity to beauty and hence an attraction to the beautiful body of the woman of color would open toward collective futures through sexual reproduction and a growing sensitivity to ethical ugliness, and while Fauset and the Walker Company present the beautification of the individual body as benefiting "the race" in various ways, *Quicksand* dismantles these logics and treats aesthetic experience as a rather solitary affair.

Nevertheless, as we have seen, the novel does not endorse fantasies of an autonomous aesthetic sensibility, since it shows how the terrain of fashion shapes aesthetic perception. Moreover, from its opening scene, *Quicksand* suggests that one cannot easily differentiate between the sensations produced by an encounter with what is merely fashionable and those generated by an engagement with art—including the novel itself. The inextricability of art and fashion also puts pressure on the distinctions between the personal and the collective that characterize Helga's aesthetic experience. Simmel, of course, understood fashion as a way to secure a sense of individuality without breaking free of the crowd. And despite the collective nature of fashion, it is often narrated and conceptualized via the individual's attraction and relation to a garment or to a specific body wearing a garment, which in turn supposedly uniquely expresses a trend. The dynamics and contradictions of Helga's "intensely personal taste" thus also characterize this individualist (il) logic of fashion.

The novel's explorations of the relationships between aesthetic perception, fashion, and art also suggest a theory of reading. *Quicksand* repeatedly associates Helga's taste for fashion and beauty with her taste for books, and (as I noted) the related phenomena of fashion, beauty, and literature welcome the reader into the text. Also, when we enter Helga's room in Naxos, our sense that we are alone with her (and perhaps the narrator) gives way to an awareness of the multiple observers who shape her image for us; the second paragraph begins, "An observer would have thought her well fitted to that framing of light and shade" (Q, 36). So as we encounter Helga as "attractive," we understand that she is already read and seen. Our reading of her is in part a reading of others' perceptions of her. Thus it will be no more or less "intensely personal" than Helga's taste. In short, fashion nicely describes the novel's treatment of reading as a solitary act that always occurs in relation to others and in time but does not necessarily direct us toward a sustained or sustainable attachment to others.

This formulation interrupts the strategies by which Du Bois, the Walkers, and Fauset imagine that fashion, beauty, and art provide or can produce desired ethical, political, and economic goods. Yet in laying out this vision, Larsen shares with them an engagement with fashion and beauty as pedagogical tools. Indeed, one way to map the connections and divergences between how Larsen, Du Bois, the Walker Company, and Fauset treat fashion and beauty is to describe what and how they might teach. While *Dark Princess* is suspicious of clothing as a form of social control—as, for example, the depictions of Sarah's obedient women's groups suggest—its hero's taste for dress orients him toward a revolutionary internationalist aesthetic education. The Walker Company, meanwhile, emphasized the educational and, at times, civilizing aspects of its project of beautification through its colleges and via its rhetoric of uplift, including an emphasis on what the company and its agents might teach those in other nations and parts of the black diaspora. *There Is Confusion* offers Maggie and her process of fashioning herself into a better woman via her expertise in fashioning hair as an instructive if not easily imitated model for the reader. A'Lelia Walker's decadent cosmopolitanism seemed to reject such modes of virtuous self-improvement. Yet her knowledge of what was fashionable in dress, art, and interior decorating was key to her celebrity, by which she promised agents, costumers, clients, and friends access or at least proximity to that knowledge. In each case, we can also understand the connections between beauty, fashion, and Afro-Orientalism in terms of pedagogy. This is in keeping with the way that Oriental objects circulated in early twentieth-century U.S. culture as sources of "an education in beauty," to borrow Kim's phrase.[117] In the context of black art and politics, however, such education might offer lessons in revolutionary subjectivity, in overlapping modes of gendered imperial violence, or in the incommensurability of aesthetic perception and existing forms of racialized subjectivity and belonging.

The next chapter more directly addresses the relationship between fashion and education, particularly as they shape forms of celebrity and thereby transform authorship and cultural production in the early twentieth century. Jennifer Wicke describes celebrity as a "fashion in people."[118] As this study has emphasized, fashion raises questions about the potential for objects to have desired effects in the world. It describes how things are subject to prevailing cultural, economic, and political forces and how they might shape those forces. Celebrity, then, is a related phenomenon that prompts us to ask if and how cultural producers who are "of the moment" might shape that moment and perhaps those that follow. Fashion and celebrity, moreover, give rise to certain theories about how particular people and objects provide privileged expressions and reflections of a given historical period. As we have seen, Woolf's and Lawrence's texts respond to fashion's influence on modern theories of history that conceive the past in terms of moments that are at once irrecoverable and understandable via cultural objects.[119] The next chapter turns to the career and work of the Jazz Age icon F. Scott Fitzgerald to explore these interdependent theories of history, influence, and transformation. I trace how these theories structure both Fitzgerald's work and contemporary historicist approaches to literary study.

4 : PROPHETS AND HISTORICISTS

F. Scott Fitzgerald and Paul Poiret

Those who give the illusion of dominating their epoch are often dominated by it, and growing terribly dated, they disappear with it.
—Pierre Bourdieu, "How Can 'Free-Floating Intellectuals' Be Set Free?"

"Can't repeat the past?" he cried incredulously. "Why of course you can!"
—F. Scott Fitzgerald, *The Great Gatsby*

Zelda and F. Scott Fitzgerald have circulated as metonyms for the Jazz Age since the early 1920s, when Scott popularized the term and the couple emerged as celebrities who embodied and spoke for a new generation. In film and fashion, the Fitzgeralds, Jay Gatsby, and Daisy Buchanan index certain Jazz Age modes—linen suits, drop-waisted dresses, glamorous and boozy parties—which in turn are periodically recast via current trends. While he does not focus on dress, Fredric Jameson argues that the proliferation of historical styles in the era of late capitalism reflects and generates an inability to think historically in a substantive and politically trenchant way; what occurs is a representation of "the past as fashion plate."[1] Yet Jameson's method also shares certain principles with popular understandings of fashion. Both draw power from their capacity to grasp the most salient characteristics of a particular historical moment, which extend beyond but are discovered in particular cultural objects. Both also deploy the logic of periodization, although they also highlight the inadequacy and multiplicity of such designations.[2] These similarities make fashion particularly threatening to what Jameson regards as a properly historical mode of understanding, which would expose capitalism's determinative power. Fashion operates as a competing means of grasping the past and its significance for the present.

While critiques of Jameson's historical techniques and imperative continue to appear, key principles of his approach remain dominant. As Jennifer Fleissner observes with respect to the study of American literature, "That literary artifacts are of interest to us chiefly for what they can tell us about a given culture (at a given historical moment) has become such a truism within our own field that it can seem scarcely possible to conceive of what alternative practices might look like."[3] The same could be said of the new modernist studies, which emerged as scholars drew on historicist and cultural studies approaches to challenge modernist claims for aesthetic autonomy as well as criticism that embraced modernism on those terms. Work in the field has shown both how various modernists were engaged in political and cultural issues and how modernist claims to disinterestedness or detachment are belied by authors' and texts' entanglements with various economic and cultural forces. To a certain degree, this chapter takes up the work of situating Fitzgerald in his historical moment; it shows how Fitzgerald and his career exemplify and generate ways of thinking about history and the relationships between creator, object, and context, which overlap with and draw from the dynamics of fashion and periodical culture in the 1910s and 1920s. I argue that Fitzgerald's self-fashioning as the so-called Prophet of the Jazz Age and his practice of producing both self-consciously literary novels and short stories for popular periodicals parallel the persona and seasonal production methods of Paul Poiret, the most famous fashion designer of the first decades of the twentieth century.

Yet I read Fitzgerald, Poiret, and their moment fashionably to argue that the connections that I trace between literature, fashion, and periodicals anticipate modes of historical thinking that shape contemporary approaches to modernism. Fitzgerald and Poiret provide contexts for their work that at once anchor them in a particular moment and can move with their texts through time. One of those contexts is a kind of romantic historicism, in which cultural figures and objects, including texts and garments, express the contours of a given era. That mode of historicism situates these men and their work as expressions of the "spirit of the age." It also helps to dignify Fitzgerald's and Poiret's focus on seemingly frivolous, fashionable material; in Fitzgerald's case, he transforms fleeting time into highly stylized, representative literary forms. For Fitzgerald, the philosopher of the flapper, as for the King of Fashion, Paul Poiret, securing their legacies requires a mastery of fashionable femininity (including their wives) as well as a turn to the didactic. They become celebrity-artist-teachers whose pedagogical stance provides a way to manage (frivolous, feminine) time and to provide the terms for the reception and preservation of their work. In the process, Fitzgerald's and Poiret's versions of historicism and formalism perform and invite the modes of analysis often practiced in modernist studies. My account of their historical thinking suggests how current reading practices perpetuate modernist modes of imagining and engaging with literature, even as scholars question the logic and limits of periodization, contextualization, and historical representativeness. While our forms of reading can be seen to extend modernist methods, however, they also represent a reemergence and reformulation of these methods—in other words, a repetition with a difference.

Fleissner offers the idea of history's repetition with a difference as an alternative to recent methods that either treat the past as inseparable from the present or conceive the past as radically different from the present. She associates the idea of the past's intertwinement with the present with a recent version of "the Benjaminian notion of repeating," which involves a romantic vision of the present as haunted by the past.[4] As Fleissner points out, such recent Benjaminian historiography replaces Benjamin's idea of the repetition of a "lost revolutionary *opportunity*" with the ongoing repetition "of a past *trauma*."[5] She thus understands that replacement and the shift to the discourse of trauma as itself a lost opportunity. Nevertheless, given Benjamin's claim that revolutionary historicism resembles fashion's "tiger's leap into the past," it is not clear that, as a whole, "On the Concept of History" presents an account of repetition that counters the idea of the past's difference. One might conclude that the leap backwards is revolutionary precisely because it moves between two distinct moments, even if those moments may not be radically different, as a bourgeois schema of periodization might hold.[6] In fact, fashion is a useful structure for reading modernism because it already involves repetition with a difference. As the first chapter discusses, for example, Woolf's "The New Dress" highlights the impossibility of repeating a fashion; moreover, in that story, the attempt to repeat the past is part of an effort to heal enduring wounds without actually grasping the contours of that present. In that sense, fashion's demonstration of the impossibility of repetition could shift the emphasis from attempts at healing to efforts at transformation that acknowledge the dynamic nature of the past and the present.

Fitzgerald and Poiret do not pursue that particular possibility. Their work and celebrity, however, engage fashion's recursive historicism—in which certain past styles represent a given moment and are recast via present forms—as a means by which authors and their work might generate iterative effects (which, however, are not necessarily revolutionary or even desirable). For if fashion involves recurrence, then the style, individual, or object that epitomizes a given moment might reemerge as newly relevant.[7] The idea that a work, person, or style might gain immortality by epitomizing a given moment resonates with the Baudelairian belief that modernist art discovers the eternal in the transitory. But by embracing repetition with a difference,

Fitzgerald's and Poiret's work and persona respond more particularly to the way that changes and continuities over time will affect how modernist art is encountered, reencountered, and remade. In that sense, their vision, though melancholy, departs from the idea of traumatic history that Fleissner describes. Fitzgerald attempts to grapple with the inevitability of changing conditions of reception by offering ready-made contexts through which readers might grasp his work; those contexts include versions of literary history, his methods of composition, and his historical moment. A number of his essays also employ particular methods for relating text to context. The result is not an embrace of aesthetic autonomy, a vision of traumatic history, or an account of the past's absolute difference. Instead, Fitzgerald's work represents an effort to secure a lasting legacy via forms of differently repeated histories *and* historicisms, which emerge from and also (re-)contextualize Fitzgerald's works.

The pursuit of the right kind of repetition with a difference structured Fitzgerald's career even during his lifetime. He attempted to repeat but also reconfigure the remarkable success of his first novel, *This Side of Paradise*, which upon its publication in 1920 was advertised and received as a paradigmatic expression of contemporary American "youth" writ large.[8] Writing to his editor, Max Perkins, in 1921, Fitzgerald laid out his ambitions for his soon-to-be-published second novel, *The Beautiful and Damned* (1922): "I do not expect in any event that I am to have the same person-for-person public this time that *Paradise* had. My one hope is to be endorsed by the intellectually élite and thus *forced* onto people as Conrad has."[9] As Loren Glass observes, a "volatile passage from the restricted elite audience of urban bohemia and 'little magazines' to the mass audience of the U.S. middlebrow became a signature career arc for American modernist writers," including Gertrude Stein and Ernest Hemingway, whom Fitzgerald considered key competition in his quest to be the "best American novelist."[10] Other modernist writers including Eliot, Pound, Joyce, and Woolf also had more established literary reputations before they gained some degree of broader popularity. Thanks to the success of *This Side of Paradise* and Fitzgerald's talents at self-promotion, that pattern did not fit; Fitzgerald's authorial persona was already entangled with his celebrity and he did not make a smooth transition from popular to elite endorsement.[11] His capacity to represent the 1920s in writing became synonymous with his own representativeness, and his literary stock rose and fell and rose again more dramatically and publicly than that of virtually any writer who was endorsed (even temporarily) by the "intellectually élite" in the 1920s or today.

Glass maintains that different temporalities of recognition—one characterized by late and often posthumous regard and the other by early, instant celebrity—map onto distinctions between modernist and postmodernist constructions of authorship (designations that themselves mark temporal boundaries).[12] Fitzgerald's example troubles such categorization and periodization. Rather than treat Fitzgerald as an aberration or an anachronism, however, this chapter focuses on how early twentieth-century fashion offers a model for understanding the complex temporalities of his texts and persona. This is at once to indicate that the reception of Fitzgerald's work is a matter of fashion and to insist on fashion's inextricability from seemingly more substantive modes of transformation. While the uneven, shifting reception of his work is the result of numerous cultural, political, and institutional factors—including changes in the study of literature—fashion provides a means for describing the dynamic of repetition and change that emerges within and shapes our encounters with his texts and persona.

In addition to this idea of fashion's returns, being fashionable can be interpreted as a sign of permanence and persistence instead of ephemerality if it is recast as evidence of the artist-celebrity's role as the source and vector of cultural trends. That is true even if the artist's name does not remain attached to the trends he propels and the forms they produce. Fashion, then, actually sets in motion two ways of thinking about a work's effects over time: one periodic and punctuated, and the other continuous and diffuse. Of course, these temporalities also intersect; for example, a periodic reappearance might reinvigorate or set off ongoing effects. I find that a number of Fitzgerald's works, including *The Great Gatsby* (1925) and his belated modernist novel *Tender Is the Night* (1934), take up these distinct and overlapping ways of thinking about the nature of cultural influence, and that they do so via fashion. Thus Fitzgerald's attention to the connections between fashion and fiction can be understood as an effort to grasp literature and the author's cultural authority and impact beyond the realm of literary history. In that sense, Fitzgerald's work and career demonstrate what I have been arguing is fashion's centrality to conceptions of literature's uses and effects. We have seen how Woolf's work grapples with fashion as a means to sense out and convey the shape of the past and present via textual forms; how Lawrence's creations deploy and compete with fashion's capacity to touch, orient, and stimulate bodies; and how texts by Du Bois, Fauset, and Larsen formulate theories of art and politics in relation to how fashion shapes aesthetic experience and brings particular political possibilities into view. Fitzgerald's writing and persona approach literature's entanglement with fashion as a way to theorize the relationship between text and context and to conceive how texts and authors might have ongoing and unanticipated effects over time. Fitzgerald's work treats fashion and literature as interdependent sources of historical information and means of instruction, a strategy that anticipates the logic if not the specific

techniques or aims of certain late twentieth- and twenty-first-century historicist approaches to literary criticism.

Poiret and Fitzgerald's Celebrity Designs

We can begin to grasp how fashion shapes and overlaps with Fitzgerald's
concepts of literary history as well as the relationship between text and context by examining his accounts of literary movements in terms of representative authors. In 1923, Fitzgerald was one of the "Widely-Known Men and
Women" who contributed to a syndicated newspaper feature titled "Ten
Books I Have Enjoyed Most." Fitzgerald chose to annotate his "List of Favor-
ites" and make predictions about the course of literary and cultural history.
Explaining why he picked *A Portrait of the Artist as a Young Man* (1916),
Fitzgerald declares Joyce would be "the most profound literary influence in
the next fifty years." True to Fitzgerald's burgeoning reputation as a "prophet"
of his age, he doubled down on this prognostication, stating that he selected
Nostromo (1904) because it was "the great novel of the last fifty years, as
Ulysses is the great novel of the future."[13] As Fitzgerald's predictions appeared
in newspapers across the country in April, they shared space with reports
on immigration and naturalization policy as well as "forecasts" about fashion, which were a common news and advertising feature, especially in the
pivotal spring season. Indeed, Fitzgerald's claims about Joyce's influence resemble contemporaneous accounts of drop-waisted frocks; in 1923, *Ulysses*
(1922) and those dresses were considered groundbreaking as much for their
scandalous display of bodies and sex as for their formal innovation.

Fitzgerald's abbreviated, speculative literary history generates a particular place for his own work amidst this aesthetic and cultural change. He does
not describe Conrad and Joyce as part of the same movement, let alone call
it modernism, but Fitzgerald's work increasingly showed Conrad's influence,
and *This Side of Paradise*, which could be described as an American Catho-
lic bildungsroman, shared subject matter with *A Portrait of the Artist as a
Young Man*. Hence Fitzgerald could position himself as a descendent of Conrad and a close contemporary of Joyce. According to Fitzgerald's list, the
shift from Conrad and Joyce sums up literary history from 1873 to 1973,
since Conrad epitomizes the first fifty years and Joyce the second. This literary historical logic of influence and representativeness provides the terms
by which Fitzgerald—with his tendency to prophesize and his status as a Jazz
Age icon—exemplifies the figure of the author as privileged source, register, and driver of cultural forms.

Nevertheless, by the end of his life, Fitzgerald seemed to have failed to achieve the right balance between being timely and timeless—a combination epitomized in fashion by the little black dress, which Coco Chanel debuted in the mid-1920s. In contrast to such timeless chic, Fitzgerald's association with 1920s youth fashion and his production of popular fiction did not encourage the perception that he could produce such classic work. While Fitzgerald did not produce according to Chanel's model or parlay literary respect into popularity like other canonical modernists, the trajectory of his career overlaps with that of the "King of Fashion," Paul Poiret, who dominated the elite world of fashion in the first two decades of the twentieth century. Both Poiret and Fitzgerald imagine a mode of celebrity according to which the ability to generate fashions constitutes a form of art and a source of masculine authority. Poiret, for example, claimed: "I am not commercial. Ladies come to me for a gown as they go to a distinguished painter to get their portraits put on canvas. I am an artist not a dressmaker."[14] Poiret, however, made this assertion to reporters during a publicity and lecture tour in the United States, which was meant to attract clientele. This irony underscores that Poiret's and Fitzgerald's positions as artists depended on the ability to generate images of femininity that would capture the interest of women as clients or readers.[15] As Poiret's reference to portraiture reminds us, he, like Fitzgerald, was famous for shaping the vision of the modern woman. Both men presented themselves as pedagogues of taste and femininity. They conceived themselves and are described as, at once, artists, prophets, and (often rather moralizing) experts on current aesthetic and cultural values. This combination involves recasting celebrity and fashionability as consonant with masculine modernist authorship. For Poiret and Fitzgerald, their entanglement with femininity involved attempts simultaneously to solicit, manage, and distance themselves from women's interests. If their work were to have an effect, it would be in part via women's minds and bodies.

Fitzgerald's and Poiret's marriages to women who were their muses and models dramatize their intricate and intimate negotiations with fashionable modern femininity. As the epitome of the American "flapper"—whom Fitzgerald was said to have invented, publicized, and educated—Zelda represented the material and audience on which Fitzgerald's fame and income relied, especially since bold young women often featured in the stories that established his long and remunerative relationship with the *Saturday Evening Post*. Zelda also gained her own degree of fame, and the Fitzgeralds have been cited as one of the first celebrity couples.[16] Denise Poiret never had the public voice or fame that Zelda did, but she was integral to Poiret's career until the couple's divorce in 1928. She modeled his designs at high-profile events (such as the debut of Stravinsky's *Rite of Spring*) and helped to host his famous, publicity-producing parties. In an interview with *Vogue* in 1913, Poiret described Denise as "the inspiration for all my creations; she is the embodiment of my ideas."[17] Later, in his memoirs, he implied that she was one of his creations; he credited his "designer's eye" with having picked out his provincial, unsophisticated wife, who became, with the proper cultural education and clothing, "one of the Queens of Paris."[18] While celebrity is often described as the epitome of individualism or as a particular relation between a subject and a collective, here it emerges as the work of a heterosexual dyad. More specifically, in the context of the Fitzgeralds' and Poirets' highly visible marriages, celebrity became a gendered scene of education, with the husbands functioning as pedagogues and the wives as their subject matter and star pupils. It follows, then, that both Fitzgerald and Poiret framed marital conflicts as a threat to the (male) artist's legacy—particularly the artist who might be mistaken as a mere trendsetter. In turn, Zelda's and Denise's roles as models and pupils helped to frame their husbands' celebrity as consonant with the work of creating aesthetic and cultural change.

The parallels between Fitzgerald's and Poiret's personas and careers prompt us to broaden our accounts of the cultural fields in which modern celebrity emerged and circulated. Hollywood is the most obvious source for discourses and ideas of celebrity, and historians often link the emergence of the cinema to the birth of modern celebrity culture and specifically the figure of the "star."[19] Accordingly, scholars who discuss literary celebrity often compare and contrast it with cinematic models as well as those flourishing in the theater.[20] Yet the similarities between Fitzgerald's and Poiret's careers and personas—including their relationships to modern femininity, negotiations with particular temporal rhythms and categories, strategies for authorizing and classifying their work, and attempts to link cultural production to forms of education—suggest that fashion design was an arena of cultural production in which distinctive and influential models of celebrity as well as creativity and pedagogy took shape.[21] These involved particular practices for using the media, especially periodicals, to promote cultural products. From its inception, modern periodical culture was unthinkable without fashion and fiction, and vice versa.

This nexus of fashion, fiction, and periodicals also bears on the way that time and history are experienced and narrated. In the early twentieth century, writing about fashion, especially in magazines, exhibited an intense, sometimes satirical interest in what distinguished the current cultural moment from its predecessors; "smart magazines" such as *Vogue* and *Harper's Bazaar*, for example, often discussed the latest trends with an irony that nevertheless reaffirmed their expertise on the subject.[22] That focus on the nature of the present moment is paradigmatic of modernity and modernism. As a medium, the periodical offers a particular version of that temporality, since it involves repetition with a difference; each issue of a magazine promises some degree of novelty as well as a consistency in layout and general subject matter. As James Mussell observes, "The promise of succession means magazine publication is haunted by haunting, by the threat of lapsing into repetition. Each successive issue must assert its difference from its predecessor, introducing enough singularity to disrupt the rhythm but not enough to break it entirely."[23] Fitzgerald was intimately acquainted with this rhythm, as his income depended on turning out consistent (and consistently new) products, first for the *Saturday Evening Post* and later for *Esquire*. This pacing helped periodicals—from mass-market weeklies to more expensive magazines such as *Vogue*—to work symbiotically with the fashion industry, particularly in the early twentieth century when the latter was more effectively controlled by a set of fashion houses that presented new styles at regular intervals, which magazines duly observed. Design houses such as Le Maison Poiret shared the serial's pace and logic, presenting periodic innovations in given forms (dress, coat, skirt, table of contents, editorial, etc.) in order to assemble a full collection or volume while maintaining a recognizable house style. Periodicals and fashion thus worked together to produce the terms and rhythm by which continuity and transformation might be perceived and disseminated. That is the context in which a literary text might depict, mediate, resist, and effect change, as well as secure its own legacy. Indeed, fashion and periodicals' capacity to set the pace of change adds to our understanding of how and why Du Bois's treatment of beauty in *Dark Princess* should be understood in relation to the interdependent worlds of periodicals and black beauty culture. While Fitzgerald's novels do not orient themselves toward international political transformation, their paces and forms also converge and compete with those of fashion and periodicals as ways of marking, resisting, and preserving time.

The Art of the "Glorified Anecdote"

In order to tease out how fashion and periodicals shape the concepts of history and exemplarity that structure Fitzgerald's and Poiret's careers in the early twentieth century, I want to make a brief detour through Woolf's *Orlando* and ideas of history in the eighteenth century. As I note in my discussion of *The Years*, Timothy Campbell argues that modern conceptions of the past as defined by particular eras and as unrepeatable yet accessible via cultural objects developed in eighteenth-century Britain through people's encounters with the growing phenomenon of changing fashions. This bourgeois philosophy of history countered the idea of the aristocracy as naturally embodying historical continuity. As Campbell emphasizes, print cultural fashion was particularly key to the circulation of bourgeois historical sensibilities, since periodicals and literature helped to frame garments as evidence of other changes over time. Campbell notes, for example, that the practice of offering a single outfit to represent the fashion of a given year promoted the idea that years were meaningful cultural as well as temporal units.[24] We can thus understand *The Years*'s use of fashion to think through and beyond the logic of annualization (reflected in its chapter titles) in terms of the longer history that Campbell traces. *Orlando* also interrogates conventional historical thinking, including periodization. In fact, it does so in a ludic, extravagant manner that actually more closely recalls the style of leading early twentieth-century fashion magazines. Moreover, if *The Years* defies the form of the realist historical novel partly through its frequent, sudden, and seemingly arbitrary movement between characters over time, *Orlando* mocks conventional ideas of character and biography by featuring a star figure who nearly blocks all others from view, lives for centuries, and experiences the salient characteristics of an entire era by donning a new outfit. *Orlando* is fashion history exaggerated to the point of absurdity. In addition, the novel bears witness to the ways that, by the twenties, aristocratic symbols of historical continuity, from individuals such as Vita Sackville-West to estates such as Knole House, became fodder for fashion magazines.[25]

   The chapter of *Orlando* set in the eighteenth century draws particular attention to how the related phenomena of fashion, periodicals, and biography help to establish the anecdote as a key literary form and mode of historical evidence. Orlando's glimpses of Addison, Johnson, and Boswell remind us that modern biography emerged alongside modern periodical culture. The novel even briefly stages a competition between journalism, dress, and biography when it claims the latter is unnecessary because we can know Addison "to the very wrinkle of his stocking" by reading a passage from one of his essays in the *Spectator*.[26] Woolf also satirizes Boswell's detailed accounts of Johnson's sayings in the scene in which Orlando peers through a window at the two men drinking tea with Anne Williams, Johnson's companion. Unable to hear their conversation, Orlando nevertheless imagines that Johnson utters "the most magnificent phrases that have ever left human lips."[27] The import and impact of anecdotes are so predictable that Orlando can produce them for herself.

This playful treatment of historical evidence is followed by a scene that indulges in hyperbolic versions of continuous and contrastive modes of history. The chapter ends as Orlando observes and recalls an improbably detailed series of tableaux of London. She contrasts the "orderly scene" of the contemporary late eighteenth-century city with recollections of Elizabethan London. Even more fantastically, Orlando makes this comparison at the very moment that dark clouds gather to inaugurate the nineteenth century and to end that chapter of the novel. The novel mocks the dominant logic of periodicity and its celebration of representative scenes, sayings, and garments. With its preternaturally youthful protagonist, it also plays with the idea of historical continuity as located in the aristocratic body. Indeed, the apparent mutability of Orlando's body helps to collapse distinctions between bourgeois contrastive, anecdotal time and aristocratic continuous time. Instead of a clear distinction between temporal registers, we get fashion's two paces of change, the one swift and periodic and the other gradual and diffuse. Of course, these rhythms can intersect to generate repetition with a difference.

Accordingly, the chapter enacts repetition with a difference through its scenes of London. Verbal and visual tableaux of the city were a characteristic feature of eighteenth-century print culture, and the scenes often depict fashionable dress as a way to indicate that they are capturing a particular moment. The chapter's concluding scenes represent a repetition with a difference, since previously in the chapter, upon Orlando's return to London in the early eighteenth century, she also imagines and contrasts scenes of Elizabethan London with images of the contemporary city. Those early eighteenth-century tableaux, moreover, register the explosion of British fashion culture as they describe women in "flowered silk" and "citizens in broidered coats."[28] Thus the novel participates in the eighteenth century's proliferation of textual fashion—that is, fashion rendered in print, whether in words or via engravings. Yet these passages also illuminate the transhistorical force of textual fashion. After all, the novel's descriptions of dress and the city are located at once in the early eighteenth century (for Orlando), in the early twentieth century (for the narrator), and in a shifting present moment (for the reader). With this collision of temporalities, the careful balance between singularity, succession, and repetition that Mussell associates with the nineteenth-century periodical is shaken. Through *Orlando*'s textual fashion, the contrastive and the continuous jostle against each other as conditions of writing and reading. This jostling, in turn, destabilizes (but does not overturn) categories of gender, sexuality, nation, and race.[29] Revealingly, *Orlando*'s chapter on the eighteenth century contains the narrator's famously ambiguous statements about the relationship between fashion and gender, which effectively establish that no clear correspondence can be established. Dress functions as the loosening clamp holding together gender, sexual, geographic, national, racial, ontological, and temporal categories, including that of the anecdote. The novel playfully displays the absurdity and interdependence of concepts of periodicity, categories of difference, perceptions of fashion, and the logic of exemplarity.

While *Orlando* parodies the enormous historical and biographical weight carried by garments and anecdotes, those phenomena also are key to Fitzgerald's version of romantic historicism, which embraces the idea that a text, individual, and style might represent an entire age. In his review of *The Great Gatsby*, H. L. Mencken famously describes the book as "a glorified anecdote" and asserts that the novel represents the emergence of "Fitzgerald, the stylist, who arises to challenge Fitzgerald, the social historian," author of *This Side of Paradise*.[30] Yet, having set up that contrast, Mencken suggests that *Gatsby* is the work of both Fitzgeralds, for it demonstrates the author's long-standing interest in "the florid show of American life—and especially the devil's dance that goes on at the top."[31] Although Fitzgerald's novel "does not go below the surface," this elite milieu

> is worth any social historian's study, for its influence upon the rest of the country is immense and profound. What is vogue among the profiteers of Manhattan and their harlots today is imitated by the flappers of the Bible Belt country clubs weeks after next. The whole tone of American society, once so highly formalized and so suspicious of change, is now taken largely from frail ladies who were slinging hash a year ago.

What Mencken describes is a version of the "democratization" of fashion and a testament to fashion's power to effect social change—with regrettable results, in his opinion. As Mencken's references to "tone" and form imply, this is an aesthetic as well as social process. In this context, Fitzgerald's newly achieved command of style is precisely what is needed to represent social history. Moreover, what Mencken describes as Fitzgerald's growing attention to "form and organization" establishes literature as the place in which the "highly formalized" still retains its hold. This analysis echoes the familiar idea that modernism turns to form as a compensation and bulwark against cultural decline. In Fitzgerald's case, this command of style is particularly crucial in distancing him from the frivolous, formless, and fashionable world that he depicts and with which he was associated; Mencken's conceit that there are multiple Fitzgeralds highlights the entanglement between what Fitzgerald writes and who he is. Nevertheless, the idea that a "glorified anecdote" might provide the basis of a representative social history recapitulates rather than overturns fashion's logic. If celebrity is a "fashion of people," then the glorified anecdote—a term that can refer to an item of gossip—is the characteristic narrative form of celebrity and fashion, and it is one that Fitzgerald deploys throughout his career.[32] Moreover, Mencken's observations provide the terms for describing formalism as a tool of the social historian, whose command of style both gives him a perspective on the chaos and allows him to give it shape.

In "Echoes of the Jazz Age," Fitzgerald offers just such an anecdotal history of the twenties—one, moreover, that presents fashion and literature as pivotal expressions and drivers of cultural change. Published in *Scribner's Magazine* in November 1931, the essay begins by asserting, "It is too soon to write about the Jazz Age with perspective," a gesture that recalls Woolf's claim in "Modern Fiction" that her proximity to developments in literature means that she lacks the "vantage ground" from which to trace its broader historical outlines.[33] Despite this caveat, Fitzgerald, like Woolf, draws on dress and its language to sense out and describe proximate but fundamental cultural shifts. Both of their accounts turn on the figure of the Bond Street tailor— and more specifically, his waning ability to dictate style. According to Fitzgerald, America's ascent to world power is best demonstrated by the fact that "with Americans ordering suits by the gross in London, the Bond Street tailors perforce agreed to moderate their cut to the American long-waisted figure and loose-fitting taste, something subtle passed to America, the style of man."[34] What follows is a comically abbreviated version of European history, which stands in for world history: "During the Renaissance, Francis the First looked to Florence to trim his leg. Seventeenth-century England aped the court of France, and fifty years ago the German Guards officer bought his civilian clothes in London. Gentlemen's clothes—symbol of 'the power that man must hold and that passes from race to race.'" Setting the fashion epitomizes and knits together cultural, economic, and political supremacy. Yet Fitzgerald also deploys the familiar antithesis between fashion and politics to describe how, in the Jazz Age, the realm of formal politics gave way to economics and culture as determinants of geopolitical power. Hence "the events of 1919" inspired some rummaging through a trunk for a "liberty cap" and "moujik blouse" but no real interest in politics among "us"—the white, male elite that is a metonymy for the nation. Fitzgerald takes up the idea that politics are more serious than fashion but suggests that fashion nevertheless trumps politics as a defining force in contemporary life.

As is frequently the case in Fitzgerald's essays, he treats his own pronouncements with some irony, at once offering and undercutting his anecdotal, fashion-conscious approach to history. For example, he creates a bit of distance from his own assertion about the symbolic importance of "gentleman's clothes" by routing it through an unattributed and (as far as I can tell) untraceable quotation about the "power of man." This tone and technique bind this account more closely to the kinds of playful histories and ironic assertions about fashion's importance that appeared in fashion magazines. The January 1930 edition of *Harper's Bazaar*, for example, featured a mock philosophical dialogue by the famous fashion photographer Baron Adolph de Meyer in which he informs his interlocutor that "the French Revolution started by being a revolt against tight lacing" and proceeds to narrate political and dress history together, mixing historical detail with campy commentary.[35] Beside the article is a photograph by de Meyer depicting a model in a cloche, with the caption "A Black Satin Felt Tiara Hat Worn Back on the Forehead." The recasting of the cloche as tiara is a clever nod to the way 1920s dress manifests the tensions between "democracy" and aristocratic extravagance, which the article describes with respect to the French Revolution.[36] Fitzgerald's combination of didacticism and irony thus figures as yet another element of his work that makes this philosopher of the flapper representative of his age. In short, Fitzgerald's treatment of clothing as a profoundly serious and thoroughly frivolous way of understanding history is characteristic of early twentieth-century fashion magazines. His ironic treatment of the idea of fashion as history embeds him more deeply in fashion culture.

Fitzgerald's and the magazine's ironic, anecdotal account of fashion as a symbol and driver of change also provides the terms by which "Echoes of the Jazz Age" describes literature's effects on cultural life. According to the essay, fiction reflects and fuels cultural shifts, particularly insofar as it serves as a source of information about sex for young people and provides an "intensive education" about current sexual mores for "people over twenty-five."[37] Fitzgerald's history-cum-syllabus for this adult education reads like a parody of cultural studies approaches to modernist literature, as he places highbrow modernist texts beside popular novels and emphasizes the discourses and phenomena that they register and convey:

We begin with the suggestion that Don Juan leads an interesting life (*Jurgen*, 1919); then we learn that there's a lot of sex around if we only knew it (*Winesburg, Ohio*, 1920), that adolescents lead very amorous lives (*This Side of Paradise*, 1920), that there are a lot of neglected Anglo-Saxon words (*Ulysses*, 1921), that older people don't always resist sudden temptations (*Cytherea*, 1922), that girls are sometimes seduced without being ruined (*Flaming Youth*, 1922), that even rape often turns out well (*The Sheik*, 1922), that glamorous English ladies are often promiscuous (*The Green Hat*, 1924), that in fact they devote most of their time to it (*The Vortex*, 1926), that it's a damn good thing too (*Lady Chatterley's Lover*, 1928), and finally that there are abnormal variations (*The Well of Loneliness*, 1928, and *Sodom and Gomorrah*, 1929).[38]

This nearly year-by-year chronology enables Fitzgerald to mention *This Side of Paradise* alongside *Ulysses*, because the latter is misdated (as are a number of other works).[39] It also establishes Fitzgerald's first novel as paradigmatic of, simultaneously, Jazz Age "adolescents," his own youth, the emerging era, and its literature, since *This Side of Paradise* appears to pave the way for subsequent literary and sexual revelations. The essay describes the Jazz Age as a ten-year period in which initial and ultimately fairly innocent expressions of adolescents' sexuality, such as those depicted in *This Side of Paradise*, yield to the more hedonistic and destructive indulgences of their elders.

Fitzgerald's method for narrating the era as a series of representative and influential works of literature resembles what Campbell notes is the long-standing practice by which popular periodicals (including, but not limited to, fashion magazines) offer a parade of fashions representing a given set of seasons, years, or decades. The importance of fashion to Fitzgerald's romantic historicism also becomes clear if we consider "Echoes of the Jazz Age" in the context of specific developments in the U.S. magazine industry of the 1920s and early 1930s. In that period, smart magazines such as *Vanity Fair* and fashion magazines such as (American) *Vogue* and especially *Harper's Bazaar* combined information about clothes and literature in each glamorous number. While fashion was often treated as synonymous with women's dress, the men's clothing industry underpinned and informed developments in magazines. *Vanity Fair*, for example, was launched in 1913 after Condé Nast bought the men's fashion magazine *Dress*; the new magazine was originally called *Dress and Vanity Fair*. That title neatly echoes Fitzgerald's pairing of "gentleman's clothes" and literature in "Echoes of the Jazz Age," particularly as Thackeray's *Vanity Fair* was on Fitzgerald's 1923 list of top ten books. While the magazine quickly dropped its clumsy compound title, it continued to try to address male and female readers. Nevertheless, in 1933 *Esquire* was launched, aimed at what it described as an underserved audience of men who wanted a magazine focused on "masculine interests." It included articles and fiction by writers including Hemingway and "The Scott Fitzgerald" alongside an extensive focus on dress, since *Esquire* proposed to be "a fashion guide for men"—but not, however, for "fops."[40] *Esquire* became a key outlet for Fitzgerald's late work; as James L. W. West III observes, in the last six years of his life, Fitzgerald "was not a [*Saturday Evening*] *Post* writer; he was an *Esquire* writer."[41] From *Esquire*'s first issue, Fitzgerald represented the intersection of literature and men's clothing; the caption under a photograph of Ring Lardner accompanying his article "Princeton Panorama" cited *This Side of Paradise* as a definitive vision of the university, which was a "fountainhead of young men's fashions."[42] So even as "Echoes of the Jazz Age" insists on a break between decades, its emphasis on the power of fashion, literature, and magazines anticipates the means by which, in *Esquire*, Fitzgerald could exemplify the twenties and serve as a model for the thirties.

Nevertheless, "Echoes" was not published in a magazine that showed much interest in fashion. *Scribner's* was a more sober, serious publication with roots in the nineteenth century and the imprimatur of a distinguished publishing house. Yet its status as a "quality" magazine also made it a fine perch from which Fitzgerald could deliver his pronouncement on the hedonistic Jazz Age after its death. *Scribner's* was not a "big magazine" catering to a wide readership, but neither was it a relatively unknown "little magazine" associated with modernism; as a "quality" magazine it addressed itself to an established, highly influential American cultural elite.[43] While it did not focus on fashion or sex, it could be depended on to provide "people over twenty-five" with timely information about the latest and greatest books. *Scribner's* is thus an example of the kind of periodical that made it possible for Fitzgerald to imagine that literature might approximate fashion's cultural influence.

In "Echoes of the Jazz Age," the connections between fashion and literature as mediums for grasping and narrating cultural history establish particular geographical and racial coordinates for that culture. While Fitzgerald asserts that "the style of man" is in America's possession, his account of Bond Street tailors moderating their cuts suggests something closer to an asymmetrical exchange in which shifting economic and geopolitical conditions lead to new, hybrid forms. That paradigm of Anglo-American style sets the groundwork for Fitzgerald's depiction of this supposedly American era in terms of British and American texts (with *Ulysses* highlighted for its "Anglo-Saxon" vocabulary and with nods to Latin America and France).[44] These mutually reinforcing descriptions of Anglo-American literature and dress also serve to downplay the power of two other forms of cultural production with a potentially greater social impact: movies and music—namely, jazz. A number of the novels that Fitzgerald lists, particularly *Flaming Youth*, became more famous as movies, but he insists that the cinema's depiction of sexuality was tamer and belated, as magazines had already begun to "celebrate" the "younger generation" by 1923. Given the essay's title, it is especially striking that it devotes greater attention to dress and print culture than to the music of the era. Fitzgerald's turn to the Bond Street tailors is also illustrative in that respect, for if the sound of jazz haunts the essay, so too does the figure of the black dandy, with its connections to both black minstrelsy and black modernity.[45] Having mentioned Bond Street and observed power passing "from race to race" via dress, Fitzgerald claims, "We were the most powerful nation. Who else could tell us what was fashionable and what was fun? Isolated during the European war, we had begun combing the unknown South and West for folkways and pastimes."[46] Though "folkways and pastimes" refers more directly to social habits and entertainment rather than dress, the pursuit of what is "fashionable" as well as the textile and capillary metaphor of "combing" keeps matters of adornment and self-fashioning in view. While Bond Street might be the location where Anglo-American style is forged, further styling occurs elsewhere; fashion becomes a medium through which the essay acknowledges and manages the influence of racialized and working-class forms of cultural production. That strategy helps to preserve a place for Anglo-American literature as a key interpreter and driver of American culture.

Representative Figures

I have been arguing that "Echoes of the Jazz Age" celebrates a kind of anecdotal, fashion-conscious cultural historicism, which Mencken associates with *The Great Gatsby* and which resembles romantic approaches to history as made up of discrete eras that are imaginable if not recoverable via particular cultural objects. Yet "Echoes of the Jazz Age" does not mention *The Great Gatsby*; in fact, Fitzgerald's odd syllabus does not include any book from 1925, thus leaving a gap at the heart of this ten-year period. Nevertheless, the essay in many ways recapitulates the dynamics and features of Fitzgerald's "glorified anecdote." Thus the essay's history of the "Age"—in which youthful romance yields to disillusionment and dissolution, amounting to "the most expensive orgy in history"—enables the novel to represent the period as a whole. In addition, Fitzgerald's claim about the symbolism of "gentleman's clothes" offers a way to see the novel as an expression of the zeitgeist.[47] If the "style of man" is transformed by American orders for Bond Street suits, then Jay Gatsby and Tom Buchanan embody that demand. Tom first appears in "riding clothes"—a sartorial sign of Anglophilia—and Gatsby, in one of the novel's most famous scenes, shows Nick and Daisy the shirts that are sent to him by "a man in England who buys me clothes. He sends over a selection every season."[48] Discussing this line, Meredith Goldsmith concludes that Gatsby "is unaccountable for his own sartorial style, relegating the job to a middleman."[49] But the sheer number of shirts that Gatsby possesses suggests he has some latitude in selecting his rather outré ensembles. Indeed, as Goldsmith also argues, Gatsby's sometimes inept self-fashioning recalls Jewish American narratives of assimilation and African American tales of passing, which hinge on the capacity and failure of men's clothing to project an upper-middle-class Anglo-American body. It is thus telling that Gatsby errs in adjusting the color as well as the cut of aristocratic British styles; Tom, for example, presents Gatsby's pink suit as evidence that he cannot be an "Oxford man" (*GG*, 122). Tom and Gatsby's aesthetics thus place them at different points in the spectrum of Anglo-American style, with the former exemplifying more tasteful adjustments to Bond Street's silhouette. Fitzgerald outfits both characters in garments that announce their capacity to represent broader social trends and forces. In that sense, the men's suits function like representative anecdotes.[50]

"Echoes of the Jazz Age" also provides the terms for perceiving *The Great Gatsby* as representative of the era because the novel, like the essay, addresses the logic of historical representativeness—specifically, the marking and understanding of change over time via exemplary cultural phenomena, especially visual and verbal depictions of fashion. *The Great Gatsby* confirms that to interrogate representativeness is to be representative of the era, while to do so spectacularly makes one spectacularly so. Moreover, both the essay and the novel specifically register the ways that this mode of historicism flourished in periodicals. "Echoes of the Jazz Age," for example, describes magazines as fueling social change by depicting "the younger generation"—a phrase that organizes all people of a certain age around a consummate set of styles, behaviors, and figures. This approach to representativeness overlaps with the logic not only of the anecdote, but also of the cliché. The relations between periodicals, anecdotes, clichés, and modes of historicism—as well as British men's fashion—emerge in the scene in which Nick describes listening to Gatsby fabricate his personal history as they drive to New York. Nick says the experience "was like skimming hastily through a dozen magazines" (*GG*, 66). This simile captures the romantic, frenetic, secondhand, and patchwork quality of Gatsby's life story, which takes him from a wealthy childhood in "the middle-west" (where Gatsby locates his fictional hometown, San Francisco), to an extravagant young manhood "living like a young rajah in the all capitals of Europe," then the war, and Oxford (*GG*, 65). Nick's comment registers the way that magazines circulate popular fantasies, which

Gatsby fails to arrange into a believable sequence. Yet Nick's doubts dissolve when presented with a photograph of Gatsby holding a "cricket bat" with a group of men in "blazers" at Oxford. Nick's conclusion—"it was all true"—can be read as a reaction to photography's purportedly more factual status. But it also presents an image of an American in British "gentleman's clothes" as the linchpin for the various clichés circulated by periodicals, which Gatsby's version of his own history otherwise fails to make cohere. Playing out Fitzgerald's concept of the Bond Street tailor, Anglo-American men's clothing gives weight and heft to the images and narratives that are otherwise quickly recognizable as fiction and fantasy.

Nick's reference to magazines in this scene also offers a way to reread his earlier proposal that "if personality is an unbroken series of successful gestures, then there was something gorgeous about him" (*GG*, 2). The scene in Gatsby's car suggests that, in a magazine- and celebrity-saturated culture, personality and personal history can be understood as a "series" not simply of "gestures" but also of the images and scenes in periodicals. The novel is in fact filled with references to serial print culture, from the *Saturday Evening Post* to New York newspapers and popular tabloids. In piecing together an unbelievable life story, however, Gatsby fails to achieve the steady pace and coherence generated by a magazine as it appears issue by issue; instead, he seems to bring together disparate material from various publications, and to present them at a frantic pace. By contrast, what Linda K. Hughes and Michael Lund describe as the periodical's "progress and pause" across and between issues parallels Nick's vision of gestures that are at once discrete and part of an "unbroken series."[51] Periodicals promise new material in each number but also a certain consistency in layout, style, and content across issues. This produces a particular temporality; as Mussell observes, "Serial publication resists the ruptures and closures, the events that mark before and after necessary for narrative."[52] Seriality offers, instead, repetition with a certain predictable degree of difference as well as a sense of time as accumulation, as back issues collect.

While this rhythm and logic resist the shape of narrative, they resemble the temporality that, according to Nick, Gatsby imagines will characterize his romance with Daisy. Gatsby seeks a repetition of a past that will be altered only by the fact that Gatsby has accumulated a fortune and hence a history. (The hint that Gatsby's wealth derives in part from bond fraud signifies his attempt to convert time into money at a breakneck pace.) This accumulation of the past—which, nevertheless, enables it to be repeated—is epitomized by a shift of dress. According to Nick, Gatsby's first seduction of Daisy was made possible by "the invisible cloak of Gatsby's uniform," which concealed that he was then "at present a penniless man without a past" (*GG*, 149). In turn, Gatsby is determined that his newer garments will display the fabricated history that he wants to bear. In short, Gatsby's conviction that one might "repeat the past" and thereby "recover" what "had gone into loving Daisy" does not just borrow images and tropes from the sentimental stories circulated by periodicals (*GG*, 116, 110). This approach to time reproduces fashion and periodicals' ways of marking, managing, and gathering time as steady accumulation. It especially highlights dress's capacity to transfigure history and time into matter and form.

Fashion and the periodical characterize Gatsby's orientation toward the future as well as the past—necessarily so, since, for Gatsby, moving into the future involves repeating the past with a carefully managed difference. This dynamic also applies to Nick and his narrative; the novel draws attention to the fact that Nick's recollection and writing of Gatsby's story takes time, and takes place after he has returned to the Midwest from New York. Mussell observes that the periodical is recursive and does not prepare for or imagine its own end; while allowing for progress and accumulation, it aims for continuity and an endless future. This is akin to the attitude that Nick ascribes to Gatsby in the book's opening passages: a "gift for hope, a romantic readiness" (*GG*, 2). Nick also attributes his own readiness to listen to other young men's "revelations" to a kind of "hope," which wavers when Gatsby falls: it is "what preyed on Gatsby, what foul dust floated in the wake of his dreams that temporarily closed out my interest in the abortive sorrows and short-winded elations of men." As Nick receives the too-brief utterances of members of his generation, he functions as a writer and as an archivist and potential editor, gathering disparate materials that speak to and for a particular cultural moment.[53] Thus both Nick and Gatsby possess a "hope" that might transcend closure and abbreviation and provide instead versions of the punctuated, accumulative time that characterizes periodicals.

If Nick operates as a kind of editor, the question remains if and how the anecdotes and stories he selects might represent a given period and theme, as the number of a serial usually promises to do. The novel raises a similar question when, in this midst of chapter 3, Nick breaks from recounting a series of events from June and July 1922 (which include his dinner at the Buchanans; meeting Myrtle, and the gathering at her and Tom's apartment; and his first party at Gatsby's). Nick notes that what he has conveyed does not accurately reflect his experience of that time: "Reading over what I have written so far I see I have given the impression that the events of three nights several weeks apart were all that absorbed me. On the contrary, they were merely casual events in a crowded summer and, until much later, they absorbed me infinitely less than my personal affairs" (*GG*, 55–56). This moment draws attention to the ways that the narrative manages and obscures the gaps between episodes; that type of time management is a characteristic task of the serial, since it must establish a particular (if potentially variable) relationship between its own intermittent appearances and the flow of time. Nick describes this technique as misleading insofar as it does not represent his experience in Long Island and New York in the early summer of 1922. But his attempt to describe this period more accurately ends up recapitulating the key features of Gatsby's story: the pursuit of unattainable women ("I would pick out romantic women from the crowd and imagine that in a few minutes I was going to enter into their lives"); exclusion from the "intimate excitement" enjoyed by other people set against the sense of the "racy, adventurous feel" of New York; and Nick's discovery of Jordan's dishonesty and bad driving, which foreshadows Daisy's betrayal of Gatsby and killing of Myrtle (*GG*, 56).

We could read this as evidence that Nick shapes Gatsby's story through the lens of his own experience or that Gatsby's story has irrevocably shaped his recollection of the other events of the summer. As Christopher P. Wilson observes, however, this passage also exhibits "many of the features of its historical moment—the city as a place of restless, flickering glances and hidden assignations" as well as a typical mode of perception. Plus, Wilson observes, Nick exhibits the combination of "voyeurism, confession, and wistful desire that is often said to characterize the readers of . . . mass literary forms" from the *Saturday Evening Post* to gossip magazines and popular westerns.[54] In short, these episodes seem representative, and not only of Nick's particular concerns and experiences. Indeed, early twenty-first-century readers—or at least a critical mass of scholars of the early twentieth-century United States—continue to accept and reproduce this vision of the period. This dynamic could be understood as evidence of both Fitzgerald's capacity to capture the feeling of the time and his continued power to shape the terms by which we perceive the era.

Wilson's interest in the way that this scene encapsulates a broader cultural phenomenon also reminds us of the prestige of the anecdote in historicist literary criticism. New Historicist scholarship is notorious for deploying historical anecdotes, often at the beginning of an academic piece, to exemplify the particular discourses that the critic then traces in, through, and around literary texts. Accordingly, in their resolutely inconclusive review of New Historicist practices, Catherine Gallagher and Stephen Greenblatt examine the literary and critical function of the anecdote. In keeping with their New Historicist principles, they emphasize the anecdote's ability to call into question the nature of historical knowledge and practices of representation and representativeness rather than its capacity to "epitomize epochal truths."[55] As I have been arguing, Fitzgerald's work and persona invest in the idea that the anecdote, like the single text or garment, can represent an era. At the same time, his texts' efforts to construct and maintain that understanding of cultural production expose the fragility of those concepts.

While Gallagher and Greenblatt disavow ideas of representativeness and periodicity, those concepts motivate much historicist work. In a critique of recent practices, Eric Hayot asserts, "Almost everyone now thinks 'new historically,' but no one is really a New Historicist anymore. Such thinking is enough, since it has inculcated a strong unstated theory of *era* as the final goal and subtending force of the intimacies of literary criticism, fixing at the ideological level a powerful theory of periods as social formations."[56] Hayot emphasizes New Historicism's skepticism about periodization as well as what constitutes historical knowledge and evidence. Thus Hayot narrates the shift in literary practices as a "loss," since contemporary "thinking" occurs without the theoretical nuance or critical force of New Historicism. Yet we could also describe the ascendance of that style of thinking as a reemergence with a difference, since it recalls the refashioned romantic historicism practiced by Fitzgerald and deployed by Mencken.

The Great Gatsby itself conceives history in terms of both repetition and loss. In addition to enshrining the anecdote, *The Great Gatsby* is structured through repetition and the manipulation of seriality. To be more specific: while periodical time is characterized by a combination of cycles and progress, *The Great Gatsby* makes it such that the movement forward in time through a series of chapters also generates a backwards and downward spiral, driving us toward Gatsby's violent death but also his past as well as the origins of the nation and of European settlement. So young Gatsby's daily schedule for self-improvement, which his father shows Nick before the funeral, is a pathetic echo of the daily plan devised by Ben Franklin, a founding figure of U.S. print culture and politics. Gatsby's Franklinesque plan invites us to read the periodical as a particularly American form, since, like Gatsby's and Franklin's planned daily routines, its regular "progress and pause" is a template for orderly reinvention. Indeed, the novel's emphasis on recurrence and imitation generates an association between Americanness and print in general, since, as Mussell observes, "the logic of print is repetition," though "of all print genres it is the serial that embodies this most fully."[57] Yet the incommensurability of Gatsby's and Franklin's careers present U.S. history and periodical time as a story of repetition and decay. If Franklin creates the press and is one of its first products, then Gatsby is a later, inevitably inferior copy. The contrast between Gatsby and Franklin also points to the economic, cultural, and racial and ethnic structures that foreclose the promise of American opportunity.

Despite these indications of decay and foreclosure, the novel implies that these cycles will continue. Narrative and readerly time converge with annual, seasonal, and daily cycles in the final scene when Nick proclaims Gatsby's romantic belief in "the orgastic future that year by year recedes before us. It eluded us then, but that's no matter—tomorrow we will run faster, stretch out our arms farther . . ." (*GG*, 180). Via Gatsby—and more specifically, Nick's vision of him—those natural and erotic temporalities fuse with periodical and fashion time, which become the rhythm by which Gatsby, *The Great Gatsby*, and readers together "beat on, boats against the current" and are "borne ceaselessly into the past." So, as Nick stands looking at the sound and shore at the end of the fashionable "season," "the current" suggests oceanic cycles and what is au courant—that is, fashions and ways of knowing. The contrast and convergence between the scales and rhythms in this scene confirm fashion and narrative (particularly, that rendered in print) as the primary means, however inadequate and even trivializing, by which "we" sense planetary rhythms and understand our relation to them.[58] This moment, then, establishes Gatsby and *The Great Gatsby*'s continued relevance, but does so based on the melancholy idea that its modes of apprehending time and space, though deeply flawed, will not be surpassed.

Philosophers of Fashion

I have argued that *The Great Gatsby* makes use of the ways that print-cultural fashion, especially in serials, was naturalized as a means of marking change over time. But while Fitzgerald's most critically acclaimed novel engages periodicals via its form and content, he insisted on its qualitative and quantitative difference from his stories published in magazines.[59] Fitzgerald asserted this distinction between his novels and his stories throughout his career, and a key means of differentiation was time: he often described his short stories as written hastily and for money, which would allow him the time to compose his novels. Fitzgerald's concern with time extended to the schedule of his work's publication; in 1928, when he believed he would soon complete *Tender Is the Night*, he proposed to Perkins that he would put out a short story collection "to follow my novel in the season *immediately* after, so as not to seem in the direct line of my so-called 'work.'"[60] Seven years later, that collection was published as *Taps at Reveille*. The idea that the literary artist might produce two categories of writing and that his reputation might rest on the aesthetically superior type diverges from what critics have described as modernist models of authorship. Aaron Jaffe, for example, argues that Eliot, Pound, Joyce, and Wyndham Lewis employed a "literary economics" of "scarcity" and rhetorics of masculine condescension in order to establish the value of their work.[61] The worth of what Jaffe terms the author's "imprimatur" or brand thus depended on the consistent quality of his output and, presumably, would be damaged or diluted by the rapid appearance of inferior products under his name. Such a system helps to organize the literary field in a condition of "overproduction," which we could also understand as a condition of insufficient time; by building expectations around selected writers, one could winnow the field and direct intellectual resources accordingly. Fitzgerald, then, did not entirely dismiss this logic. Rather, he insisted on the scarcity of his own "so-called 'work'" while, in effect, overproducing his own writing.

This strategy has proven largely effective, at least in terms of the academic reception of Fitzgerald's oeuvre, since scholars (myself included) focus far more frequently on his novels. Nevertheless, Fitzgerald's attempts to draw categorical distinctions between his publications belie the many connections between his novels and short fiction. For example, late in his career, Fitzgerald often took—in his words, "stripped"—material from his short stories to use in his novels; *Tender Is the Night* contains numerous passages from previously published stories in which Fitzgerald worked out key themes and ideas, and crafted the sorts of gorgeous descriptions for which he was and is known.[62] Observing this practice, Bryant Mangum describes the short stories as "workshops" for the novels, especially *Tender*.[63] Indeed, this practice suggests another type of temporal relationship between his stories and the novel, with the former constituting potential and actual first drafts of the latter. In turn, the short stories often recapitulated themes, figures, and ideas—mostly famously in the case of the flapper heroine—and some of those also had appeared earlier in novels. In that sense, the stories can be conceived as partial copies of each other *and* of parts of the novels. Despite such reproduction, Fitzgerald's plans for *Taps at Reveille* show him negotiating the distinction between a stylistic stamp and a reproducible copy. He tried to ensure that none of the stories contained any passages that also appeared in *Tender*, despite the fact that the stories had already been published in periodicals with those passages. This strategy shaped Fitzgerald's selections and required a substantial amount of excising and rewriting the stories before *Taps at Reveille* could be issued. Fitzgerald thus sought to distinguish not only between his novels and his short stories, but also between his published volumes of short stories and those in periodicals, thereby creating three overlapping categories of work. Branding was key to that scheme. Fitzgerald insisted that the binding of all of his books, including those of short stories, "be absolutely uniform," thereby signaling that, timing notwithstanding, all of his volumes were in line with each other.[64]

Fitzgerald's mode of production differs in key respects from that of modernists with whom he hoped to be and is associated. But it resembles the strategies developed by elite fashion designers just before and after World War I, particularly as they addressed the growing U.S. market. The "democratization" of fashion in this period involved an increased demand for designer clothing, which included both unauthorized copies of designs from famous houses and attempts by designers to market less expensive garments. Once again, Poiret helps to elucidate the logic of Fitzgerald's career, as the designer was at the forefront of efforts to battle piracy and to devise ways of profiting from changes in the market. As Nancy Troy notes, Poiret effectively created a new category of goods, the so-called genuine reproduction, when he designed a spring 1917 collection for the U.S. market.[65] Rather than selling patterns or producing the clothing in France and attempting to ship it to the United States (which was nearly impossible due to the war and otherwise expensive due to import taxes), Poiret advertised designs that could be ordered at lower (though hardly modest) prices, and which were produced by selected companies. Each garment bore a Poiret label containing its signature image of a rose and also the phrase "reproduction autorisée," thereby indicating each piece's affiliation with and difference from Poiret's more exclusive creations.

Advertising for the items emphasized that they displayed Poiret's distinctive method and aesthetic. In the luxurious catalog, for example, a coat bearing the name "Cecile" was said to have "been created . . . by a gesture, in a flash of time, with that incomparable *élan* that gives the Poiret coats their unmistakable character."[66] Even if the garment is made outside of Maison Poiret, it shows his inimitable touch. Bolstered by such rhetoric, Poiret's innovative, two-tiered classification system provided a potential way for him to benefit from the commercial value of his name without undermining that value insofar as it depended on an economics of scarcity. This scheme offered, in short, a solution to Fitzgerald's dilemma. Yet this approach was more available to (if not entirely successful for) Poiret precisely because the status of the designer as an artist was even less certain than that of the novelist. Whereas the author's signature was tied to romantic conceptions of the artist's singular vision, the designer's label by this period was more clearly a corporate sign. It is for that reason that the catalog refers to Poiret's unique touch, and it is why he insisted so strenuously on his status as an artist. Nevertheless, as Mencken's references to "Fitzgerald the social historian" and "Fitzgerald the stylist" suggest, Fitzgerald's output pushed the boundaries of contemporary constructions of authorship such that he might even be said to produce under different labels. Because fashion was an arena in which ideas of creativity were renegotiated, it offered Fitzgerald a method for preserving the aura of authorship and originality.

Poiret's venture was not particularly successful, but it represented an innovative and symptomatic response to changes in the fashion industry, as more rapid forms of communication and systems of production made copying designer garments easier. By 1929, Poiret was forced to sell his business, and he never recovered anything like his former glory and influence. Fitzgerald's decline was less precipitous, but in the 1930s both men ended up publishing reflections on the earlier period during which they were figures of fashion. The year 1931 saw the publication of "Echoes of the Jazz Age" and *King of Fashion*, the English translation of Poiret's memoir *En habillant l'époque* (1930). Like "Echoes" (but without Fitzgerald's irony), *King of Fashion* provides an anecdotal history that embraces fashion as a form of authority and a material expression of history (as its French and English titles suggest). Poiret also discusses the extent to which designers in the postwar period were forced to adapt the "lines of the American mode," although he focuses on women's dress and harshly condemns this trend, which he associates with his own declining authority.[67] Though Poiret studiously avoids mentioning her in *King of Fashion*, Coco Chanel is the couturier most closely tied to the new "lines" of the 1920s as well as to the culture of the copy. As Jessica Burstein notes, Chanel's often relatively simple designs could be more easily imitated, yet this served to bolster the visibility of her brand. Meanwhile, for those in the know, an authentic Chanel remained recognizable and more valuable.[68] So, despite their different attitudes toward copying, both Chanel and Poiret tried to use imitation to bolster the value of their original creations.

In *King of Fashion*, Poiret attempts to reclaim his authority by describing how he shaped fashion and, especially, art. A chapter titled "My Influence" begins, "People have been good enough to say that I have exercised a powerful influence over my age, and that I have inspired the whole of my generation."[69] Though he feigns modesty, he sets out to substantiate this claim. But while Poiret asserts that his impact on fashion was profound, he also notes that it is once again needed, insofar as the bright colors with which he transformed dress are no longer seen. His influence on theater and art seems more lasting. With respect to the former, Poiret makes an unusual and repeated address to the reader, prompting "you" to "remember" his costumes and the scenery for *Le Minaret* and (the fittingly titled) *Plus ça change*.[70] With this gesture, Poiret's own memory and that of the reader become evidence of his influence as he closes the gap between the present and the time of those performances. Regarding art, Poiret is more definite about describing his impact over time, as he celebrates the careers of Paul Iribe and André Dunoyer de Segonzac, whom he claims to have discovered and influenced. The evidence of his influence on art also is more concrete, as he announces that the "well known" book of Iribe's illustrations of Poiret's designs—*Les Robes de Paul Poiret, racontées par Paul Iribe*—"to-day is to be found in every artist's and art lover's library."[71] Though Poiret does not emphasize it, this album was most remarkable for the unusual intersection between fashion illustration, art, advertising, and journalism that it represented.[72] In 1908, Poiret commissioned Iribe to create images of Poiret's recent dress designs, which were then gathered in the album and distributed to Poiret's top clients. The book thus elevates the ephemeral media of fashion illustration, dress catalogue, and fashion journal into high art. *Les Robes de Paul Poiret* is the most specific material evidence of his glorious career that Poiret proffers; his own possessions have been sold, and he even remains uncertain whether there are any remaining examples of one his most important designs—a coat made from material decorated by Raoul Dufy. Yet the image of Iribe's book in "every artist's and art lover's library" invites us to imagine that *King of Fashion*—the very book that readers hold in their hands—might find a place there as well. It is fitting then that the final chapter, "The Philosopher," draws attention to the imperfect formula that converts time and body into sheets of paper and text: "Here it is, whole and entire, this life that has lasted fifty years. It has gone into a volume of three hundred and thirty-one pages."[73] If fashion fails to reflect Poiret's lasting influence, writing provides a more tangible and lasting archive, whereby time is gathered and preserved thanks to the taste of so-called art lovers rather than the whims of female clients.

For Poiret, writing extends his techniques for managing time, particularly the tensions between ephemerality and immortality that characterize fashion and fashion design, since he can set down in print the fleeting accomplishments that took on meaning precisely because of their exquisite timing. Another fleeting form of art that Poiret seeks to capture in print is that of hosting parties. He describes in some detail his most famous fêtes, including the "Thousand and Second Night," a luxurious Orientalist fantasy in which Poiret played the role of a sultan, cast Denise as his "favourite," and required his guests to don "Persian" outfits in order to enter his home and garden, which served as the setting for many of his events.[74] As Poiret describes, at the height of the party, he let Denise out of a cage where he had her locked and she fled through the crowd. "Did we know, on that evening" he sighs, "we were rehearsing the drama of our lives?" As Ilya Parkins suggests, Denise in this moment epitomizes Poiret's frustrated attempt to master femininity, which is also an attempt to master time; femininity represents the ephemerality that Poiret must control and surpass, but also the inexhaustible matter from which his reputation and immortality might be made. Parkins argues that the need to establish and manage one's relationship to time is fundamental to the career of any fashion designer.[75] As she shows, for Poiret, this struggle especially occurs via his relationship to American women, whose growing power in the fashion industry coincides with his eclipse.

King of Fashion works to secure Poiret's legacy in part by linking writing and design to transformative education, specifically that of girls and women. This education is woven into the processes of producing and consuming Poiret's creations. One of the ventures that Poiret celebrates and mourns is his "School of Decorative Arts." The school gathered girls from "working class districts of Paris" (apparently without payment, save for "prizes") and encouraged them to go about "copying nature" in their sketches, which he compares to Henri Rousseau's compositions.[76] Poiret then selected some of these "motifs" for the "stuffs" he sold at his interior design studio, Maison Martine, which bore the name of one of his daughters. He also had the pupils learn to "weave with their own hands" so that the "fresh and living" quality of their designs might not be lost in translation. Poiret credits his laissez-faire teaching methods for the success of this venture, which helped him to become the first couturier to sell a lifestyle along with clothes—a phenomenon that inspired Roger Fry and was particularly resented by D. H. Lawrence. Poiret regrets that the school had to close, and invites the reader to imagine what artistic innovations it could have spurred ("Where would the *Martine* school have arrived by now, if it had been able to continue?").[77]

While the Martine school may be irrecoverable, *King of Fashion* archives and reanimates Poiret's efforts as a teacher. Poiret describes his marriage to Denise as a process of education, and the volume devotes its antepenultimate chapter to excerpts from lectures that Poiret delivered during trips to the United States. Most of the material seems to come from his 1927 tour rather than those of 1913 or 1922 (and he provides locations but not dates for these talks).[78] The speeches offer philosophical reflections on fashion and the nature of fashion design, as well as comments on American women's resistance to innovation. Poiret makes a few specific, timely comments about dress—such as the prediction that women would wear jupes-culottes—but he mostly offers generalities about the nature of design and fashion, which he explains, variously, in terms of "evolution" and women's "caprice."[79] In these lectures, Poiret's designs, his experiences, and the women whom he dressed and addressed become the material out of which he fashions potentially more lasting ideas. By including his lectures in the memoir, Poiret transforms belatedness into current wisdom that might shape the future.

While Fitzgerald's reputation as the philosopher of the flapper encapsulates his attempt to fashion and explain yet also transcend his frivolous, feminized era by appearing as a celebrity, artist, and educator, so, too, does Poiret's bid for immortality rely on the seemingly paradoxical idea of the philosopher of fashion. In that sense, Fitzgerald's and Poiret's careers demonstrate how various forms of modernist cultural production anticipate the afterlives they will lead in the realms of consumer culture and education. But rather than exemplifying the familiar stories of modernism's midcentury commodification and its institutionalization in universities, Fitzgerald and Poiret resemble something closer to celebrity artist-intellectuals, who combine commodification with extramural instruction. Their celebrity also involves forms of education that transcend the dynamics of emulation associated with the Hollywood star and that flourish beyond the university. Indeed, their pedagogical approaches resemble those found in various early twentieth-century periodicals, from the didacticism exhibited in "quality" magazines such as *Scribner's* to the cosmopolitan, often ironic instruction offered by leading fashion journals such as *Harper's Bazaar*. Moreover, the role of the celebrity artist-intellectual provides a way to occupy distinct and potentially reinforcing temporalities. While celebrity and fashion involve often unpredictable repetition (if not simply obsolescence), the time of education appears more accumulative, progressive, static, or steadily cyclic and thus more manageable. Fitzgerald's and Poiret's shifts to retrospection and didacticism mark the ways that the pedagogical work of generating historical and philosophical order out of such chaotic material as fashion can help to secure a place in some order. The next section addresses how Fitzgerald and Poiret reconcile the logic and temporality of education with those of fashion in order to secure a future for themselves and their work. These strategies represent further means by which modernist cultural production has shaped the terms of its reception.

Teaching Design/History in Tender Is the Night

Tender Is the Night examines the relationships between celebrity, fashion, art, and education, as well as what it means to set a fashion—and to be surpassed by newer trends. The ill-fated hero, Dick Diver, is a kind of fashionable philosopher, whose lifestyle is a form of art and a means of education, particularly for women. He is also briefly perceived as a king of fashion; he and his wife, Nicole, are credited with having "invented" the expatriate summer season on the French Riviera, although, by the end of the novel, he is "deposed" as its ruler.[80] In settling on the Riviera, Dick steps away (temporarily but ruinously) from a promising career as a psychiatrist, which had led him to Nicole, a former patient and heiress who underwrites their lavish lifestyle. Dick shows a tendency for philosophizing and pedantry in his personal and professional lives, which become inextricable; a fellow student in Vienna warns him not to model himself too much on a "romantic philosopher" and a colleague later jokes that Dick's weakness for "generalities" will lead him to "writing little books called 'Deep Thoughts for the Layman'" (*TN*, 117, 138). Psychiatric treatment is also described as a process of being "'re-educated'" and of being "stitched" together (*TN*, 153, 137). But while Nicole becomes "well-knit," Dick unravels; though his first book, *A Psychology for Psychiatrists*, finds some success, he struggles to finish his second project as their relationship collapses (*TN*, 171). Over the course of the novel, Dick's lessons in how to live are absorbed and superseded by Nicole and his admirer-turned-lover, Rosemary Hoyt. When the novel begins in June 1925, Rosemary is a Hollywood starlet who encounters the Divers while holidaying on the Riviera with her mother, who recognizes that the Divers can provide a kind of finishing school for Rosemary, whose career depends on her sophistication and feminine allure. But while Dick may provide an education for these women, he cannot claim to be the exclusive source of his lessons. As Nicole's sister observes, Dick himself was "educated" to be a good husband to Nicole—a comment that encompasses both Dick's psychiatric training and his cultivation as a gentleman (*TN*, 312). Like Poiret and Fitzgerald, Dick is left behind by the lessons in lifestyle and in modern femininity that he helped to generate, but for which he cannot claim sole authorship.

Dick's aesthetics and his methods for educating American women also resonate with Poiret's Orientalist and primitivist styles and extend, via Nicole, to landscape and interior design. The novel emphasizes that the Mediterranean setting of the Divers' idyll is oriented eastward, away from Europe. The opening passage describes the beach, which Dick himself has cleared of rocks, as a "bright tan prayer rug," while "deferential palms cool" the hotel behind (*TN*, 1). A later dip in the sea is compared to "a tingling curry eaten with chilled white wine" (*TN*, 21). This is the stage for the Divers' performance of their exquisite lifestyle, punctuated and epitomized by the gracious parties set in their garden. That space at the Divers' Villa Diana is Nicole's sanctuary and project—that is, until she leaves Dick for a French American soldier who, as Chris Messenger observes, resembles a "desert sheik."[81] In turn, the Villa Diana provides inspiration for the expensive psychiatric facility that Nicole and Dick design and help to run near Zurich. Facilities for the patients include workshops for "carpentry," "book-binding," and "beadwork, weaving, and work in brass" (*TN*, 181). These offer some relief, but no cure. Although "the bright colors of the stuffs gave strangers a momentary illusion that all was well, as in a kindergarten," the patients think "not in a line as with normal people but in the same circle. Round, round, and round. Around forever" (*TN*, 181, 182). This repetition is demonstrated by an English woman patient who unfailingly comments to Dick about the quality of the hospital's musical entertainments. As Dick does with his guests at his parties on the Riviera, he tactfully encourages this performance, inviting her to imply that she is an accomplished pianist, although it is her sisters who are the "brilliant musicians" (*TN*, 182). The repetitive, childish handiwork that the patients undertake highlights the narrow distinctions between artistic accomplishment, feminine "re-education," and the repetitive rhythms of fashion, which Dick masters and is mastered by. Design work in the bright, primitivist style and method of Maison Martine becomes a symbol of how fashion generates and helps to conceal the individual and collective maladies that Fitzgerald discovers among the European and American elite.

If "Echoes of the Jazz Age" provides a context for reading *The Great Gatsby* as representative of that era, this is more obviously the case for *Tender Is the Night*. Like the Jazz Age, Dick's life becomes an "expensive spree," and he stands with Gatsby and Tom as an iconic consumer of Anglo-American "gentleman's clothes." Dick and Nicole's resemblance to the socialite, painter, and businessman Gerald Murphy and his wife, Sara (which is highlighted by the book's dedication "to Gerald and Sara many fêtes") confirms the novel's focus on the economic and cultural power of Anglo-American style (*TN*, vii). Murphy was voted "Best Dressed" as well as "Greatest Social Light" and "Thorough Gent" for the Yale class of 1912, and his father ran the Mark Cross Company, which had transitioned from a nineteenth-century saddlery and harness maker to a purveyor of luxury leather goods and men's accessories.[82] By 1924, when the Fitzgeralds met the Murphys on the Riviera, Gerald had some experience designing goods for the company as well as leather bags for his own use.[83] Given this history, it is apt that Dick first appears in the novel as "the man in the jockey cap"—a bit of apparel from the sport of kings that has become a symbol of masculine American style via its descendent, the baseball cap (*TN*, 6). The Mark Cross Company was rebooted in

2011 with a line of luxury bags for men and women, and its website highlights its connection to the Murphys and, through them, the Fitzgeralds, *Tender Is the Night*, and artists including Picasso.[84] Like Fitzgerald, the Murphys
and their life on the Riviera remain symbols of twenties glamour. Fitzgerald's
choice of subject matter did help to keep his name in circulation. Popular
depictions of the Murphys and Fitzgeralds, including ads for the company,
also suggest the Jazz Age is the context for *Tender Is the Night*, despite the
fact that the novel was published in 1934. That is also true of most scholarship on the novel, even if critics do not ignore completely its apparent belatedness and Depression-era publication date. My point is not that this is
incorrect, but that it highlights the way that Fitzgerald's oeuvre and association with the twenties work with the novel's fixation on that decade to shape
what counts as the important context for the book.

Dick Diver's narrative also corresponds with Fitzgerald's claim in "Echoes
of the Jazz Age" that expatriate life at the Riviera between 1926 and 1929
was "indicative of something that was taking place in the homeland—
Americans were getting soft."[85] As with *The Great Gatsby*, *Tender Is the
Night* establishes its significance on the grounds of an anecdotal historicism
that deploys fashion and the periodical's logic of repetition with a difference
while casting that repetition as decline. Among the many repeating tropes
and scenes in *Tender Is the Night* are the series of tableaux on Dick's beach,
which demonstrate his deterioration and the generational and cultural shifts
that overtake him. *Tender Is the Night* also recapitulates *The Great Gatsby*'s
technique of describing its central figure's youth and his encounter (in uniform) with his wealthy, gorgeous beloved via an episode near the middle of
the book. While *Tender* devotes far more space to this flashback and uses a
more varied set of narrative techniques and points of view, both novels move
backwards as well as downwards.[86] Finally, *Tender* provides a framework for
understanding repetition within Fitzgerald's oeuvre. Regarding Dick's struggle to compose his second book, the narrator observes, "Like so many men,
he had found that he had only one or two ideas—that his little collection of
pamphlets now in its fiftieth German edition contained the germ of all he
would ever think or know" (*TN*, 165). Fitzgerald might have objected to
the conclusion that he, too, had so few ideas. But the reference to pamphlets and editions highlights the centrality of repetition to print culture
generally, and specifically to Fitzgerald's mode of production, especially in
the nine years since the appearance of *Gatsby*, during which he increasingly
published short fiction. Unlike *Gatsby*, *Tender Is the Night* appeared in a
serialized edition (in *Scribner's Magazine*) before being published as a
book.[87] So, although Fitzgerald made changes to the novel that he urged

Perkins to emphasize, *Tender* could more easily be seen as a "collection" of shorter works.

If Dick's successful book comprises a series of works, the references to a "germ" and multiple editions also suggest the possibility that his ideas, however few, may find other, fertile ground. At the same time, the pairing of "German" and "germ" underscores that what Dick knows condenses what he was taught in Vienna. His ideas have not sprung de novo from his brain—or loins. This comparison between germ and idea, as well as the indebtedness to other practitioners, reemerges in a letter that Fitzgerald wrote to John Peale Bishop days before *Tender* was published in order to explain (and defend) the novel's supposed lack of drama. Proposing to pass on a bit of "advice from fellow-craftsmen," Fitzgerald writes, "I believe it was Ernest Hemingway who developed to me, in conversation, that the dying fall was preferable to the dramatic ending under certain conditions and I think we both got the germ of the idea from Conrad."[88] In a letter to Mencken a few weeks later, Fitzgerald refers to "the motif of the dying fall" as "the greatest 'credo' of my life, ever since I decided that I would rather be an artist than a careerist. I would rather impress my image (even though an image the size of a nickel) upon the soul of a people than be known, except in so far as I have my natural obligation to my family—to provide for them."[89] Here the "dying fall" encompasses the novel's technique and Fitzgerald's faded celebrity, while Fitzgerald's "image" suggests both his artistic vision and his own profile.[90] A coin is a particularly apt image for describing Fitzgerald's influence. It brings us back to the mechanism of the printing press and the idea of Gatsby as a faded copy of Franklin. After all, Fitzgerald's novels—that is, the objects that are printed with his stamp and by which he makes an impression on his readers—are stories about those "who have too much money to spend, and too much time for the spending of it," as Mencken said in his review of *Gatsby* almost a decade earlier.[91] In the letter to Mencken, however, Fitzgerald's reference to a nickel helps to distinguish between, on the one hand, making an impression and, on the other, gaining notoriety and thus capital. This distinction also rewrites Fitzgerald's own history; his early fame as the king of what Mencken once referred to as "flapperish Fitzgeraldistas"—a literary fashionista avant la lettre—is recast as part of the obligations of a family man.[92] Creating those frivolous characters thus becomes a sign of Fitzgerald's *character*—a word that, as J. Hillis Miller notes, comes from the Greek word for stamp.[93]

Tender Is the Night provides an anecdotal historicism that situates its Fitzgeraldian protagonist as the preceptor of a way of life and modes of femininity that at once bear his stamp and become unworthy of it. The novel thus offers a means for understanding Fitzgerald's fashionability as evidence of his importance rather than triviality. Like Woolf, Fitzgerald understands fashion as a means of sensing and describing the contours of the present, but he is particularly anxious that present and future reflect his imprint without reducing him to a fashionable brand. Fitzgerald's concern with the impression he has made is also a concern with the context in which his work will be read. This is perhaps clearest regarding the way the novel offers a way of conceptualizing Fitzgerald's career via Dick's; while they are not identical, Dick's function as a representative American figure invites us to read Fitzgerald in those terms. Fitzgerald's design of Dick's character or stamp is a way to make the right kind of impression on his readers. Through Dick, Fitzgerald provides both content and context that establishes the author figure as the dominant horizon or referent for the novel.

While Fitzgerald and Poiret provide certain contexts to ensure their works' endurance and to shape the terms by which they will reemerge, that effort reveals the permeability of text and context and the impossibility of setting boundaries for appropriate context. In particular, the slight belatedness of *Tender Is the Night* reminds us that "context" might refer to material from the time and place that a work depicts, from the time and place of publication, or from the scene of reading. With its accelerated pace of transformation, fashion highlights the complexity of the reception of styles and objects. It also provides a framework for perceiving the reproduction of styles and objects via both continuous and punctuated temporalities. Finally, fashion draws attention to the perpetuation and reemergence of certain modes of historicizing, for current methods remain entangled with modes of romantic historicism, which emerged (in part) from print-cultural fashion.

Recognizing the recapitulation of this romantic historicism allows us to reframe discussions of current literary methods. It makes clear that our contextual reading practices are not simply something we apply to texts but have been developed in those texts. That realization leads us to take a longer, broader view of the sources and histories of our critical approaches. We can better see that our literary methods emerge not only in relation to each other (with, for example, New Historicism giving way to thinking "new historically"), but also in relation to methods of reading that function in and through other forms of cultural production, from print-cultural fashion to literature. At the same time, as my reading of *The Great Gatsby* suggests, skepticism about such concepts as representativeness and periodization does not release us from the operating logic of those terms. In addition, the examples of Fitzgerald and Poiret prompt us to be wary about if and how education might counter other, less reflective rhythms, paces, and logics of accumulation. As we have seen, both men set themselves in contrast to fashion by claiming the slower, broader, more meditative pace and perspective of pedagogy. That move, however, involves a trivialization of fashion that belies their dependence upon it. Furthermore, the connections I have traced between Fitzgerald, Poiret, fashion, periodicals, and periodicity bear upon the way that literary studies is itself circulated largely through periodicals that are organized according to a given period and that promise to deliver new material in each issue. That situation makes clear that print-cultural fashion's romantic historicism not only operates as a prevailing theoretical paradigm, but also as the material structure that shapes the production of literary scholarship.

Yet, as this book has sought to show, modernism and fashion generate other ways of conceiving and experiencing cultural production that can intervene in the contemporary moment. In the coda that follows, I demonstrate how the ways of reading fashionably in Woolf's, Lawrence's, Du Bois's, Larsen's, and Fitzgerald's texts appear in a contemporary piece of installation art that thinks with and across periodicity and political transformation. As I show, modernist methods of feeling one's way, of animating bodies, of imagining collectivities, and of conceiving time nonlinearly operate in Mariam Ghani's *A Brief History of Collapses* (2012), which contemplates the cycles of destruction and reconstruction that characterize modern nation states. Ghani engages with fabric and dress—as well as with buildings and fabrication—to trace transhistorical, translocal connections between the processes of rending and restitching the political and cultural fabric of two nations. Ghani's work is pedagogical in that she leads the reader towards ways of sensing the past, present, and future that draw upon modernism and fashion without treating either as definitive or redemptive. Indeed, one of her strategies is to use those interwoven cultural phenomena to prompt nimble, non-teleological ways of reading comparatively across time and space.

CODA

The Pedagogies of Fashion and Modernism

This book has argued for fashion's importance to understanding what modernist texts do, and how. In doing so, it has described various forms of literary pedagogy, meaning both the ways that literature teaches and the ways that one might teach literature (which can involve teaching what literature teaches). These pedagogies provide ways of describing modernism's continued relevance. Woolf's "frock conscious" mode of making legible an unfolding scene, for example, suggests how her modernism intersects with and enriches contemporary critical, theoretical, and social scientific approaches to knowing, representing, and reimagining texts and the world. In turn, Fitzgerald's anecdotal historicism draws attention to the potential and limits of approaches to modernism that present cultural objects as a privileged way of learning about the contours of a given historical moment. These resemblances can be understood as evidence of continuities between the early twentieth century and the present. But it is just as accurate and revealing to understand these connections as resonances between two distinct historical moments and methods that illuminate, amplify, and—to some degree—alter each other.[1] Nevertheless, it also is too reductive to understand historical moments, cultural objects, or literary and critical methods as discrete and unified. They are made up of forces, bodies, phenomena, events, and concerns, each of which, like a cut of sleeve, can persist and periodically re-emerge without, however, detaching entirely from the other elements to which they are (tightly or loosely) stitched.

This sartorial metaphor and method of understanding modernism is particularly useful given the way that the language of fashion already shapes discussions of methodologies and approaches to literary study. In their account of modernism's relationship to what they describe as contemporary "metamodernist" fiction, for example, David James and Urmila Seshagiri argue for an "unfashionable" understanding of modernism as an early twentieth-century phenomenon because, they assert, such periodization provides more leverage for describing the particular aesthetic qualities and political investments of contemporary fiction.[2] They resist what they describe as a recent tendency to treat modernism as "inherently positive, transportable across time, and transferable to the work of contemporary writers."[3] I agree that modernism should not be thought of as necessarily positive, portable, or unaltered when moved across time and space. But, as this book suggests, fashion provides a heuristic for thinking of modernism as made up of forces and characteristics that are historically and geographically situated but not fixed, and that become perceptible in relation to the contemporary moment, which in turn may sustain or recast modernist strategies, techniques, and concerns. In short, fashion does not necessarily empty the past of meaningful historical content (as Jameson's account of postmodernism would suggest), but rather can heighten our attention to how, where, and why what is seemingly past persists or reemerges. Fashion's rhythm of periodic if unpredictable reemergence is particularly useful for modernist studies as the field turns its gaze forward to midcentury and contemporary moments, for it reminds us that modernism's aesthetic, ethical, and political configurations are part of an irregular series rather than an origin or end point. By the same logic, fashion provides tools for interrogating modernism's and modernist studies' purported break from Victorian literature and culture. In other words, via the lens of fashion, early twentieth-century modernism appears as a site of creative rearticulation and reassemblage.

Part of what this book has argued is that fashion is a way of thinking of style and history together. Though she does not focus on fashion per se, Elizabeth Freeman draws out such possibilities in her account of "temporal drag." She describes how dressing in an "outmoded" form of femininity might constitute a kind of "disruptive anachronism" that conveys the latent possibilities of radical lesbian politics.[4] Freeman's vision recalls Benjamin's idea of fashion as "the tiger's leap into the past" that epitomizes Marx's dialectics of the revolution but takes place "in an arena where the ruling class gives commands."[5] Instead of a revolutionary leap, however, Freeman tells "a story of disjunctive, sticky entanglements and dissociations."[6] Freeman's "temporal drag," that is, explores part of the vast, textured middle ground between, on the one hand, fashion's enforcement of bourgeois power and, on the other, its revolutionary temporal sensibility. *Modernism à la Mode* has shown how early twentieth-century writers also mapped this terrain.

This ground continues to be well traversed. While completing this project in the summer of 2016 I made a trip to see family in New York City, and one afternoon we made an excursion to the Guggenheim Museum. The big exhibition was on László Maholy-Nagy, but the main attraction was a small show called *But a Storm Is Blowing from Paradise: Contemporary Art of the Middle East and North Africa*, which was tucked into two levels of the "tower" galleries that extend beyond the building's famous central modernist spiral.[7] This location and the fact that a quotation from "On the Concept of History" was the show's title—as well as the title of a piece (by Rokni Haerizadeh) in the exhibition—hints at the fraught relationship between the museum's enshrinement of early and midcentury U.S. and European modernism and the works displayed, which were recent acquisitions meant to help "diversify" the Guggenheim's holdings.[8] The Guggenheim's efforts at diversification coincide, not coincidentally, with its establishment of new museums around the world, including a controversial building in Abu Dhabi. Indeed, just days before *But a Storm . . .* opened in April 2016, the Guggenheim's board of trustees cut off talks with the Gulf Labor Artist Coalition, a group that was formed to advocate for the rights of workers at the Abu Dhabi site and that included artists shown at this exhibition. In response, ten of the eighteen artists in the show issued an open letter to the Guggenheim protesting its decision.[9] Among them was Mariam Ghani, a New York–born artist of Lebanese and Afghan descent, whose father, Ashraf Ghani, became president of Afghanistan in 2014. Her captivating video installation, titled *A Brief History of Collapses*, filled a separate, darkened space at the back of one of the tower galleries. Its nonlinear treatments of history, which engage extensively with Benjamin's work, and its meditation on the relationships between modernization, art, and state making all hinge on the lively matter of dress. Her work demonstrates the persistence, reemergence, and relevance of the treatments of sartorial fashion—as a mode of perception and display, a way of touching and orienting audiences, and a means of historical thinking—which this book has explained. Like Woolf, Lawrence, Du Bois, and Fitzgerald, Ghani finds in dress a resource for advancing the pedagogical aims of her art.

Ghani's dual-channel twenty-two-minute video installation, which is shown on loop, displays simultaneous sets of tracking shots that seem to pursue two different female figures as they move through two neoclassical buildings. The structure displayed on the left-hand screen is the Fridericianum in Kassel, Germany; it was completed in 1779 at the order of King Friedrich II and stands as one of the oldest public museums built for that purpose. The other building—shown on the right-hand screen—is Dar ul-Aman Palace in Kabul, Afghanistan; it was built in 1929, having been designed by a German architect and commissioned as a government building by King Amanullah Khan. The construction of Dar ul-Aman was part of King Amanullah's attempt to "[enact] modernism from above," as Ghani says in *Afghanistan: A Lexicon* (2011), a book she coauthored with her father, who was trained in the United States as a cultural anthropologist with an expertise in failed states.[10] Both the Fridericianum and the Dar ul-Aman Palace were nearly destroyed by political violence. The Fridericianum hosted art exhibitions while still in ruins after World War II, but it has since been rebuilt and now (as the film shows) displays the pristine, white walls of a contemporary state-sponsored European cultural institution. Every five years it hosts a leading international art show, *documenta*, which commissioned *A Brief History of Collapses* and the Ghanis' accompanying coauthored book. Dar ul-Aman Palace was periodically patched up after sustaining damage, but currently is crumbling under the impact of decades of military action; the halls are filled with rubble and its walls are marked by bullet holes and graffiti, including writing by Taliban, Soviet, and U.S. soldiers. Ghani's films of the two buildings are projected onto eight-foot-high screens set at a roughly 120-degree angle from each other—"hinged like a book."[11] The viewer thus is positioned as a reader, albeit one who glances back and forth between pages, rather than reading left to right (as in Latin scripts) or right to left (as in Arabic and Semitic scripts).

The viewer-reader is also a listener, for as the two cameras move steadily through the buildings, a feminine voice (Ghani's in the English version) delivers a series of reflections. She comments on storytelling and "the power of words" in German and Afghan traditions, discusses the two structures and their royal sponsors, and describes nonlinear ways of conceiving history (a "hall of mirrors, a spiral maze . . . a door that swings back and forth on its hinges").[12] The script conveys a wealth of historical detail, yet the narrator begins by disavowing claims to absolute accuracy, opting instead for the approach of the "brothers Grimm," "Arabic folktales," and Afghan storytelling traditions, which together suspend distinctions between past and future, truth and belief, creative and academic work.[13] The intricate script, however, is hard to grasp while attending to the two screens, an effect exacerbated by the speaker's rather flat, academic tone, which slips by the listener who might otherwise respond to emotional cues. At the same time, one's attention is sometimes caught and pulled away by a particularly loud or ominous note in the minimalist, atonal score. This density of visual and auditory information and the piece's focus on building design recall Benjamin's claim that architecture anticipates film insofar as each offers an "artwork that is received in a state of distraction and through the collective."[14] Yet whereas

Benjamin emphasizes the "percussive effect" of film's "successive changes of scene and focus," Ghani forgoes the (no longer shocking) modernist aesthetic of shock for more subtle if distracting affects and effects.[15] The result of the piece's visual, verbal, and historical cross-references, some of which are displayed in the work and some of which involve contextual knowledge, is a sense of interwoven times and spaces. Within this fabric, modernism and textiles are dense nodes and epistemological, cultural, and historical sites from which one might feel one's way toward other places, moments, and ways of knowing.

The feeling of grasping and losing the thread is visually expressed by the intermittent appearance in each video of a woman, whom the camera seems to follow through the building as she turns corners, exits rooms, and repeatedly escapes the camera's frame. These figures—played by Erin Ellen Kelly, Ghani's sometime collaborator, in the German location and by Parwana Riaza in Afghanistan—animate the entire piece. Their performances transform its somewhat academic meditations—which touch on narrative, history, violence, and connections between making and preserving art and making and preserving states—into a form of physical pursuit. More specifically, these performers' animation of the piece occurs through dress; the performers generally remain at a distance, are clothed nearly from head to toe, and usually are seen from behind, so that they mostly appear to us as lively garments. Kelly's costume resembles a 1930s or early 1940s women's tailored suit complete with a tight-fitting hat, but the ankle-length black skirt is semitransparent rather than opaque, as a garment of the period would have been. Riaza wears a simple, white, flowing version of a *firaq partug* with a pink chador whose gauzy fabric recalls the material if not the color of the other woman's skirt. Instead of a predictable contrast between "Western" and "Eastern" dress or a focus on the veil as a mark of radical difference, the gauzy, semitransparent fabric provides a material connection and relay between these two figures.

This fabric also dislocates these figures temporally, since they help to mark the outfits as costumes, which fuse elements of the past, present, and a possible future, and which remind us that other times are accessible only via the contemporary moment. In each case, the woman embodies but also defies the building's history. Both performers wear pumps, but they move quite differently, with Kelly walking haltingly, as if wounded, over the polished floors and Riaza gliding smoothly despite the rubble. The seemingly injured woman in a fictional version of thirties or forties European dress recalls the Fridericianum and Germany's wartime collapse, while the white garments of the woman in the Dar ul-Aman Palace help to generate a sense of loss and anxi-

Simultaneous stills from *A Brief History of Collapses* by Mariam Ghani (2012).

ety as well as possibility and promise as she moves through the ruined building. As with the work of Woolf, Lawrence, Du Bois, Fauset, Larsen, and Fitzgerald, in *A Brief History of Collapses*, dress makes palpable the need, difficulty, and possibility (but not the means) for the ongoing work of understanding and representation to become that of action and transformation.

Ghani's piece specifically recalls the links between fashions of femininity and spaces that cultivate particular models for political and cultural collectivities, which are also forged by Du Bois's *Dark Princess* and the Walkers' black (business) empire amidst a shift in the global international order. Ghani's installation, however, places a greater emphasis on the repeated failure of these sites to give rise to sustainable state forms and geopolitical systems. In turn, those failures become legible through their effects on women's bodies (hence the limping figure in the Fridericianum). Ghani's piece also undertakes Woolf's modernist mood work insofar as it draws on dress's capacity to conjure and epitomize a collective feeling, which encompasses and involves objects, structures, and historical events as well as bodies. For Ghani and Woolf, stylish dress functions as a means to feel out the contours of an unfolding present, which is filled with a sense of the past and future. It also highlights women's absent presence in public spaces and properly "political" institutions. Both performers dress in outfits that facilitate their movement in public, but also highlight the fragility of that access, not least because it depends on garments; the transparency of the German performer's skirt, for example, draws attention to the shifting but deeply consequential distinction between garments that might facilitate or trouble the wearer's access to public spaces. The outfit's anachronism also underscores that, in certain times and places, no dress could help to protect one from harm or ensure access to redress via political institutions.

Even as dress makes legible the connections and resonances between Ghani's contemporary practices and early twentieth-century objects and forms of cultural production, clothing's association with specific times and places interrupts a tendency to collapse difference into singularity. Hence, in *A Brief History of Collapses*, the narrator's reflections on the possibilities and pitfalls of the work of comparison focus on dress. Commenting on how an Afghan folktale about a doomed heroine might be interpreted "in another country," the narrator observes: "We would do well to remember that the outward signs of victory, defeat, love and grief are different in different places; the mourning dress may be white here, but black there; a veil assumed here would be thrown off there."[16] For much of *A Brief History of Collapses*, the audience and narrator seem suspended between the two places and different times, but the deictic "here" shifts the piece's center of gravity toward contemporary Kabul and in particular the woman in white. Thus, in this highly conceptual work, dress styles help to prompt a situated, textured, and nimble mode of perception that brings disparate times and places into a dense, textured relation without falling back on a sense of absolute difference or simplistic similarities.

Like many of Woolf's texts, Ghani's installation treats garments as objects and phenomena that hold information about the world, which art points to and seeks to translate into other forms. Nevertheless, for both artists—as for Lawrence, Du Bois, Fauset, Larsen, and Fitzgerald—the ways of knowing contained, inspired, or represented by textiles are available only intermittently and serve to make perceptible grander possibilities. In Ghani's piece, a sense of pursuing elusive and consequential knowledge emerges not only via the unbridged distance between camera and the performers, but also via the camera's refusal or inability to linger on details of the buildings, especially Dar ul-Aman Palace. Yet the camera suddenly achieves unexpected closeness with the palace at a moment when the structure most resembles a fabric. About a third of the way through the video, as the camera turns to take in the arched doorways and window on the other side of a large room, the foreground is suddenly filled for a few seconds by part of a collapsed ceiling that hangs into the space like a semitransparent textile made of wires studded with cement. As the moment unfolds, the narrator proposes, "An abandoned building becomes its own archive, its history inevitably written on its own skin. Perhaps this is why Dar ul-Aman remains so important to Afghans, who invest it with all the memories about which they do not speak."[17] The reference to "skin" and the echo of "vestments" in "invest" announces the convergence of body, fabric, and building, the conflation of material and memory, and the connection between the dressed bodies of the performers and the buildings they inhabit.[18] While the camera scans the ceiling-turned-textile and the narrator pauses (uncharacteristically) after delivering these lines, the potential for these memories to find expression and form becomes palpable. As with the woman performers, the fragile, fabric-like quality of this unplanned drape in the building's structure injects a sense of contingency—not to say, optimism—into the seemingly inevitable cycles of collapse that the buildings otherwise represent. At the same time, the idea that the building-fabric might simply be restitched into the existing building or, more fantastically, might take the shape of the injured woman's skirt or the chador highlights the limitations of existing forms for fashioning not simply garments, but institutions that could harbor and gather bodies into cultural and political collectivities.

We can understand the sudden switch from a wide to a close-up shot of the Dar ul-Aman in terms of what Laura U. Marks describes as "the sliding relationship between haptic and optical" visuality in which "distant vision gives way to touch, and touch reconceives the object seen from a distance."[19] As I note in my discussions of Woolf and Lawrence, optical visuality (for Marks) accords with Western idealism, particularly the Renaissance perspective embraced by neoclassicism, in which a disembodied subject gains knowledge about an object or being through sight. Haptic visuality, by contrast, destabilizes distinctions between viewer and object and prompts a more textured, less determinative, and decentered way of looking. This process of touching also, Marks claims, changes both the viewer and that which is viewed. Marks's concept of haptic visuality recalls Sedgwick's account of reading for texture, particularly insofar as both approaches describe less hierarchical, more embodied modes of feeling one's way. Marks also shares Sedgwick's concern with what these forms of reading and criticism *do* in the world, particularly what they do to and for the textual or cinematic object, the critic, and those who read the resulting criticism. My point in citing Marks' theories, however, is to argue that Ghani's brief deployment

Still depicting part of Dar ul-Aman Palace from *A Brief History of Collapses* by Mariam Ghani (2012).

of haptic visuality represents a cinematic version of Woolf's and Lawrence's textual efforts to make use of fabric's capacity for virtual but intimate touch—that is, not via actual contact between bodies, but touch through other senses. Marks's descriptions of the erotic dimensions of haptic visuality resonate particularly powerfully with the techniques and concerns of Lawrence's work. She writes, "What is erotic is being able to become an object with and for the world, and to return to being a subject in the world; to be able to trust someone or something to take you through this process; and to be trusted to do the same for others."[20] *Women in Love* and especially *Lady Chatterley's Lover* attempt to take Lawrence's reader through this process, whereas *A Brief History of Collapses* engages such erotic methods and possibilities only briefly. Indeed, Ghani's installation also seems suspicious of this presumption of intimacy and touch, as well as its outcomes. Given the haptic qualities of garments, it is particularly fitting that the suspicion of closeness and understanding across national and, implicitly, ethnic boundaries ("in another country") is articulated in terms of dress.

While they differ in approach, works by Ghani and Lawrence as well as Woolf, Du Bois, and Fitzgerald are all pedagogical insofar as they offer, encourage, or orient readers toward various ways of knowing, feeling, and sensing via dress. Their work remains invested in the possibility of instruction, however oblique, contingent, and noninstrumental. That said, if fashion has a dominant pedagogical function, it would seem to be one of imitation—hence Du Bois's association between fashion and Sara's mimicry of white bourgeois femininity, as well as Lawrence's antifashion proposal in "Education of the People" that each student learn to make his own apparel "to the satisfaction of his own desire."[21] Yet, precisely for that reason, fashion provides a way to explore the tenuous but real distinction between reproducing existing power relations and developing ways of thinking and being that might generate or sustain something better—a vibrant social fabric. Indeed, I turn to *A Brief History of Collapses* because it shows that the alternative relationships between historically situated garments (i.e., fashion), literature, and pedagogy that this book recovers remain critical and aesthetic resources. That is not because Ghani necessarily responds to any of these artists; rather, her piece hinges on aspects of early twentieth-century history, culture, and thought that inform and intersect with their work. In turn, Woolf's, Lawrence's, Du Bois's, Fauset's, Larsen's, and Fitzgerald's modish modes of reading and representation provide ways of grasping the strategies and aims of *A Brief History of Collapses* that also point toward other positions from which to engage her work. In short, these modish modes are resources both because they provide ways of understanding contemporary work like Ghani's and because, as Ghani's work demonstrates, they can be redeployed and recirculated as a way to grapple with contemporary challenges, not least by showing how the contemporary moment repeats and perpetuates past phenomena.

Ghani's piece also suggests a story about the institutionalization of modernism (loosely and fashionably understood) that does not involve the familiar process of once radical energies becoming part of more conservative systems. This book's account of early twentieth-century textual, political, and aesthetic engagements with fashion is, in part, a description of how cultural producers grappled with their own relations to and positions within, outside, and beside various institutions and existing structures of power. It follows that Ghani's use of similar strategies of representation and pedagogy can be understood as a way to negotiate her work's fraught relationship to modern and modernist institutions. Consider, for example, her position as the daughter of a U.S.-trained, globally recognized Afghan politician; her inclusion in the Guggenheim exhibition thanks to what could be described as a trend for mainstream cultural institutions to "diversify"; and her protest against the Guggenheim's practices of globalizing. More particularly, *A Brief History of Collapses* raises questions about the relationship between (artistic) installation and institutionalization. The piece depicts and has been shown at different sites of public education and governance; it debuted near the Fridericianum as part of the quintennial art exhibition *documenta*, which nearly simultaneously hosted a show that included Ghani's piece at Kabul's Tajbeg Palace, a building that was reconstructed by Amanullah and recently restored after the end of Taliban rule. In this situation, modernism describes forms of institutionalization (via, for instance, the Guggenheim and political processes of modernization) as well as strategies to reconceive, recast, and make more sustainable ways of resisting and creating lasting structures. Modernism thus helps to describe the textured terrain in which cultural and political activity take place.

A Brief History of Collapses deploys what we can recognize as fashion-conscious modernist literary pedagogies in another medium and as a way to grapple with how institutions of cultural production, preservation, and education relate to state making. As an installation that appears in and through institutions around the globe, Ghani's piece reminds us that the writers whom I have discussed engage with fashion not only to manage and thematize the pedagogical dimension of their works, but also to negotiate their relationship to institutions, including the state. For example, when *Three Guineas* indicates that the art of dress should be part of a university education that will teach peace, but it cannot be offered until other material and affective conditions have been realized, the text shows how fashion prompts Woolf to think subjunctively beyond existing institutional contexts while addressing how her work is entangled with them. Lawrence's account of liberated boot making likewise imagines alternative educational institutions whose relationship to the state is strong yet unspecified; the impossibility of determining what makes certain fashions catch on helps Lawrence to elide the question of cause and effect regarding the relationship between individual desires and institutional forms, as well as between educational practices and systems of governance. Du Bois, in turn, enshrines a form of sartorial and natural beauty that transcends fashion at the heart of his vision for a black radical aesthetic education that can sustain a fantastically democratic, anticapitalist, yet imperial state. For Fitzgerald, the ability to teach fashion—its forms, its philosophies, and its dangers—becomes a way to locate himself and his work within historical and artistic patterns that predate and may outlast the United States. While many of these writers' cultural and political investments diverge from Ghani's, they all turn to fashion to evoke temporalities and ways of knowing through which to sense out the force and fragility of existing institutions and their relation to those institutions.

Scholars of modernism participate in installing and reinstalling modernist texts in existing institutions in various ways over time. And, on a smaller scale, the issue of what modernist literature and culture teaches, and how, is one that academics face in classrooms every day. This book has offered a few answers using a method of explanation that acknowledges that such answers should always be shifting. I would describe those shifts as matters of fashion and of reading fashionably, in part because they are driven by economic, aesthetic, and political forces that are not reducible to simple cause and effect or narratives of progress. But they are also matters of fashion in that we should change how we teach modernism and what we think modernism teaches so that such pedagogies can address and intervene in the ways that institutions are being refashioned all the time.

Notes

INTRODUCTION

1. Pound used the phrase as a title for a book of his essays published in 1934, but it first appeared in his work in 1928, as part of a footnote to a translation of Confucian philosophy. In *Novelty*, Michael North traces the history of this phrase as "a dense palimpsest of historical ideas about the new" in order to demonstrate the complexity of modernist ideas of novelty (165). Yet, while North carefully draws out the visions of recombination and recurrence that characterize ideas of novelty across history and especially in modernist art and criticism, his study describes fashion as "the love of change for its own sake" and associates it with a debased, simplistic vision of novelty (73). I argue, however, that fashion is not so easily bracketed off from the seemingly more substantive visions of transformation and innovation that North describes.

2. See Spencer, *Principles of Sociology*, Vol. II, pt. 4; Simmel, "Philosophy of Fashion"; and Flügel, *The Psychology of Clothes*.

3. Benjamin, "On the Concept of History," in *Selected Writings*, 395.

4. Woolf, "Modern Fiction," in *Common Reader*, 149.

5. Theodor Adorno asserts that modernist art achieves partial autonomy from commodity culture via innovative form and that its pursuit of the new represents a utopian desire for an alternative to capitalist modernity. See, for example, Adorno *Aesthetic Theory*, 5, 32. In *A Singular Modernity*, Fredric Jameson calls into question Adorno's claims for modernism on the basis of its "innovative mechanism" (128). He also employs a Marxist framework to describe modernism's formal characteristics as symptoms of imperialism. See especially Jameson, *Modernist Papers*, 152–69. Beginning in the late 1980s, a wave of scholarship explored modernist writers' participation in consumer culture, including through the marketing of their work as well as convergences between modernist and commercial aesthetics. That work helped give rise to the field of new modernist studies. See, for example, Wicke, *Advertising Fictions*; Dettmar and Watt, eds., *Marketing Modernisms*; Diepeveen, *Difficulties of Modernism*. While scholars continue to investigate the fraught relationship between modernism and consumer culture, work such as Rebecca Walkowitz's *Cosmopolitan Style* and Jessica Berman's *Modernist Commitments* place greater emphasis on how modernist aesthetics function as means of political critique and modes of commitment. Walkowitz's and Berman's books also exemplify the practice of treating modernism as a way of constructing and interrupting categories and experiences of difference, including those of race, nation, gender, and sexuality.

6. Celia Marshik's *At the Mercy of Their Clothes* shows that, in interwar Britain, garments were perceived to exert forces and forms of agency well beyond their role as commodities.

7. Wilson, *Adorned in Dreams*, 3, emphasis in original.

8. In her influential study, Evelyn Brooks Higginbotham describes how women in the black Baptist church employed what she describes as the politics of respectability; while clothing is not a focus on Higginbotham's study, she does note its role in that strategy. See Higginbotham, *Righteous Discontent*, 15, 195–96, 216.

9. Pham, "The Right to Fashion in the Age of Terrorism," 392 and passim.

10. Lipovetsky, *The Empire of Fashion*, 11.

11. Pham, "The Right to Fashion in the Age of Terrorism," 400.

12. Breward, *Fashion*, 25–26.

13. Breward, 14–15.

14. Mao and Walkowitz, "The New Modernist Studies," 745.

15. Walkowitz's *Cosmopolitan Style* is in fact a model for scholarship that interrogates rather than reinforces distinctions amongst culture, economics, and politics, as it argues that political theories of cosmopolitanism depend upon "the concept of style more broadly conceived—as attitude, stance, posture, and consciousness," which modernism also deploys (2).

16. The conservative paper the *Daily Mail*, then owned by Lord Rothmere, popularized the term *"flapper vote"* and led the cause against extending suffrage to women under the age of thirty. The *Daily Mail* claimed that young women's interest in fashion betrayed their manipulability and lemming-like behavior, which in turn would allow them to be easily seduced by the socialist party. For contrasting accounts of this debate, see Melman, *Women and the Popular Imagination, in the Twenties*, 15–37, and Bingham, "'Stop the Flapper Vote Folly.'" Melman argues that the *Daily Mail*'s attack on the flapper vote was representative of prevailing views and currents in the culture, while Bingham argues that the anti-antiflapper vote campaign was an anomaly and that the *Daily Mail* and the popular press evinced relatively favorable attitude towards young, fashionable women. On fashion and politics, see also Enstad, "Fashioning Political Identities."

17. Green, *Spectacular Confessions*, 1.

18. Simmel, "Philosophy of Fashion," 196.

19. Flügel, *The Psychology of Clothes*, 110.

20. Flügel, 113.

21. For a history of the women's dress reform movement, including a discussion of the Wiener Werkstätte, see Cunningham, *Reforming Women's Fashion*.

22. On Simmel and Van de Velde, see Lehmann, *Tigersprung*, 183–4.

23. Burman, "The Better and Brighter Clothes," 279.

24. The dynamics and fate of those investigations into aesthetic environments are the subject of Douglas Mao's *Fateful Beauty*.

25. Spencer, *Principles of Sociology*, Vol. II, Part 4, 210.

26. See Edelman, *No Future*.

27. Benjamin, "On the Concept of History," 395.

28. Lehmann, *Tigersprung*, 203.

29. Baudelaire, "The Painter of Modern Life," 12.

30. In *Tigersprung*, Lehmann compares Benjamin's use of fragmentation in "On the Concept of History" and *The Arcades Project* to the ephemeral, transitory character of fashion (278).

31. Berlant, *Cruel Optimism*, 5.

32. See Stanford-Friedman, *Planetary Modernisms*. Sean Latham and Gayle Rogers offer an illuminating history of the term *modernism*, including its redefinition via recent work in modernist studies, in *Modernism*.

33. Saint-Amour, *Tense Future*, 38.

34. Saint-Amour, 40.

35. In *Touching Feeling*, Eve Kosofsky Sedgwick writes, "to read from a repartive position is to surrender the knowing, anxious paranoid determination that no horror, however apparently

unthinkable, shall ever come to the reader *as new*; to a reparatively positioned reader, it can seem realistic and necessary to experience surprise" (146). Wai Chee Dimock's essay "Weak Theory" begins by asking, "How to theorize the extended and continually changing relations among genres? . . . Would it make sense to begin, not with formal properties, but with a phenomenal register more or less ad hoc, more or less episodic, namely, the impromptu meetings occasioned by citations and cross-references, and the proliferating thread of association that result" (732).

36. Sedgwick, *Touching Feeling*, 16.

37. Sedgwick, 149.

38. Sedgwick also implies that reading will involve shifts between the paranoid and depressive positions. On this point, see Love, "Truth and Consequences," 235–41.

39. Sedgwick, 134.

40. Stallybrass, "Marx's Coat," 184.

41. Sedgwick, *Touching Feeling*, 21.

42. In invoking forms here, I am thinking of Caroline Levine's argument that political and social structures and institutions as well as literary patterns and genres should be understood as forms that interact and collide "without presuming that one is the ground or cause of the other" (*Forms* 22). *Forms* exemplifies recent scholarship that shows how formalist methods facilitate rather than oppose analysis that embraces the political methods and aims that are more often associated with historicism.

43. Burstein, *Cold Modernism*, 2. The contrast that I am describing between form and history as the grounds for meaning can also be described in terms of debates about modernist autonomy— that is, the extent to which modernist writers claim or establish the autonomy of their art. Revealingly, Andrew Goldstone's discussion in *Fictions of Autonomy* about whether James Joyce's cosmopolitanism embraces aesthetic detachment or political community hinges on an analysis of Stephen Dedalus's hat (138–48). Goldstone concludes that Stephen's Parisian hat signals the way that Joycean style distances the cosmopolitan aesthete from political community. His argument depends on a reading of sartorial style as antithetical to political community, which may be true in the case of Stephen's Paris hat, but is certainly not necessarily the case. Georg Simmel's "The Philosophy of Fashion," for example, emphasizes that to be fashionable is to appear to be individual but to represent a group in ways that parallel the functions of constitutional democracy (194). What Goldstone helps us to see, then, is that fashion poses the question of the relationship between style and politics, autonomy and belonging, and formalism and historicism.

44. Brown, *Glamour in Six Dimensions*, 5. Both Burstein and Brown acknowledge that the aesthetics they describe are commodified, but contend that does not fully account for their force or significance. Brown, for example, argues that glamour's "aesthetic power" exceeds its commodification (12).

45. Du Bois, *Dark Princess*, 22; Miller, *Slaves to Fashion*, 137–75.

46. For an account of the emergence of the New Modernist Studies, see Latham and Rogers, *Modernism*, 149–209.

47. Ross, "Introduction," 3. As Stanford-Friedman points out in her contribution to the volume, precisely what Ross means by "theory" remains a bit unclear, though he seems to privilege critical theory associated with the Frankfurt School and poststructuralism over cultural theory, including "feminist theory, lesbian/gay theory, race studies, and multicultural and class theory" ("Theory," 239). Ross's focus may help to explain his sense of theory as involving a break, as the rhetoric of revolution has itself been a target of feminist and antiracist theorists, even as they aim toward radical transformation.

48. In her "Appreciation, Depreciation," Jennifer Wicke asserts that "modernism is a brand name" and that new modernist studies as an attempt at rebranding (394). She thus urges scholars to acknowledge their "own investment in modernism's speculative bubble" (395).

49. See Ahmed, "Imaginary Prohibitions."

50. In one of the many commentaries on Pound's phrase, Charles Altieri in "Afterword: How the 'New Modernist Studies' fails the Old Modernism" argues that what is new for Pound

is not so much the object as the mode of perception (765). Altieri also distinguishes such new modes from the work of critique, which he describes as making way or even clearing the ground for the former. My account of modernism as (in part) a kind of attunement accords with aspects of Altieri's argument, but I treat the work of critique and the offering of new ways of thinking as more entangled. In part, that is because I employ a broader understanding of critique, which does not aim simply toward subversion, but rather, like Ahmed's queer phenomenology, also involves bringing new things into view or bringing things into view in a new way.

51. Love, "Close but not Deep," 375. Sedgwick's influence on affect studies and debates about literary methodology help to explain the connections between these fields. Love responds to Sedgwick, as do Stephen Best and Sharon Marcus, who propose surface reading as a means of avoiding subsuming texts into readers' pre-existing social and political schemas. See Best and Marcus, "Surface Reading." Given that Love began her career focusing partly on modernist literature, it is striking that her recent work on modes of reading involves a turn to realist projects and aesthetics; she focuses, for example, on moments of realist description in Toni Morrison's *Beloved* (in "Close but not Deep") and emphasizes the documentary impulses of experimental works including Claudia Rankine's *Citizen*. On *Citizen*, see Love, "Small Change."

52. With respect to discussions of fashion, Burstein's *Cold Modernism*, and Brown's *Glamour in Six Dimensions* can be seen as part of a longer tradition of work that focuses on modernist impersonality and nonhuman objects. For work on modernist garments in that vein, see Marshik, *At the Mercy of Their Clothes*, and Anne Anlin Cheng, *Second Skin*.

53. Berlant, 9. In this sense, these texts offer a type of what Berlant describes as "affective realism" (52). The presumed distinction between realism and modernism has been reconsidered in the midst of work on late modernism. See, for example, Davis, *Extinct Scene*, especially 12–14.

54. On mood work, see Highmore and Taylor, eds., "Mood Work," For recent considerations of how literary and cultural studies might deploy the concept of mood, see also Felski and Fraiman, eds., "In the Mood." Highmore and Taylor's and Felski and Fraiman's introductions to their respective special issues are especially illuminating.

55. See Heidegger, *Being and Time*, 172–7.

56. Mao, *Fateful Beauty*, 7.

57. See Coole and Frost, "Introducing the New Materialisms," especially 5, 26–27.

58. Cheng, "Shine," 1026.

59. As Thomas W. Kim points out in "Being Modern," in the late nineteenth- and early twentieth-century United States, the Orient (specifically, East Asia) functioned as at once past and present, "the a priori signifier of beauty and grace, but also of goods and merchandise," which could convey Japan's "education in beauty and order" (383). On the British context in relation to modernist literature, see Marx, *The Modernist Novel and the Decline of Empire*, 122–66.

60. Marx, *Modernist Novel*, especially 140–63.

61. See Wollen, "Fashion/Orientalism/The Body."

62. See Cheng, "Shine."

63. See Woolf, *Roger Fry*, 199–200.

64. As Jed Esty notes in *Unseasonable Youth*, a "pair of Turkish trousers is the pivotal device that allows Woolf to pull off her gender-shifting plot with subtle nonchalance" (105).

65. Woolf, *Letters of Virginia Woolf*, 2:92.

66. Urmila Seshagiri teases out these dynamics in her discussion of how primitivism and Orientalism shape the Bloomsbury group, including the Omega and especially the work of Virginia Woolf, in *Race and the Modernist Imagination*, 140–91.

67. Nieland, *Feeling Modern*, 6.

68. Jennifer L. Fleissner provides an insightful account of how such disavowals function in feminist historicist work in "Is Feminism a Historicism?"

1. MOODS, MODES, MODERNISM

1. Carlson and Stewart, "Legibilities of Mood Work," 114.

2. Carlson and Stewart, 115.

3. Williams, "Structures of Feeling," 132.

4. Williams, 131.

5. Highmore and Taylor, "Introducing Mood Work," 6. Like Highmore and Taylor's, my thinking about mood is also shaped by the special issue of *New Literary History* on mood, which is titled "In the Mood" and edited by Rita Felski and Susan Fraiman.

6. Woolf, *Diary of Virginia Woolf,* 3:12.

7. In *The Cultural Politics of Emotion,* Sara Ahmed asserts that "feelings do not reside in subjects or objects, but are produced as effects of circulation" (8).

8. Ruth Leys critiques affect studies for reinforcing that distinction in "The Turn to Affect." For a response to Leys that draws on mood, see Flatley, "How a Revolutionary Counter-Mood Is Made." Felski and Fraiman also note that mood helps to bypass such dichotomies in their introduction to "In the Mood" (vi). In addition, see Flatley, *Affective Mapping.*

9. See Stewart, *Ordinary Affects,* 4–5.

10. See especially Berlant, *Cruel Optimism,* and Ahmed, *Cultural Politics of Emotion* and *Promise of Happiness.*

11. For this connection between mood and "women's style," I am indebted to Hemmings, "In the Mood for Revolution."

12. Woolf, *Essays of Virginia Woolf,* 3:422.

13. Heidegger, *Being and Time,* 177.

14. Ahmed, "Not in the Mood," 14, emphasis in original. Fashion's capacity to form our perception of forms provides a way to discuss how and why formalist reading practices must acknowledge the historical contingency of forms as well as their varying visibility. This is true even, or especially, in the case of more politically attuned approaches to formalism, such as that offered by Caroline Levine, whose *Forms* encourages literary critics to think in terms of how social and aesthetic forms interact and overlap, rather than treating the latter as subordinate or reactive to the former.

15. This trend in affect studies also can be connected to a long tradition of feminist and antiracist work that attends to feeling and the writer's entanglement or attachment to what they examine. So, for example, Ahmed cites Audre Lorde as a key influence and inspiration for her work in *The Cultural Politics of Emotion* and *The Promise of Happiness.*

16. Two touchstones for these views are Eve Kosofsky Sedgwick's work on affect and the hermeneutics of suspicion and Bruno Latour's critique of critique. See in particular Sedgwick, "Paranoid Reading and Reparative Reader" in *Touching Feeling,* 123–51, and Latour, "Why Critique Has Run Out of Steam."

17. See Felski, *Limits of Critique,* especially 18–26.

18. Ricoeur, *Freud and Philosophy,* 9.

19. Woolf, *Orlando,* 172. For an analysis of a number of Woolf's works—including *Orlando* and *The Waves* as well as *Mrs. Dalloway* and *Three Guineas*—through the lens of fashion, see Koppen, *Virginia Woolf, Fashion and Literary Modernity.*

20. "Modern Fiction," however, had appeared in a slightly different form in 1919 as "Modern Novels" in the *Times Literary Supplement.*

21. Woolf, "Modern Fiction," in *Common Reader,* 150 (hereafter cited in text as "MF").

22. Woolf, *Diary of Virginia Woolf,* 2:319. On Bloomsbury's and Woolf's relationships to *Vogue,* see Garrity, "Selling Culture to the 'Civilized'" and her "Virginia Woolf, Intellectual Harlotry"; Luckhurst, *Bloomsbury in Vogue*; and Reed, "Design for [Queer] Living."

23. The emphasis on feeling as a method of reading and writing appears in many of Woolf's essays on those subjects. "On Re-reading Novels," for example, proposes "a book itself is not a form which you see, but emotion which you feel" (340). Ten years later, in the revised version of "How Should One Read a Book?," Woolf states that "we learn through feeling" (581).

24. On the language of fashion in "Modern Fiction," see Gaipa, "Accessorizing Clarissa," and Garrity, "Woolf and Fashion."

25. The connection between mood and textiles has inspired various recent design innovations. See, for example, Stylios and Yang, "Concept of Mood Changing Garments." With respect to literary studies, see Eve Kosofsky Sedgwick's observations about the relationship between affect and texture, including in the form of textiles and textile art in *Touching Feeling*, 16–24.

26. Many scholars have made similar points. For discussions of Woolf's engagement with material objects and things, see Mao, *Solid Objects*, and Brown, "The Secret Life of Things."

27. Cheng, "Skin, Tattoos, and Susceptibility," 98.

28. As Ahmed writes in *The Cultural Politics of Emotion*, "We need to remember the 'press' in an impression. It allows us to associate the experience of having an emotion with the very affect of one surface upon another, an affect that leaves its mark or trace" (6).

29. Best and Marcus, "Surface Reading," 9, 1.

30. Best and Marcus, 17. For an overview of spatial metaphors in contemporary methodological debates, see Felski, *Limits of Critique*, especially 52–84.

31. Ahmed, *On Being Included*, 185.

32. For a related exploration of how Bruno Latour's concept of the social as composed of a network of actors might illuminate Woolf's work, see Outka, "Dead Men, Walking."

33. On the history of shopping on Bond Street, see Adburgham, *Shopping in Style*.

34. For an analysis of *Mrs. Dalloway* in light of those historical changes, see Abbott, "What Miss Kilman's Petticoat Means."

35. Woolf, *Mrs. Dalloway*, 17 (hereafter cited in text and notes as *MD*).

36. Benjamin, "Central Park," in *Selected Writings*, 46.

37. On the revival of "Queen Victoria," see, for example, Dixon, "Woman's Ways."

38. See, for example, English, *Cultural History of Fashion*, and Breward, *Fashion*.

39. Marshik, *At the Mercy of Their Clothes*, 33, emphasis in original. My reading of Clarissa's gown also accords with Marshik's argument that Woolf as well as Jean Rhys and Rebecca West "frame the garment as embodying conservative gender roles but also as expressing its own trajectory toward public life" (53).

40. For a discussion of how folds of fabrics—in this case, in the curtains—draw out the ethical implications of this scene, see Berman, *Modernist Commitments*, 60–62.

41. As Jessica Burstein shows in *Cold Modernism*, this temporal signature operated simultaneously in literary modernism and fashion in the 1920s, as Coco Chanel's "little black dress" offered a vision of "classic chic" that could at once epitomize and transcend fashion (125–50).

42. This sense of belatedness results from the fact that, although Woolf revised parts of the earlier version of the essay (including updating a reference to bicycles so it referred to motor cars), the edition published in *The Common Reader* still describes *Ulysses* as "now appearing in the *Little Review*" (Woolf, "Modern Fiction," 151). By 1925, Woolf's prediction about *Ulysses*'s importance (if not her criticisms) would have been borne out, thus at once undermining the impact of her prediction and confirming her authority.

43. Nevertheless, Woolf and Best and Marcus suggest they are motivated by a wish that prevailing modes of writing might more precisely capture the nature of an essential, central thing: in Woolf's case, "life," and in Best and Marcus's, the cultural objects they read (rather than "the absent cause that structures the text's inclusions and exclusions," which symptomatic methods of analysis seek to disclose) (Woolf, "Modern Fiction," 150; Best and Marcus, "Surface Reading," 3). As I've suggested, however, Woolf's mode of reading attends more to texture and the way things surface.

44. My claims about the relationship between modernism and literary criticism echo and extend Felski's illuminating analysis in *Limits of Critique* of the ways that the rhetoric of critique echoes that of the avant-garde. While Felski focuses particularly on critique (which includes ideology critique, Foucauldian historicism, and symptomatic reading), I would emphasize how the less strident rhetoric exemplified by Woolf's "Modern Fiction" describes a wider range of scholarship, including that which, like Best and Marcus's, seeks alternatives to critique.

45. Saint-Amour, *Tense Future*, 38.

46. Ahmed, "Not in the Mood," 13.

47. For a discussion of the relationship between fashion and anxiety in modernity, see Clarke and Miller, "Fashion and Anxiety."

48. Ngai, *Ugly Feelings*, 247.

49. Heidegger, *Being and Time*, 174.

50. Heidegger, 175.

51. Mulhall, *Heidegger and* Being and Time, 110.

52. Heidegger, *Being and Time*, 232.

53. Nieland, *Feeling Modern*, 173.

54. Ngai, *Ugly Feelings*, 212.

55. Ngai, 236.

56. Woolf, "The New Dress," 63 (hereafter cited in text as "ND").

57. Sedgwick, *Touching Feeling*, 124–26.

58. Burstein, *Cold Modernism*, 129. Marshik, in turn, draws out how the story explores how a garment, and specifically a gown, has "the power to render the character a thing" (*At the Mercy of Their Clothes*, 60).

59. Heidegger, *Being and Time*, 176.

60. Sedgwick notes that discussions of epistemology in queer theory (including her own) exemplify paranoid reading, so it is fitting that "The New Dress" has been read through the lens of the "open secret." See Cohen, "'Frock Consciousness.'"

61. Tomkins, *Affect Imagery Consciousness* 2: 433 quoted in Sedgwick, *Touching Feeling*, 134.

62. "We Nominate for the Hall of Fame," 49. For discussions of this photograph, see Garrity, "Virginia Woolf, Intellectual Harlotry," and Reed, *Bloomsbury Rooms*, 24.

63. For a discussion on the limitations of critique as a form of critical distance for feminist critics, see Fleissner, "Is Feminism a Historicism?"

64. Rooney, "Live Free or Describe," 129.

65. Woolf, "Sketch of the Past," in *Moments of Being*, 70–73. What precisely Woolf means by "moments of being," however, remains somewhat ambiguous. She associates them with "sudden shocks" and often with "sudden horror," yet her account of one exemplary moment of being does not include any mention of pain, but rather an overwhelming sense of connection between a plant and the earth and a sense of wholeness, which resembles one of Mabel's visions (72). For a discussion of "moments of being" as pedagogical, see Hagen, "Feeling Shadows."

66. *Price tag* also comes to mind, though at the time it was almost exclusively an American term (*OED*).

67. Sedgwick, *Touching Feeling*, 128.

68. For a discussion of the importance of the context in which Sedgwick first wrote her critique of paranoid reading, see Weigman, "The Times We're In," 4–25.

69. On the role of suspicion to Sedgwick's essay on paranoid and reparative reading, see Love, "Truth and Consequences."

70. Heidegger, *Being and Time*, 177.

71. Marshik, *At the Mercy of Their Clothes*, 2.

72. Felski and Fraiman, for example, note that "mood is like the weather" (introduction to "In the Mood," v).

73. Consider, for example, that Clarissa and Hugh's first encounter pivots on his display of and her reaction to his "well-upholstered body" and "hat," as well as Clarissa's self-consciousness about whether her own hat fits the time of day (*MD*, 6). In addition, Clarissa's mending her dress sets the scene for her reunion with Peter and provides a trope through which he imagines her life, while Kilman's mackintosh becomes a focal point for her and Clarissa as they consider their relationship to each other.

74. Woolf, *Diary of Virginia Woolf*, 3:12.

75. This is not to dismiss the importance of the kiss between Clarissa and Sally. Indeed, a number of critics describe this moment as exhibiting a queer temporality because the kiss's ongoing impact on Clarissa in the past and present counters linear, normative temporalities. In making these claims, these scholars draw implicitly and explicitly on Sedgwick's comments on the temporality of what is queer. See, for example, Haffey, "Exquisite Moments."

76. Sedgwick, *Touching Feeling*, 128, emphasis in the original.

77. Indeed, Clarissa's thoughts of Othello and of Sally also are entwined with her own clothing, as she recalls "her feeling—Othello's feeling, and she felt it, she was convinced, as strongly as Shakespeare meant Othello to feel it, all because she was coming down to dinner in a white frock to meet Sally Seton" (*MD*, 34). Moreover, in the earlier version of Clarissa's shopping trip offered in "Mrs. Dalloway in Bond Street," she encounters the line on an excursion to get gloves. Woolf's shift from gloves to flowers obviously decenters fashion in that scene, but, as I note above, it still figures prominently in the account of the atmospheric effects of the motor car's appearance. The short story's focus on garments (specifically, gloves) as a means to consider how the war has shifted certain economic aspects of British life (the influence of "Rich Americans," difficulty getting luxury products) without dislodging other social networks of power and privilege is also recapitulated in the novel via Mrs. Dalloway's mending of her dress (Woolf, "Mrs. Dalloway in Bond Street," 15).

78. Woolf, *Moments of Being*, 64, 65. Woolf writes, "If life has a base that it stands upon, if it is a bowl that one fills and fills and fills—then my bowl without a doubt stands upon this memory" (64).

79. Clare Hemmings's "In the Mood for Revolution" argues that Emma Goldman seeks to dislodge women from such an understanding of mood and *la mode* for these reasons.

80. Bell to Fry, n.d. ["Monday," Summer 1915], Charleston Trust, 8010.8.179, Tate Gallery Archive, London.

81. For a discussion of Bloomsbury as a subculture sustained in part through design work, see Reed, *Bloomsbury Rooms*.

82. An important exception is Seshagiri's "Orienting Virginia Woolf," which argues that the Omega exemplifies the Orientalist modernist aesthetics, which, in *To the Lighthouse*, seem paradoxically to offer an alternative to the racialized imperialist systems that fuel war.

83. Ahmed, *On Being Included*, 176.

84. On Bloomsbury's Orientalism, see Seshagiri, "Orienting Virginia Woolf," and her expanded version of that essay in *Race and the Modernist Imagination*. This idea of Orientalism as expressing a sense of reach and access comes from Ahmed, *Queer Phenomenology*, 109–56.

85. On the role of the fashion world in shaping and advancing Bloomsbury's vision of civilization, see Garrity, "Selling Culture to the 'Civilized.'"

86. On Bloomsbury interior design, see Reed, *Bloomsbury Rooms*. While Reed associates this style with Bloomsbury's nonnormative gender and sexual relations, this association with style underpins Raymond Williams's claim that the Bloomsbury group amounts to a particular "style" of the bourgeoisie that was ahead of its time, but did not amount to an "oppositional" force. At stake in their different views are questions about what difference sexual difference might make, especially when expressed and experienced as style. Indeed, Bloomsbury's popularity for fashion designers bears out Williams's observations about modernism's "integration into the new international capitalism" (Williams, *Politics of Modernism*, 35).

87. For histories of Bloomsbury design, see Anscombe, *Omega and After* and Collins, *Omega Workshops*.

88. For a discussion of the relationship between interior design and modernist interiority, including in Bloomsbury, see Rosner, *Modernism and the Architecture of Private Life*.

89. Burberry, "Burberry Prorsum Womenswear." The collection reflected Burberry's new "partnership" with the Charleston Trust.

90. For a discussion of the Omega's political activism, see Brockington, "Omega and the End of Civilisation" and her *Above the Battlefield*, 98–111.

91. Woolf, *Letters of Virginia Woolf*, 2:92.

92. For a discussion of Woolf's shifting public image in the twentieth century, see Silver, *Virginia Woolf, Icon*.

93. On Omega garments, see Sheehan, "Experiments in Art and Fashion." On Poiret, see Koda and Bolton, *Poiret: Exhibition Catalogue*.

94. Parliamentary Recruitment Committee, "Why Aren't *You* in Khaki?" and Central London Recruiting Depot, "Which Ought You to Wear?"

95. On the British discourse of khaki during the First World War, see Tynan, *British Army Uniform*.

96. Marshik shows that the mackintosh in particular bore associations with war and violence well after the conclusion of the war, in *At the Mercy of Their Clothes* (66–101).

97. Bell, *Selected Letters of Vanessa Bell*, 174.

98. For an illuminating analysis of Morrell's modernist fashion design sensibility, see Marshik, *At the Mercy of Their Clothes*, 54–64.

99. On Tree's bathing suit, see Sheehan, "Experiments in Art and Fashion," 57. For a discussion of *Women in Love* as a roman à clef, see Latham, *Art of Scandal*, especially 141–56.

100. Fry, "Preface to the Omega Workshops Catalog," 201.

101. Fry, 201. Fry's theory can be understood in light of Sedgwick's point that even texture that seems to bear historicity—what Renu Bora describes as texxture—may be subject to "a kind of fetish" when produced by "the cheap, precious work of many foreign hands" (Sedgwick, *Touching Feeling*, 15). See also Bora, "Outing Texture," 99–103. In the case of Omega textiles, their texture is produced and sold at considerable cost by British hands that make modern the work of foreign hands. Yet this also bears out Anne Cheng's argument that, at the level of surface, the distinction between what is modernist and what is primitivist becomes indistinguishable. See Cheng, *Second Skin*.

102. Fry, "Omega Workshops Fundraising Letter," 196.

103. This point echoes Seshagiri's argument in *Race and the Modernist Imagination* about the racial politics of Bloomsbury aesthetics and the Omega, although I add a particular emphasis on the way that primitivism served to make Omega style visible and legible within and beyond Britain.

104. Woolf, *Letters of Virginia Woolf*, 2:111.

105. Seshagiri notes a similar paradox in Bloomsbury's Orientalist anti-imperialist strategies when discussing the *Dreadnought* hoax. Sarah Cole explores Woolf's late work in light of the paradox of pacifist movements that fought for peace in *At the Violet Hour*, especially 224–28.

106. Woolf, *Roger Fry*, 213 (hereafter cited in text as *RF*). On Bloomsbury's values, including civilization, art, and personal relationships, see Froula, *Virginia Woolf and the Bloomsbury Avant-Garde*. For a discussion of how Bloomsbury participated in British *Vogue*'s civilizing project, see Garrity, "Selling Culture to the 'Civilized.'"

107. Koppen, *Virginia Woolf, Fashion and Literary Modernity*, 22.

108. Woolf, *Three Guineas*, 5 (hereafter cited in text as *TG*).

109. Jessica Berman draws out the ways that *Three Guineas* offers "a narrative politics of hiatus, involution, and substitution" in place of the anger and propaganda that prompt her to write the book in the first place (*Modernist Commitments*, 63). In making this argument, Berman responds to critics who emphasize the anger of *Three Guineas*. See, for example, Silver, "Authority of Anger." On the affective nuances of the text, see also Hsieh, "Other Side of the Picture."

110. For an illuminating discussion of how *Three Guineas* troubles Flügel's gendered theories of dress, see Green, *Spectacular Confessions*, 148–53.

111. For an account of the spectacular nature of consumer culture and ways that "modern women" in the early twentieth century negotiated that optical regime, see Conor, *Spectacular Modern Woman*. On the gaze in *Three Guineas*, see Pawlowski, "Virginia Woolf's Veil."

112. Marks, *Touch*, xiii.

113. See Marks, xi–xvii

114. Marks writes, "In a haptic relationship our self rushes up to the surface to interact with another surface. When this happens there is a concomitant loss of depth—we become amoeba-like, lacking a center, changing as the surface to which we cling changes. We cannot help but be changed in the process of interacting" (xvi).

115. Ahmed, *Queer Phenomenology*, 172.

116. Ahmed, *On Being Included*, 173.

117. Woolf concludes, "We can best help you to prevent war not by repeating your words and following your methods but by finding new words and creating new methods" (*TG*, 169–170). Yet, as I have been arguing, Woolf emphasizes that the "new methods" she uses have been practiced all along. It is also telling that the next, penultimate paragraph of *Three Guineas* describes the questionnaire that the interlocutor has sent as a "form," which she will not "fill up" (*TG*, 170).

118. Davis, "Historical Novel at History's End," 19.

119. James, "Preface to *The Tragic Muse*," 84.

120. See Campbell, *Historical Style*.

121. Woolf, *The Years*, 54 (hereafter cited in text as *TY*).

122. Woolf, "Sketch of the Past," 73.

123. Whittier-Ferguson, "Repetition, Remembering, Repetition," 235.

124. Ahmed, *Queer Phenomenology*, 178–79.

125. Sedgwick, *Touching Feeling*, 13.

126. Evans, "Air War, Propaganda," 70.

127. I am indebted to Rishona Zimring for pointing out this allusion to Wordsworth's poem.

128. Cole, *At the Violet Hour*, 255.

129. This proposal is in keeping with Saint-Amour's account of how *The Years* shows us that all thinking (and hence all of Woolf's writing) occurs "against the threat of thought's extinction," and, more generally, his analysis of how many modernist texts grapple with the possibility, even likelihood, of a foreclosed future by imagining subjunctively (*Tense Future*, 125). Saint-Amour specifically offers Eleanor's earlier revelations about human connection during a 1917 bombing of London as evidence that, for Woolf, "to think at all is to think in a raid." However, I would emphasize that, in this final moment, we are invited to perceive and undertake such thought during a moment of peace that resonates with a violent past and future, but is not necessarily filled with dread. This also helps us to imagine that peace rather than destruction will have occurred and will be the pattern according to which we read.

2. MATERIAL CONCERNS

1. D. H. Lawrence, "Red Trousers," 138.

2. D. H. Lawrence, *Letters of D. H. Lawrence*, 2:470.

3. As David Bradshaw notes, the newspaper appears to have rejected and replaced Lawrence's chosen title, "Red Trousers," as it was published as "Oh! for a New Crusade" (Bradshaw, "Red Trousers," 352).

4. Lawrence, "Red Trousers," 138.

5. Lawrence, 137.

6. Bradshaw makes a similar point in his essay "Red Trousers" (353).

7. Whereas in *Aaron's Rod*, *Kangaroo*, and *The Plumed Serpent* Lawrence describes protagonists who flee England for less industrialized regions, those works offer tentative visions for collective transformation within the nation, if not within the existing national framework.

8. Lawrence, "Red Trousers," 137.

9. Lawrence, 137.

10. Lawrence writes, "I shall always be a priest of love" in a letter to Sallie Hopkin dated December 25, 1912 (*Letters of D. H. Lawrence*, 1:493). Harry T. Moore uses the phrase for the title of the second, revised version of his biography of Lawrence, published in 1974, and it was

the title of a 1981 film about D. H. and Frieda Lawrence based on Moore's book, directed by Christopher Miles and starring Ian McKellen.

11. For example, on Lawrence and critical animal studies, see Rohman, *Stalking the Subject.* For a study of the posthumanist aspects of Lawrence's work and his engagements with science, see Wallace, *D. H. Lawrence, Science, and the Posthuman.* Wallace is, however, hardly the first to address Lawrence's engagement with science. As Christina Walters observes, claims about Lawrence's rejection of science have given way to a "sense that Lawrence often disagreed on the surface with scientists and scientific philosophers only to commit to them at a more fundamental level," and she cites Craig Gordon and Granofsky as examples of that approach (*Optical Impersonality,* 172). Walters, in turn, argues that Lawrence's objection was to "positivism" rather than "modern science" per se (173).

12. There has, however, been scattered work on Lawrence and fashion. In addition to Bradshaw, "Red Trousers," see Carter, "Lorenzo the Closet-Queen"; Gilbert, "Costumes of the Mind"; and Ruderman, *Race and Identity in D.H. Lawrence.* See also a related discussion of Lawrence's treatment of glamour in Brown, *Glamour in Six Dimensions,* 13–15.

13. Celia Marshik's *At the Mercy of Their Clothes* shows how early twentieth-century British literary texts and other forms of cultural production register and react to the power of garments, particularly as they constrain individual human agency. While her study emphasizes the historical dimensions of this phenomenon, Marshik also notes the lack of attention to garments in the contemporary field of thing theory (in which she includes work by Bruno Latour, Bill Brown, and Elaine Freedgood), "which tends to prioritize things that are around, but not on, the body" (13). Thing theory overlaps with aspects of new materialism, though the latter (usually) names a broader field of inquiry, which includes work in political theory, science studies, and feminist theory, among other areas.

14. Coole and Frost, "Introducing the New Materialisms," 3. Coole and Frost, like Jane Bennett, are political theorists, so it follows that their account of the field of new materialism emphasizes its political dimensions.

15. In Coole and Frost's volume, Grosz and Ahmed touch on how aspects of feminist theory and new materialism intertwine. See Grosz, "Feminism, Materialism, and Freedom," and Ahmed, "Orientations Matter." Ahmed, however, remains skeptical of the term *new materialism* precisely because it can serve to erase the existing body of feminist and queer work on matter and corporeality, particularly "feminist engagements with phenomenology"; she prefers "critical materialism" ("Orientations Matter," 234). See also Ahmed, "Imaginary Prohibitions." With respect to Lawrence, Wallace proffers the author's critique of Cartesian dualism as "the foundation of a 'posthuman' Lawrence" (*D. H. Lawrence, Science, and the Posthuman,* 158). On Lawrence's rejections and alternatives to Cartesian dualism, see also Walters, *Optical Impersonality,* 171–203.

16. Coole and Frost, "Introducing the New Materialisms," 30.

17. Bennett, *Enchantment of Modern Life,* 111.

18. Bennett, 105.

19. Bennett, 112.

20. Bennett, 118.

21. Bennett, 112.

22. Bennett, 113.

23. Various critics have argued that the apparent authoritarianism, misogyny, and racism in Lawrence's texts give way to a more complex treatment of politics, gender, race, and difference. For example, on Lawrence and authoritarianism, see Frost, *Sex Drives,* 38–58; on socialism, see Ferrall and McNeill, *Writing the 1926 General Strike,* 83–103; on gender, see Williams, *Sex in the Head*; on race and difference, see Chaudhaury, *D. H. Lawrence and "Difference."*

24. Bennett, *Enchantment of Modern Life,* 4.

25. Masschelein, "Rip the Veil of the Old Vision Across, and Walk through the Rent: Reading D. H. Lawrence with Deleuze and Guattari," 24–25. Though she does not discuss the place of garments in Lawrence's or Deleuze and Guattari's thought, Masschelein's title and her

epigraph invite an exploration of their treatment of how these tropes and materials overlap. This mutual deployment of ideas of clothing and fabric is borne out by Deleuze and Guattari's praise for Lawrence's understanding of sexuality in *Anti-Oedipus*, which resists "uniform figures" and "torniquets." They write: "Lawrence shows in a profound way that sexuality, including chastity, is a matter of flows, an infinity of different and even contrary flows. Everything depends on the way in which these flows—whatever their object, source, and aim—are coded and broken according to uniform figures, or on the contrary taken up in chains of decoding that reset them according to mobile and nonfigurative points (the flows-schizzes). Lawrence attacks the poverty of the immutable identical images, the figurative roles that are so many torniquets cutting off the flows of sexuality" (*Anti-Oedipus*, 351).

26. Bennett, however, points out that her account of the vitality of materiality departs from traditional vitalist ideas of "a spiritual supplement or 'life force' added to the matter said to house it" (*Vibrant Matter*, xiii). On Lawrence and Bergson, see Wallace, *D. H. Lawrence, Science, and the Posthuman*, passim, and Wientzen, "Automatic Modernism."

27. Clarke, *Energy Forms*, 11. See Masschelein, "Rip the Veil" for a discussion of Lawrence and Deleuze and Guattari's shared vocabulary.

28. Cole, *At the Violet Hour*, especially 39–81.

29. Cole notes that among modernist forms of "(re)enchantment" are "Yeats's occultism, Eliot's celebration of Frazer, Weston, et al.; E. M. Forster's Eastern idealizations; D. H. Lawrence's theories of primal sexuality; and surrealism's investigation of the unconscious mind as source of creativity and transgression" (*At the Violet Hour*, 42). For Felski's defense of enchantment as a mode and aim of reading literature, see her *Uses of Literature*, 51–76.

30. This point follows from Felski's discussion of how Berthold Brecht's drama offers the pleasures of disenchantment (*Uses of Literature*, 56). Felski, too, uses a modernist text to point out the pleasures of literary and cultural critique, including the hermeneutics of suspicion.

31. For example, Wientzen notes that in her influential study *D. H. Lawrence: Aesthetics and Ideology*, Anne Fernihough defines politics as involving "large, controlling organizations" and, on those grounds, concludes that Lawrence is "ultimately apolitical" (Fernihough quoted in Wientzen, "Automatic Modernism," 45). Wientzen takes up Fernihough's characterization of politics, but argues that Lawrence's engagement with vitalist political thought in *The Plumed Serpent* qualifies as political in those terms.

32. For an influential account of Lawrence's turn from politics to sex and myth, see Sanders, *D. H. Lawrence*.

33. Literary and cultural studies already often employ the expanded sense of the political prompted by aspects of Michel Foucault's work, especially his accounts of subjectivization, for which Jeremy Bentham's panopticon is a paradigmatic image. Coole and Frost also draw on Foucault to describe what they say is the "multimodal materialism" that characterizes new materialism ("Introducing the New Materialisms," 32). In doing so, they emphasize both the material specificity of Foucault's genealogical approach and the extent to which "the matter whose materialization Foucault describes is malleable, socially produced, and inscribed with its histories; paradoxically, it is obliged to acquire (additional, redirected) agentic capacities as an aspect of its subjection" (33). Coole and Frost's account of new materialism emphasizes the potential for such agency to be redirected once again.

34. Barbara Langell Miliaras has also noted Lawrence's anxieties about clothing at this time, and connected them what she reads as his "warfare" against fashion and fashionability, which are "held up to ridicule" in *The White Peacock* ("Fashion, Art and the Leisure Class," 74).

35. Lawrence, *Letters of D. H. Lawrence*, 1:286. See also the letters dated May 7, 1911 and May 9, 1911 (1:265–66).

36. Lawrence also repeatedly mentions his poorer pupils who are "crippled with broken boots" (1:125).

37. Lawrence, 1:145.

38. Lawrence, 1:165. Miliaras also notes Lawrence's great interest in Pound's clothing and observes that Lawrence was "still too much his mother's son to adopt such Bohemian rags as Pound" ("Fashion, Art and the Leisure Class," 74).

39. Lawrence, *Letters of D. H. Lawrence*, 1:166.

40. Pound's penchant for marketing and advertising helped to inspire a wave of scholarship in modernist studies on modernism's relationship to consumer culture. See, for example, Materer, "Make It Sell!," and Rainey, *Institutions of Modernism*.

41. Lawrence, *Letters of D. H. Lawrence*, 1:259.

42. Pound, *Letters of Ezra Pound, 1907–1941*, 17.

43. Lawrence, *White Peacock*, 305 (hereafter cited in text as *WP*). James T. Boulton points out this connection to Pound in his notes (Lawrence, *Letters of D. H. Lawrence*, 1:165).

44. Pease, *Modernism, Mass Culture*, 93.

45. Indeed, the novel's title may refer obliquely to Beardsley's print from *Salomé* called "The Peacock Skirt," which depicts Salomé in a sweeping garment and head feathers. See Wilde, *Salomé*, between pages 14 and 15.

46. Williams, *Sex in the Head*, 14–15.

47. On censorship laws and their effects on late nineteenth- and early twentieth-century British literature, see Marshik, *British Modernism and Censorship*.

48. Pease observes, "by writing the body as against culture, [Lawrence] was still writing the body, by necessity of the medium he used, into culture" (*Modernism, Mass Culture*, 137). Pease understands this as conflict between pure bodily knowledge and the corrupted ideas of culture, while Linda Williams describes it as a tension between unseen bodily knowledge and the corrupted visual.

49. Derrida, *Animal that Therefore I Am*, 5.

50. On this connection, see Sproles, "Shooting *The White Peacock*," 247, and Stewart, *Vital Art of D. H. Lawrence*, 11–13.

51. Sproles also notes Annable's resemblance to the white peacock, though surprisingly few critics take up this point ("Shooting *The White Peacock*," 244).

52. Sproles, 251.

53. Lawlor, *This Is Not Sufficient*, 78.

54. Rohman also grapples with the ways that Lawrence's primitivism intersects with his interest in animality, particularly in *The Plumed Serpent*, but concludes, "While Lawrence appears to rely upon an outmoded, imperialistic equation of racial and animal otherness in the novel, the European and Mexican characters are depicted in a complicated ideological framework that troubles the distinctions between human and animal consciousness" (*Stalking the Subject*, 61).

55. Grosz, *Becoming Undone*, 132.

56. Grosz, 131.

57. Grosz, 128.

58. Grosz, 119.

59. Grosz, 62.

60. See, for example, Lawrence's essay "Democracy" (Lawrence, *Reflections on the Death of a Porcupine*, 61–84).

61. Grosz, *Becoming Undone*, 131.

62. In 1918 Lawrence wrote four essays for publication in the *Times Literary Supplement*, which nevertheless rejected them. He then revised and added to these pieces in 1920, but was never able to get them published during his lifetime. See Herbert, introduction to *Reflections on the Death of a Porcupine*, xxxi.

63. Lawrence, *Women in Love*, xxxii (hereafter cited in text and notes as *WL*).

64. Hopkins, "An Intimate Pen Picture."

65. For more details about Lawrence's talents as a sewer, see Ruderman, *Race and Identity in D.H. Lawrence*, especially 149–50. Among the witnesses to Lawrence's trimming hats for Frieda

is Katherine Mansfield, who in a letter in May 1916 described Lawrence doing so the morning after a violent fight with Frieda. Mansfield interprets the hat trimming as a sign of Lawrence's "slavery" to Frieda, and thus as part of the violent struggles for power that she perceived as central to their relationship (Kinkaid-Weekes, *D. H. Lawrence*, 319–20). Kinkaid-Weekes also offers a few comments on Lawrence and "needlework" (844).

66. Thomas, "Two Pieces of Advice," 12.

67. DiBattista, *First Love*, 148.

68. Levenson, *Modernism and the Fate of Individuality*, 147.

69. Cole, *At the Violet Hour*, 42.

70. Buck-Morss, *The Dialectics of Seeing*, 101, quoted in Evans, *Fashion at the Edge*, 186.

71. Leslie, *Walter Benjamin*, 10, quoted in Evans, 187.

72. In addition, this comparison to a military trumpet dovetails with the allusion to the attire of students at bluecoat charity schools, since the latter wear uniforms that signal both their access to education and their relative poverty—two circumstances that lead Gudrun to work for the Criches, and which she defies through her mocking, defiant attitude.

73. Andrew Harrison maintains that Birkin achieves (a beneficial) "articulacy" through a futurist vocabulary, whereas "the violence and the destructive surface trappings of Futurism get associated in the novel with Gerald Crich" (*D. H. Lawrence and Italian Futurism*, 129). For a nimble reading of futurism and *Women in Love*, which describes Leorke as "quasi-Futurist" and emphasizes Gerald's connection to futurism, see Wollaeger, "D. H. Lawrence and the Technological Image," 81, 88–89. The most extended consideration of Gudrun's relationship to futurism is Stewart, *Vital Art of D. H. Lawrence*, 117–30.

74. Schnapp, "Fabric of Modern Times," 199. Schnapp shows how conceptions of nonliving matter as autonomous and agential led the futurists, including Marinetti, to embrace Italian-made artificial fabrics as part of their fascist project, particularly in the 1930s. In addition, on the manifestoes on dress and for English translations of the texts, see Braun, "Futurist Fashion."

75. Braun, "Futurist Fashion," 39.

76. Lawrence, *Letters of D. H. Lawrence*, 2:183.

77. Lawrence, 2:181.

78. Lawrence, "Education of the People," 152 (hereafter cited in text as "EP").

79. On fashion and dress in the suffrage movement, see Green, *Spectacular Confessions*.

80. "Fashion and the Vote," 11. In the subsequent days, the *Times* also published a series of letters responding to the article, which expressed a range of views on the relationship between fashion, aesthetics, suffrage, and political subjectivity. One signed "O. K. H.," for example, correlates masculinity, rationality, and uniform dress when it announces: "Fashions succeed each other with such rapidity that only the woman with a large dress allowance can hope to keep pace with them; but man, serene and unmoved, goes on his way, and in the comparative unchangeableness of his attire proclaims his superiority" (O. K. H., "A Fatal Mistake," 5).

81. Braun, "Futurist Fashion," 40.

82. Braun, 40.

83. Braun, 41.

84. Joel H. Kaplan and Sheila Stowell note that the adjective *futurist* was used to discuss a range of dress styles (*Theatre and Fashion*, 78–81).

85. "New Ideas in Room Decoration," 126.

86. "Shocking Stocking," 34.

87. For example, as the men dress after wrestling, Birkin "was looking at the handsome figure of the other man, blond and comely in the rich robe, and he was half thinking of the difference between it and himself—so different; as far, perhaps, apart as a man from woman, yet in another direction" (*WL*, 283). "It" seems to refer to Gerald's figure, but it also seems to encompass the robe.

88. Cheng, *Second Skin*, 6, emphasis in original. As its title intimates, Cheng's study hinges on the crisis of legibility produced by Josephine Baker's skin, since "with Baker, *being unveiled often also means being covered over*" (8, emphasis in original). This phenomenon, Cheng shows, points

to the way that the modernist focus on surface "led to profound engagements with and reimaginings of the relationship between interiority and exteriority, between essence and covering" (11). One implication of Cheng's argument is that modernist primitivism, which involves an obsession with what is naked and natural, is inextricable from modernist experiments with artificial, minimalist style, which might seem to have nothing to do with racial and colonial fantasies.

89. Wollaeger refers to such ambiguities elsewhere in the novel as a form of veiling, although here he says "the human body is not simply veiled as it was in 'Excurse': it is distorted beyond recognition into a headless octopus a 'tense, white knot of flesh'" ("D. H. Lawrence and the Technological Image," 87). Wollaeger understands this transformation from men to octopus and knot as a form of violence that provides a "metacommentary" on the problem of representation. My reading, however, emphasizes that Lawrence critiques sight as a means of perceiving human beings and thus the ways his texts seek other ways to feel out and describe bodies and flesh. In that sense, metaphors may be preferable to mimesis.

90. Bennett, *Enchantment of Modern Life*, 114.

91. Lackey, "D. H. Lawrence's *Women in Love*," 279.

92. Marks, *Touch*, xvi.

93. Marks, 4.

94. Marks, xvi.

95. Jed Esty, however, contrasts Lawrence's modernist primitivism and elegiac sense of rural Englishness with the revivalist visions of the 1930s (*A Shrinking Island*, 48). My point is that this elegiac mood alternates with visions for revival, such as those offered in "Education of the People" and *Lady Chatterley's Lover*.

96. *Oxford English Dictionary*, s.v. "brave, adj., n., and int."

97. Grosz, *Volatile Bodies*, especially xii–xiii.

98. Lawrence, *The Letters of D. H. Lawrence*, 6:119.

99. Lawrence, 6:119.

100. Lawrence, 6:120.

101. Lawrence, 6:125.

102. This argument is in keeping with Brown's claim that *Women in Love* reveals "the very *queerness* of glamour," although Brown understands glamour as an attraction, in part, to modern technology, while here the queerness of the garments and the location arises from their (temporary) suspension of modernity (*Glamour in Six Dimensions*, 13, emphasis in original).

103. Lawrence, *Letters of D. H. Lawrence*, 6:120.

104. Lawrence, *Lady Chatterley's Lover*, 233.

105. Lawrence, 319.

106. Lawrence, 320.

107. Lawrence, 321–22.

108. For an account of how the passage emphasizes the body's constitution through history, see Kellogg, "Reading Foucault Reading Lawrence," 46. For a reading of this scene as equating writing with erotic sublimation, see Polhemus, *Erotic Faith*, 290.

3. "THIS GREAT WORK OF THE CREATION OF BEAUTY"

1. Lorde, *Collected Poems*, 63.

2. Lorde, 64. The resonance between the conclusion of Lorde's poem and W. H. Auden's line in "September 1, 1939"—"We must love each other or die," which he revised as "We must love each other and die"—also raises the issue of what place modernist aesthetics might have in such a political project.

3. Du Bois quoted in Levering-Lewis, *W. E. B. Du Bois*, 219. Levering-Lewis points out that Du Bois's celebration of *Dark Princess* in *Dusk of Dawn: An Essay towards an Autiobiography of a Race Concept* (1940) predates Du Bois's post–World War II "Marxist phase," and Levering-Lewis speculates "he must have come to feel that the novel's racialist romanticism was

unworthy of the scientific socialism of his final decades" (219, 218). Critics including Alys Weinbaum and Bill V. Mullen, however, note the Marxist dimensions of *Dark Princess*—without, however, claiming that they reflect Du Bois's later political beliefs; Weinbaum in particular grapples with the novel's investment in romance as well as Marxism. See Mullen, *Afro-Orientalism*, 13–21, and Weinbaum, *Wayward Reproductions*, 202–12.

4. I follow Edwards in using black internationalism to refer broadly to movements drawing on communist, socialist, and liberal internationalisms (*Practice of Diaspora*, 3).

5. I am indebted to discussions of the diasporic, political dimensions of the Walkers' work in Noliwe M. Rooks's *Hair Raising* and Davarian Baldwin's *Chicago's New Negroes*.

6. My work thus joins scholarship such as the Modern Girl around the World Research Group's *Modern Girl around the World*, which addresses the relationship between feminized beauty practices and nationalism in a range of geographic and cultural contexts.

7. Mullen, *Afro-Orientalism*, xv, xvii.

8. While I agree with Mullen that "Afro-Orientalism" is most productive if it refers to a "counterdiscourse," I underscore the difficulty (which of course the term itself signals) in distinguishing it from Orientalism (*Afro-Orientalism*, xv). This chapter thus gestures toward possible continuities between Afro-Orientalism and what Helen Jun discusses as nineteenth-century U.S. black Orientalism, a discourse in which "narratives of black inclusion . . . converged with the rhetoric and logic of the anti-Chinese movement" (*Race for Citizenship*, 6). Fiona I. B. Ngô emphasizes continuities between upholding and resisting empire but differentiates between Afro-Orientalism and queer Orientalism, explaining, "because these queer aesthetic practices took aim at the solidity of boundaries that marked identity categories, they did not fall into the category of Afro-Orientalist works that spoke to needs for alliance; rather, they worked to deconstruct the very categories of race on which notions of alliance rely" (*Imperial Blues*, 96). Distinctions between practices and works that uphold rather than trouble such boundaries are, however, themselves quite unstable.

9. Kim, "Being Modern," 383.

10. Du Bois, *Dark Princess*, 8 (hereafter cited in text as *DP*).

11. Du Bois, "Color Line Belts the World," 34. Japan may have offered Du Bois an ideal convergence of aesthetics and politics, as it symbolized aesthetic refinement and nonwhite political self-determination. See Onishi, *Transpacific Antiracism*, 54–93.

12. Roberts, *Artistic Ambassadors*, 128. Monica L. Miller makes a similar point about the novel's efforts at inclusion (*Slaves to Fashion*, 158).

13. Du Bois, "Criteria of Negro Art," 296.

14. On *Dark Princess*'s generic hybridity and diasporic vision, see Ahmad, "'More than Romance'" and Goyal, *Romance, Diaspora, and Black Atlantic Literature*, especially 59–103.

15. Weinbaum, "Interracial Romance and Black Internationalism," 101.

16. Miller, *Slaves to Fashion*, 136, 151. This chapter draws on Miller's illuminating analysis of *Dark Princess* but disagrees about the extent to which the depiction of Matthew, whom Miller describes as "a queer Race Man," challenges gender and sexual norms (145).

17. Craig, "Race, Beauty, and the Tangled Knot," 174.

18. It also could be said to anticipate the contemporary market for Indian hair.

19. The intersection of politics and beauty culture is suggested by the May 1924 issue of *Crisis*. It included an "East India Girl" advertisement, while the cover featured a drawing titled "The Head of a Hindu" and the issue contained an article about a virtuous young man from Pune, India that was illustrated by a photograph of Gandhi.

20. Mullen addresses Du Bois's links to India in the 1920s, especially his relationship with Indian nationalist Lala Lajpat Rai (*Afro-Orientalism*, xiv–xv, xxxv–xxxvi, 4–23). On Raj and *Dark Princess*, see also Ahmad, "More than Romance." For a more detailed historical account of Du Bois's relationship to Indian nationalist movements, see Slate, *Colored Cosmopolitanism*.

21. Ahmed, *Queer Phenomenology*, 114–15, emphasis in original.

22. Ahmed, 120.

23. On the politics of respectability, see Higginbotham, *Righteous Discontent*. On beauty culture, see Peiss, *Hope in a Jar* and Rooks, *Hair Raising*.

24. The novel glimpses the possibility of an organization headed by a woman when we learn in retrospect that Kautilya has led a box makers' union. The members, however, reject her when they learn of her adulterous relationship with Matthew, which underscores the need to link political resistance with erotic desire and aesthetic and ethical beauty.

25. On pageantry in *Dark Princess*, see Tate, "Race and Desire" and Stokes, "Father of the Bride."

26. Du Bois, "Browsing Reader," 202, quoted in Vogel, *Scene of Harlem Cabaret*, 160; Vogel, 160.

27. Du Bois, "Browsing Reader," 202 quoted in Vogel, *Scene of Harlem Cabaret*, 132.

28. Holcomb, "Diaspora Cruises," 721.

29. The status of feminism in Du Bois's work and his treatment of black women's political agency has long been a subject of debate. For foundational work on this question, see James's discussion of Du Bois's "protofeminism" in her "Profeminism and Gender Elites" and Hazel Carby's critique of the construction of the black male intellectual in her "Souls of Black Men." Tate addresses the entwinement of gender, sexual, and racial politics in *Dark Princess* specifically in her "Race and Desire." For a recent discussion on the figuration of women in McKay's work, see Reed, "'A Women Is a Conjunction.'"

30. Walker to Normal Industrial and Agricultural College, March 27, 1917, Box 1, Folder 7, Madam C. J. Walker Collection. Walker Company materials like this letter often use terms such as *art* and *beauty culture*. Rooks discusses how the Walker Company promoted itself by promising economic and political opportunities to agents in *Hair Raising* (51–74). The ways that Walker's business provided black women with economic and political agency are discussed in Peiss's *Hope in a Jar* (89–95), and Tiffany Gill's *Beauty Shop Politics*. See also Bundles, *On Her Own Ground*, 96, 179–80, 211. Baldwin addressed that dynamic and emphasizes the international dimensions of Walker's activism in his *Chicago's New Negroes* (55–56, 63–80).

31. Bundles, *On Her Own Ground*, 212.

32. "Press Releases from the First National Convention of Madam Walker Agents," 1917, Box 12, Folder 1, Madam C. J. Walker Collection.

33. Bundles, *On Her Own Ground*, 212.

34. Baldwin, *Chicago's New Negroes*, 62.

35. Baldwin, 79.

36. On the ILDP and Walker's activism, see Bundles, *On Her Own Ground*, 251–65, and Baldwin, *Chicago's New Negroes*, 68–80.

37. "League of Darker Peoples," 2.

38. "League of Darker Peoples," 1.

39. "Villa Lewaro-on-the-Hudson," 3. The article is unattributed and may have been intended to secure Walker's continued patronage.

40. Walker Company advertisement.

41. Bundles, *On Her Own Ground*, 253.

42. On the Walkers' real estate strategies, see Dudley, "Seeking the Ideal African-American Interior."

43. Walker's support for these periodicals often went beyond buying advertising space. Her business, for example, supported the launch of the *Messenger* and the *Negro World*. See Watkins-Owens, *Blood Relations*, 98–99, 113.

44. "Villa Lewaro-on-the-Hudson," 3. The flowers accompanied a letter in English and Japanese to the "Japanese Envoys" praising their anticipated "mission of securing equal rights for all the people . . . regardless of race, creed or color" (International League of Dark Peoples to Chairman of the Japanese Envoys to the Peace Council, December 30, 1918, Box 1, Folder 14, Madam C. J. Walker Collection).

45. Finch, *Correspondence of the Military Intelligence Division*, 89–90.

46. The proposals in the *World Forum* include demands to return "Africa to her own," "for abolition and prohibition of all economic and social discrimination," "freedom of immigration and emigration," and an "International Commission of Darker Peoples," which together were more radical than what Du Bois advocated ("Memorandum of Peace Proposals," 3–4). Randolph was quite critical of imperial Japan at this time. See, for example, Foley, *Spectres of 1919*, 105.

47. "Japanese Representatives Urge Fight," 1.

48. "Members of Race Confer with Japanese," 1.

49. On Walker's advertising strategies, see Rooks, *Hair Raising*, 69–74.

50. On Walker's travels, see Bundles, *On Her Own Ground*, 154–56.

51. "Madam C. J. Walker, of Indianapolis."

52. Nguyen, "Biopower of Beauty," 359–60.

53. Nguyen, 366.

54. Du Bois, "Hayti."

55. Weinbaum, *Wayward Reproductions*, 211.

56. Ahmad makes a similar point with respect to the novel's use of genres in her "'More than Romance.'"

57. On the politics of African American women's hair and Walker's response to critiques of her method as a form of hair straightening, see Rooks, *Hair Raising*, 63–65.

58. Du Bois, "A Great Woman," 131.

59. Du Bois, *Souls of Black Folk*, 1.

60. Du Bois, "Color Line Belts the World," 34.

61. An overdetermined imperial symbol, the sun also recalls the famous claim that it never sets on the British Empire.

62. Reddy, "Beauty and the Limits," 339.

63. For an illuminating analysis of Du Bois's review of and relation to *Home to Harlem*, see Vogel, *Scene of the Harlem Cabaret*, 132–66. On Du Bois and *Fire!!*, see Levering-Lewis, *W. E. B. Du Bois*, 180.

64. Hughes, *Big Sea*, 228.

65. A'Lelia made thinly disguised appearances in a number of Harlem Renaissance-era novels, including Carl Van Vechten's notorious *Nigger Heaven*, which became a lightning rod for disagreements between Du Bois and many of the writers associated with *Fire!!*

66. Hughes, *Big Sea*, 245, 227.

67. Ngô, *Imperial Blues*, 76.

68. Louise Siddons reads A'Lelia Walker's turbans as evidence that she takes an "interest in the headwrap as an Africanism" ("African Past or American Present?," 451).

69. It also romanticizes Russia's imperial past, which cuts against the turn at this time toward socialism and communism among many black artists and intellectuals (including Du Bois). Thanks to A'Lelia Bundles for pointing out that it is an imitation of a Cossacks uniform. On the connection between the Harlem drag balls and the proliferation of fashion shows in and beyond Harlem, see White and White, *Stylin'*, 215–18.

70. Dossett, "'I Try to Live,'" 104. Dossett's article discusses the transition in Walker Company advertising practices in terms of citizenship and consumption, including A'Lelia Walker's luxury travel.

71. See Bundles, *On Her Own Ground*, 279.

72. Du Bois, "A'Lelia Walker," 351.

73. Hutchinson, *In Search of Nella Larsen*, 264.

74. Braddock, "Poetics of Conjecture."

75. Bundles, *On Her Own Ground*, 286.

76. Reliable information about the Dark Tower is relatively scarce, but Richard Bruce Nugent gives a vivid retrospective account of its creation in "The Dark Tower." See Nugent, *Gay Rebel of the Harlem Renaissance*, 217–20.

77. Levering-Lewis, *W. E. B. Du Bois*, 221.

78. Daylanne K. English discusses the significance of the wedding with respect to Du Bois's construction of a racial family romance in *Unnatural Selections* (35–64). Mason Stokes analyzes the event in terms of Du Bois's participation in the ongoing construction of heterosexuality during the era in his "Father of the Bride" (289–316).

79. See Patton to Du Bois, March 19, 1928, W. E. B. Du Bois Papers.

80. Du Bois, "So the Girl Marries," 193.

81. Du Bois, 207.

82. On Fauset's internationalism, see, for example, Wall, *Women of the Harlem Renaissance*, especially 48–52; Allen, *Black Women Intellectuals*, 47–76; Edwards, *Practice of Diaspora*, 134–44; and Zackodnik, "Recirculation and Feminist Black Internationalism." Larsen's work is even less often discussed in terms of internationalism per se, but Laura Doyle situates it in the sweep of transatlantic history. See her *Freedom's Empire*, especially 393–412. Cherene Sherrard-Johnson reads Larsen's depictions of the "mulatta" in relation to the circulation of Orientalist tropes in her *Portraits of the New Negro Woman*, 21–48. For other work on Orientalist and Asian and Asian American identity in Larsen's work, see note 107.

83. Hughes, *Big Sea*, 247.

84. Hughes, 244. andré m. carrington notes the emphasis on speaking French at Fauset's salons as evidence of the kind of cosmpolitan training in "preferred ways of cultural life" that Fauset sought to provide young black writers ("Salon Cultures and Spaces," 253). carrington also notes connections between Fauset's salon and the Dark Tower, specifically its literary society (254).

85. Castronovo, *Beautiful Democracy*, 132, 130.

86. The name Harkness suggests both wealth and philanthropy, especially in art and education, since Edward Harkness, heir to a Standard Oil fortune, was one of the United States's most famous benefactors in the interwar period.

87. Fauset, *There Is Confusion*, 129 (hereafter cited in text as *TIC*).

88. Miller, "Femininity, Publicity," 217. Miller touches on the connection between Maggie's work and Madam C. J. Walker's business as a way of thinking about class-bound ideologies of black women's publicness, again in a U.S. context.

89. Levering-Lewis, *When Harlem Was in Vogue*, xxviii.

90. Kim, *Writing Manhood in Black and Yellow*, 30. Ngô argues that Wallace Thurman and Richard Bruce Nugent draw on the figure of Madame Butterfly and particularly Puccini's opera "to escape referential certainties, even while they rely on empire's signs and symbols. In this way, the wielding of imperial logic both set the stage for an assertion of queer sexuality and imposed limits on the representations of that sexuality" (*Imperial Blues*, 29).

91. Fauset's association between black and Asian femininities via the image of the geisha in this brief scene does not address the fact that Japan was a global imperial power by 1924. But my argument does not depend on the assumption that Fauset sees Japan as unable to challenge U.S. imperialism.

92. I discuss that dynamic in Sheehan, "Face of Fashion."

93. This paragraph in particular and my argument about *There Is Confusion* more broadly are adapted from my "Fashioning Internationalism," especially 148–49.

94. Levering-Lewis, *When Harlem Was in Vogue*, 90.

95. Baldwin, "Introduction," 7.

96. Fauset, "Gift of Laughter," 167.

97. Fauset, 167. See Kuenz, "Face of America"; Olwell, *Genius of Democracy*, 210–12; and Levison, "Performance and the 'Strange Place,'" 833–35.

98. Miller's "Femininity, Publicity, and the Class Division of Cultural Labor" also discusses Maggie's capacity for performance and discusses her as a complement and alternative to Joanna.

99. That is not to imply that this domestic ending signals the abandonment of political aspirations or a commitment to racial justice. As Ann duCille argues in her foundational *The*

Coupling Convention, the trope of coupling in black women's fiction of the nineteenth and early twentieth centuries is a means of critique and reimagination.

100. Miller describes Maggie's beauty parlors as "a . . . fantasy that working-class womanhood be unencumbered in an empowering publicity of the free market" ("Femininity, Publicity," 217). I am indebted to this argument, but emphasize that the beauty parlor is imagined as less "public" than the stage or the street, whose privacy is suggested in part by its absence from the text.

101. carrington, "Salon Cultures and Spaces," 254. We also can see the beauty parlor as an alternative to the church, which *There Is Confusion* associates with the legacy of slavery via Peter's family bible (which contains the secret of his family's tangled history during legalized slavery) as well as with patriarchal authority via Joel Marshall (who holds various positions at his local church).

102. Larsen, *Quicksand,* 36 (hereafter cited in text as Q).

103. For example, Sherrard-Johnson builds on Thadious Davis's account of *Quicksand* as "a portrait of a failed artist" by showing how that failure exposes the Orientalist and painterly dimensions of the novel (*Portraits of the New Negro Woman,* 24).

104. Reddy, *Freedom with Violence,* 118. Reddy argues that *Quicksand*'s modernist style conveys the contradictions produced by the failure of the bildungsroman to address how race and gender shape the experience of its mixed-race protagonist. Whereas the bildungsroman narrates the development of the individual in a national context, *Quicksand* points to the disorder resulting from the protagonist's multiple and incipient affiliations as well as the inadequacy of available subject positions. On the way that scenes in *Quicksand* resemble tableaux, see also Sherrard-Johnson, *Portraits of the New Negro Woman,* 21–48.

105. Sherrard-Johnson, 22.

106. Sherrard-Johnson, 28. For discussions of Orientalism in this passage, see also Reddy, *Freedom with Violence,* 119–24. Julia H. Lee argues that it is more accurate and illuminating to describe *Quicksand* in terms of its depiction of chinoiserie rather than Orientalism per se. See her *Interracial Encounters,* 114–37.

107. Sherrard-Johnson, *Portraits of the New Negro Woman,* 46.

108. The literary history of this passage also raises questions about what distinguishes the "intensely personal" from the fashionable and generic and how one perceives things as Orientalist, modernist, or "New Negro" (insofar as that term, particularly when referring to black women, implies more conservative modes of representation). As Erika Renée Williams shows in "A Lie of Omission," Larsen's opening scene nearly reproduces the wording and syntax of the opening passage of John Galsworthy's short story "The First and the Last." Galsworthy's tale is, in part, a critique of conventional morals and a commentary on the relationship between ethical conduct and a sensibility to beauty and emotion, as the protagonist's sensitive, sentimental brother sacrifices himself first for his lover and then for the innocent man who is accused of the crime he himself has committed. Moreover, Galsworthy's writing, including this story, occupies the border between modernism and Edwardian realism, a stylistic categorization that also operates to distinguish Larsen's more formally experimental texts from Fauset's and Du Bois's. Larsen's narrative technique throughout *Quicksand* is, in fact, a bit more recognizably modernist than Galworthy's, both in its more disorienting use of free indirect discourse and in its more disjunctive transitions between scenes. But her use of Galsworthy puts pressure on such imperfect and imprecise categorizations as realism and modernism.

109. Reddy, *Freedom with Violence,* 131.

110. See Weinbaum, "Racial Masquerade."

111. On Audrey as a queer figure whom Helga desires, see Doyle, *Freedom's Empire,* 401–5. On Audrey's subjectivity, see Vogel, *Scene of the Harlem Cabaret,* 95. On Audrey's apparent transcendence of race, see Sherrard-Johnson, *Portraits of the New Negro Woman,* 35–48.

112. Ngai, *Ugly Feelings,* 205, 208, emphasis in original.

113. Ngai, 208.

114. Doyle, *Freedom's Empire*, 404.

115. McDowell provides a foundational reading of *Passing* as a story of lesbian desire in her introduction to *Quicksand and Passing*.

116. This reading extends to *Passing*, as Clare is intermittently associated with Oriental aesthetics and with iconic beauty. Clare's skin is described as "ivory" and, in the moments after Clare's sudden fall from the window, Irene gazes at "a ridiculous Japanese print" and thinks, "Gone! The soft white face, the bright hair, the disturbing scarlet mouth, the caressing smile, the whole torturing loveliness that had been Clare Kendry. That beauty that had torn at Irene's placid life. Gone!" (Larsen, *Complete Works of Nella Larsen*, 177, 272).

117. Kim, "Being Modern," 383.

118. Wicke, "Enchantment, Disenchantment, Re-Enchantment," 130.

119. On the connection between print-cultural fashion and theories of history, see Campbell, *Historical Style*.

4. PROPHETS AND HISTORICISTS

1. Jameson, *Postmodernism*, 118.

2. Jameson at once affirms and undercuts the idea that the postmodern constitutes a new epoch (xii–xiii).

3. Fleissner, "Historicism Blues," 708.

4. Fleissner, 704.

5. Fleissner, 704, emphasis in original.

6. Ted Underwood describes how particular bourgeois concepts of periodization came to shape literary study and now are in decline in *Why Literary Periods Mattered*. Timothy Campbell's *Historical Style* argues more specifically that print-cultural fashion was at the heart of those ideas about history and periods.

7. Benjamin's account of fashion as "the tiger's leap into the past" refers to its capacity to sniff out what is once again "topical." Benjamin, however, focuses on fashion's backwards look as a way of thinking about how the past might provide revolutionary resources for the present. Fitzgerald's work is more concerned with how what is currently fashionable might later re-emerge as newly relevant, and his aim is not necessarily radical transformation—as it is for Benjamin and for Jameson.

8. The book's jacket copy, for example, declared the "novel so full of the unexpressed experiences, the true adventures and realities of youth, which conventional novelists leave untouched, that it seems rather an amazingly frank autobiography of a man's actual experiences—written with the unexpected freshness of youth itself and a touch of its insolence—than a work of fiction."

9. Fitzgerald, *Dear Scott/Dear Max*, 47, emphasis in the original. Fitzgerald may have been thinking specifically of H. L. Mencken, then arguably the most influential critic in the United States and a proponent of Conrad. Indeed, in a letter to Perkins in February 1920, Fitzgerald praised Mencken ("who is certainly a factor in present day literature") and admitted that he had helped him to see that "this fellow Conrad seems to be pretty good after all" (28). During Mencken's tenure as an editor of the *Smart Set*, the magazine published work by Joyce, Eliot, Pound, and Huxley, among others. Mencken's endorsement of *This Side of Paradise* was pivotal to establishing Fitzgerald's reputation and launching his career.

10. Glass, *Authors Inc*, 6; Fitzgerald, *Life in Letters*, 131.

11. On this point, see Galow, "Literary Modernism."

12. Glass, "Zuckerman/Roth," 224.

13. "Prediction Is Made about James Joyce Novel," 91.

14. "Paul Poiret Here to Tell of His Art," 11.

15. Ilya Parkins shows that Poiret's negotiations with femininity (including via his clients) are also ways to situate himself in the complex temporality of modernity. My discussion of Poiret is indebted to her *Poiret, Dior, Schiaparelli*, 47–78.

16. On the Fitzgeralds as celebrity couple, see Churchwell, "'Most Envied Couple in America'" 30.

17. Evans, "Denise Poiret," 27.

18. Poiret, *King of Fashion*, 82, 83.

19. Inglis, *Short History of Celebrity*, 155.

20. See, for example, Moran, *Star Authors* and, in modernist literary studies, Hammill, *Women, Celebrity, and Literary Culture between the Wars* and Goldman, *Modernism Is the Literature of Celebrity*. Rhonda K. Garelick, by contrast, traces contemporary forms of celebrity, including that of literary critics (namely, Derrida and de Man), to the literary figure of the dandy. Fitzgerald's and Poiret's work and lives recall aspects of the dandy persona as Garelick describes it, including an apparent mastery of fashionable femininity. Their dependence on women as consumers and even collaborators, as well as their public positions as parts of heterosexual dyads, however, depart from what Garelick argues is an increasingly strong association between dandyism and homosexuality in the late nineteenth and early twentieth centuries (which she associates in particular with the figure of Oscar Wilde). See Garelick, *Rising Star*.

21. Ilya Parkins shows how early twentieth-century fashion designers, including Poiret, exemplify particularly modern visions of celebrity and the artist, in her *Poiret, Dior, Schiaparelli*.

22. While the term *smart magazines* is used by George H. Douglas to categorize aspirational, middlebrow publications including *Vanity Fair* and the *New Yorker*, Catherine Keyser's *Playing Smart* takes up the idea of smartness to describe the strategies by which women magazine writers in the 1920s negotiated gender, racial, and class norms, including those enforced and refitted through fashion.

23. Mussell, "Repetition," 351.

24. Campbell, *Historical Style*, especially 57–67.

25. We can also connect that visibility of aristocratic women in fashion magazines to the novel's interrogations of gender and sex, given what Laura Doan shows is the varying visibility of lesbian identity in the twenties thanks to the trend for masculine dress. See Doan, *Fashioning Sapphism*, 95–125.

26. Woolf, *Orlando*, 154.

27. Woolf, 163.

28. Woolf, 137.

29. For example, for a discussion of the relationship between the transgender and transnational dynamics of the novel, see Berman, "Is the Trans in Transnational the Trans in Transgender?" and for an analysis of the link between its transsexual and transtemporal dimensions, see Caughie, "Temporality of Modernist Life Writing in the Era of Transsexualism."

30. Mencken, Review of *The Great Gatsby*, 111, 114.

31. Mencken, 114.

32. Wicke, "Enchantment, Disenchantment, Re-Enchantment," 130.

33. Fitzgerald, "Echoes of the Jazz Age," 13. Woolf, "Modern Fiction," 146.

34. Fitzgerald, 14.

35. "Evolution of Style," 49, 52–55, 110.

36. "Evolution of Style," 48.

37. Fitzgerald, "Echoes of the Jazz Age," 16.

38. Fitzgerald, 16–17.

39. *Ulysses*'s final serial installment in the *Little Review* appeared in December 1920, and its publication as a book was in 1922.

40. Tables of contents, *Esquire*, June 1934 and September 1934.

41. West, "Fitzgerald and *Esquire*," 149.

42. Lardner, "Princeton Panorama," 69.

43. For a discussion of these distinctions and insights about Fitzgerald's relationship to early twentieth-century magazine culture, see Harris, *On Company Time*, 1–28.

44. Fitzgerald, "Echoes of the Jazz Age," 17.

45. For a relevant analysis of *The Great Gatsby*'s whitening of jazz, see Breitwieser, "*The Great Gatsby*" and his "Jazz Fractures." On the way jazz exemplifies the novel's handling of black and Jewish bodies and culture, see Goldsmith, "White Skin, White Mask."
46. Fitzgerald, "Echoes of the Jazz Age," 14.
47. Fitzgerald, 21.
48. Fitzgerald, *The Great Gatsby*, 11, 97 (hereafter cited in text as *GG*).
49. Goldsmith, "White Skin, White Mask," 448.
50. I am indebted to Megan Ward for this observation.
51. Hughes and Lund, *Victorian Serial*, 63.
52. Mussell, "Repetition," 350.
53. Christopher P. Wilson observes, "Nick's own sequential revisions—his own cycling of disclosure and closure—implicitly captures the typical routine of the tabloids' own operations: revelations that not only allowed a story to grow, but to acquire sensational excess through retelling, often keyed to the promise of the next edition" ("'He Fell Just Short of Being News,'" 126).
54. Wilson, 120. Wilson focuses on this passage in his discussion of how tabloids structure the aesthetic of *The Great Gatsby*, particularly the uncertain relationship between foreground and background. He also emphasizes that periodicals—specifically tabloids—are not just sources and context for the novel, but shape its form and epistemology.
55. Gallagher and Greenblatt, *Practicing New Historicism*, 51.
56. Hayot, "Against Periodization; or, On Institutional Time," 742.
57. Mussell, "Repetition," 345.
58. Walter Benn Michaels reads this moment as confirming Lothrop Stoddard's nativist, eugenicist vision of American history as heritage rather than an achievement as it connects Nick to the Dutch sailors (*Our America*, 35). My reading suggests, however, that the novel's conclusion underscores that that understanding of history is artificial and fashionable, if hard to displace or replace.
59. This attitude is displayed in Fitzgerald's famous letter to Hemingway in which his postscript notes with "a last flicker of the old cheap pride:—the *Post* now pay the old whore $4000. a screw" (Fitzgerald, *A Life in Letters*, 169). With respect to *Gatsby*, when writing to Perkins as he was completing the book, Fitzgerald contrasted the content of the novel with the "trashy imaginings" that made up his stories (67). Fitzgerald also asserted to Perkins that *The Great Gatsby* was "not a very serialized book" and hence not well fitted for magazine publication, although he also mentioned that he had a plan for splitting the novel into ten sections should he get the right offer (84). One can only guess what Fitzgerald thought made the book particularly ill-fitted for serial publication; perhaps it was the lack of narrative suspense in each chapter, the difficulty that readers might find in orienting themselves in the midst of the often elliptical text, or—as he insisted elsewhere—that *Gatsby* was a "man's book," but women drove the market for fiction.
60. Fitzgerald, 158, emphasis in original.
61. Jaffe, *Modernism and the Culture of Celebrity*, 69.
62. For an account of the passages taken from various short stories, see Bruccoli, *Composition of Tender is the Night*.
63. Mangum, "Short Stories of F. Scott Fitzgerald," 61, 57–78. Matthew Bruccoli proposes that the short stories can be seen as "the equivalent of a more orderly writer's notebooks" (*Composition of Tender Is the Night*, 70).
64. Fitzgerald, *A Life in Letters*, 84.
65. See Troy, *Couture Culture*, 266–326. Troy's study unpacks the implications of Poiret's system of production, as well as his positioning as an artist, and shows how these overlap with the shifts in discourses of originality that were key to developments in early twentieth-century art.
66. *Les modèles de Paul Poiret*, 12.
67. Poiret, *King of Fashion*, 47.

68. See Burstein, *Cold Modernism*, 150. Garelick also offers a compelling account of how Chanel built her business on others' desire to copy her (as well as her ability to incorporate aspects of other people); for example, Garelick describes Chanel as having a "wearable personality" (*Mademoiselle*, xvii).

69. Poiret, *King of Fashion*, 93.

70. Poiret, 94, 95.

71. Poiret, 99.

72. For a discussion of Poiret's albums in relation to his self-presentation as an artist and art collector, see Troy, *Couture Culture*, especially 52–54.

73. Poiret, *King of Fashion*, 329.

74. Poiret, 192.

75. See Parkins, *Poiret, Dior, and Schiaparelli*, especially 47–78.

76. Poiret, *King of Fashion*, 161.

77. Poiret, 163.

78. Poiret travelled to the United States in 1913, 1922, and 1927, and gave lectures in 1913 and 1927. For coverage by the *New York Times* of the 1913 and 1927 trips, see "Poiret, Creator of Fashions, Here," x3, and "Poiret Decries Trend of Modern Fashions," 2, respectively.

79. Poiret, *King of Fashion*, 292, 294.

80. Fitzgerald, *Tender Is the Night*, 17, 280 (hereafter cited in text as *TN*).

81. Messenger, "'Out Upon the Mongolian Plain,'" 165.

82. Vaill, *Everybody Was So Young*, 46, 18. Given Dick's role as an educator of women, it is worth noting that in 1939, the Murphys gave a loan to Fitzgerald that, he claimed, allowed him "to send Scottie back to Vassar" (Fitzgerald, *A Life in Letters*, 463).

83. Vaill, *Everybody Was So Young*, 86–87, 156.

84. Mark Cross, "Our Story."

85. Fitzgerald, "Echoes of the Jazz Age," 6.

86. Fitzgerald's dissatisfaction with this structure in *Tender Is the Night*, however, led him to begin creating what has been described as an "eighteenth draft" of the novel, which told the story in chronological order and was the basis of the version of *Tender* published in 1948.

87. Since as George Anderson notes, Fitzgerald was scrupulous about not allowing any passages that had been "stripped" for *Tender Is the Night* from short stories that were published in magazines to then appear in those stories as published in *Taps in Reveille*, Fitzgerald seems to have bet, in effect, on the ephemerality of magazines ("F. Scott Fitzgerald's Use of Story Strippings," 218).

88. Fitzgerald, *A Life in Letters*, 255.

89. Fitzgerald, 256.

90. Perhaps Fitzgerald imagined his nickel-sized imprint would replace the head of a Native American, which was then featured on the nickel and in fact was the work of a fellow Minnesotan, the sculptor James Earle Fraser.

91. Mencken, Review of *The Great Gatsby*, 114.

92. Mencken, Review of *The Beautiful and the Damned*, 106.

93. Miller, *Ariadne's Thread*, 56.

CODA

1. Wai Chee Dimock offers resonance as a model for thinking transtemporally in "A Theory of Resonance."

2. James and Seshagiri, "Metamodernism," 91.

3. James and Seshagiri, 88.

4. Freeman, *Time Binds*, 71.

5. Benjamin, "On the Concept of History," in *Selected Writings*, 395.

6. Freeman, *Time Binds*, 70.

7. Nico Israel's *Spirals* shows how the spiral functions as a way of representing and theorizing the relationship between the local and global and between past, present, and future in twentieth-century art. What Israel notes as the spiral's vision of history of "repetitions-with-a-difference" in various early Cold War works neatly expresses what I am arguing is modernism's status in Ghani's work as well as her vision of history (19).

8. Guggenheim Foundation, "Solomon R. Guggenheim Museum and Rockbund Art Museum." As this press release explains, the show on "the Middle East and North Africa" was "the final installment of the UBS MAP Global Art Initiative," which included shows focused on art from South and Southeast Asian as well as Latin America. Ghani's piece helps to expose the particular logic of inclusion not only through its form, but also through its focus on her identification with Afghanistan, which of course has a peripheral relationship to "the Middle East and North Africa" as a region.

9. Gulf Labor Artist Coalition, "Gulf Labor Responds."

10. Ghani and Ghani, *Afghanistan*, xx.

11. Ghani, "Work: *A Brief History of Collapses.*"

12. Ghani, *A Brief History of Collapses* (voice-over script), 6, 1.

13. Ghani, 1.

14. Benjamin, "The Work of Art in the Age of Its Technological Reproducibility," 40.

15. Benjamin, 267.

16. Ghani, *A Brief History of Collapses* (voice-over script), 4.

17. Ghani, 3.

18. As Peter Stallybrass notes in "Marx's Coat," the word *memory* itself has a material dimensions that underscore the ways that dress can serve as an archive: "In the language of nineteenth century clothes-makers and repairers, the wrinkles in the elbows of a jacket or a sleeve were called 'memories'" (196).

19. Marks, *Touch*, xvi.

20. Marks, xvi.

21. Lawrence, "Education of the People," 152.

Works Cited

Abbott, Reginald. "What Miss Kilman's Petticoat Means: Virginia Woolf, Shopping, and Spectacle." *Modern Fiction Studies* 38, no. 1 (Spring 1992): 193–216.

Adburgham, Alison. *Shopping in Style: London from the Restoration to Edwardian Elegance*. London: Thames and Hudson, 1979.

Adorno, Theodor. *Aesthetic Theory*. Edited by Gretel Adorno and Rolf Tiedemann. Translated and edited by Robert Hullot-Kentor. Minneapolis: University of Minnesota Press, 1997.

Ahmad, Dohra. "'More than Romance': Genre and Geography in *Dark Princess*." *ELH* 69, no. 3 (2002): 775–803.

Ahmed, Sara. *The Cultural Politics of Emotion*. New York: Routledge, 2004.

Ahmed, Sara. "Imaginary Prohibitions: Some Preliminary Remarks on the Founding Gestures of the 'New Materialism.'" *European Journal of Women's Studies* 15, no. 1 (2008): 23–39.

Ahmed, Sara. "Not in the Mood." *New Formations* 82 (2014): 14.

Ahmed, Sara. *On Being Included: Racism and Diversity in Institutional Life*. Durham, NC: Duke University Press, 2012.

Ahmed, Sara. "Orientations Matter." In *New Materialisms: Ontology, Agency, and Politics*, edited by Diana Coole and Samantha Frost, 234–57. Durham, NC: Duke University Press, 2010.

Ahmed, Sara. *The Promise of Happiness*. Durham, NC: Duke University Press, 2010.

Ahmed, Sara. *Queer Phenomenology: Orientations, Objects, Others*. Durham, NC: Duke University Press, 2006.

Allen, Carol. *Black Women Intellectuals: Strategies of Nation, Family, and Neighborhood in the Works of Pauline Hopkins, Jessie Fauset, and Marita Bonner*. New York, Garland, 1998.

Altieri, Charles. "Afterword: How the 'New Modernist Studies' Fails the Old Modernism." *Textual Practice* 26, no. 4 (2012): 763–82.

Anderson. George. "F. Scott Fitzgerald's Use of Story Strippings in *Tender Is the Night*." In *Reader's Companion to F. Scott Fitzgerald's* Tender Is the Night, edited by Matthew J. Bruccoli, 213–62. Columbia: University of South Carolina Press, 1996.

Anscombe, Isabelle. *The Omega and After: Bloomsbury and the Decorative Arts*. London: Thames and Hudson, 1981.

Baldwin, Davarian L. *Chicago's New Negroes: Modernity, the Great Migration, and Black Urban Life*. Chapel Hill: University of North Carolina Press, 2007.

Baldwin, Davarian L. "Introduction: New Negroes Forging a New World." In *Escape from New York: The New Negro Renaissance beyond Harlem*, edited by Davarian L. Baldwin and Minkah Makalani, 1–27. Minneapolis: University of Minnesota Press, 2013.

Barthes, Roland. *The Fashion System*. Berkeley: University of California Press, 1983.

Baudelaire, Charles. "The Painter of Modern Life." In *The Painter of Modern Life and Other Essays*, translated and edited by Jonathan Mayne, 1–41. London: Phaidon, 2003.

Bell, Vanessa. *The Selected Letters of Vanessa Bell*. Edited by Regina Marler. New York: Pantheon Books, 1993.

Benjamin, Walter. *The Arcades Project*. Translated by Howard Eiland and Kevin McLaughlin. Cambridge, MA: Belknap Press of Harvard University Press, 1999.

Benjamin, Walter. *Selected Writings*. Vol. 4, *1938–1940*. Translated by Edmund Jephcott, Howard Eiland, et al. Edited by Howard Eiland and Michael W. Jennings. Cambridge, MA: Belknap Press of Harvard University Press, 2003.

Benjamin, Walter. "The Work of Art in the Age of Its Technological Reproducibility." In *The Work of Art in the Age of Its Technological Reproducibility and Other Writings On Media*, edited by Michael W. Jennings, Brigid Doherty, and Thomas Y. Levin, 19–55. Cambridge, MA: Belknap Press of Harvard University Press, 2008.

Bennett, Jane. *The Enchantment of Modern Life: Attachments, Crossings, and Ethics*. Princeton, NJ: Princeton University Press, 2001.

Bennett, Jane. *Vibrant Matter: A Political Ecology of Things*. Durham, NC: Duke University Press, 2010.

Berlant, Lauren. *Cruel Optimism*. Durham, NC: Duke University Press, 2011.

Berman, Jessica. "Is the Trans in Transnational the Trans in Transgender?" *Modernism/Modernity* 24, no. 2 (2017): 217–44.

Berman, Jessica. *Modernist Commitments: Ethics, Politics, and Transnational Modernism*. New York: Columbia University Press, 2011.

Best, Stephen, and Sharon Marcus. "Surface Reading: An Introduction." In "The Way We Read Now." Special issue, *Representations* 108, no.1 (Fall 2009): 1–21.

Bingham, Adrian. "'Stop the Flapper Vote Folly': Lord Rothmere, the *Daily Mail*, and the Equalization of the Franchise 1927–1928." *Twentieth Century British History* 13, no. 1 (2002): 17–37.

Bora, Renu. "Outing Texture." In *Novel Gazing: Queer Readings in Fiction*, edited by Eve Kosofsky Sedgwick, 94–127. Durham, NC: Duke University Press, 1997.

Boucher, François. *20,000 Years of Fashion: The History of Costume and Personal Adornment*. New York: Harry N. Abrams, 1987.

Braddock, Jeremy. "The Poetics of Conjecture: Countee Cullen's Subversive Exemplarity." *Callaloo* 25, no. 4 (Autumn 2002): 1250–71.

Bradshaw, David. "Red Trousers: *Lady Chatterley's Lover* and John Hargrave." *Essays in Criticism* 55, no. 4 (October 2005): 352–73.

Braun, Emily. "Futurist Fashion: Three Manifestoes." *Art Journal* 54, no. 1 (Spring 1995): 34–41.

Breitwieser, Mitchell. "*The Great Gatsby*: Grief, Jazz and the Eye-Witness." *Arizona Quarterly* 47, no. 3 (1991): 17–70.

Breitwieser, Mitchell. "Jazz Fractures: F. Scott Fitzgerald and Epochal Representation." *American Literary History* 12, no. 3 (2000): 359–81.

Breward, Christopher. *Fashion.* Oxford: Oxford University Press, 2003.

Brockington, Grace. *Above the Battlefield: Modernism and the Peace Movement in Britain, 1900–1918.* New Haven, CT: Yale University Press and Paul Mellon Center for British Art, 2011.

Brockington, Grace. "The Omega and the End of Civilisation: Pacifism, Publishing, and Performance in the First World War." In *Beyond Bloomsbury: Designs of the Omega Workshops 1913–19,* edited by Alexandra Gerstein, 61–70. London: Courtauld Gallery and the Fontanka Press, 2009.

Brown, Bill. "The Secret Life of Things (Virginia Woolf and the Matter of Modernism)." *Modernism/Modernity* 6, no. 2 (April 1999): 1–28.

Brown, Bill. *A Sense of Things: The Object Matter of American Literature.* Chicago: Chicago University Press, 2003.

Brown, Judith. *Glamour in Six Dimensions: Modernism and the Radiance of Form.* Ithaca, NY: Cornell University Press, 2009.

Bruccoli, Matthew J. *The Composition of* Tender is the Night. Pittsburgh, PA: University of Pittsburgh Press, 1963.

Bruccoli, Matthew J. *Some Sort of Epic Grandeur: The Life of F. Scott Fitzgerald.* Rev. ed. Columbia: University of South Carolina Press, 2002.

Bruccoli, Matthew J., Scottie Fitzgerald Smith, and Joan P. Kerr, eds. *The Romantic Egoists.* New York: Scribner's, 1974.

Bryer, Jackson R., ed. *F. Scott Fitzgerald: The Critical Reception.* New York: Burt Franklin, 1978.

Buck-Morss, Susan. *The Dialectics of Seeing: Walter Benjamin and the Arcades Project.* Cambridge, MA: M.I.T. Press, 1991.

Bundles, A'Lelia. *On Her Own Ground: The Life and Times of Madam C. J. Walker.* New York: Scribner's, 2001.

Burberry. "Burberry Prorsum Womenswear Autumn/Winter 2014 Show." *Burberry.* February 17, 2014. http://www.burberryplc.com/media_centre/press_releases/2014/burberry-prorsum-womenswear-autumn-winter-2014-show (page discontinued).

Burman, Barbara. "The Better and Brighter Clothes: The Men's Dress Reform Party, 1929–1940." *Journal of Design History* 8, no. 4 (1995): 275–90.

Burstein, Jessica. *Cold Modernism: Literature, Fashion, Art.* University Park: Pennsylvania State University Press, 2012.

Campbell, Timothy. *Historical Style: Fashion and the New Mode of History, 1740–1830.* Philadelphia: University of Pennsylvania Press, 2016.

Carby, Hazel. "The Souls of Black Men." In *Next to the Color Line: Gender, Sexuality, and W. E. B. Du Bois,* edited by Susan Gillman and Alys Eve Weinbaum, 234–68. Minneapolis: University of Minnesota Press, 2007.

Carlson, Jennifer D., and Kathleen C. Stewart. "The Legibilities of Mood Work." *New Formations* 82 (2014): 114–33.

carrington, andre m. "Salon Cultures and Spaces of Culture Edification." In *A Companion to the Harlem Renaissance,* edited by Cherene Sherrard-Johnson, 251–66. West Sussex, UK: Wiley Blackwell, 2015.

Carter, Angela. "Lorenzo the Closet-Queen." In *Shaking a Leg: Collected Writings,* 498–503. New York: Penguin Books, 1998.

Castronovo, Russ. *Beautiful Democracy: Aesthetics and Anarchy in a Global Era*. Chicago: University of Chicago Press, 2007.

Caughie, Pamela. "The Temporality of Modernist Life Writing in the Era of Transsexualism: Virginia Woolf's *Orlando* and Einer Wegener's *Man into Woman*." *Modern Fiction Studies* 59, no. 3 (2013): 501–25.

Chaudhaury, Amit. *D. H. Lawrence and "Difference."* Oxford: Oxford University Press, 2003.

Cheng, Anne Anlin. *Second Skin: Josephine Baker and the Modern Surface*. Oxford: Oxford University Press, 2011.

Cheng, Anne Anlin. "Shine: On Race, Glamour, and the Modern." *PMLA* 126, no. 4 (October 2011): 1022–41.

Cheng, Anne Anlin. "Skin, Tattoos, and Susceptibility." *Representations* 108, no. 1 (Fall 2009): 98–119.

Cheng, Anne Anlin. "Wounded Beauty: An Exploratory Essay on Race, Feminism, and the Aesthetic Question." *Tulsa Studies in Women's Literature* 19, no. 2 (2000): 191–217.

Churchwell, Sarah. "'The Most Envied Couple in America in 1921': Making the Social Register in the Scrapbooks of F. Scott and Zelda Fitzgerald." In *First Comes Love: Power Couples, Celebrity Kinship and Cultural Politics*, edited by Shelley Cobb and Neil Ewen, 29–52. New York: Bloomsbury, 2015.

Clarke, Allison, and Daniel Miller. "Fashion and Anxiety." *Fashion Theory* 6, no. 2 (2012): 191–213.

Clarke, Bruce. *Energy Forms: Allegory and Science in the Era of Classical Thermodynamics*. Ann Arbor: University of Michigan Press, 2001.

Cohen, Lisa. "'Frock Consciousness': Virginia Woolf, the Open Secret, and the Language of Fashion." *Fashion Theory* 3, no. 2 (1999): 149–74.

Cole, Sarah. *At the Violet Hour: Modernism and Violence in England and Ireland*. New York: Oxford University Press, 2012.

Colebrook, Claire, and Rita Felski, eds. "Beauty." Special issue, *Feminist Theory* 7, no. 2 (2006): 131–282.

Collins, Judith. *The Omega Workshops*. London: Martin Secker, 1983.

Conor, Liz. *The Spectacular Modern Woman: Feminine Visibility in the 1920s*. Bloomington: Indiana University Press, 2004.

Coole, Diane, and Samantha Frost. "Introducing the New Materialisms." In *New Materialisms: Ontology, Agency, and Politics*, 1–46. Durham, NC: Duke University Press, 2010.

Craig, Maxine Leeds. "Race, Beauty, and the Tangled Knot of a Guilty Pleasure." In "Beauty." Special issue, *Feminist Theory* 7, no. 2 (2006): 159–77.

Cunningham, Patricia A. *Reforming Women's Fashion: Politics, Health, and Art*. Kent, OH: Kent State University Press, 2003.

Davis, Mary E. *Classic Chic: Music, Fashion and Modernism*. Berkeley: University of California Press, 2006.

Davis, Thomas S. *The Extinct Scene: Late Modernism and Everyday Life*. New York: Columbia University Press, 2015.

Davis, Thomas S. "The Historical Novel at History's End: Virginia Woolf's *The Years*," *Twentieth Century Literature* 60, no.1 (Spring 2014): 1–26.

Diepeveen, Leonard. *The Difficulties of Modernism*. New York: Routledge, 2003.

Deleuze, Gilles, and Felix Guattari. *Anti-Oedipus: Capitalism and Schizophrenia*. Translated by Robert Hurley et al. Minneapolis: University of Minnesota Press, 2003.

Derrida, Jacques. *The Animal that Therefore I Am*. Edited by Marie-Louise Mallet. Translated by David Wills. New York: Fordham University Press, 2008.

Dettmar, Kevin J. H., and Stephen Watt, eds. *Marketing Modernisms*. Ann Arbor: University of Michigan Press, 1996.

DiBattista, Maria. *First Love: The Affections of Modern Fiction*. Chicago: University of Chicago Press, 1991.

Dimock, Wai Chee. "A Theory of Resonance." *PMLA* 112, no. 5 (1997): 1060–71.

Dimock, Wai Chee. "Weak Theory." *Critical Inquiry* 39, no. 4 (Spring 2013): 732–53.

Dixon, Ella Hepworth. "Woman's Ways." *Sketch*, June 23, 1915.

Doan, Laura. *Fashioning Sapphism: The Origins of Modern English Lesbian Culture*. New York: Columbia University Press, 2001.

Dossett, Kate. "'I Try to Live Somewhat in Keeping with My Reputation as a Wealthy Woman': A'Lelia Walker and the Madam C. J. Walker Manufacturing Company." *Journal of Women's History* 21, no. 2 (2009): 90–114.

Doyle, Laura. *Freedom's Empire: Race and the Rise of the Novel in Atlantic Modernity, 1640–1940*. Durham, NC: Duke University Press, 2008.

Du Bois, W. E. B. "A'Lelia Walker." *Crisis*, October 1931.

Du Bois, W. E. B. "The Browsing Reader: Two Novels." *Crisis*, June 1928.

Du Bois, W. E. B. "The Color Line Belts the World." In *W. E. B. Du Bois on Asia: Crossing the World Color Line*, edited by Bill V. Mullen and Cathryn Watson, 33–34. Jackson: University Press of Mississippi, 2005.

Du Bois, W. E. B. "Criteria of Negro Art." *Crisis*, October 1926.

Du Bois, W. E. B. *Dark Princess: A Romance*. Jackson, MS: Banner, 1995.

Du Bois, W. E. B. "A Great Woman." *Crisis*, July 1919.

Du Bois, W. E. B. "Hayti." *Crisis*, September 1915.

Du Bois, W. E. B. "The Problem of Amusement." In *W. E. B. Du Bois on Sociology and the Black Community*, edited by Dan S. Green and Edwin D. Driver, 226–37. Chicago: University of Chicago Press, 1978.

Du Bois, W. E. B. *The Souls of Black Folk*. New Haven, CT: Yale University Press, 2015.

Du Bois, W. E. B. "So the Girl Marries." *Crisis*, June 1928.

DuCille, Ann. *The Coupling Convention: Sex, Text, and Tradition in Black Women's Fiction*. New York: Oxford University Press, 1993.

Dudley, Tara. "Seeking the Ideal African-American Interior: The Walker Residences and Salon in New York." *Studies in the Decorative Arts* 14, no. 1 (2006–2007): 80–112.

Edelman, Lee. *No Future: Queer Theory and the Death Drive*. Durham, NC: Duke University Press, 2004.

Edwards, Brent Hayes. *The Practice of Diaspora: Literature, Translation, and the Rise of Black Internationalism*. Cambridge, MA: Harvard University Press, 2003.

English, Bonnie. *Cultural History of Fashion in the 20th and 21st Centuries: From the Catwalk to the Sidewalk*. London: Bloomsbury Academic, 2007.

English, Daylanne K. *Unnatural Selections: Eugenics in American Modernism and the Harlem Renaissance*. Chapel Hill: University of North Carolina Press, 2004.

Enstad, Nan. "Fashioning Political Identities: Cultural Studies and the Historical Construction of Political Subjects." *American Quarterly* 50, no. 4 (1998): 745–82.

Esty, Jed. *A Shrinking Island: Modernism and National Culture in England*. Princeton, NJ: Princeton University Press, 2003.

Esty, Jed. *Unseasonable Youth: Modernism, Colonialism and the Fiction of Development.* Oxford: Oxford University Press, 2012.

Evans, Caroline. "Denise Poiret: Muse or Mannequin?" In *Poiret: Exhibition Catalogue*, edited by Harold Koda and Andrew Boulton, 27–29. New York: Metropolitan Museum of Art Publications, 2007.

Evans, Caroline. *Fashion at the Edge: Spectacle, Modernity and Deathliness.* New Haven, CT: Yale University Press, 2003.

Evans, Elizabeth F. "Air War, Propaganda, and Woolf's Anti-Tyranny Aesthetic." *Modern Fiction Studies* 59, no. 1 (Spring 2013): 53–82.

"The Evolution of Style." *Harper's Bazaar*, January 1930.

"Fashion and the Vote: Women's Dress as Hindrance to Her Cause." *Times* (London), April 11, 1914.

Fauset, Jessie. "The Gift of Laughter." In *The New Negro: Voices of the Harlem Renaissance*, edited by Alain Locke, 161–67. New York: Touchstone, 1999.

Fauset, Jessie Redmon. 1989. *There Is Confusion.* Foreword by Thadious M. Davis. Boston, MA: Northeastern University Press.

Felski, Rita. *The Limits of Critique.* Chicago: University of Chicago Press, 2015.

Felski, Rita. *Uses of Literature.* Malden, MA: Blackwell Publishing, 2008.

Felski, Rita, and Susan Fraiman, eds. "In the Mood." Special issue, *New Literary History* 43, no. 3 (Summer 2012).

Felski, Rita, and Susan Fraiman, eds. Introduction to "In the Mood." Special issue, *New Literary History* 43, no. 3 (Summer 2012): v–xii.

Fernihough, Anne. *D. H. Lawrence: Aesthetics and Ideology.* Oxford: Oxford University Press, 1993.

Ferrall, Charles, and Dougal McNeill. *Writing the 1926 General Strike: Literature, Culture, Politics.* New York: Cambridge University Press, 2015.

Finch, R. W. *Correspondence of the Military Intelligence Division Relating to "Negro Subversion," 1917–1941.* March 5, 1919. National Archives and Records Administration.

Fitzgerald, F. Scott. *Conversations with F. Scott Fitzgerald.* Eds. Matthew J. Bruccoli and Judith S. Baughman. Jackson: University Press of Mississippi, 2004.

Fitzgerald, F. Scott. *Dear Scott/Dear Max: The Fitzgerald-Perkins Correspondence.* Edited by John Kuehl and Jackson R. Bryer. New York: Scribner's, 1991.

Fitzgerald, F. Scott. "Echoes of the Jazz Age." In *The Crack-Up*, edited by Edmund Wilson, 13–22. New York: New Directions, 1945.

Fitzgerald, F. Scott. *The Great Gatsby.* Notes and preface by Matthew Bruccoli. New York: Scribner's, 1992.

Fitzgerald, F. Scott. *Letters of F. Scott Fitzgerald.* Edited by Andrew Turnbull. New York: Dell, 1965.

Fitzgerald, F. Scott. *A Life in Letters.* Edited by Matthew J Bruccoli. New York: Macmillan, 1994.

Fitzgerald, F. Scott. *Tender Is the Night.* New York: Scribner's, 2004.

Flatley, Jonathan. *Affective Mapping: Melancholia and the Politics of Modernism.* Cambridge, MA: Harvard University Press, 2008.

Flatley, Jonathan. "How a Revolutionary Counter-Mood Is Made." *New Literary History* 43 (2012): 503–25.

Fleissner, Jennifer. "Historicism Blues." *American Literary History* 25, no. 4 (Winter 2013): 699–717.

Fleissner, Jennifer. "Is Feminism a Historicism?" *Tulsa Studies in Women's Literature* 21, no. 2 (2002): 45–66.

Flügel, J. C. *The Psychology of Clothes.* London: Hogarth Press, 1930.

Foley, Barbara. *Spectres of 1919: Class and Nation in the Making of the New Negro.* Urbana: University of Illinois Press, 2008.

Freeman, Elizabeth. *Time Binds: Queer Temporalities, Queer Histories.* Durham, NC: Duke University Press, 2010.

Frost, Laura. *Sex Drives: Fantasies of Fascism in Literary Modernism.* Ithaca, NY: Cornell University Press, 2002.

Froula, Christine. *Virginia Woolf and the Bloomsbury Avant-Garde: War, Civilization, Modernity.* New York: Columbia University Press, 2005.

Fry, Roger. "Omega Workshops Fundraising Letter." In *A Roger Fry Reader*, edited by Christopher Reed, 196–97. Chicago: University of Chicago Press, 1996.

Fry, Roger. "Preface to the Omega Workshops Catalog." In *A Roger Fry Reader*, edited by Christopher Reed, 201. Chicago: University of Chicago Press, 1996.

Gaipa, Mark. "Accessorizing Clarissa: How Virginia Woolf Changes the Clothes and the Character of Her Lady of Fashion." *Modernist Cultures* 4 (2009): 24–47.

Gallagher, Catherine, and Stephen Greenblatt. *Practicing New Historicism.* Chicago: University of Chicago Press, 2000.

Galow, Timothy W. "Literary Modernism in the Age of Celebrity." *Modernism/Modernity* 17, no. 2 (2010): 313–29.

Garelick, Rhonda K. *Mademoiselle: Coco Chanel and the Pulse of History.* New York: Random House, 2014.

Garelick, Rhonda K. *Rising Star: Dandyism, Gender, and Performance in the Fin de Siècle.* Princeton, NJ: Princeton University Press, 1998.

Garrity, Jane. "Selling Culture to the 'Civilized': Bloomsbury, British *Vogue*, and the Marketing of National Identity." *Modernism/Modernity* 6, no. 2 (1999): 29–58.

Garrity, Jane. "Virginia Woolf, Intellectual Harlotry, and 1920s British *Vogue*." In *Virginia Woolf in the Age of Mechanical Reproduction: Technology, Mass Culture, and the Arts*, edited by Pamela L. Caughie, 185–211. London: Garland, 2000.

Garrity, Jane. "Woolf and Fashion." In *The Edinburgh Companion to Virginia Woolf and the Arts*, edited by Maggie Humm, 195–211. Edinburgh: Edinburgh University Press, 2010.

Ghani, Mariam. "Work: A Brief History of Collapses." *Mariam Ghani*. Accessed October 15, 2017. http://www.mariamghani.com/work/357.

Ghani, Mariam, and Ashraf Ghani. *Afghanistan: A Lexicon: 100 Notes—100 Thoughts.* Ostfildern, Germany: Hatje Cantz Verlag, 2011.

Gilbert, Sandra M. "Costumes of the Mind: Transvestism as Metaphor in Modern Literature." *Critical Inquiry* 7, no. 2 (Winter 1980): 391–417.

Gill, Tiffany. *Beauty Shop Politics: African American Women's Activism in the Beauty Industry.* Urbana: University of Illinois Press, 2010.

Glass, Loren. *Authors Inc.: Literary Celebrity in the Modern United States, 1880–1980.* New York: New York University Press, 2004.

Glass, Loren. "Zuckerman/Roth: Literary Celebrity between Two Deaths." *PMLA* 129, no. 2 (2014): 223–36.

Goldman, Jonathan. *Modernism Is the Literature of Celebrity.* Austin: University of Texas, 2011.

Goldsmith, Meredith. "White Skin, White Mask: Passing, Posing, and Performing in *The Great Gatsby.*" *Modern Fiction Studies* 49, no. 3 (Fall 2003): 443–68.

Goldstone, Andrew. *Fictions of Autonomy: Modernism from Wilde to de Man.* Oxford: Oxford University Press, 2013.

Goyal, Yogita. *Romance, Diaspora, and Black Atlantic Literature.* Cambridge: Cambridge University Press, 2010.

Green, Barbara. *Spectacular Confessions: Autobiography, Performative Activism, and the Sites of Suffrage 1905–1938.* New York: Palgrave, 1997.

Grosz, Elizabeth. *Becoming Undone: Darwinian Reflections on Life, Politics, and Art.* Durham, NC: Duke University Press, 2011.

Grosz, Elizabeth. "Feminism, Materialism, and Freedom." In *New Materialisms: Ontology, Agency, and Politics,* edited by Diana Coole and Samantha Frost, 139–57. Durham, NC: Duke University Press, 2010.

Grosz, Elizabeth. *Volatile Bodies: Toward a Corporeal Feminism.* Bloomington: Indiana University Press, 1994.

Guggenheim Foundation. "Solomon R. Guggenheim Museum and Rockbund Art Museum, Shanghai, Present Exhibition of Middle Eastern and North African Art from April 15 to June 11, 2017." *Guggenheim.* https://www.guggenheim.org/press-release /solomon-r-guggenheim-museum-and-rockbund-art-museum-shanghai-present -exhibition-of-middle-eastern-and-north-african-art-from-april-15-to-june-11-2017.

Gulf Labor Artist Coalition. "Gulf Labor Responds to Guggenheim Breaking off Negotiations." *Gulf Labor Artist Coalition.* April 18, 2016. https://gulflabor.org/?s =gulf+labor+responds.

Haffey, Kate. "Exquisite Moments and the Temporality of the Kiss in *Mrs. Dalloway* and *The Hours.*" *Narrative* 18, no. 2 (2010): 137–64.

Hagen, Benjamin D. "Feeling Shadows: Virginia Woolf's Sensuous Pedagogy." *PMLA* 123, no. 2 (2017): 266–80.

Hammill, Faye. *Women, Celebrity, and Literary Culture between the Wars.* Austin: University of Texas Press, 2007.

Harris, Donal. *On Company Time: American Modernism in the Big Magazines.* New York: Columbia University Press, 2016.

Harrison, Andrew. *D. H. Lawrence and Italian Futurism: A Study of Influence.* Amsterdam: Rodopi, 2003.

Hayot, Eric. "Against Periodization; or, On Institutional Time." *New Literary History* 42, no. 4 (Autumn 2011): 739–56.

Heidegger, Martin. *Being and Time.* Translated by John MacQuarrie and Edward Robinson. Foreword by Taylor Carman. New York: Harper Perennial, 2008.

Hemmings, Clare. "In the Mood for Revolution." *New Literary History* 43, no. 3 (Summer 2012): 527–45.

Herbert, Michael. Introduction to *Reflections on the Death of a Porcupine,* edited by Michael Herbert, xvii–lvii. Cambridge: Cambridge University Press, 1988.

Higginbotham, Evelyn Brooks. *Righteous Discontent: The Woman's Movement in the Black Baptist Church, 1880–1920.* Cambridge, MA: Harvard University Press, 1993.

Highmore, Ben, and Jenny Bourne Taylor. "Introducing Mood Work." In "Mood Work." Special issue, *New Formations* 82 (2014): 5–12.

Highmore, Ben, and Jenny Bourne Taylor. "Mood Work." Special issue, *New Formations* 82 (2014).

Holcomb, Gary. "Diaspora Cruises: Queer Black Proletarianism in Claude McKay's *A Long Way from Home.*" *Modern Fiction Studies* 49, no. 4 (2003): 714–45.

Hopkins, William E. "An Intimate Pen Picture of D. H. Lawrence: The Soul of a Genius—by an Eastwood Friend." *Nottingham Journal*, March 6, 1930.

Hsieh, Lili. "The Other Side of the Picture: The Politics of Affect in Virginia Woolf's *Three Guineas.*" *Journal of Narrative Theory* 36, no. 1 (Winter 2006): 20–52.

Hughes, Langston. *The Big Sea.* New York: Hill, 1993.

Hughes, Linda K., and Michael Lund. *The Victorian Serial.* Charlottesville: University of Virginia Press, 1991.

Hutchinson, George. *In Search of Nella Larsen: A Biography of the Color Line.* Cambridge, MA: Belknap Press of Harvard University Press, 2006.

Inglis, Fred. *A Short History of Celebrity.* Princeton, NJ: Princeton University Press, 2010.

Israel, Nico. *Spirals: The Whirled Image in Twentieth-Century Literature and Art.* New York: Columbia University Press, 2015.

Jaffe, Aaron. *Modernism and the Culture of Celebrity.* Cambridge: Cambridge University Press, 2010.

James, David, and Urmila Seshagiri, "Metamodernism: Narratives of Continuity and Revolution," *PMLA* 129, no. 1 (2014): 87–100.

James, Henry. "Preface to *The Tragic Muse.*" In *The Art of the Novel*, introduction by R. P. Blackmur and foreword by Colm Tóibín, 79–97. Chicago: University of Chicago Press, 2011.

James, Joy A. "Profeminism and Gender Elites: W. E. B. Du Bois, Anna Julia Cooper, and Ida B. Wells-Barnett." In *Next to the Color Line: Gender, Sexuality, and W. E. B. Du Bois*, edited by Susan Gillman and Alys Eve Weinbaum, 69–95. Minneapolis: University of Minnesota Press, 2007.

Jameson, Fredric. *The Modernist Papers.* London: Verso, 2007.

Jameson, Fredric. *Postmodernism, or the Cultural Logic of Late Capitalism.* Durham, NC: Duke University Press, 1991.

Jameson, Fredric. *A Singular Modernity: Essay on the Ontology of the Present.* London: Verso, 2012.

"Japanese Representatives Urge Fight on Race Prejudice at Waldorf Astoria." *World Forum* 1, no. 1 (1919): 1.

Jun, Helen Heran. *Race for Citizenship: Black Orientalism and Asian Uplift from Pre-Emancipation to Neoliberal America.* New York: New York University Press, 2011.

Kaplan, Joel H., and Sheila Stowell. *Theatre and Fashion: Oscar Wilde to the Suffragettes.* Cambridge: Cambridge University Press, 1994.

Kellogg, David. "Reading Foucault Reading Lawrence: Body, Voice, and Sexuality in *Lady Chatterley's Lover.*" *D. H. Lawrence Review* 28, no. 3 (1999): 31–54.

Keyser, Catherine. *Playing Smart: New York Women Writers and Modern Magazine Culture.* New Brunswick, NJ: Rutgers University Press, 2010.

Kim, Daniel Y. *Writing Manhood in Black and Yellow: Ralph Ellison, Frank Chin, and the Literary Politics of Identity.* Stanford, CA: Stanford University Press, 2005.

Kim, Thomas W. "Being Modern: The Circulation of Oriental Objects." *American Quarterly* 58, no. 2 (June 2006): 379–406.

Kinkaid-Weekes, Mark. *D. H. Lawrence: Triumph to Exile, 1912–1922.* Cambridge: Cambridge University Press, 1996.

Koda, Harold, and Andrew Bolton, eds. *Poiret: Exhibition Catalogue.* New York: Metropolitan Museum of Art Publications, 2007.

Koppen, Randi. *Virginia Woolf, Fashion and Literary Modernity.* Edinburgh: Edinburgh University Press, 2009.

Kuenz, Jane. "The Face of America: Performing Race and Nation in Jessie Fauset's *There Is Confusion.*" *Yale Journal of Criticism* 12, no. 1 (1999): 89–111.

Lackey, Michael. "D. H. Lawrence's *Women in Love*: A Tale of the Modernist Psyche, the Continental 'Concept,' and the Aesthetic Experience." *Journal of Speculative Philosophy* 20, no. 4 (2006): 266–86.

Lardner, Ring W., Jr. "Princeton Panorama." *Esquire,* October 1933.

Larsen, Nella. *The Complete Fiction of Nella Larsen: Passing, Quicksand, and the Stories.* Edited by Charles Larson. Foreword by Marita Golden. New York: Anchor Books, 2001.

Latham, Sean. *The Art of Scandal: Modernism, Libel Law, and the Roman à Clef.* New York: Oxford University Press, 2009.

Latham, Sean, and Gayle Rogers. *Modernism: Evolution of an Idea.* London: Bloomsbury, 2015.

Latour, Bruno. *Reassembling the Social: An Introduction to Actor-Network-Theory.* New York: Oxford University Press, 2005.

Latour, Bruno. "Why Critique Has Run Out of Steam: From Matters of Fact to Matters of Concern." *Critical Inquiry* 30 (Winter 2004): 225–48.

Lawlor, Leonard. *This Is Not Sufficient: An Essay on Animality and Human Nature in Derrida.* New York: Columbia University Press, 2007.

Lawrence, D. H. "Education of the People." In *Reflections on the Death of a Porcupine and Other Essays,* edited by Michael Herbert, 85–166. Cambridge: Cambridge University Press, 1988.

Lawrence, D. H. *Lady Chatterley's Lover.* New York: Signet Classic, 2003.

Lawrence, D. H. *The Letters of D. H. Lawrence.* Vol. 1, *September 1901–May 1913.* Edited by James T. Boulton. Cambridge: Cambridge University Press, 1979.

Lawrence, D. H. *The Letters of D. H. Lawrence.* Vol. 2, *June 1913–October 1916.* Edited by George J. Zytaruk and James T. Boulton. Cambridge: Cambridge University Press, 1981.

Lawrence, D. H. *The Letters of D. H. Lawrence.* Vol. 6, *March 1927–November 1928.* Edited by James T. Boulton and Margaret H. Boulton. Cambridge: Cambridge University Press, 1991.

Lawrence, D. H. "Red Trousers (Oh! For a New Crusade)." In *Late Essays and Articles,* edited by James T. Boulton, 135–38. Cambridge: Cambridge University Press, 2004.

Lawrence, D. H. *Reflections on the Death of a Porcupine and Other Essays.* Edited by Michael Herbert. Cambridge: Cambridge University Press, 1988.

Lawrence, D. H. *The White Peacock.* Edited by Andrew Robertson. New York: Penguin Books, 1983.

Lawrence, D. H. *Women in Love.* New York: Modern Library, 1999.

"The League of Darker Peoples: What It Is and What It Can Accomplish." *World Forum* 1, no. 1 (1919): 1–2.

Lee, Julia H. *Interracial Encounters: Reciprocal Representations in African and Asian American Literatures, 1896–1937.* New York: New York University Press, 2011.

Lehmann, Ulrich. *Tigersprung: Fashion in Modernity.* Cambridge, MA: MIT Press, 2000.

Les modèles de Paul Poiret: 1917 Printemps. Paris: Poiret, 1917.

Leslie, Esther. *Walter Benjamin: Overpowering Conformism*. London and Sterling, VA: Pluto Press, 2000.

Levenson, Michael. *Modernism and the Fate of Individuality: Character and Novelistic Form from Conrad to Woolf*. Cambridge: Cambridge University Press, 1998.

Levering-Lewis, David. *W. E. B. Du Bois: The Fight for Equality and the American Century, 1919–1963*. New York: Holt, 2000.

Levering-Lewis, David. *When Harlem Was In Vogue*. New York: Knopf, 1997.

Levine, Caroline. *Forms: Whole, Rhythm, Hierarchy, Network*. Princeton, NJ: Princeton University Press, 2015.

Levison, Susan. "Performance and the 'Strange Place' of Jessie Redmon Fauset's *There Is Confusion*." *Modern Fiction Studies* 46, no. 4 (2000): 825–48.

Leys, Ruth. "The Turn to Affect: A Critique." *Critical Inquiry* 37, no. 3 (Spring 2011): 434–72.

Lipovetsky, Giles. *The Empire of Fashion: Dressing Modern Democracy*. Translated by Catherine Porter. Princeton, NJ: Princeton University Press, 1994.

Lorde, Audre. *The Collected Poems of Audre Lorde*. New York: W. W. Norton, 2000.

Love, Heather. "Close but not Deep: Literary Ethics and the Descriptive Turn." *New Literary History* 41, no. 2 (Spring 2010): 371–391.

Love, Heather. "Small Change: Realism, Immanence, and the Politics of the Micro." *Modern Language Quarterly* 77, no. 3 (2016): 419–445.

Love, Heather. "Truth and Consequences: On Paranoid Reading and Reparative Reading." *Criticism* 52, no. 2 (Spring 2010): 235–41.

Luckhurst, Nicola. *Bloomsbury in Vogue*. London: Cecil Woolf Publishers, 1998.

Madam C. J. Walker Collection. Indiana Historical Society, Indianapolis.

"Madam C. J. Walker, of Indianapolis Seeing the Islands of the Southern Seas." *Freeman* 17 (January 1914): 8.

Mangum, Bryant. "The Short Stories of F. Scott Fitzgerald." In *The Cambridge Companion to F. Scott Fitzgerald*, edited by Ruth Prigozy, 57–78. Cambridge: Cambridge University Press, 2002.

Mansfield, Katherine. *The Collected Letters of Katherine Mansfield*. Vol. 1, *1903–1917*. Edited by Vincent O'Sullivan and Margaret Scott. Oxford: Clarendon Press, 1984.

Mao, Douglas. *Fateful Beauty: Aesthetic Environments, Juvenile Development, and Literature, 1860–1960*. Princeton, NJ: Princeton University Press, 2008.

Mao, Douglas. *Solid Objects: Modernism and the Test of Production*. Princeton, NJ: Princeton University Press, 1999.

Mao, Douglas and Rebecca Walkowitz. "The New Modernist Studies." *PMLA* 123, No. 3. (May 2008): 737–48.

Mark Cross. "Our Story." Accessed January 25, 2017. https://www.markcross.com/our -story.

Marks, Laura U. *Touch: Sensuous Theory and Multisensory Media*. Minneapolis: University of Minnesota Press, 2002.

Marshik, Celia. *At the Mercy of Their Clothes: Modernism, the Middlebrow, and British Garment Culture*. New York: Columbia University Press, 2016.

Marshik, Celia. *British Modernism and Censorship*. Cambridge: Cambridge University Press, 2006.

Marx, John. *The Modernist Novel and the Decline of Empire*. Cambridge: Cambridge University Press, 2005.

Masschelein, Anneleen. "Rip the Veil of the Old Vision Across, and Walk through the Rent: Reading D. H. Lawrence with Deleuze and Guattari." In *Modernism and Theory: A Critical Debate*, edited by Stephen Ross, 24–25. London: Routledge, 2009.

Materer, Timothy. "Make It Sell! Ezra Pound Advertises Modernism." In *Marketing Modernisms: Self-Promotion, Canonization, Rereading*, edited by Kevin J. H. Dettmar and Stephen Watt, 17–36. Ann Arbor: University of Michigan Press, 1996.

McDowell, Deborah E. Introduction to *Quicksand and Passing*, by Nella Larsen, ix–xxxi New Brunswick, NJ: Rutgers University Press, 1986.

Melman, Billie. *Women and the Popular Imagination in the Twenties: Flappers and Nymphs*. New York: St. Martins, 1988.

"Members of Race Confer with Japanese." *Philadelphia Tribune*, January 18, 1919.

"Memorandum of Peace Proposals of the International League of Darker Peoples." *World Forum* 1, no. 1 (1919): 3–4.

Mencken, H. L. Review of *The Beautiful and the Damned*. In *F. Scott Fitzgerald: The Critical Reception*, edited by Jackson R. Bryer, 106. New York: Burt Franklin, 1978.

Mencken, H. L. Review of *The Great Gatsby*. In *H. L. Mencken on American Literature*, edited by S. T. Joshi, 111–14. Columbus: Ohio University Press, 2002.

Mendes, Valerie D., and Amy de la Haye. *Lucile Ltd: London, Paris, New York, and Chicago 1890s–1930s*. London: V&A Publishing, 2009.

Messenger, Chris. "'Out Upon the Mongolian Plain': Fitzgerald's Racial and Ethnic Cross-Identifying in *Tender Is the Night*." In *Twenty-First Century Readings of* Tender Is the Night, edited by William Blazek and Laura Rattray, 160–76. Liverpool: Liverpool University Press, 2007.

Michaels, Walter Benn. *Our America: Nativism, Modernism, and Pluralism*. Durham, NC: Duke University Press, 1995.

Miles, Christopher, dir. *Priest of Love*. Milesian Films, 1981. Film.

Miliaras, Barbara Langell. "Fashion, Art and the Leisure Class in D. H. Lawrence's *The White Peacock*." *Journal of the DH Lawrence Society* (1994–1995): 67–81.

Miller, J. Hillis. *Ariadne's Thread: Story Lines*. New Haven, CT: Yale University Press, 1992.

Miller, Monica L. *Slaves to Fashion: Black Dandyism and the Styling of Black Diasporic Identity*. Durham, NC: Duke University Press, 2009.

Miller, Nina. "Femininity, Publicity, and the Class Division of Cultural Labor." *African American Review* 30, no. 2 (Summer 1996): 205–20.

"Mme. C. J. Walker's Return Home." *Freeman*, February 7, 1914.

Modern Girl around the World Research Group (Alys Eve Weinbaum, Lynn M. Thomas, Priti Ramamurthy, Uta G. Poiger, Madeleine Yue Dong, and Tani E. Barlow), eds. *The Modern Girl around the World: Consumption, Modernity, and Globalization*. Durham, NC: Duke University Press, 2008.

Moore, Harry T. *The Priest of Love: A Life of D. H. Lawrence*. Rev. ed. Carbondale: Southern Illinois University, 1977.

Moran, Joe. *Star Authors: Literary Celebrity in America*. New York: Pluto Press, 2000.

Mulhall, Stephen. *Heidegger and* Being and Time. London: Routledge, 1996.

Mullen, Bill V. *Afro-Orientalism*. Minneapolis: University of Minnesota Press, 2004.

Mussell, James. "Repetition: Or, 'In Our Last." *Victorian Periodicals Review* 48, no. 3 (2015): 343–58.

Neiland, Justus. *Feeling Modern: The Eccentricities of Public Life.* Urbana: University of Illinois Press, 2008.

"New Ideas in Room Decoration." *Sketch*, November 10, 1915.

Ngai, Sianne. *Ugly Feelings.* Cambridge, MA: Harvard University Press, 2005.

Ngô, Fiona I. B. *Imperial Blues: Geographies of Sex and Race in Jazz Age New York.* Durham, NC: Duke University Press, 2013.

Nguyen, Mimi Thi. "The Biopower of Beauty: Humanitarian Imperialisms and Global Feminisms in an Age of Terror." *Signs* 36, no. 2 (2011): 359–83.

North, Michael. *Novelty: A History of the New.* Chicago: University of Chicago Press, 2013.

Nugent, Richard Bruce. "The Dark Tower." In *Gay Rebel of the Harlem Renaissance: Selections from the Work of Richard Bruce Nugent,* edited by Thomas H. Wirth, 217–20. Durham, NC: Duke University Press, 2002.

O. K. H. "A Fatal Mistake." *Times* (London). April 15, 1914.

Olwell, Victoria. *The Genius of Democracy: Fictions of Gender and Citizenship in the United States, 1860–1945.* Philadelphia: University of Pennsylvania Press, 2011.

Onishi, Yuichiro. *Transpacific Antiracism: Afro-Asian Solidarity in 20th-Century Black America, Japan, and Okinawa.* New York: New York University Press, 2013.

Outka, Elizabeth. "Dead Men, Walking: Actors, Networks, and Actualized Metaphors in *Mrs. Dalloway* and *Raymond.*" *Novel: A Forum on Fiction* 46, no. 2 (2013): 253–74.

Parkins, Ilya. *Poiret, Dior, Schiaparelli: Fashion, Femininity, and Modernity.* London: Berg, 2012.

Patton, Sari Price. Letter to W. E. B. Du Bois. March 19, 1928. MS. W. E. B. Du Bois Papers. Special Collections and University Archives, University of Massachusetts Amherst Library.

"Paul Poiret Here to Tell of His Art." *New York Times*, September 21, 1913.

Pawlowski, Merry M. "Virginia Woolf's Veil: The Feminist Intellectual and the Organization of Public Space." *Modern Fiction Studies* 53, no. 4 (2007): 722–51.

Pease, Allison. *Modernism, Mass Culture, and the Aesthetics of Obscenity.* Cambridge: Cambridge University Press, 2000.

Peiss, Kathy. *Hope in a Jar: The Making of America's Beauty Culture.* New York: Metropolitan, 1998.

Pham, Minh-Ha T. "The Right to Fashion in the Age of Terrorism." *Signs* 36, no. 2 (Winter 2011): 385–410.

"Poiret, Creator of Fashions, Here." *New York Times*, September 21, 1913.

"Poiret Decries Trend of Modern Fashions." *New York Times*, November 12, 1927.

Poiret, Paul. *King of Fashion.* London: Gollancz, 1931.

Poiret, Paul. "Paul Poiret on Dress." In *Principles of Correct Dress*, by Florence Hull Winterbourne, 237–45. New York: Harper, 1914.

Polhemus, Robert M. *Erotic Faith: Being in Love from Jane Austen to D. H. Lawrence.* Chicago: University of Chicago Press, 1990.

Pound, Ezra. *The Letters of Ezra Pound, 1907–1941.* Edited by D. D. Paige. New York: Harcourt, Brace, and Company, 1950.

"Prediction Is Made about James Joyce Novel: F. S. Fitzgerald Believes *Ulysses* Is the Great Book of Future." *F. Scott Fitzgerald on Authorship*, edited by Matthew J. Bruccoli with Judith S. Baughman, 91. Columbia: University of South Carolina Press, 1996.

Rainey, Lawrence. *Institutions of Modernism: Literary Elites and Public Culture*. New Haven, CT: Yale University Press, 1998.

Reddy, Chandan. *Freedom with Violence: Race, Sexuality, and the U.S. State*. Durham, NC: Duke University Press, 2011.

Reddy, Vanita. "Beauty and the Limits of National Belonging in Bharati Mukherjee's *Jasmine*." *Contemporary Literature* 54, no. 2 (2013): 337–68.

Reed, Anthony. "'A Women Is a Conjunction': The Ends of Improvisation in Claude McKay's *Banjo: A Story Without a Plot*." *Callaloo* 36, no. 3 (2013): 758–72.

Reed, Christopher. *Bloomsbury Rooms: Modernism, Subculture, and Domesticity*. New Haven, CT: Yale University Press, 2004.

Reed, Christopher. "Design for [Queer] Living: Sexual Identity, Performance, and Décor in British *Vogue*, 1922–1926." *GLQ* 12, no. 3 (2006): 377–404.

Ricoeur, Paul. *Freud and Philosophy: An Essay on Interpretation*. Translated by Denis Savage. New Haven, CT: Yale University Press, 1970.

Roberts, Brian Russell. *Artistic Ambassadors: Literary and International Representation of the New Negro Era*. Charlottesville: University of Virginia Press, 2013.

Rohman, Carrie. *Stalking the Subject: Modernism and the Animal*. New York: Columbia University Press, 2009.

Rooks, Noliwe M. *Hair Raising: Beauty, Culture, and African American Women*. New Brunswick, NJ: Rutgers University Press, 1996.

Rooney, Ellen. "Live Free or Describe: The Reading Effect and the Persistence of Form." *differences* 21, no. 3 (2010): 112–39.

Rosner, Victoria. *Modernism and the Architecture of Private Life*. New York: Columbia University Press, 2005.

Ross, Stephen. "Introduction: The Missing Link." In *Modernism and Theory: A Critical Debate*, edited by Stephen Ross, 1–17. New York: Routledge, 2009.

Ruderman, Judith. *Race and Identity in D. H. Lawrence: Indians, Gypsies, and Jews*. London: Palgrave Macmillan, 2014.

Saint-Amour, Paul. *Tense Future: Modernism, Total War, Encyclopedic Form*. New York: Oxford University Press, 2015.

Sanders, Scott. *D. H. Lawrence: The World of the Five Major Novels*. New York: Viking Press, 1974.

Schnapp, Jeffrey T. "The Fabric of Modern Times." *Critical Inquiry* 24, no. 1 (1997): 191–245.

Sedgwick, Eve Kosofsky. *Touching Feeling: Affect, Pedagogy, Performativity*. Durham, NC: Duke University Press, 2003.

Seshagiri, Urmila. "Orienting Virginia Woolf: Race, Aesthetics, and Politics in *To the Lighthouse*." *Modern Fiction Studies* 50, no. 1 (Spring 2004): 58–84.

Seshagiri, Urmila. *Race and the Modernist Imagination*. Ithaca, NY: Cornell University Press, 2010.

Sheehan, Elizabeth M. "Experiments in Art and Fashion: Vanessa Bell's Dress Design." In *Beyond Bloomsbury: Designs of the Omega Workshops 1913–19*, 50–59. London: Courtauld Gallery and the Fontanka Press, 2009.

Sheehan, Elizabeth M. "The Face of Fashion: Race and Fantasy in James VanDerZee's Photography and Jessie Fauset's Fiction." In *Cultures of Femininity in Modern Fashion*, edited by Ilya Parkins and Elizabeth M. Sheehan, 180–202. Durham: University of New Hampshire Press, 2011.

Sheehan, Elizabeth M. "Fashioning Internationalism in Jessie Redmon Fauset's Writing." In *A Companion to the Harlem Renaissance*, edited by Cherene Sherrard-Johnson, 137–53. Oxford: Wiley-Blackwell, 2015.

Sherrard-Johnson, Cherene. *Portraits of the New Negro Woman: Visual and Literary Culture in the Harlem Renaissance*. New Brunswick, NJ: Rutgers University Press, 2007.

"Shocking Stockings." *Sketch*, July 14, 1915.

Siddons, Louise. "African Past or American Present?: The Visual Eloquence of James VanDerZee's Identical Twins." *African American Review* 46, no. 2–3 (2013): 439–59.

Silver, Brenda. "The Authority of Anger: *Three Guineas* as Case Study." *Signs* 16, no. 2 (1991): 340–70.

Silver, Brenda R. *Virginia Woolf, Icon*. Chicago: University of Chicago Press, 1999.

Simmel, Georg. "The Philosophy of Fashion." In *Simmel on Culture*, edited by David Frisby and Mike Featherstone, 187–206. London: Sage, 1997.

Slate, Nico. *Colored Cosmopolitanism: The Shared Struggle for Freedom in the United States and India*. Cambridge, MA: Harvard University Press, 2012.

Spencer, Herbert. *Principles of Sociology*. Vol. 2, pt. 4: *Ceremonial Institutions*. New York: D. Appleton and Company, 1880.

Sproles, Kathryn. "Shooting *The White Peacock*: Victorian Art and Feminine Sexuality in D. H. Lawrence's First Novel." *Criticism* 34, no. 2 (1992): 237–59.

Stallybrass, Peter. "Marx's Coat." In *Border Fetishisms: Material Objects in Unstable Spaces*, edited by Patricia Spyer, 183–207. New York: Routledge, 1998.

Stanford-Friedman, Susan. "Definitional Excursions: The Meanings of Modern/Modernity/Modernism." *Modernism/Modernity* 8, no. 3 (2001): 493–513.

Stanford-Friedman, Susan. *Planetary Modernisms: Provocations on Modernity across Time*. New York: Columbia University Press, 2015.

Stanford-Friedman, Susan. "Theory." In *Modernism and Theory: A Critical Debate*, edited by Stephen Ross, 237–46. New York: Routledge, 2009.

Stephens, Michelle Ann. *Black Empire: The Masculine Global Imaginary of Caribbean Intellectuals in the United States, 1914–1962*. Durham, NC: Duke University Press, 2005.

Stewart, Jack. *The Vital Art of D. H. Lawrence*. Carbondale: Southern Illinois Press, 1999.

Stewart, Kathleen. *Ordinary Affects*. Durham, NC: Duke University Press, 2007.

Stewart, Kathleen. "Weak Theory in An Unfinished World." *Journal of Folklore Research* 45, no. 1 (2008): 71–82.

Stokes, Mason. "Father of the Bride: Du Bois and the Making of Black Heterosexuality." In *Next to the Color Line: Gender, Sexuality, and W. E. B. Du Bois*, edited by Susan Gillman and Alys Eve Weinbaum, 289–316. Minneapolis: University of Minnesota Press, 2007.

Stylios, George K., and Dan Ying Yang. "The Concept of Mood Changing Garments Made from Luminescent Woven Fabrics and Flexible Photovoltaics 'MoodWear.'" *Advances in Science and Technology* 80 (2012): 22–29.

Tate, Claudia. "Race and Desire: *Dark Princess: A Romance*." In *Next to the Color Line: Gender, Sexuality, and W. E. B. Du Bois*, edited by Susan Gillman and Alys Eve Weinbaum, 150–208. Minneapolis: University of Minnesota Press, 2007.

Thomas, Helen. "Two Pieces of Advice from D. H. Lawrence." *Times* (London). February 13, 1963.

Times (London). "Fashion and the Vote: Women's Dress as Hindrance to Her Cause." April 11, 1914.

Tomkins, Silvan S. *Affect Imagery Consciousness*. Vol. 2. New York: Springer, 1963.

Troy, Nancy J. *Couture Culture: A Study in Modern Art and Fashion.* Cambridge, MA: MIT Press, 2003.

Tynan, Jane. *British Army Uniform and the First World War: Men in Khaki.* London: Palgrave Macmillan, 2013.

Underwood, Ted. *Why Literary Periods Mattered: Historical Contrast and the Prestige of Literary Studies.* Stanford, CA: Stanford University Press, 2013.

Vaill, Amanda. *Everybody Was So Young: Gerald and Sara Murphy.* New York: Houghton Mifflin, 1998.

"Villa Lewaro-on-the-Hudson, Birthplace of International League of Darker Peoples." *World Forum* 1, no. 1 (1919): 2–3.

Vogel, Shane. *The Scene of Harlem Cabaret: Race, Sexuality, Performance.* Chicago: University of Chicago Press, 2009.

Walkowitz, Rebecca L. *Cosmopolitan Style: Modernism Beyond the Nation.* New York: Columbia University Press, 2005.

Wall, Cheryl. *Women of the Harlem Renaissance.* Bloomington: Indiana University Press 1995.

Wallace, Jeff. *D. H. Lawrence, Science and the Posthuman.* Basingstoke, UK: Palgrave Macmillan, 2005.

Walters, Christina. *Optical Impersonality: Science, Images, and Literary Modernism.* Baltimore: Johns Hopkins University Press, 2014.

Watkins-Owens, Irma. *Blood Relations: Caribbean Immigrants and the Harlem Community, 1900–1930.* Bloomington: Indiana University Press, 1996.

"We Nominate for the Hall of Fame." *Vogue* (London), Late May 1924.

Weigman, Robyn. "The Times We're In: Queer Feminist Criticism and the Reparative 'Turn.'" *Feminist Theory* 15, no. 1 (2014): 4–25.

Weinbaum, Alys Eve. "Interracial Romance and Black Internationalism." In *Next to the Color Line: Gender, Sexuality, and W. E. B. Du Bois,* edited by Susan Gillman and Alys Eve Weinbaum, 96–123. Minneapolis: University of Minnesota Press, 2007.

Weinbaum, Alys Eve. "Racial Masquerade: Consumption and Contestation of American Modernity." In *The Modern Girl around the World: Consumption, Modernity, and Globalization,* edited by the Modern Girl around the World Research Group, 120–46. Durham, NC: Duke University Press, 2008.

Weinbaum, Alys Eve. *Wayward Reproductions: Genealogies of Race and Nation in Transatlantic Modern Thought.* Durham, NC: Duke University Press, 2004.

West, James L. W., III. "Fitzgerald and *Esquire.*" In *The Short Stories of F. Scott Fitzgerald: New Approaches in Criticism,* edited by Jackson R. Bryer, 149–66. Madison: University of Wisconsin Press, 1982.

White, Shane, and Graham White. *Stylin': African-American Expressive Culture, from Its Beginnings to the Zoot Suit.* Ithaca, NY: Cornell University Press, 1998.

Whittier-Ferguson, John. "Repetition, Remembering, Repetition: Virginia Woolf's Late Fiction and the Return of War." *Modern Fiction Studies* 57, no. 2 (Summer 2011): 230–53.

Wicke, Jennifer. *Advertising Fictions: Literature, Advertisement, and Social Reading.* New York: Columbia University Press, 1988.

Wicke, Jennifer. "Appreciation, Depreciation: Modernism's Speculative Bubble." *Modernism /Modernity* 8, no. 3 (2001): 389–403.

Wicke, Jennifer. "Enchantment, Disenchantment, Re-Enchantment: Joyce and the Cult of the Absolutely Fabulous." *Novel: A Forum on Fiction* 29, no. 1 (Autumn 1995): 128–37.

Wientzen, Timothy. "Automatic Modernism: D. H. Lawrence, Vitalism and the Political Body." *Genre* 46, no. 1 (2013): 33–55.

Wilde, Oscar. *Salomé: A Tragedy in One Act.* London: Melmoth, 1904.

Williams, Erika Renée. "A Lie of Omission: Plagiarism in Nella Larsen's *Quicksand.*" *African American Review* 45, no. 1–2 (Spring/Summer 2012): 205–16.

Williams, Linda R. *Sex in the Head: Visions of Femininity and Film in D. H. Lawrence.* Detroit, MI: Wayne State University Press, 1993.

Williams, Raymond. *Politics of Modernism: Against the New Conformists.* New York: Verso Books, 2007.

Williams, Raymond. "Structures of Feeling." In *Marxism and Literature*, 128–35. New York: Oxford University Press, 2009.

Wilson, Christopher P. "'He Fell Just Short of Being News': *Gatsby*'s Tabloid Shadows." *American Literature* 84, no. 1 (March 2012): 119–49.

Wilson, Elizabeth. *Adorned in Dreams: Fashion and Modernity.* Rev. ed. New Brunswick, NJ: Rutgers University Press, 2003.

Wollaeger, Mark A. "D. H. Lawrence and the Technological Image: Modernism, Reference, and Abstraction in *Women in Love.*" *English Language Notes* 51, no. 1 (Spring/Summer 2013): 75–92.

Wollen, Peter. "Fashion/Orientalism/The Body." *New Formations* 1 (Spring 1987): 5–33.

Woolf, Virginia. *The Common Reader: First Series.* Annotations and introduction by Andrew McNeillie. New York: Harcourt, 2002.

Woolf, Virginia. *Diary of Virginia Woolf.* Vol. 2, *1920–1924.* Edited by Anne Olivier Bell, assisted by Andrew McNeillie. New York: Harvest, 1978.

Woolf, Virginia. *The Diary of Virginia Woolf.* Vol. 3, *1925–1930.* Edited by Anne Olivier Bell, assisted by Andrew McNeillie. New York: Harvest, 1980.

Woolf, Virginia. "How Should One Read a Book?" In *The Essays of Virginia Woolf.* Vol. 5, *1929–1932*, edited by Stuart N. Clarke, 572–84. New York: Houghton Mifflin, 2009.

Woolf, Virginia. *Letters of Virginia Woolf.* Vol. 2. Edited by Nigel Nicholson and Joanne Trautmann. New York: Harcourt Brace Jovanovich, 1976.

[Woolf, Virginia]. "Modern Novels." *Times Literary Supplement.* April 10, 1919.

Woolf, Virginia. *Moments of Being.* Edited by Jeanne Schulkind. New York: Harvest, 1985.

Woolf, Virginia. *Mrs. Dalloway.* Annotations and introduction by Bonnie Kime Scott. New York: Harcourt, 2005.

Woolf, Virginia. "Mrs. Dalloway in Bond Street." In *Mrs. Dalloway's Party*, edited by Stella McNichol, 11–23. New York: Harvest, 1973.

Woolf, Virginia. "The New Dress." In *Mrs. Dalloway's Party*, edited by Stella McNichol, 61–73. New York: Harvest, 1973.

Woolf, Virginia. "On Re-reading Novels." In *The Essays of Virginia Woolf.* Vol. 3, *1919–1924*, edited by Andrew McNeillie, 336–46. New York: Harcourt, 1991.

Woolf, Virginia. *Orlando: A Biography.* Annotations and introduction by Maria DiBattista. New York: Harcourt, 2006.

Woolf, Virginia. *Roger Fry: A Biography*. New York: Harcourt, 1976.

Woolf, Virginia. *Three Guineas*. Annotations and introduction by Jane Marcus. New York: Harcourt, 2006.

Woolf, Virginia. *The Years*. Annotations and introduction by Eleanor McNees. New York: Harcourt, 2008.

Zackodnik. Teresa. "Recirculation and Feminist Black Internationalism in Jessie Fauset's 'The Looking Glass' and Amy Jacques Garvey's 'Our Women and What They Think.'" *Modernism/Modernity* 19, no. 3 (2012): 437–59.

Index

Page numbers in *italics* refer to images.

CPSIA information can be obtained
at www.ICGtesting.com
Printed in the USA
BVHW08*1817090918
526773BV00002B/5/P